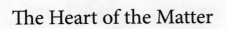

The Heart of the Matter

Arthur Green. Courtesy of Hebrew College

UNIVERSITY OF NEBRASKA PRESS | LINCOLN

JPS דור דור
SCHOLAR ודורשיו
OF DISTINCTION
SERIES

The Heart of the Matter

Studies in Jewish Mysticism and Theology

Arthur Green

THE JEWISH PUBLICATION SOCIETY | PHILADELPHIA

© 2015 by The Jewish Publication Society

Acknowledgments for the use of copyrighted material appear on pages 359–60, which constitute an extension of the copyright page.

Library of Congress Cataloging-in-Publication Data

Green, Arthur, 1941–, author.
The heart of the matter: studies in Jewish mysticism and theology / Arthur Green.
pages   cm

Includes bibliographical references and index.
ISBN 978-0-8276-1213-6 (cloth: alk. paper)
ISBN 978-0-8276-1227-3 (pdf)
1. Mysticism—Judaism. I. Title.

BM723.G727 2015
296.7′12—dc23
2014047514

Set in Minion Pro by Lindsey Auten.
Designed by A. Shahan.

Dedicated to

RABBI SHARON COHEN ANISFELD

Student, Friend, Partner

ותורת חסד על לשונה

It is like walking through a meadow, gathering beautiful blossoms and flowers, adding one to another to make a bouquet. But you cannot stop, you take one more flower and one more until you have created another bouquet, and you combine the two. And you go on and on adding one flower
to the next, creating yet another beautiful bouquet, and another, and another . . .

R. NACHMAN OF BRESLAV, *Likutei Moharan* 65:2

How can we thank the teacher who teaches us Torah?

We are blessed to be part of the rabbinical school you created.
Together we have learned
to become a circle of listening companions
to open our hearts to the seventy faces of Torah.
You have enabled us to spread our wings and find our own ways of
serving the Jewish people.

We who have been privileged to witness the Torah that you live
are honored to help bring this collection of your written Torah to
the world.
In this volume and in the school you founded,
your work will endure long after we are gone.

How can we thank the teacher who teaches us Torah?

We walk through your garden.
We gather the flowers.
We do our part in passing them on.

With deepest gratitude,
The alumni, faculty, and students of the
Rabbinical School of Hebrew College

Contents

Preface

Looking Back

Writing a retrospective is a sobering exercise. While I by no means feel that I am at the end of my run as a scholar or thinker, I have to accept the fact that the bulk of my creative years are behind me and that my areas of interest and my approach to them are already well established and not likely to undergo significant change. The several projects, both minor and major, that I see in front of me are mostly predictable ones.

A quick look at this volume's table of contents will make it clear that I include historical and phenomenological treatments of classical Judaic subject matter (i.e., "academic" articles) together with more personal theological reflections. I do so because I consider my intellectual/spiritual project to be of a piece. To paraphrase my mentor Rabbi Nahman of Bratslav ("I *am* a 'Know what to answer the heretic'"), I *am* a bridge between Jewish scholarship and Jewish theology, between intensive study of the Jewish past and the construction of a believable Judaism for the future. A look back at my professional history will reveal the fact that I have twice left tenured positions at major universities to lead what might be considered relatively fly-by-night rabbinical schools. In a sense this move has happened three times, the first while I was still a doctoral student. In 1967, after my ordination at the Jewish Theological Seminary, I returned to my undergraduate home at Brandeis University to pursue a doctorate with Professor Alexander Altmann. Proper training for a scholarly career in the study of Jewish mysticism, Altmann assured me, would involve studying medieval Latin and Arabic, learning Jewish philosophy as well as Kabbalah, and preparing a manuscript for publication, probably a text of the Zohar circle. I found these requirements both daunting and uninteresting, especially in the heady atmosphere of the late 1960s. After completing my coursework, I withdrew from graduate studies for several years, eventually returning on my own terms to write *Rabbi Nahman of Bratslav: A Critical Biography*, later published as *Tormented Master*.

In 1968 I joined with several friends to create the Havurat Shalom Community Seminary, an attempt to offer higher Jewish education in a different key. The models we had in mind for that different sort of learning were primarily the early Hasidic community (partly as idealized by Martin Buber) and the Frankfurt Lehrhaus of Franz Rosenzweig.

Those models bespoke a serious engagement with classical Jewish sources, but one focused on a devotional stance (*Torah le-shem heh* [= *ha-shem*], "learning for God's sake," rather than *li-shemah,* "for its own sake," in Hasidic parlance) and a quest for personal meaning. We had an early intuitive sense of what now would be called an emerging postmodern relationship to the sources—one that understood and accepted the legitimacy and conclusions of historical scholarship but sought to go beyond it, treating the texts, both biblical and later (in my case especially the Zohar and Hasidic writings), as potential sources of wisdom and truth, even of divine presence in our midst.

In 1973 (still ABD at Brandeis) I accepted a position in the Religious Studies Department at the University of Pennsylvania. I did indeed learn something about the methodology of religious studies during those years, but I learned much more about the struggle to teach humanities in a corporate university, where the very enterprise of the humanities (and *kal va-homer* that of Religious Studies) seemed to be something of an afterthought. I was there until 1984, when I left Penn to become dean (and president, two years later) of the Reconstructionist Rabbinical College.

Rabbinical students, I discovered there (and again today, in a different context) are wonderful to teach. They are mature, serious, devoted to learning the material, and anxious that they will never know enough. They are interested in discussing questions raised by their own struggles with faith as well as in the historical setting from which the texts emerged. My most treasured teaching experiences have all involved working with present and future rabbis.

In 1993, I was deeply honored to be offered the Philip W. Lown chair at Brandeis, formerly occupied by my own teacher, Professor Altmann. I was there until 2003, when I took a leave and then retired to the emeritus faculty in order to create the Hebrew College Rabbinical School, where I continue to serve as rector and which I see as my greatest educational achievement. My wife, Kathy, says that some men, when they reach a certain age, get a little red sports car every few years. I seem to get a little red rabbinical school. ("Red" refers mostly to the ink color in the financial records of those institutions, rather than to the politics of their students. But then there is some of that, too.)

This alternation in career decisions coordinates fully with my literary output, and thus a recounting of it seems appropriate for introducing this volume, in which I seek to make, indeed to be, the bridge of which I have spoken. The choice to work in a seminary rather than a university context has about it both a "push" and a "pull." I will begin with the latter, which is the reason for my decision to work at training future rabbis rather than teaching in an academic department of religion or Judaic studies, both of which I have done with some success. I find myself as committed to the Jewish future as I am to the Jewish past. Living in an era of tremendously rapid change in North American Jewish life as well as in worldwide Jewish history, it is not clear to me that our heterodox and progressive Jewish community (to which I firmly belong) will withstand the pressures of assimilation already so apparent.

As will become clear from some of the more personal essays in this volume, I became the Jew I am because I was partially raised by my mother's parents, essentially *shtetl* Jews who had grown up in late nineteenth-century Eastern Europe. Because of various complications in my family history, these grandparents had an unusual degree of influence on me. The echoes of Yiddish speech, old-world *shul* melodies, attitudes, humor, superstitions, and kitchen aromas were all part of my childhood. When I began teaching at Penn in the mid-1970s, I realized I was teaching fourth- and fifth-generation American Jews. They were bright young people, products of suburbia and the upper middle class, totally untouched even by memories of anti-Semitism (with the exception of a small but significant sprinkling of Holocaust survivors' children), well on their way to lucrative careers, and fully at home in this country. "Why should these people remain Jewish?" I began to ask myself. Is there anything we have to offer that is sufficiently compelling, both intellectually and spiritually, to keep them within our orb?

The conventional apologetic instinct of defending the tradition at all costs, including that of intellectual integrity, simply did not work for me. An overly strong dose of adolescent piety (stimulated by the influence of those grandparents) set me up for a crisis of faith in my college years. That experience seemed to have immunized me against both excessive devotion to halakhic behavior and all sorts of superficial "answers" to the great spiritual challenges of life, especially in our times. I had already tried them all on for size, thank you, and had found them wanting. I came to see myself as a seeker, one comfortable with ongoing questions, challenges, and an intense but "stormy" religious life.

Among my university students, as among my own peers, I detected a small subset of such seekers—people for whom personal and spiritual quest was going to be an important theme in their lives. I sensed that these were the potential leaders of a future generation of Jewish thinkers and leaders. Most of them, however, were opting for the seemingly much more accessible spiritualities imported from the East and so much in vogue throughout the past half century. The task of articulating a Jewish faith that would speak to such people, perhaps even to broader audiences of both Jews and non-Jews, became paramount to me. I began to feel that in an age such as ours we could ill afford devoting ourselves entirely to the study and investigation of the Jewish past, filling journals with learned articles that hardly anyone would read. Unlike earlier generations of *Wissenschaft* scholars, including some of my own teachers, I no longer believed that the nobility of Jewish history, or even the profundity of classic Jewish teachings, would serve to compel Jews to carry the tradition forward. Those insights of the past would need to be recast into a language that contemporary seekers— open-minded, exposed to teachings from diverse sources, and unbounded by prior commitment to Judaism—would find worthy of further inquiry, perhaps even of devotion.

This was clearly the work of seminary, not university. I wanted to teach in an institutional setting that was openly committed to the values of Jewish creativity and Jewish survival. For me those two are the same: we will only have a chance of surviving and a reason to survive as a distinctive community if we think creatively and boldly about what our tradition has to offer and how we structure its message for new generations of Jews. I hope that the future rabbis we teach will be the bearers and creators of this renewed Jewish spiritual language. Many of those applying to rabbinical schools were in fact the Jewish seekers I was looking for, people who (like myself) were attracted to Jewish learning because in one way or another it fulfilled their souls. For many of them the rabbinic career came second, a way of justifying and continuing their own deep engagement with the Jewish sources and way of life.

In response to this need to address the contemporary seeker, I added two more parts to the course of critical/historical scholarship in the field of Jewish mysticism and Hasidism for which I had been trained. One was a commitment to translation, making texts available in English, in formats that might be attractive to readers, sometimes giving special attention to how those sources might be reread in the context of a contemporary Jewish spiritual quest. I am especially grateful to my teacher Nahum N. Glatzer for inspiring this effort. My ongoing translation project began with *Your Word Is Fire*, a little booklet of Hasidic prayer instructions (which I translated together with Barry Holtz in 1969); continued in *The Language of Truth*, my rendering of the Hasidic classic *Sefat Emet* for the contemporary reader; and finds its fullest expression in the recently published *Speaking Torah: Spiritual Teachings from around the Maggid's Table*. Currently I am engaged in a complete translation of my favorite Hasidic classic, *Me'or 'Eynayim*, by Rabbi Menahem Nahum of Chernobyl. The second addition was a series of personal theological writings, especially the trilogy *Seek My Face, Speak My Name* (1992), *EHYEH: A Kabbalah for Tomorrow* (2003), and *Radical Judaism* (2010). A number of shorter pieces of such personal writing are included in the present volume.

In my comments (I hope not overly unkind) about my years at Penn, I alluded to the "push" that sent me from the secular academy into seminary education. The enterprise of humanistic education, meant to enlighten and excite the mind and make the human spirit soar, is in drastic decline in the American university. Such an approach to education, involving literature, classical studies, religion, intellectual history, and the arts has come to be seen as a luxury, among the first things to be cut as we drift toward positioning the university as a glorified vocational school. To be sure, the masters of these disciplines themselves are complicit in this decline, first by having allowed the statistics-driven aspect of social science into their temple, second by an excessive bow to political correctness, and more recently by tying their writings and ultimately themselves into such knots of postmodernist jargon that few are either able to or interested in figuring out what they have to say. These successive rounds of internal weakening in the humanities have made it easy for those who never had much regard for them to drive them toward marginalization within the world of what is still called "higher education" —a phrase that did not originally mean "advanced professional training."

I mean to suggest here that a certain sacred trust has been broken within the western educational mission. The liberal academic tradition fought a great battle against ecclesiastical domination over the course of several centuries, seeking a freedom that was certainly necessary for its own integrity. Nevertheless, a certain spirit of sacredness continued to hover over it. Education saw itself as having a *mission* of creating a more thoughtful citizenry, one respecting artistic and intellectual creativity. The "Temple of Learning" was still there to cultivate discernment and perhaps even wisdom in its students' minds. Today no one would think of going to most American universities in search of wisdom. The thought is almost laughable.

But Jewish learning, as I understand it, is precisely about that. It is a process of inquiry and a meeting with sources, study partners, and teachers in which the human heart and its ability to embrace the mystery of the divine within the text and the learning experience is precisely "the heart of the matter." Deep learning requires one to become open to human awareness that reaches beyond the superficial level of discourse where our daily lives are conducted. Thoughtful and open dialogue around the sources opens us up to deeper perceptions of both self and other, as well as the world around us.

Let me restate some of this in what has become my own symbolic language as a neo-Hasidic thinker. Franz Kafka's little collection of *Parables and Paradoxes* (edited by Professor Glatzer) contains a remark to the effect that humans were expelled from the Garden of Eden not because we ate of the Tree of Knowledge but because we detached it from the Tree of Life. Unbeknown to Kafka, a Kabbalist named Rabbi Ezra of Gerona had reached the same conclusion some seven hundred years earlier, in a text only to be rediscovered and published from manuscript by Gershom Scholem several decades after Kafka's death. For the Kabbalist, the two trees represent the essential male/female or giver/receiver duality that stands at the core of Kabbalistic symbolism; the Tree of Life is *tif'eret,* the central "male" figure of God, and the Tree of Knowledge of Good and Evil is *malkhut,* the receptive and liminal "female" body at the edge of the divine world that can be turned in either moral direction. Separating these two, the primal pair to be ever united in *heiros gamos,* is the root of all sin. But the Torah is known to be "A Tree of Life to those who hold fast to her (Prov. 3:18)," so the two aspects of divinity are also symbolized as written and oral Torah, *malkhut* serving as the ever-refreshing channel of interpretation through which the inscrutable written text is brought to earth. Separated from the text, she will go astray.

But surely Kafka had something else in mind, as do I. The great human fault ("original sin") lies in the bifurcation of knowledge and life, making the quest for knowledge an independent and self-justifying end, one that can then be turned against life itself as well as toward it, both for the individual and for the world as a whole. In our era, the diversion of brilliant minds toward creating weapons of ever-greater destructive power is only the most blatant example of this detachment. It is knowledge gone astray, no longer linked to its root in life itself, no longer a blessing that enhances our shared humanity, but rather a possession that will serve to divide us, leading toward violence and strife.

All this is a long way of saying that my life has been about a quest for a way of learning that might heal this breach between life and knowledge or wisdom and learning, an approach to the Jewish sources that might paradigmatically demonstrate to moderns or postmoderns what it is to learn for the sake of inner growth, cultivating a search for truth that broadens and deepens the human spirit. Religious learning may be the last refuge of what I see as the true humanistic spirit. Of course we Jews are not entirely alone in this matter. In the classical and medieval scholastic traditions of all three western faiths, wisdom and learning were seen as only slightly different aspects of a single enterprise: one sought knowledge in order to become wise or enlightened. In the West, this remains the case perhaps only in some monastic or quasi-monastic settings: among Benedictines and perhaps a few other Catholic orders and in the Hasidic and Sufi traditions of learning. A few small "oddball" colleges continue to keep the faith as well. But the special devotion of Jews to the study of our classic sources, together with our closeness to the world of the western academy, gives us a special opportunity and obligation to make this point.

The spirit of learning that we created in the early years of Havurat Shalom has remained my inspiration over the course of a half century. The work that our little band of twenty or thirty remarkable young Jews undertook in 1968 was intended as the cutting edge of an educational revolution, one that aimed to transform Jewish life and then reach far beyond it. (You understand now that I am a person not lacking in grandiosity of vision.) I take great pride in the accomplishments of our original *haverim,* many of which I believe are still colored by the values of those early and formative years in all of our lives. For myself, I can report some modest success in imbuing generations of both rabbinic and doctoral students with their spirit. I ask the reader of these essays to look at them with an eye open for that spirit and with an appreciation of the bridge I have sought to build between the openhearted study of the Jewish past and the articulation of a faith and spiritual path that will lead toward a creative Jewish future.

In preparing the essays for republication in this volume, I have chosen to leave them essentially in their original form. The reader should take note of the date of each article, listed in the bibliography at the end of this volume.

The text reflects my views at the time each article was written. In many cases these views have evolved since then, as may be reflected in other essays within the collection. It also means that some of the footnotes are hopelessly dated. This is particularly noticeable in the historical essays. With but a few exceptions, I have not included references to scholarly works appearing since the articles were originally published. To do so would have involved not only listing but discussion, and I felt that would require too much reshaping of the original pieces. I have made just occasional exceptions to this policy where I feared that reprinting a view I no longer hold to be true might seriously mislead the reader. I also apologize to the reader for some repetition, particularly in the theological essays. Each was originally written (or occasionally spoken) for a particular occasion or audience.

Arthur Green
Sivan 5773
June 2013

Acknowledgments

As this project of collection, selection, and editing draws to a close, I want to express my gratitude to the Jewish Publication Society for choosing to honor my work in this way. I am grateful to the society's director, Rabbi Barry Schwartz, and especially to Carol Hupping, who went beyond the call of duty and patience in working with me. I am also grateful to the alumni of our Hebrew College Rabbinical School, including Rabbis Minna Bromberg, Van Lanckton, and Suzanne Offit, who were touched by my choice to dedicate this volume to our beloved Sharon and who helped to raise funds to support its publication. Their dedication touches me deeply. As always, I am also grateful to my faithful student Ariel Mayse for his help in various technical matters required in seeing the project to completion.

The Heart of the Matter

PART 1

Judaism

The Religious Life

1

Introduction to *Jewish Spirituality*

Hear, O Lord, when I cry aloud;
have mercy on me, answer me.
In Your behalf my heart says:
"Seek My face!"
O Lord, I seek Your face.
Do not hide Your face from me;
do not thrust aside Your servant in anger;
You have ever been my help.
Do not forsake me, do not abandon me,
O God, my deliverer.

PSALM 27:8–9

Seeking the face of God, striving to live in His presence and to fashion the life of holiness appropriate to God's presence—these have ever been the core of that religious civilization known to the world as Judaism, the collective religious expression of the people Israel. Such a statement of supreme value—aside from questions of how precisely it is to be defined and how it is achieved—could win the assent of biblical priest and prophet, of Pharisee and Essene sectarian, of Hellenistic contemplative and law-centered rabbi, of philosopher, Kabbalist, hasid, and even of moderns who seek to walk in their footsteps.

Life in the presence of God—or the cultivation of a life in the ordinary world bearing the holiness once associated with sacred space and time, with Temple and with holy days—is perhaps as close as one can come to a definition of "spirituality" that is native to the Jewish tradition and indeed faithful to its Semitic roots. Within this definition there is room for an array of varied types, each of which gives different weight to one aspect or another of the spiritual life. For some, the evocation of God's presence includes an "ascent" to a higher realm and implies knowledge other than that vouchsafed to most mortals. Others content themselves with "preparing the table of the Lord" or, alternatively, seek to discover "the tabernacle within the heart" and allow the *shekhinah* (Presence) to find a dwelling there. The ultimate vision may be one of a highly anthropomorphic Deity seated on His throne, an utterly abstract sense of mystical absorption within the presence, the imminent arrival of messiah, or simply that of a life lived in the fulfillment of God's will. What all these have in common is a commitment to the life of holiness, a faith in the power of Israel's ancient code to embody that holiness, and a knowledge that such a life fulfills God's intent in creation and in the election, however understood, of His "kingdom of priests," the people Israel. This consensus has lasted until modern times when we find Jews in search of the spiritual life who can no longer accept its premises as classically outlined by Judaism.

The definition of Jewish spirituality offered here has rather little to do with the term "spirituality" itself, for which there is a precise Hebrew equivalent, *ruhaniyyut*. The reader sensitive to the nuances of Hebrew speech will recognize this word as a latecomer to the ancient Hebrew tongue. It is an artifice of the medieval translators that was created first to express philosophical and scientific concepts that were Hellenic in origin. It was taken over only later by Kabbalists and pietists to describe a religious ideal that by then indeed was a thorough amalgam of the spiritual legacies of Israel and Greece. Spirituality in the western sense, inevitably opposed in some degree to "corporeality" or "worldliness" (all apologies to the contrary notwithstanding), is unknown to the religious worldview of ancient Israel; it is rather a late element, though an important one, among those factors that make up the religious legacy of medieval and later Jewry. Defining spirituality as the cultivation and appreciation of the "inward" religious life, we find both assent and demurral in the sources of Judaism. Surely the Psalmist was a master, indeed perhaps the original western master, of inwardness, and the early rabbis knew well to speak of "the service within the heart" and the values of silence and solitude. There are latter-day Hasidic treatises focused almost entirely on the cultivation of *ruhaniyyut* and *penimiyyut* ("inwardness"). At the same time, concern is aroused lest the inner be praised at the expense of the outer. The rabbi, spiritual descendant of both priest and prophet in this matter, will perforce rise to defend the externals. If inwardness implies a depreciation of the outer and dismisses religious behavior (in the moral as well as the ritual realm) as *mere* ceremony or trappings, the rabbi will find this a notion hard to tolerate. Religion, as far as the rabbi is concerned, is the living word of God, ever evolving through interpretation, a word that concerns itself with proper behavior in every domain of life at least as much as it does with matters of the heart.

Aware of these reservations, and wary generally of applying to a particular tradition terms and categories that are alien to it ("mysticism" too is a category that does not exist within classical Jewish sources), we nevertheless permit ourselves to speak of Jewish spirituality, defining it as we have: Israel's striving for life in the presence of God. This should allow talmudist, halakhist, and commentator to take their deserved place within the collective "spiritual" enterprise alongside the more obvious prophet, philosopher, and mystic.

This view is also meant to dispel the ancient and widely held notion that there are in fact two Judaisms, one of the flesh or the law and the other of the spirit, or one of the mind and the other of the heart. This idea has a surprisingly long history and has been held by Christian detractors of Judaism who reflect the biases of the New Testament, but also by many Jews themselves. The Kabbalists supported a version of this idea, claiming that their teaching was the "soul" of Judaism and that without it rabbinic practice was but a lifeless body. Students of Judaism in the early twentieth century, themselves rebels against the stultifying world of the Eastern European *shtetl* ("small town"), also put forth a version of this idea (one thinks here of Buber, Berdyczewski, and Horodezky), by which they hoped to save and renew the heart of Judaism while casting off its outer shackles. From the historian's point of view, there is no single secret doctrine that serves to quicken Judaism, to save it from becoming a life-threatening morass of detail. Jews throughout the ages, including the early rabbis themselves, have struggled with this issue of providing meaning and spiritual content to the tradition. Some have done so in highly systematic fashion, creating such grand edifices as Jewish Aristotelianism and classical Kabbalah. Others, including the Hasidic preacher, have chosen to do so in a more spontaneous and sporadic manner. The very notion of a divine or primordial Torah, a thought that has accompanied rabbinic Judaism since its earliest days, seems, as Gershom Scholem has pointed out, to call forth a sense that there is some deeper esoteric meaning to the text at hand, some secret that is more than any ordinary human reading of Torah can provide. All of the systems of meaning that have emerged within the classical Jewish context have made use of this idea and have found within it the theological license for that exegetical creativity which is in fact the tradition's very lifeblood. "Turn it over, turn it over, for all is in it" has allowed sages and seekers of the most varied sorts to see their own thought, influenced as it may be by spiritual currents far from those of ancient Israel, as the true meaning of their own religious legacy. There are not *two* Torahs, a revealed and a hidden, but rather both *one* and *many*—as many as the ongoing creativity of the Jewish people can provide.

A history of Judaism from the viewpoint of the phenomenology of religion has yet to be written. The ways in which classic patterns of myth, symbol, and archetype survive the great transformations wrought by biblical religion and reappear, *mutatis mutandis*, in rabbinic and later Judaism are yet to be fully traced. The unique element of diaspora, spreading the Jews throughout the Western world at an early and crucial stage in their religion's development, also needs here to be taken into account. The traditions that grew out of that monotheistic and iconoclastic revolution in ancient Canaan, overlaid with memories of the Babylonian exile and its Persian aftermath as well as with evidence of the early contacts of Israel with Greece and Rome, were carried throughout the known world by bands of faithful wanderers. Yet who would dare say that Judaism, even of the most pious and traditionalist sort, remained unaffected by the cultural patterns of those in whose midst particular groups of Jews happened to settle? It is not at all clear that a Jew in Spain in the twelfth century and one in Poland or Bohemia some five hundred years later, even if performing the very same ritual actions, were in fact "doing the same thing." Distinctive religious subcultures emerged within the history of Jewry. Even in latter-day terms, if one thinks of Lithuania, Italy, and Yemen, highly diverse images of Judaism come to mind. These, it should be added, were not simply mirror images of the respective non-Jewish cultures amid which they were created: Jewish communities themselves, separated by distances of both time and space, created cultural and religious life patterns that differed greatly both from one another and from those of the host cultures in whose shadow they flourished.

Nor were differences in religious types attributable only to variations in historical or geographical circumstance. The same Amsterdam of the seventeenth century was home to rationalists and messianic Kabbalists, both of them probably nurtured by the same combination of Marrano past and expanding future. Warsaw at the turn of the twentieth century housed Hasidim of various stripes alongside socialists, Zionists, Yiddishists, and Hebraists in every imaginable combination—all of them products of, some of them rebels against, the same cultural milieu. Any account of the spiritual life of Jewry undoubtedly is in need of the word "varieties" somewhere in its title. Indeed it may be that a major lesson the Jewish experience has to offer the historian of religion is just that: even within this "smallest of all the nations" there lie a vast array of different religious types, spiritual activities, and attempts at self-understanding. No single characterization or typology of "Jewish spirituality" could possibly comprehend them all. How much more true must this be for religious empires far more vast than the relatively circumscribed realm of Jewry!

What then is it that coinhabitants of this religious and cultural phenomenon known as Judaism have in common? First, it must be said that they all are Jews, and this is no mere tautology. Judaism is the religious path of a distinct national group, one that has defined itself in ethnic as well as religious terms throughout the ages. The shared legacy of national symbols, including language, land (held dear, as history has shown, despite long absence), and common history, including but not limited to a history of persecution, is quite inseparable from Jewish religious identity. Yet the historian of religion must probe further, asking what it is within this legacy of the past that makes for the vital and ongoing thread of Judaism as a religious enterprise. In this search, one is first tempted to go the route of essentialism: somewhere at the core there must be an essence of Judaism that all its many bearers hold in common. This was, in fact, the path taken by most presentations of Judaism for the western reader, including both attempts at "objective" religious history and works of advocacy by Jewish theologians, in the nineteenth and early twentieth centuries. Of course this essence was usually articulated in theological terms—and then often in terms not unsurprisingly accommodating either to the writer's particular religious stance within the Jewish community or to the properly liberal and western values that an author might have thought his readers would find most comfortable. Thus ethical monotheism, the struggle against idolatry, and a vague commitment to "the rule of law"—though not to particular laws—were emphasized by liberal Jewish writers, whereas *halakhah* in its specific sense, but also expanded to "the halakhic mind," was brought to the fore by traditionalists.

Aside from the obviously self-serving quality of some of these presentations (and our selection from them admittedly borders on caricature), the attempts at arriving at such an essence have been largely discredited in Jewish scholarly circles because of recent developments in historical research. Essentialism always wound up positing a "mainstream" in the history of Jewry; those who diverged from whatever the particular set of norms was said to be were then characterized as minor groups of dissenters, who cut themselves off from the ongoing stream of Jewish history. But the work of mid-twentieth-century Jewish scholarship has almost entirely discredited the notion of *any* theological mainstream. Erwin R. Goodenough, researching the archaeological remains of Jewry throughout the eastern Mediterranean world, gave the lie to the widely held view that a rabbinic mainstream, puritanical, iconoclastic, and uncompromisingly anti-syncretistic, dominated Palestinian and Babylonian Jewry in the first centuries of the common era. Harry A. Wolfson has shown how thoroughly Jewish philosophers from Philo to Spinoza were part and parcel of the Western philosophical tradition, at times having more intellectually in common with their Christian and Muslim counterparts than they did with Jews who stood outside philosophy. Above all, Gershom Scholem and his studies of medieval Jewish mysticism and seventeenth-century Sabbatian messianism have had a revolutionary impact on the field of Jewish studies as a whole. Scholem has forced us to realize that notions of mainstream were posited largely out of ignorance and were sustained by the selective suppression of evidence. This process reflects the cultural biases to which historians, perhaps only slightly less than theologians, were themselves subject.

The elusive quality of any essentials that might still be said to underlie, even in an unspoken way, most or all Jewish theologies is heightened by the nonfundamentalist relationship that traditional Jewry has always had with its sacred scripture. Although the veracity and theoretical authority of the Bible were taken for granted from the Hellenistic era down to modern times, unanimity about the meaning of any but the blandest biblical phrases was utterly lacking. There is no postbiblical Jewish theology in any age that could claim to base itself on a *peshat*, that is, an obvious and straightforward reading of the biblical text. The contest between interpreters is not about which have scripture on their side, but rather about which display the greater ingenuity in marshaling scriptural support for their views. When in medieval times certain dogmatic formulations achieved a status that was nearly canonical (belief in divine omnipotence, or in creation *ex nihilo*), Kabbalists and others played freely with these, reinterpreting their meaning to suit their own ideas.

What then, if not theological essentials, will serve as the binding substance for the variety of Jewish spiritual expressions? It seems safe to begin with the text itself. All Judaisms since approximately the second century CE have had in common a defined body of sacred scripture, the Hebrew bible. Though exegetical license has indeed reigned free, it is not fair to assume that the text has made no claims on those who are faithful to it. These claims, the ones least bendable by interpretation, exist first in the realm of religious deed and second in that of religious language, imagery, and style.

The relative unanimity of premodern Jews in matters of religious action, codified as *halakhah* or the "path," is well known. The commandments of the Torah as defined and elaborated by the early rabbis were accepted as binding by all Jews except the Karaite minority, at least from the early Middle Ages down to the seventeenth century. There were, to be sure, ongoing debates concerning both details of the law and the seemingly large matter of what exactly it was that constituted the 613 commandments of the Torah itself. But these were dwarfed by the overwhelming unanimity in most matters of praxis, including both those matters "between man and God" and those "between man and man," or the ritual-devotional and the moral-ethical spheres. It is worthy of note that neither premodern Hebrew nor Yiddish has a term that may be properly used to translate "orthodox"; *shomer mizwot* ("observer of the commandments") or, in the more casual Yiddish vernacular, *shoimer shabes* ("Sabbath keeper") is as close as one could come. It was this unanimity of life pattern that allowed for Moses Mendelsohn's claim in the eighteenth century that Judaism was in fact a matter of "revealed legislation." This, of course, allowed for the wide berth of intellectual freedom that he as an enlightener sought. This view of Judaism, though thoroughly discredited by the nineteenth-century "essentialists," was based in the reality of long experience with one aspect of the tradition, the relative unanimity of deed and form.

Deeds, of course, are an aspect of symbolic speech, especially so when they take the regularized and repeated form of ritual. Alongside this type of speech-act, then, contemporary scholarship suggests that Judaism (like any religious tradition) has a unique pattern of verbal tropes and rubrics that constitute a unifying style of expression, one that transcends even great chasms in theological meaning. Any theology of Judaism, for example, must claim to believe in one God; monotheism is embodied in the essential trope of *shema' yisra'el* ("Hear, O Israel, the Lord our God, the Lord is one" [Deut. 6:4, recited in the daily liturgy]). A theology that denies the truth of the *shema'* or openly proclaims belief in a multiplicity of heavenly powers can hardly claim a place within Judaism. But the range of meaning given to the *shema'* remains quite open; the One may be a unity of ten powers, as for the Kabbalistic, or the *shema'* may attest to the absolute oneness of God and world, as for the *HaBaD Hasid*. The fact that both of these views stand in utter contradiction to the theology of Hebrew scripture constitutes no real problem in the history of Judaism, but stands rather as a monument to the exegetical success and freedom of these latter-day thinkers.

Another such basic trope is the belief in Torah as revealed at Mount Sinai. Again, a Judaism without some sort of Sinaitic revelation is inconceivable, but the range of beliefs about exactly what was given at Sinai, or what it means to speak of revelation, or the degrees of difference between inspiration and revelation, is tremendous, even before one takes into account the great variety of modern Jewish positions on this matter. Realistically speaking, the traditional claim that "whoever says 'This verse' or 'This word' is not from heaven is one who 'despises the word of the Lord'" (Num. 15:31) comes down to mean that those who can find no place for *some* concept of *Torah mi-Sinai* have rejected an essential rubric of Jewish discourse and thus have placed themselves outside the theological consensus of Israel.

Do we then propose naught but a new essentialism, one of tropes and rubrics rather than of dogmas and ideas? It should not be difficult to compile a list of essential religious vocabulary of which the would-be Jewish theologian could make rather free use. Of course (Heaven be praised! we should perhaps add), the matter is not so simple. Having used rather obvious and easily labeled examples, we speak of a literary and theological *style*, one carried in part by the mention of certain key terms but hardly reducible to them. The ways in which these terms are used, the frequency with which they appear, how they are juxtaposed with one another, and a whole host of other more or less intangible elements collectively constitute the religious language of Judaism. The well-trained eye of a text scholar or ear of a native speaker learns to detect unusual patterns, changes in meaning, and shifts of emphasis even in the seemingly most standard bit of rabbinic discourse. Especially interesting here are two late genres of premodern Jewish theological literature. Scholem's studies of the seventeenth- and eighteenth-century documents in which Sabbatian heresy was masked behind the language of traditional piety are instructive in illuminating the outermost limits of Jewish religious language and the ways in which even an exaggeratedly pietistic Jewish style can be distorted to produce radically new meanings. Similarly, the literature of Hasidism, though hardly heretical in the same way, offers the careful reader a chance to explore the traditional language and style of Judaism pushed to the extreme, as the masters used it to legitimize the particular religious values for which they stood.

The Judaism that all held in common was, we are claiming, a shared religious *language*, rooted in a body of sacred Scripture and anchored to daily life by a prescribed pattern of deeds. Like any language in currency over a wide geographical area and through the course of many centuries, it evolved, changed, grew, and developed its own varied "dialects." A multiplicity of religious types found within it sufficient breadth and depth to express their differences of vision and understanding; even those labeled "sinners" or "heretics" in times of controversy continued to make use, often the most creative use, of this religious language. Only in modern times has the language itself suffered a serious challenge, as the weakening of its own faith-claims has combined with the tremendous assimilatory pressures on Jewry to diminish greatly the hold it has maintained over the Jewish people. But the challenge to tradition, the various attempts to buttress it, and the large and highly variegated movements of modern or postmodern Jews seeking to return to its fold are themselves all a part of the ongoing history of Jewish spirituality.

2

Sabbath as Temple

Some Thoughts on Space and Time in Judaism

In 1945, just as the European Holocaust (and with it the second great age in Jewish history) was drawing to a close, Abraham Joshua Heschel gave voice to a hope that later Jewish history would one day be recognized and sanctified by the world, as has the history of biblical Israel:

> When Nebuchadnezzar destroyed Jerusalem and set fire to the Temple, our forefathers did not forget the Revelation at Mount Sinai and the words of the Prophets. Today the world knows that what transpired on the soil of Palestine was sacred history, from which mankind draws its inspiration. A day may come when the hidden light of the East European period will be revealed.[1]

We look at Jewish history throughout the Diaspora period—going here beyond Heschel and extending back from Eastern Europe to the Roman destruction—and ask ourselves what sort of inspiration we hope humanity might derive from the collective experience of the Jew. Surely the basic insights of our religion, moral as well as spiritual, are by now accessible outside of Judaism, whether through her younger sister faiths or altogether independently. The particularizing nuances of Jewish faith and expression, vital as they may seem from within, will not constitute a major new source of understanding. It is rather from the experience of Jewish history, and within this overwhelmingly from the experience of *galut*, that the world has to learn. Homelessness, alienation, permanent insecurity, the feeling of living as unwelcome guests in a society not of our making: these long-known characteristics of life as a Jew are now increasingly the lot of millions of others in a world where the uprooting of populations, the migration of labor forces, and, above all, the ongoing urbanization and de-traditionalization of people are taking place far faster than anyone can record.

Surely the great miracle of Jewish existence is our survival of *galut*. But if we ask ourselves what exactly *galut* is, and what means the Jewish people used to combat its corrosive power, our answer will necessarily be manifold. Our interest here is in the specifically religious quality of *galut*, in distinction (a historical artificiality, to be sure) from its political, economic, linguistic, and other aspects. It was in religious terms, after all, that premodern Jews generally and most successfully expressed themselves, and it is around religious symbols, not surprisingly, that a great deal of the discussion of *galut* is focused.

Umi-penei hata'enu galinu me-'arzenu—"because of our sins we were exiled from our land." Such phrases abound in Jewish liturgy, alternating always with the prayers for restoration. If we take such liturgical expression as a standard for the Jews' images of their history, it becomes clear that *hurban* and *galut*, the destruction of the Temple and the exile from the land, are invariably treated as one. This is the case despite the fact that they did not come at the same time in the all-important second destruction. Erez Yisrael remained a major center of Jewish life and activity for four or five hundred years after the Temple was destroyed. The paradigmatic event for classical Jewish self-understanding was the *first* destruction, even though it was in the crucible of the second that rabbinic Judaism had its birth. Sin and prophetic warning followed by destruction and exile as one event: this is the way the Jewish people chose to remember it.

In order to see the meaning of this exile in religious terms, some patterns perceived elsewhere in the study of the history of religions should be recalled. Israel is a people living in what its God has designated a holy land, proclaimed as such through the various deeds of revered ancestors in times long gone. In that holy land God has chosen one place "to cause His name to dwell there" (Deut. 12:11) and at that spot has commanded His faithful servant to build a Temple. True, many among Israel had learned, especially by the second Temple period, that their God was not purely a local tribal deity, that the Creator could be worshipped from anywhere and by others as well as Israelites. And yet the religion of Israel had never fully abandoned its tribal roots. The Land of Israel, Jerusalem, and the Temple were still the *right* places—if not the only places—for Israel to stand before its God. The dearest expression of this viewpoint in the Bible is probably the prayer of Solomon, with which he reportedly dedicated the House of God. It is worth calling to mind some excerpts:

But will God really dwell on earth? Even the heavens and their uttermost reaches cannot contain You, how much less this house that I have built! Yet turn, O Lord my God, to the prayer and supplication of Your servant, and hear the cry and prayer which Your servant offers before You this day. May Your eyes be open day and night toward this House, toward the place of which you have said: "My name shall abide there," may You heed the prayers which Your servants will offer toward this place. And when You hear the supplications which Your servant and Your people offer toward this place, give heed in Your heavenly abode— give heed and pardon.

In any plague or in any disease, in any prayer or supplication offered by any person among all Your people Israel—each of whom knows his own affliction—when he spreads his palms toward this House, O hear in Your heavenly abode, and pardon, and take action!

When Your people take the field against their enemy by whatever way You send them, and they pray to the Lord in the direction of the city which You have chosen, and of the House which I have built to Your name, O hear in heaven their prayer and supplication and uphold their cause. (1 Kings 8:27–30, 38–39, 44–45)

Although this prayer was probably composed long after Solomon, and possibly after the first exile, it shows how central the chosen city and Temple remained in Israelite eyes. Historians of religion have shown that early societies are generally constructed around a geographical "sacred center." Such a center serves to embody the values and aspirations of each society. It is also in one way or another the very real dwelling place of the deity, the locus out of which divine power radiates, or at least the place on earth where humans are most apt to be touched by the Presence. The Bible is somewhat reserved about expressing this concept, at least in some of its more mythological aspects. The notion that the Temple is the opening to heaven and hell, or stands on the spot where Creation began, or is located just below a great heavenly Temple, does not find direct narrative expression in scripture. Such is of course indicated by biblical language and terminology: *Beth El* and *Sha'ar ha-Shamayim* are two of the more obvious examples. The fact that these terms grow forth into full and explicit narratives in the postbiblical sources, where less care was taken with regard to such anti-mythic "orthodoxy," and sometimes in forms quite strikingly parallel to expressions in Mesopotamian literature of more than a millennium earlier, makes it rather likely that these concepts were indeed a part of the unrecorded folk legacy of ancient Israel.[2] This notion of center ties together visions of ideal past or origins and restoration in the harmonious future, which is to say that it stands at the very core of what the Bible understands as both cosmology and history. It has also been suggestively argued that the biblical narrative itself, taken as a literary whole, may be said to have underlying it an ongoing sense of sacred center, extending from the tree of Eden down through Abraham's discovery of the Holy Land, Jacob's Bethel vision, and the tabernacle in the wilderness, until it receives its final articulation in the city of David and the Temple of his son.[3]

Bearing in mind this view of Temple as the center of cosmic orientation, we can now pose more clearly our question about the religious meaning of *galut* to the Jewish people and how postbiblical Judaism has been a reaction to it. First, we should reiterate that the destruction of the Temple made *galut* a fact; a visit or even settlement in the Holy Land could not change that. The Land of Israel *sans* Temple and altar was still sacred, to be sure, but it had lost much of its luster in Jewish eyes. Medieval Jewish visitors to the Land, rather than glorying in their return home, joined the land in *its* mourning. It was as though the burning of Jerusalem had caused the land itself to go into exile. Our primary focus, however, should not be upon Judaism's mourning but upon its growth and renewal. Given the role that the Jerusalem center played in the cosmology of ancient Israel, and given the later biblical insistence that only there could the cult of Israel be practiced, how was the transition made in the religious life of the Jewish people from Temple to synagogue, from a sacrificial cult at the Center to a liturgical faith that could thrive anywhere?[4] To answer this we should look at the attitudes of the early synagogue and its religion, especially as reflected in the liturgy, toward the old cult and Temple. Fortunately, this very question has been addressed in an illuminating study by Robert Goldenberg entitled "The Broken Axis."[5] In examining early rabbinic liturgy, the author notes that the rabbis never resolved the dilemma of whether or not their religion of prayer, *halakhah*, and study successfully superseded the Jerusalem cult. With Hosea (14:3) they proclaimed, "We shall render for bullocks the offering of our lips," and they structured their daily *'amidah* prayers as though they were filling the role of sacrifices. But they also made sure, in the midst of those prayers, to express a longing that "the Temple be rebuilt soon, in our own days," that "You restore the priests to their service and the Levites to their song and music," and, quite explicitly, that "there we shall eat of the sacrifices and the Paschal offerings as their blood reaches the side of Your altar, in fulfillment of Your will."[6] Goldenberg reaches the following conclusion:

> The self-conception of rabbinic Judaism is built on the contradictory assumptions that the earlier worship in the Temple has been successfully left behind, but that things will never be quite right until it has been restored. If considered theologically, that amounts to a stark contradiction or at best an ambivalent paradox; seen as an effort to preserve the old religious orientation after its basis has been swept away, it makes sense. We can then see here the outlines of a system which took advantage of the disorientation caused by the fall of Jerusalem, but did not fall victim to it. The continuity of religious life was thus protected, even as all the forms of religious life had to be changed.

This ambivalence toward the sacred center is placed into clearest relief when the position of rabbinic Judaism is contrasted with that of its rival and fellow heir to ancient Hebrew cosmology, the early Church. Classical Christianity took the clear and unambiguous step that the rabbis declined to take: the old Temple has been replaced. Christ has become the center; sacred space has been recast into Christ the Temple. Sacred person completely dominates the cosmological stage; as Jesus the Christ is Torah enfleshed, so is he God's house reestablished. His cross and his body are the meeting place of heaven and hell. His body, through its presence in the Eucharist, is able thus to consecrate real sacred space over and over again. It is the clear negation of the old *axis mundi* that allows Christianity the power to create new sacred space symbolically in a way that Judaism was never able (nor did it seek) to do. The cathedral and its architecture seek to re-create and embody the primal world; through the death of sacred space and its rebirth, creation can happen anew. The synagogue, though sometimes called *miqdash me'at* ("little Temple"), is viewed so much as a temporary replacement for the only *real* sanctuary that its structure, however loved and sometimes embellished, could not be granted such significance.

Lacking an unambiguous resolution of this question, the Judaism of the rabbis moved on several fronts at once. The Day of Atonement, liturgy, and good deeds all serve in one or another rabbinic pronouncement to replace the altar. Sacred person has a very limited role in early post-exilic Judaism and assumes major proportions only—to the distress of many—in the Hasidism of the eighteenth century.[7] An area that is less obvious, largely because it is not articulated directly by the rabbis, is our concern here: the transfer of attention from sacred space to sacred time. Diaspora Israel are deprived of space; the land they are in is profane in their sight, not capable or worthy of sanctuary. The only truly holy place, far off from most, in any case lies in presently irreparable ruin. What has remained untouched by the conqueror, however, and, moreover, what remains consistently portable for a wandering community, is the realm of time. It is to time, and of course particularly to the Sabbath, that the rabbis sought to turn Israel's attention. The development of the already ancient Sabbath as the central ritual/halakhic institution of rabbinic Judaism was a specific reaction to the era of destruction, and it represented an unconscious shifting of primary Jewish allegiance from the spatial to the temporal realm.

It was Heschel who first called the attention of modern Jews to the Temple-like quality of the Jewish Sabbath. His book *The Sabbath* made frequent reference to Shabbat as a "palace in time" and went on to describe Judaism as a time- oriented rather than space-oriented way of viewing the world. Heschel did not, however, set the centrality of Shabbat in historical context, a move that might have been inappropriate to an essentially poetic work.[8] In asserting the superiority of time over space as an eternal Jewish value, however, and in consigning the love of space to the realms of the ancient pagan and the modern materialist, the work inevitably wound up in deprecation of space, despite Heschel's claims to the contrary.

The remainder of this study may be viewed as an extended footnote to *The Sabbath*, a claim that Shabbat-centered piety belongs specifically to the second era of Jewish history, the result of particular spiritual/historical circumstances.

Anyone familiar with the life of a traditional Jewish community needs no proof of the centrality of Shabbat in Jewish religious life. The ongoing love affair between Jew and Shabbat is so well attested in Jewish folk literature, and has been so beautifully described by Heschel and others that it would be worse than superfluous to try to capsulize it here. It might be worth noting that there are ways in which the Jewish community actually *defined* itself religiously as a community of Sabbath observers: one who keeps the Sabbath is part of the group, but one who profanes it (for the Sabbath was proclaimed holy at Creation) is not. A Sabbath observer may be trusted as a witness before a rabbinic court; a Sabbath profaner may not. Food served in the home of a known Sabbath observer may be assumed ritually fit; among others one could take no chances. Probably the closest one could come to speaking of an "Orthodox" Jew in premodern Jewish parlance, as used within the community, was *shomer shabbos*. Such evidences are, of course, popular and informal; they reflect general opinion rather than *halakhah* and are not necessarily early.[9] One might wonder, however, whether the Talmudic tale of the final encounter between Elisha ben Abuya and Rabbi Meir does not represent something similar. It is as Elisha rides off on his horse beyond the Sabbath barrier, leaving Meir behind, that the final break is made by the heretic who has left the rabbinic fold.[10]

The observance of the Sabbath has always been one of the major concerns of Jewish law: definitions and categorizations of forbidden labors, punishments for Sabbath violation, and the application of old categories of forbidden labor to ever-new situations of advancing human technology have occupied Jewish legalists since very early times. While we do not know as much as we would like about the observance of the Sabbath in pre-rabbinic times, there is much evidence from the later period of the Second Temple, both internal and external, to indicate that Sabbath rest was a central part, if not actually the defining characteristic, of the religion of the Jews.[11] Evidence from the Dead Sea sectarians shows that their Sabbath was rather like that of the later rabbis in terms of its halakhic nature.[12] Some indications are now found that lead scholars to trace later forms of Sabbath observance back to biblical times, despite the lack of written evidence for them.[13]

Our claim is *not*, then, that Sabbath became important only after the destruction of the Temple. This would be foolish; the Ten Commandments are ample testimony to the contrary. It is rather this: *the Sabbath gradually supplanted the Temple as the central unifying religious symbol of the Jewish people.* This shift took place originally in the context of the sectarian strife of the Second Temple period and was ultimately confirmed by the destruction of the Temple.

The best symbol for this movement from space-oriented to time-oriented piety is in the formula that the rabbis use to encapsulate the Sabbath regulations; the thirty-nine categories of forbidden labor.[14] According to Talmudic report (originally disputed but later widely accepted by the tradition), the biblical basis for almost the entirety of the Sabbath prohibitions lies in Exodus 31:13: "Moreover you shall keep My Sabbaths." This Sabbath command is inserted, seemingly without reason, in the midst of the ongoing discussion of the building of the tabernacle, the Torah's prototype of an ideal Temple. Since the word 'akh, with which this Sabbath verse opens, is a term of exception in the technical vocabulary of rabbinic exegesis (i.e., it comes to teach that what follows is an exception to the previously stated rule), the rabbis conclude that all forms of labor involved in any way in the construction of the tabernacle were meant to be forbidden on the Sabbath. These include such general categories as planting, shearing, dyeing, sewing, and striking a hammer. The point seems to be obscure and arbitrary, that so much of Sabbath law should be unmentioned in scripture and derived from a seemingly innocuous two-letter Hebrew word. The rabbis themselves called it "mountains hanging by a hair."[15] But perhaps it is neither arbitrary nor obscure. The commandments for the tabernacle tell how to construct sacred space, elaborating in full and rich detail the place that was to be Israel's center and opening to heaven. Now, because of changed circumstances, a new such center was needed, temporal rather than spatial in character. The ancient and revered institution of Shabbat is the vehicle, of course, but the detail of Shabbat observance is lacking in biblical basis and especially lacking in a coherent structure to lend it meaning. By the deft interpretation of an 'akh, the rabbis have succeeded in transferring all that biblical detail from the realm of space, where it had been rendered useless, to that of time. The phenomenon is one of reversal: by *doing* all these labors in the particular prescribed configuration, one creates sacred space. By *refraining* from these same acts, in the context of the Sabbath, one creates sacred time. Here the legalistic device, far from being arbitrary, is used in a highly sophisticated way to effect a basic change in religious modality.

The Talmudic rabbis had not read Mircea Eliade. For them such notions as "sacred time" and "sacred space" hardly existed as categories of thought. There was, of course, no conscious decision taken one fine day at Yavneh to fashion the Sabbath after the fallen Temple.[16] How then, according to our reading, could such a transference have come about? How could Temple and Shabbat, two seemingly unrelated institutions of ancient Judaism, be so linked? The question requires a brief examination of the theological rationale provided for these institutions in the biblical and rabbinic sources, one that will uncover a deep though mostly unspoken link between the two, a link that makes this shift of focus after the destruction considerably more understandable.

Rav Judah in the name of Rav (Babylonia, third century) teaches that Bezalel, architect of the tabernacle, "knew how to perform those permutations of letters through which heaven and earth were created."[17] Why should Bezalel, of all people (and not Moses or Aaron), be privy to this secret? The tradition makes sense only if his single task is somehow especially related to the original Creation. We do not have to go far to see that this is the case:

"These are the accounts of the tabernacle" (Ex. 38:21). . . . Said Rabbi Jacob ben Assi: Why does Scripture say "Lord, I love the habitation of Your House and the place where Your Glory dwells" (Ps. 26:8)? Because it [God's house] is parallel to the Creation of the world. How is this?

Of the first day it is written: "In the beginning God created the heaven and the earth." It is also written "He stretched forth the heavens like a curtain" (Ps. 104:2). And what is written regarding the tabernacle? "You shall make curtains of goatskins" (Ex. 26:7).

On the second day: "Let there be a firmament," and separation is mentioned, as it says: "Let it separate waters from waters." And of the tabernacle: "And the veil shall separate for you between the holy and the holy of holies" (Ex. 26:33).

On the third day water is mentioned: "Let the waters be gathered." And in the tabernacle: "You shall make a brass basin with a brass base . . . and place water there" (Ex. 30:18).

On the fourth day He created the lights, as it says: "Let there be luminaries in the heavenly firmament." And in the tabernacle: "You shall make a gold candelabrum" (Ex. 25:31).

On the fifth day He created the birds: "Let the waters swarm with every living thing and let birds fly." Parallel to them in the tabernacle are sacrifices of lambs and birds. [Alternative reading: "And in the tabernacle: 'The cherubim spread their wings upward' (Ex. 25:20)."]

On the sixth day man was created, as it says: "He created man in His image. He created him through the glory.[18] Man (Adam) in the tabernacle is the high priest, anointed to serve and minister before the Lord.[19]

The continuation of this midrash will be quoted below, but there is enough here for our present purpose. The parallel raises to an ultimate height the cosmic significance of the drama that takes place within the tabernacle or Temple. The priest is now Adam or the embodiment of all mankind, the candelabrum gives off the radiance of the sun, and so forth. While the language is that of metaphor, the intent seems clearly symbolic: thus is the cult to be understood. The rabbis speak of sacred space as microcosm, the tabernacle reproducing in a sacralized context the entirety of Creation. In other passages the relationship between Creation and the tabernacle is adumbrated somewhat differently: Creation is not quite complete or secure until it has been "sealed" by the erection of the sacred shrine:

"Who has established all the ends of the earth?" (Prov. 30:4). The tent of meeting, as it says: "It was on the day that Moses completed setting up the tabernacle" (Num. 7:1). The world was set up with it. Rabbi Joshua ben Levi in the name of R. Simeon ben Yohai: It does not say *LeHa-*QYM *HaMiSHKaN*, but rather *LeHa-*QYM *'et* [with] *Ha-MiSHKaN*. What was set up "with" it? The world, for until the tabernacle was erected the world trembled; when the tabernacle was set up the world was firmly established.[20]

Here too we see a theme that is familiar from other cultural contexts. The shrine finally validates (and hence guarantees) the existence of the world itself; only at this point is Creation complete.

Viewing the tabernacle/Temple from this perspective, we understand that the rabbis took it as no coincidence that the Sabbath command of Ex. 31:12 followed immediately upon the details of its construction. Only then is Moses told (31:1ff.) that God has called upon Bezalel and his associates to execute the work. The Sabbath warning comes before work can actually begin. Theologically as well as halakhically, there is no arbitrariness; as God rests on the seventh day after His work of Creation, so do you rest on the seventh of yours. The repetition of the Sabbath command in Ex. 35:1–3, just as the actual work is to get under way, makes it clear that in this case what the rabbis saw was probably *peshat*, at least the intent of a scriptural editor.

The Sabbath, according to Genesis, is the apex of Creation. There is no holiness in God's world until He finds rest. Only after Creation has been completed and He ceases from work does He bless and hallow. And it is not the fruit of His labors that is sanctified, but the day of His rest.

The building of a Temple is, for religious societies, the most meaning-ful of human labors; in it man makes an earthly dwelling place for the presence of his God or, in Israel's case, a symbol of His presence in their midst. But this labor too remains unhallowed until completion. The labor-ers who constructed the Temple, we are told, were able to come and go throughout, even walking through what was to become the holy of holies, until their work was done.

No wonder then that the closing chapter of Exodus repeats the step-by-step structure of the opening chapter of Genesis, concluding with the unmistakable refrain *Va-yekhal Mosheh et ha-mel'akhah*.[21] A biblical redactor, having before him an account that reached from Creation to the tabernacle, sought to "seal" that account with a conclusion that has an appropriate parallel to its beginning. Creation is completed by its rep-etition as a human act; God's work finds fulfillment only as something of His power to create is imitated by humans. In this linking of sacred-space construction to the original Creation, the Torah also implies a link, spo-ken only with the subtlety of juxtaposition and linguistic parallel, between Temple and Sabbath.

Now we may conclude the passage from *Midrash Tanhuma* that we cited above. The six days of Creation, we recall, have already found their match in the tabernacle. And now:

> On the seventh day: "Heaven and earth were completed." And in the tab-ernacle: "All the work was completed" (Ex. 39:32). Of Creation: "And God blessed [the seventh day]," and of the tabernacle: "And Moses blessed them" (Ex. 39:43). Of Creation: "God completed," and of the tabernacle: "On the day when Moses completed" (Num. 7:1). Of Creation: "And He made it holy," and of the tabernacle: "He anointed it and made it holy."

It was the rabbis' sensitivity to this nuance of biblical meaning, barely hinted at in text but deeply implanted in the structure of the two institutions, that allowed them, in the face of the need of their age, to perform the delicate manipulation of an 'akh[22] that had so great a meaning for all of the Judaism that was to come.

Jewish thinkers writing under the influence of Kabbalah, beginning in the thirteenth century, were able to articulate most fully this link between Temple and Sabbath. In the works of the Spanish Kabbalists, well known for their deft use of symbols and their ability to rapidly translate from one symbol system into another, it is frequently made clear either that Temple (or tabernacle) and Sabbath are one or else that they are the classic pair which need to be drawn together. Here we are dealing with a literature of mysticism, one in which both time and space will perforce be relativized. The chief focus of the Kabbalists' interest is the realm of the *sefirot*, seen at once as the stages of divine unfolding or emanation and as the rungs in the ladder of the mystic's ascent to the One. As the adept moves by successive degrees ever "upward" or "inward" toward realization, points along the journey must perforce somehow be designated. These designations, drawn especially by the Zohar in a full array of colorful symbols, may be characterized by terms that have their origins either in the temporal or the spatial realm. Either is acceptable for this purpose because neither is quite adequate. The divine effulgence does not first flow through spatially locatable points or temporally determined moments; neither does the mystic in his ascent to God. In order to speak of his universe in human language, however, he must designate the stages in symbols taken from one realm or the other. It is not surprising, then, to find in his writings moments in "time" and objects in "space" that turn out to be identical with one another. As symbols of light may turn into water as one proceeds from line to line on the same page of Zohar, so may figures in space "reveal themselves" to be figures in time. What we have here is no merely external literary device, but a representation in symbolic language of an essential characteristic of mystical experience.

The central figures in most discussions of the sefirotic universe are the sixth and the last of these ten manifestations. The sixth *sefirah* represents the deity as generally depicted in the earlier biblical and rabbinic sources. This is the God-figure, Father and King, who is the source of the written Torah, the object of nonmystical prayer, and whose being represents a constant balance of the potentially warring forces of justice and love, the "blessed Holy One," as He is most frequently called by the rabbis. The tenth *sefirah* is the *shekhinah*, the presence of God indwelling, the hypostatized Community of Israel, and most important, the object of divine affection, the bride of the mystical Song of Solomon. The most essential and daring theological innovation of the Kabbalah was the claim that the Canticle, long read by the rabbis as a love song between God and His people Israel, was now to be seen as documenting a love that takes place *within* God, between two poles of the divine self symbolically designated as male and female, a relationship in which the people Israel were no longer seen as the direct object of divine *eros* but rather as its offspring and devotees.

The association of the Sabbath with the feminine aspect of the divine world is widespread in the Kabbalah and is quite well known, if only through its presentation in the Sabbath hymn *Lekha Dodi*. Many Kabbalistic writings speak of two Sabbaths or of male and female aspects within the Shabbat itself (these resting on earlier speculations around *zakhor*— "remember" the Sabbath [Ex. 20:8] and *shamor*—"keep" the Sabbath [Deut. 5:12]). But it is with the *shekhinah* as bride and queen that the mystics' Sabbath is finally identified:

> The secret of Sabbath: *She* is Sabbath as she cleaves to the mysterious One, causing that One to shine upon her. . . . When Sabbath comes, she is unified and separated from the "other side." All evil forces of judgment are removed from her, and she dwells in union with the holy light. She is crowned with many crowns as she faces the holy king . . . her face shines with a sublime radiance as she is crowned from below by the holy people.[23]

The tabernacle/Temple too is identified with the *shekhinah* throughout the literature of the Kabbalah. House, Tent, Temple are all classic symbols of the feminine archetype: that which is entered, gathering place, womb, etc. It is in this symbolic garb that the last *sefirah* serves as the meeting place for God and Israel: the flow of divine energy from the *sefirot* "above" and the devotion of Israel's prayers "below" are joined together in this *bet mo'ed le-khol hai*. It was in some of their most daring moments that the Kabbalistic authors allowed Moses (or the adept in the guise of Moses?) to share with God the role of bridegroom of the *shekhinah*. Hence this rather startling passage is made possible:

"They brought the tabernacle unto Moses" (Ex. 39:33). Why did they bring the tabernacle? Because that was the hour of Moses' marriage—for this reason "they brought the tabernacle unto Moses"—just as the bride is brought to the bridegroom. First the bride must be brought to her groom, as Scripture says: "I have given my daughter to this man as a wife" (Deut. 22:16). Only afterwards may he [the bridegroom] come to her, and it says, "and he came unto her," as is written, "Moses came unto the tent of testimony" (Num. 17:23). Here, however, what is written? "Moses could not come in to the tent of meeting for the cloud abode upon it" (Ex. 40:35). For what reason? She was preparing herself for him, as a woman prepares and adorns herself for her husband. At the time when she is adorning herself it is not proper for her husband to come in to her. That was why "Moses could not come in to the tent of meeting" and it was for that reason that "They brought the tabernacle unto Moses."[24]

This rather courtly vignette of Moses and the *shekhinah* as bridegroom and bride is paralleled by a number of passages, particularly in the Zohar, where the lovely damsel or chaste and faithful wife appears as symbolic representation of the *shekhinah*. It is generally understood that these refer in the first place to *shekhinah* as the bride of God, but not exclusively so. With regard to the Sabbath, too, it should be recalled, there is reason in old Midrashic sources to think of her as Israel's bride: "Israel will be your mate," God says to the lonely seventh day.[25] The poetic genius of Alkabez's *Lekha Dodi* lies in his steadfast refusal to name the *dod* to whom the hymn is addressed, thus maintaining a certain enriching ambiguity in the identity of the Sabbath's bridegroom.[26] This Shabbat, for whom one must prepare "as one prepares a canopy for a bride," is also the one who is "shut and sealed on the six weekdays," in a passage that quotes from Ezekiel's vision of the restored Temple (46:1): "but on the seventh day she is open to receive her husband."[27] The identification of Temple and Sabbath is sometimes associated with the exegesis of Lev. 19:30: "You shall keep My Sabbaths and fear My Temple." So, for example, Rabbi Bahya ben Asher of Barcelona, a contemporary of the Zohar:

"You shall keep My Sabbaths." . . . One is the Great Sabbath, that of "remember," and the other is the Temple, the Community of Israel, mate of [the upper] Sabbath. This one is "keep," and for that reason it was not proper that the work of [building] the Temple supersede this Sabbath/Temple.[28]

Here the lower Sabbath, that of "keep" and thus particularly identified with the prohibitions among the Sabbath commands, is identified at once with *shekhinah* and Temple. For the Kabbalist it is perfectly a matter of course that the command of Sabbath was so placed in the Bible as to infer that the work of construction had to cease on the seventh day: anything else would have been self-contradictory, for the Sabbath, and particularly the cessation from labor, *is* the Temple.[29]

If the medieval Kabbalists were able by means of their mystical symbolization of space and time to bring Temple and Sabbath to a state of identification, the free-wheeling associative patterns of the later Hasidic homilies were able to do the same. Popular impressions to the contrary, their method was not at all that of the Kabbalists, but rather an extension, sometimes seemingly *ad absurdum*, of the classical methods of Midrashic exegesis. Although the rubric of the *sefirot* is formally preserved in Hasidic discourse, its content has been largely vitiated. The Kabbalistic system is generally used (*HaBaD* is the great exception here) as only one more device in the hands of the homilist. Thus "Sabbath" and "Temple" in the following passages are no longer ciphers for the *shekhinah* but once again the real Sabbath and Temple of time and space, with perhaps just a slight added nuance of Kabbalistic meaning.

The first Hasidic passage comes from the *Degel Mahaneh Ephraim*, the collected homilies of Rabbi Moses Hayyim Ephraim of Sudilkov, first published in 1810/11. Ephraim was the grandson of the Ba'al Shem Tov,[30] and his teachings often reflect the thoughts of the movement's first central figure:

The children of Israel shall keep the Sabbath, observing the Sabbath throughout their generations as an everlasting covenant; it is a sign forever between Me and the children of Israel" (Ex. 31:13). The *Ba'al ha-Turim* notes that the words *'et ha-shabbat le-dorotam* may be abbreviated as *'HL* (consonantally) *'ohel*, "tent."

In commenting on this we must first recall the verse "They shall make Me a tabernacle and I will dwell in their midst" (Ex. 25:8). We might then think that without such a tabernacle it would not be possible for the *shekhinah* to dwell amidst us! But the matter must be understood thus: "A foretaste of the world to come is the Sabbath day of rest." The best counsel [since there is no tabernacle] is to keep the Sabbath properly. In this way may we merit, as it were, the indwelling of the Presence, for the Sabbath is a sort of sanctuary. In that way too is it a foretaste of the future world [i.e., of the rebuilt Temple].

It was for this reason that the Torah hinted at the word "tent" in the phrasing of this verse, showing that the Sabbath too is a form of tent or tabernacle. The word *le-dorotam* also hints at the notion of "dwelling" (*DoRoTaM = DiRaTaM*), as in the dwelling of a Temple. In this way God dwells in our midst, and that is why Scripture continues: "as an everlasting covenant": by means of the Sabbath, the Lord, blessed be He, dwells in our midst . . . and the words *'ot hi' le-'olam* again form the word *'ohel*, showing that this sign goes on without interruption. Even in times when there is no Temple, the Sabbath has not been negated, *and it is the Temple.*[31]

Operating here outside that symbol-structure that had so utterly relativized space and time, the Hasidic master produces his own spiritualized rereading of the scriptural command. His spirituality remains halakhic, to be sure, for it is only by "keeping the Sabbath properly (*kehilkhato*)" that this new Temple is maintained. His essential point, however, is far-reaching, one that goes to the very core of the religious radicalism of the Hasidic movement: The destruction of the Temple does not represent an *essential* change in the relationship of God to His world and to Israel. The Presence remains in our midst as previously; only the medium of primary access to it has been shifted. The immanentism that the Ba'al Shem Tov's religion represented had to find a way to overcome the sense of divine distance that permeates so much of rabbinic and later Judaism.

A second Hasidic example, as likely to have been well known to Heschel as was the first, is found in the *Mey ha-Shiloah*, by Rabbi Mordecai Joseph Leiner of Izbica (1800/01–1854). Izbica was an important school of Hasidic thought in central Poland; its founder, Mordecai Joseph, had at one point been quite close to Rabbi Mendel of Kotzk, whose latter-day disciples Heschel knew so well in Warsaw. R. Mordecai Joseph writes:

"You shall keep My Sabbaths and fear My Temple" (Lev. 19:30). 'My Sabbaths' [in the plural], for every dwelling of the *shekhinah* at any time, no matter how temporary, is called a Sabbath. The blessed Lord commanded us to honor all the places where His *shekhinah* has dwelt, however temporarily. "And fear My Temple"—the Targum renders this as "be in fear for My Temple": you still should long for the deepest [eschatological] good to be found in each of the commandments. The Sabbath as we have it now is much diminished; only in the future will God grant us "the day that is wholly Sabbath," when we shall have no need for any labors. We must long for this, while still giving honor, meanwhile, to that which God has commanded us.

This may be compared to a king who moves from place to place: you show honor to each of his lodgings, while still looking forward to his own resting place. . . .

This was the mistake of Hophni and Phinehas: they saw that God's dwelling in Shiloh was only a temporary one, and therefore they treated it lightly. Of such conduct Scripture says: "You have despised My Temple."[32]

Here we have the lesson drawn out for us in a strikingly modern-sounding formulation: the juxtaposition of Sabbath and Temple teaches us that any place where the glory of God appears, in however transient a manner (and indeed what place is not capable of such description?) is to be treated as God's holy Temple. Yes, Judaism has become a religion of sacred time, learning through the bitter experience of exile that geographical locus alone could not suffice to describe the manner in which God dwells on earth. This time-centeredness, however, also served to expand and "liberate" the notion of sacred space, a process we see reaching its culmination here in the *Mey ha-Shiloah*. The history of exile teaches Israel that a sacred day, unlike a sacred mountain or a sacred shrine, may be carried anywhere and remain safe from outward attack. The hidden lesson here learned also inevitably points to the idea that any place where that Sabbath is proclaimed holy comes to have just a touch of Jerusalem residing within it. The legacy of wandering Israel to the world may lie precisely in this: home does not have to be abandoned as you are forced to leave it. The transformation of space into time may allow us to be bearers of our homes and origins, however far away from them modernity may lead us, so that the values they represented in our lives need not fade into mere pleasant memories of things past.

1. *Der Mizraḥ-Eiropeisher Yid* (New York: Schocken Books, 1946), 44–45. Expanded translation as *The Earth Is the Lord's* (New York: Schuman, 1950), 99.

2. These sources have been collected and discussed by Raphael Patai in *Man and Temple* (London: T. Nelson, 1947). See also the dated but still important treatment by Victor Aptowitzer in "*Bet ha-Miqdash shel Maʿalah*," *Tarbiz* 2 (1931). For the older Mesopotamian parallels, see particularly the works of Geo Widengren, including *Sakrales Konigtum im Alten Testament und im Judentum* (Stuttgart, 1955), and the various ancillary studies.

3. Michael Fishbane, "The Sacred Center in the Bible," in *Texts and Responses: Studies Presented to Nahum N. Glatzer* (Leiden, 1975), 6ff. See also his *Text and Texture: Close Readings of Selected Biblical Texts* (New York: Schocken, 1979). I am grateful to Professor Fishbane for several suggestions he has made in connection with this article.

4. I do not mean to oversimplify a long and complex process. Of course, I am aware that the synagogue began to come into being before the Temple was destroyed, etc. The question is asked from a long-range historical vantage point.

5. Robert Goldenberg, "The Broken Axis," *JAAR* 45 (1977): 353ff.

6. The phrases are all from the liturgy: daily *ʿamidah*, festival *mussaf ʿamidah*, and Passover *haggadah*.

7. See my article "The *Zaddiq* as *Axis Mundi* in Later Judaism," in *JAAR* 45 (1977): 327ff. and in this volume.

8. It is perhaps noteworthy, however, that the tale of Rabbi Simeon ben Yohai and his son plays so prominent a role in that volume, certainly serving to focus the reader's attention on the generation immediately after the destruction.

9. As to witnessing, for example, Maimonides's *Mishneh Torah*, Laws of Testimony 10:2, makes it clear that a violator of any Torah law of a certain magnitude may not testify; no special point is made of the Sabbath.

10. Yer. Hagigah 2:1 (77b).

11. The Sabbath attracted a good deal of attention among Latin writers and not only those who had a particular interest in the Jews. For the sources, see Max Radin, *The Jews among the Greeks and Romans* (Philadelphia: Jewish Publication Society of America, 1915), 245ff., and J. Hugh Michael, "The Jewish Sabbath in the Latin Classical Writers," *AJSLL* 40 (1923/24): 117ff.

12. See the thorough treatment by Lawrence Schiffman in *The Halakhah at Qumran* (Leiden, 1975), 77ff.

13. See the treatment by Y. D. Gilat, "*Le-Qadmutam shel Issurey Shabbat ʿAhadim*," in *Bar-ʾIlan* 1 (1963): 106ff. A summary of Sabbath ritual in the Second Temple is found in *EJ* 15, col. 977. See further M. Fishbane's "Revelation and Tradition as Religious Categories in the Bible" in a forthcoming *JBL*.

14. The "derivation" of the thirty-nine labors from the construction of the tabernacle is given in Shabbat 49b; see also 96b. It is clear that this is a rubric added

later to an accumulation of forbidden labors of diverse origins. *Tosafot* seems nearly to admit as much. On the thirty-nine labors, see Y. D. Gilat, "39 'Avot Mel'akhot Shabbat" in *Tarbiz* 26 (1959/60): 226ff.

15. Hagigah 1:8, Tosefta Hagigah 9:9 and 'Eruvin 11:23. The actual derivation from 'akh is not found in the extant rabbinic sources but only in the Middle Ages: RaSHI to Ex. 31:13. We do have a source in the Mekilta (ed. Horwitz/Rabin, 345) that derives the relationship from the similar juxtaposition in Ex. 35:1ff. On the question of 'akh, see the extended discussion by M. M. Kasher in *Torah Shelemah*, 21: 56n34.

16. But consider the parallel between our matter and the decision recorded in Rosh Hashanah 4:1: "When the holiday of Rosh Hashanah occurs on the Sabbath, the *shofar* is blown in the Temple but not in the town. When the Temple was destroyed, Rabbi Yohanan ben Zakkai decreed that it should be blown wherever there is a *bet din*." Here is a rather clear symbolic statement that the seat of rabbinic authority takes on something of a Temple-like quality. On this see Jacob Neusner, *A Life of Yohanan ben Zakkai*, 2nd ed. (Leiden: Brill, 1970), 205f., and *Development of a Legend* (Leiden: Brill, 1970), index s.v. "Sabbath."

17. Berakhot 55a. The biblical text itself already seeks to link Hiram, architect of Solomon's Temple, with Bezalel. Note the linguistic parallel of I Kings 7:14 with Ex. 31:3. Further material on Bezalel of a similar sort is found scattered in rabbinic sources. See Ginzberg, *Legends*, s.v. Bezalel.

18. I am emending *bi-khevod yosero* to *ba-kavod yesaro*, which seems to make more sense, particularly if the phrase is a medieval gloss. I find no way of understanding the text as it stands.

19. Tanhuma, *Pequdey* 2. A parallel version is found in *Leqah Tov*, ad loc., and a somewhat better text of the Tanhuma is preserved in R. Bahya to Ex. 38:21. A rather different version is found in *Midrash Tadshe'* 2 (*Bet ha-Midrash* 3, p. 164f.) See also the sources discussed in Ginzberg's *Legends*, 6:67n346, and by Chavel in his edition of the Bahya commentary See Bahya also on Ex. 40:16.

20. *Pesikta de-Rav Kahana*, ed. Buber 5b–6a, as emended by the editor. Perhaps an even stronger statement is found regarding Solomon's Temple in *Pesikta Rabbati* 6, ed. Friedmann 25a. There it is suggested that Solomon's very name (SHeLoMoH) indicates that it was he who completed (hiSHeLyM) the making of heaven and earth.

21. This has been noticed by Cassutto, *Commentary on the Book of Exodus* (Jerusalem, 1967), 476 and 483. Cassutto does not mention that he had been preceded by the Midrash and especially by R. Bahya in this insight. M. Fishbane informs me that "there is an ancient Near Eastern pattern embedded in Enumaelish, that the end of Creation is construction of a temple for the victor god." Fragments of this, he notes, appear in the Bible (Ex. 15, Ps. 29), and this concluding pattern of Exodus is to be seen as a transformation of that pattern.

22. Taken symbolically; see note 15 above.

23. Zohar 2:135a–b. Recited in the Hasidic liturgy to introduce the Shabbat evening service. On the two Sabbaths in early Kabbalah, see Nahmanides on Ex. 20:8 and 31:13. His comments are based on those in Bahir 181–82 (ed. Scholem 124). See further Tishby's *Mishnat ha-Zohar*, 2: 487ff. Sabbath as bride in the Kabbalah is, of course, also based on earlier motifs; the figure of Sabbath as queen is mentioned occasionally in rabbinic literature. Much is made of this theme in the Falasha treatise *Ta'azaza Sanbat*, but that development seems entirely unrelated to the Kabbalistic expansion of this idea.

24. Zohar 2:235a. "And he came unto her" is not part of the verse in Deut. 22:16, but has slipped into the author's mind from elsewhere.

25. Bereshit Rabbah 11:8. Elsewhere, however (e.g., Shemot Rabbah 25:11), Shabbat is taken as a token of the intimacy that exists between God as king and His lady Israel.

26. See the extended discussion of the bride and queen motifs in Heschel's *The Sabbath*, 126ff., n. 4. The rabbinic sources to which I refer in n. 23 above are there listed in full.

27. Zohar 3:272b; Tiqquney Zohar 36, ed. Margaliot 78a.

28. Bahya to Lev. 19:30; ed. Chavel 2:532.

29. One cannot help but wonder also whether the Safed Kabbalists did not have this association somehow in mind when they chose Psalm 95 as the opening to Kabbalat Shabbat. The closing line of that psalm stands before the Sabbath as a liturgy of entry: "So I vowed in My anger that they would not come in to my *menuhah*." Of course in the context of the psalm *menuhah* clearly refers to the Land of Israel. Here, however, it cannot but refer to the Sabbath, and the psalm then challenges the worshiper, much as does Psalm 24, to examine whether he is ready to "enter" the Sabbath as Sanctum. This same verse, by the way, was used earlier, exactly as one might expect, with regard to the Temple. See *Yalqut Shime'oni*, 2:189. I am indebted to Rabbi Jack Riemer for this insight.

30. On R. Ephraim, see the references in my *Tormented Master*, a study of his nephew, R. Nahman of Bratslav. The sources on him have been collected by M. Y. Guttman, *Geza' Qodesh* (Tel Aviv, 1950/51), and in Horodezky, *Ha-Hasidut weha-Hasidim*, 3:7ff.

31. *Degel Mahaneh Ephraim, Ki tissa'* (Jerusalem, 1962/63), 131–32 (emphasis mine).

32. *Mey ha-Shiloah*, pt. 1, *Qedoshim* 38b. The verse with which he concludes is not to be found in scripture. He seems to be misquoting from 1 Sam. 2:29ff.

3

Some Aspects of Qabbalat Shabbat

As is well known, *seder qabbalat shabbat* is an innovation of Kabbalistic circles in Safed of the sixteenth century.[1] It was accepted by Jewish communities throughout the world over the course of the succeeding two hundred years, spreading with the popularity of the Safed-based Kabbalistic revival and the image of the ARI and other Kabbalists as conveyed in the highly successful hagiographic literature of the age. The liturgical form represented by *qabbalat shabbat* can best be appreciated in the context of some parallel liturgical creations of these circles. These would include tiqqunim or sedarim for midnight vigils, for Yom Kippur Qatan on the eve of the New Moon, for the nights of Shavu'ot and Hosh'ana Rabbah, and so forth.[2]

My interest here is in exploring the meaning of this ritual and certain details within it in the context of Kabbalistic manuals and commentaries on the liturgy of the age in which it developed and spread. This study does not seek to treat those sources exhaustively, but rather to use them selectively in order to highlight certain key themes. Before proceeding to do so, however, I wish to acknowledge the contributions of two other scholars in this field whose work has been important to me. My student Elliot Ginsburg, originally in a doctoral dissertation under my supervision, studied the *sod ha-shabbat* in Tola'at Ya'aqov by Rabbi Meir Ibn Gabbai (Constantinople, 1560), the highly influential Kabbalistic prayer manual of the generation immediately preceding the Safed revival. While there is no *seder qabbalat shabbat* in that work, the spiritual climate in which it was to emerge is well on its way to full development, as Ginsburg portrays so richly.[3] My present Brandeis colleague Reuven Kimelman has written a book-length commentary on *Lekha Dodi*, which he kindly made available to me in manuscript form, and he has been of great help in the preparation of this paper.[4]

I turn first to the phrase *qabbalat shabbat* to discuss its origin and meaning in several contexts. Two verbs are used in the sources for the beginning of Shabbat: *QaBBeL* and *KaNeS*, *qabbalat shabbat* and *kenisat* or *hakhnasat ha-shabbat*. *Hakhnasah* has direct roots in the Talmud, where R. Yosi is quoted as saying *yehi helki 'im makhnissey shabbat bi-Teveriah*, "may my lot be with those who bring in the Sabbath in Tiberias,"[5] referring to those who "bring it in" at the earliest hour and are thus first to welcome the holy day. The precise intent of this phrase—exactly into what are they bringing Shabbat?—into the world? into their homes? into their hearts?—is ambiguous, and this ambiguity may have a role in the later development of Shabbat's rich and varied imagery.

The phrase *qabbalat shabbat* does not appear in the Talmudic sources. It seems to be a coinage of the Geonic age; the halakhic compendia of the Middle Ages—*Shibboley ha-Leqet* and Abudraham—quote it in the name of *Halakhot Gedolot*. Its earliest meaning seems to be halakhic, referring to acceptance of Sabbath obligations and the obligation to cease work. This applies in particular where one follows the rabbinic urging to begin Shabbat before its solar occurrence, *'ad she-lo qiddesh 'alav ha-yom*. In that case, a person who has recited Shabbat prayers, either the *'arvit* service or kiddush, has performed an act of *qabbalat* shabbat and is obligated to observe it. In this case "accept" seems to be the proper translation for the *qabbalah* of *qabbalat shabbat*. Kimelman analogizes this usage to *qabbalat 'ol*, "accepting an obligation (literally 'yoke')" or *qabbalat ta'anit*, "accepting a voluntary fast." Of the many examples of this usage, one particularly striking one from the fourteenth-century Abudraham is worthy of quotation:

> If the day is cloudy and one believes the sun has set before it really has and he (for that mistaken reason) *qibbel 'alaw shabbat*, "accepted the Sabbath upon himself," he may light fire and add oil to the lamps, since the acceptance was mistaken.[6]

Here we see the phrase *qabbalat shabbat* in a usage that is clearly halakhic/instrumental and entirely of a nonmythical character.

But another dimension of *qabbalat shabbat* has equally ancient roots. The Talmud (B. Shabbat 119a) describes Rabbi Hanina saying, "Let us go forth to greet the Shabbat queen!" and he tells of Rabbi Yannai, who would enwrap himself and proclaim: "Come O bride, come O bride."[7] While neither of these descriptions uses the verb *QaBBeL*, both offer a sense of greeting, going forth to greet Shabbat as one would an honored guest. With time *qabbalat shabbat* came to have this meaning as well, derived from the *hif'il* use of the stem *le-haqbil*, to "greet" Shabbat. Also associated with this motif of greeting is an *aggadah* whose source is lost but that is quoted by the Tosafists,[8] in which God calls for the singing of Psalm 92 as a song to Shabbat under the rubric of greeting a guest: *panim hadashot ba'u le-khan, nomar shirah,* "a new face has arrived; let us recite a verse." In this case *hakhnasat shabbat* is parallel to *hakhnassat oreah,* greeting and welcoming a newly arrived guest.

In the interpretation of Ibn Gabbai, based on Kabbalislic readings going back at least to the thirteenth century, the meaning of *malkah* and *kallah* in the words of the two Talmudic masters is quite clear.

> These two holy men were referring to the same matter, for Queen Esther is the secret bride in the Song of Songs; she is the glory of night. "They would go forth early to greet her, receiving the bride and bringing her along in joy. (*U-maqdimim hayu le-qabbel paneha we-la-tset li-qrat kal-lah le-havi'ah be-simhah.*)[9]

The term *la-tset,* "to go forth," here is taken directly from the Talmudic source. As we shall see, in Safed and later the word is understood quite literally, and this "greeting" aspect of *qabbalat shabbat* included an obligation to go outdoors. It would be interesting to know how Ibn Gabbai understood it. But he is referring only to a custom of the ancients, described in what is clearly the past tense. This language constitutes important negative testimony; it tells us that there was no such practice in his time. If there were, he surely would have said: *la-khen maqdimim anahnu la-tset,* "therefore we go forth," or something of that sort.

For Ibn Gabbai, as for all Kabbalists, the Talmudic references to *kallah,* "bride," and *malkah,* "queen," have been fully integrated into the Kabbalistic symbol system, where Shabbat is associated with *shekhinah* and *qabbalat shabbat* is greeting the *shekhinah*. The dual male/female aspects of Shabbat, represented by the duality of *zakhor ve-shamor,* "remember" and "keep"[10] along with a host of other symbols, refer to *yesod* and *malkhut,* but the overwhelmingly female symbolism especially of the Sabbath eve makes this the festival of the *shekhinah,* and all later Kabbalistic embellishments are based on that foundation.

But it is a third sort of *qabbalah* in *qabbalat shabbat* that is of the greatest interest to me here. That is the literal *receiving*—now joined to the acceptance and the greeting—of *neshamah yeterah*, that "extra soul" or extra degree of soulfulness that a Jew has on the Sabbath. The notion is based on a single Talmudic source, a saying of R. Shim'on ben Lakish:

On the Sabbath eve God gives an extra soul to the person and as the Sabbath departs it is taken away. Thus it is written (Gen. 2:3) *shavat va-yinafash*—once the rest has departed, Woe! the soul is lost.[11]

This highly graphic description of the coming and going of Shabbat from the human soul is open to a number of interpretations. RaSHI has a notably naturalistic view of it. He defines *nefesh yeterah* as *rohav lev*: "relaxation," one might say. Living at a slower pace in rest and joy allows one to be more expansive, wide open, as it were. This allows one to eat and drink more lavishly than usual without revulsion. Sources quoted by Ginsburg locate R. Abraham Ibn Ezra and Maimonides, as would be expected, in this same vein of naturalistic understanding.[12]

It is the Kabbalists, understanding *neshamah yeterah* supraliterally, not as mere metaphor but as describing an ontological reality, who make it into a pillar of Shabbat symbolism. While both Nahmanides and R. Azriel of Gerona make brief mention of the extra soul, it is primarily the circle of the Zohar, including the Hebrew writings of R. Moshe De Leon, that is responsible for the development of this motif. Ginsburg treats the various aspects of *neshamah yeterah* in the Zohar quite thoroughly, including the extremes to which this description is taken in the Tiqquney Zohar literature, where the *neshamah yeterah*, itself divided into three parts, replaces the weekday soul completely. An important part of Ginsburg's discussion is what he calls "images of internalization"; that is, the receiving of *neshamah yeterah* into oneself.

The exact moment of *qabbalat neshamah yeterah*, "receiving the extra soul," is defined by the Zohar and De Leon in several ways. The completion of pre-Sabbath bathing, *ha-'aliyah min ha-rahatsah* in the poetic language of the Song of Songs, is the first stage in that process; allowing for the possibility of the soul to enter the body, since she too has been bathed in the waters of Eden to prepare for her descent into the world, like the bride immersing before entering the bridal canopy. In the famous *raza de-shabbat*, "secret of the Sabbath" passage,[13] the Zohar seems to say that the new soul has entered before the beginning of Sabbath eve prayers: "All of them (Israel) are crowned with new souls, and then the prayer begins." But elsewhere both the *hashkivenu* prayer and *qedushat ha-yom* in the *'amidah*[14] are seen as moments of receiving the extra soul. In fact, the most complete and beautiful description of that soul's arrival is that associated with *hashkivenu*:

> Come and see: In the hour when Israel bless and welcome that Tabernacle of Peace, a holy guest, saying, "who spreads the Tabernacle of Peace . . . ," a sublime holiness descends and spreads its wings over Israel, sheltering them as a mother does her child. All sorts of evil are removed from the world, and Israel dwells beneath the holiness of their Lord. Then this Tabernacle of Peace bestows new souls to Her children. Why? Because that is where souls dwell and from which they come forth. When She is present, spreading Her wings over Her children, She causes a new soul to enter each one of them.[15]

The nature of this event of receiving the *neshamah yeterah* is described in a number of ways. Here it is intimate communion between mother and child, in which the *shekhinah* in bird-like fashion feeds her child as she hovers over the nest. Elsewhere it is described in the language of a coronation rite, Israel crowned with new souls in the same moment, or as an earthly embodiment of *shekhinah* being crowned under the *huppah* as she is united with her spouse and king.[16] A noteworthy passage in De Leon's Sefer ha-Rimmon associates this entry of the soul with *qabbalat malkhut shamayim*, "accepting the kingdom of heaven" but then goes on to a most interesting description.

> It should therefore be known that an extra soul is added to every Jew on the Sabbath eve. Their heads are crowned as they enter the tabernacle of peace that stands over them. As "the spirit settles upon them" and "they are *ba-ketuvim*" (cf. Num. 11:25–26) each of the noble ones is obliged to testify to the creation of heaven and earth.[17]

While these Zoharic sources referring to the entry of *neshamah yeterah* in *hashkivenu* or in saying *qedushat ha-yom* were certainly known to the later Kabbalists, the general conclusion seems to have been that the extra soul must be received before the beginning of the evening service, which is the opinion of the *raza de-shabbat* passage. The reason for this is the strong polemic found in the Kabbalistic writings on the issue of recit- ing *ve-hu rahum*, "He is compassionate, forgiving sin" as the introduc- tion to the evening service. According to *Sefer ha-Manhig* of R. Avraham ha-Yarhi (c. 1155–1215), the old Spanish custom was to recite these verses on Shabbat as well as on weekdays. The Zohar decries this custom with some passion.[18] As Yaakov Katz and Yisrael Ta-Shma have informed us, this is one of the places where the Zohar prefers French over Spanish liturgical practice.[19] The strong feeling around this issue still seems to be alive in the generation of Ibn Gabbai, the period when Spanish cus- toms are just finding a new home in the Ottoman East, and when clari- fication of proper ritual practice takes on new importance. Gabbai is a tireless fighter for the rightness of Kabbalistic custom. He says firmly that the *barekhu* of Shabbat eve is not to be recited until the *neshamah yeterah* has been received. This of course renders the recital of *ve-hu rahum* inappropriate; one should hardly begin the joyous Sabbath thinking about one's sins.[20]

To summarize all these pre-Safed materials, I am suggesting that three motifs combine in the notion of *qabbalat shabbat*, those of accepting, greeting, and receiving, with the Kabbalistic emphasis especially on the last of these three. I would now like to examine the emergence of the liturgical form called *qabbalat shabbat* as it reflects the interrelationship among these three notions of reception. I will do so by reviewing several Kabbalistic compendia on the liturgy beginning with the period when this rite came into practice, younger siblings, if you will, of Ibn Gabbai's *Tola'at Ya'aqov*. Here I am especially indebted to Kimelman's efforts in compiling the sources.

The idea of greeting shabbat *be-shirot we-tishbahot*, "with hymns and praises," without further definition, begins to appear in medieval France and Spain. It is mentioned in ha-Yarhi's *Sefer ha-Manhig*, to which we have just referred,[21] and in a number of sources in the late fourteenth and fif- teenth centuries. R. Ovadiah of Bertinoro, writing from Jerusalem to his father back home in Italy, refers to this as "a custom (of the Jews) through- out the Islamic world."[22] Even earlier there is some evidence that Psalm 92, the Song for the Sabbath Day, was added before the evening service.[23]

Sefer ha-Qaneh, a highly inventive Kabbalistic work probably written in early fifteenth-century Byzantium, reflects a home-based version of what may be considered a prototype of *qabbalat shabbat*:

> Afterwards one should wrap oneself up in a *tallit*, calling out to one's companions, one's wife, and one's household: "Let us go forth and greet the Sabbath queen!" They join together and respond: "Come, O bride, come, O bride!"[24]

Here the Talmudic accounts of R. Hanina and R. Yannai's practice have been combined into a simple household ritual. This may be the first stage in the revival of these ancient testimonies and their conversion into an active rite.

The first Siddur to print a *Qabbalat Shabbat*, including *Lekha Dodi*, was published in Venice in 1584. But reference to *Lekha Dodi* in the context of a ceremony for greeting Shabbat is found in several versions of the customs of Safed as recorded by contemporaries. Rabbi Avraham Galanti, a disciple of R. Moshe Cordovero, writes in his *Minhagey Hasidut*:

> Every Sabbath eve they go out to the field or the synagogue courtyard to greet the Sabbath, all of them dressed in Sabbath garments. They recite: "Ascribe to the Lord, O sons of the mighty (Psalm 29)," *pizmon shel shabbat*, "a Sabbath hymn," and afterward "A Song for the Sabbath Day (Psalm 92)."[25]

Kimelman refers to four other versions of this *hanhagah* from contemporary sources, with minor variations. It is interesting here that going outdoors seems to be an essential part of the rite, acting out the meaning of *qabbalat shabbat* with emphasis on the aspect of greeting. We should recall that the phrase *lekha dodi* comes from Song of Songs 7:12, "Come, my beloved, let us go out to the field." Going out to the field, or at least to the synagogue courtyard during the cold Safed winter, was the ritual act for which the hymn *Lekha Dodi* was written. R. Moshe Cordovero is a lone voice in distancing himself from this practice, preferring to greet Shabbat from within the synagogue.[26]

The most detailed description of the *qabbalat shabbat* ritual is found in R. Hayyim Vital's *Sha'ar ha-Kavvanot*:

Here is a brief order of *qabbalat shabbat*: Go out to the field and say: "Come, let us go forth to greet Shabbat the queen, field of holy apples."[27] . . . Stand still in a fixed place in the field, better if atop a high hill. The place should be as clean as need be in front of you, as far as you can see, and for a space of four ells behind you. Turn your face to the west, where the sun is setting. Just as it sets, close your eyes, place your left hand on your chest and your right hand over your left. Have the intent, in the fear and awe of one standing before the king, to receive the addition of Sabbath holiness (i.e., the *neshamah yeterah*). Begin by reciting "Ascribe to the Lord, you sons of the mighty" (Ps. 29), all of it with a melody. Then say three times "Come, O bride, come, O bride, Sabbath queen!" Then recite "A Psalm for the Sabbath Day" (Ps. 92) in its entirety, and then "The Lord reigns" (Ps. 93) to "for all time." Then open your eyes and go home.[28]

This is a most interesting account of what is clearly a developing ritual. There does not seem to be a full *Lekha Dodi* here (although perhaps its omission is what is meant by "a brief order"), nor are the full six prior psalms mentioned. The ritual positioning of the hands and the closing of eyes have about them the sense of a newly created and intentionally elaborate ritual practice of the Kabbalistic community, one meant to deeply impress the participant with the seriousness of the moment.

The recitation of six psalms prior to *Lekha Dodi* is first mentioned in two Kabbalistic compendia written toward the close of the sixteenth century. The first we will treat (it is unknown which was first written) is a local Safed product, *Sefer Seder ha-Yom* by R. Moshe hen Machir, published in Venice, 1599, still in its author's lifetime. R. Moshe lived in Safed in the latter decades of the sixteenth century and is an important source for local customs. He later established a small *yeshivah* outside Safed in Eyn Zetim. Moshe ben Machir does not make any point of the number six in listing these psalms, nor does he say that Psalm 92, the psalm for the Sabbath, is then the seventh psalm recited. He lists the six psalms, the same that exist in our contemporary *qabbalat shabbat*, under the rubric *u-mihagenu keshe-anu holkhim le-qabbel shabbat lomar elu ha-mizmorim*, "and it is our custom to recite these psalms as we go to greet the Sabbath," listing them, and then following with *ve-ahar kakh nomar pizmon ehad o shenayim ve-elu hem*, "afterwards we recite one or two hymns, and these are they." He then records a version of *Lekha Dodi* with the refrain that we know but with entirely different verses. The relationship between the *Lekha Dodi* recorded by Ben Machir (his own?) and that of Alkabetz has not been fully clarified. Did the refrain become standard practice in the Safed community, while different circles each freely composed verses of their own? Or was the Ben Machir version, not quite as lovely as that of Alkabetz, an earlier attempt on which R. Shlomo ha-Levi then built his own poem? Might *pizmon ehad o shenayim* mean just one or two verses, far less than we have with the entire *Lekha Dodi*?

Parallel to the work of Moshe ben Machir is *Sefer Hekhal ha-Qodesh*, written by R. Moshe Elbaz in Morocco. Elbaz tells us in his introduction that he began writing the book in 1575 in his home city of Taroudant in southern Morocco. The work, his only book, remained unfinished for many years and he took the manuscript with him when the community was forced to flee to Akka in the anti-Atlas because of a plague in 1598. Elbaz never tells us that he visited Eretz Yisrael. The book was completed in that same year but was published half a century later by R. Jacob Sasportas in Amsterdam, 1653. I mention this chronology in some detail because it is quite surprising that Elbaz already knows the custom of reciting the six psalms of *qabbalat shabbat* (although he apparently considers them to number five):

> Some are accustomed (*ve-yesh nohagin*) to recite, "Let us go forth in joy," Psalm 95 and 96, 97, and 98, as well as the Psalm "Ascribe to the Lord, O sons of the mighty (29)." For all these psalms teach of *qabbalat shabbat* and the rule of heaven, which spreads forth through all the worlds on Sabbath eve. All the *qelipot* are hidden away and secreted in fear and trembling before Her. This is made explicit in Psalm 98: "The Lord rules, the nations fear." In these psalms we are helping the side of holiness to cause the *shekhinah* to rule over the world.
>
> The prayer leader then begins "A Psalm for the Sabbath Day (Psalm 92)." He stands before the ark and says: "*Barekhu* . . . Bless the Lord to whom blessing is due!"[29]

Elbaz makes no mention of *Lekha Dodi* and says nothing about going outside. Reading Elbaz's work gives one the impression that *qabbalat shabbat* did not emerge as a single unit but that its various elements—reciting Psalm 92 (the oldest and most obvious part of the rite),[30] going outdoors to greet Shabbat and chanting *Lekha Dodi*, the use of Psalm 29 (famed for its eighteen invocations of the name YHWH), and beginning the ceremony with the five kingship psalms—each developed as a separate unit, and parts or all of the package were accepted in varying combinations by individuals and communities over the course of half a century or more, until the custom became firmly rooted, due in part to its acceptance by the printers of prayerbooks, who gave it a fixed form.[31]

Elbaz's interpretation of these psalms and their meaning in this liturgical context is quite correct. They represent the powerful arrival of God or "the kingdom of heaven," the scattering of God's foes, and the universal joy at His arrival. It is interesting to see how close the Kabbalists are here to the original meaning of these psalms, although they have now applied them to their own mythic context. They naturally understand the theme of majesty in these sublime poems; the arrival of Shabbat is in many Kabbalistic sources described as the coming of the queen (an obviously important gender change from the biblical setting) or as a moment of coronation. The universal joy expressed in these psalms, in which both nature and the idolatrous nations join into the great chorus of God's praise, is here applied to the Kabbalists' own version of the uprooting of the forces of cosmic evil on Shabbat and the freeing of all the worlds from their yoke, so that they can unite in accepting God's kingdom. We will probably never be sure whether the much discussed "enthronement ritual" proposed by biblical scholars as the original setting of these psalms actually took place in ancient Israel.[32] But its transformed offspring, the greeting coronation ritual of Shabbat, using the very same texts, is indeed a reality.

Surely a key phrase in the Kabbalists' rereading of these ancient songs is the conclusion of Psalm 95, the opening creation-hymn of *qabbalat shabbat*. The warning not to be hard-hearted like those at Meribah is being reread to mean that there is no room for hard-heartedness in this sacred time. Those who harden their hearts "may not come into My rest (verse 11)." The *menuhah* of the verse is of course the Land of Israel, a holy place into which that hard-hearted generation could not enter. But here the meaning has been shifted from the dimension of space to that of time, and the text stands as a liturgy of entrance guarding the gateway to this sacred time.[33] Its recitation as the first act on the way into Shabbat reminds the one who speaks it that hard-heartedness, like the weapons of war in ancient times, has to be left outside when entering this temporal *miqdash*, "holy place."

The third work to which I would like to turn is the greatest and most elaborate of all the liturgical compendia of Kabbalah: the *Hemdat Yamim*, written by an anonymous Jerusalem Kabbalist in the early eighteenth century and first published in Izmir in 1731–32.[34] In the course of a very lengthy and detailed description of the beginning of Shabbat—he has page after page about the Kabbalistic meanings of such details as setting the table, making the bed, and preparing the *cholent*—the author makes only brief mention of the recitation of Psalm 95ff. He discusses the ascent of souls from Gehinom to Gan Eden on Friday afternoon before Shabbat, an old Kabbalistic notion that was important also to his Ashkenazic contemporary R. Yisrael Ba'al Shem Tov. Here he gives us an account of Rabbi Isaac Luria's vision of the coming of these souls, and he also finds a special role for Moshe Rabbenu in the raising up of souls.

> Our holy teacher the ARIZaL, as he went forth with his disciples outside the town to greet the Sabbath, would stand atop the mountain and see troops of souls rising from their graves (in the cemetery below). They were going upward toward Gan Eden above. So too he would see innumerable souls, tens of thousands, coming down, parallel to those others. These were the extra souls being added to the proper people (*anashim kesherim*) every Sabbath. Because of the great chaos and confusion caused by all those multitudes of souls, his sight began to fail him and he was forced to close his eyes. But even with eyes closed he saw them. . . .
> Moshe Rabbenu takes great care about this matter, each Sabbath eve raising up all those souls that are given over to the *qelipot* and are unable to ascend (on their own). So too the souls of other people that do not have the merit to ascend. Moshe Rabbenu comes down every Sabbath eve with several *zaddiqim* accompanying him. In accord with their own qualities they raise up the souls of both the living and the dead. This is hinted at in Psalm (92) *Mizmor Shir Le-yom Ha-shabbat*, the acronym reading *Le-MoSheH*. That psalm goes on to talk about the righteous and the wicked, "as the wicked sprout like grass" and "the righteous blossom like a palm tree," for they reach upward like the palm to receive the light that is prepared for them.[35]

Here *Hemdat Yamim* adds a crucial reference to the practice of *qabbalat shabbat*:

I believe this is the reason for the custom of the early hasidim (*hasidim ha-rishonim*) to recite the psalms *lekhu neranenah* (95) and following, since these psalms were authored by Moses. They chose these six parallel to the six days of the week.[36]

The author of *Hemdat Yamim* neither defends nor argues with this custom, but moves on immediately to discuss the recitation of *Shir ha-Shirim* on the Sabbath eve and the many mystical meanings he finds within it. There is something surprisingly abrupt about his brief mention of this custom, given the length and affection with which he lingers on every other detail of the Sabbath ritual. But several pages later he gives us his own order of psalms for *qabbalat shabbat*, which is entirely unrelated to this "custom of the early hasidim," and seems to be offered in place of it. It might be, in that case, that we should translate *rishonim* in the above text as "former," rendering the phrase "it was the custom of *hasidim* in former times." *Hemdat Yamim* begins its own *qabbalat shabbat* with the following meditation:

To unify the name of the blessed Holy One (and His *shekhinah*), etc., I hereby come to recite the psalms of *qabbalat shabbat* the queen, to glorify and raise up the higher worlds. May it be Your will, Lord our God and God of our fathers, that You turn toward my reading of these psalms to cut down the proud[37] and to cut off the *qelipot* that have dominated and overwhelmed the worlds of *'asiyah*, *yesirah*, and *beri'ah*. Scatter them! May the wind take them away and the storm disperse them. Let them dare not come up and join into the ascent of the worlds. May You uproot, smash and destroy all the thorns and brambles that surround the sublime Rose. Join the tent so that it be one, the youthful wife together with her beloved; let the tabernacle be one. Spread over us their shining flow so that our persons (*nefesh*) be enlightened with added spirit (*ruah*) and soul (*neshamah*). "As with a rich feast sate my soul; I will sing praises with joyous lips" (Ps. 63:6). "Create a pure heart for me, O God; renew a proper spirit within me" (Ps. 51:12). "I will thank the Lord with all my heart, in the secret of the upright assembly" (Ps. 111:1). "For as long as my soul is within me and the spirit of God in my nostrils" (Job 27:3). "May the sweetness of God be upon us" (Ps. 90:17), "May the words of my mouth be acceptable" (Ps. 19:15)," etc.[38]

Here the purpose of reciting the psalms is similar to that offered by R. Moshe Elbaz, namely, the defeat of Kabbalistic "foes" in the spirit world. But the ceremony of *qabbalat shabbat* here is defined more fully and positively as the ascent of the worlds, the union of *shekhinah* and her beloved. All that provides the dramatic background for the entry of *neshamah yeterah*. The ascent of the worlds and the descent of the soul are simultaneous events, completely inseparable from one another, manifestations on the cosmic plane and the interior plane of the same sublime moment.

Now the author of *Hemdat Yamim* offers his list of psalms for *qabbalat shabbat*, one that seems quite original and that I have not seen documented in any other source. He begins with Ps. 24, "The earth is the Lord's." This is followed by Psalms 148, 45, 48, 87, 133, and 122. It is possible to characterize this list as one that reflects the sensibilities of Shabbat in Jerusalem of old, combining the beauty and praises of nature and the wonders of the holy city. But it is also interesting to speculate on the reason or setting for this new order of psalms. Why should *Hemdat Yamim* be interested in changing the custom of *hasidim rishonim*? He who is so very conservative not only about *halakhah* but also with regard to Lurianic custom, here sets aside the practice he himself attributes to the ARIZaL in favor of a new order of *qabbalat shabbat* psalms. I suspect that this important change may have some relationship to the alleged Sabbatianism of the work. I would tentatively suggest that what we have here is a new *qabbalat shabbat* service for the dawning messianic age. To support this claim, let us examine his list a bit more closely.

Psalm 24 concludes with the dramatic announcement of the king's arrival. The Sephardic liturgy uses this psalm very powerfully in the evening service for the Days of Awe. Of course the king in the psalm is God Himself, and Luria's *qabbalat shabbat* psalms are also filled with kingship themes. Nevertheless, the dramatic opening announcing the royal arrival is important, and it is continued with the chorus of praises offered by heaven and earth in Psalm 148. Psalm 45 speaks of God's chosen annointed one, his power over the nations, noting the presence of his concubine next to him. The verses of that psalm, when read in the early eighteenth century, must have been heard as referring to the messiah:

You are fairer than all men;
your speech is endowed with grace;

rightly has God given you an eternal blessing.
Gird your sword upon your thigh, O hero,
in your splendor and glory . . .
let your right hand lead you to awesome deeds. . . . Your divine
   throne is everlasting;
your royal scepter is a scepter of equity. You love righteousness and
   hate wickedness;
rightly has God, your God, chosen to anoint you
with oil of gladness, over all your peers.[39]

These descriptions of the ancient king, more than any other single passage in the entire psalter, can be applied readily to the messiah and certainly would be fitting as a Sabbath ritual for messianic times. Read in this way, the use of Psalm 24 combines with that which follows to welcome and proclaim the divine king and his human representation in king messiah. Psalms 48, 87, and 133 are all hymns to Jerusalem, very much befitting the theme of the king (God, messiah, or both) entering the holy city. Of course the image of the triumphant messiah entering Jerusalem remained central to the imagination of Sabbatian loyalists throughout their history. I would thus like to tentatively suggest that what we have here is a new *qabbalat shabbat* service for the messianic age or for a Sabbatian community. The author of *Hemdat Yamim* has taken a liturgical event that is a key to Kabbalistic practice and imagination, but not yet firmly rooted in *halakhah*. He is thus free to propose this very dramatic change, strongly suggestive of the surge of messianic energy that underlies his entire oeuvre, without trespassing formal authority. Indeed, to my knowledge this innovation has remained unnoticed by scholars until now. It would be most interesting to know if this liturgy was followed anywhere and whether a prayerbook with this order for *qabbalat shabbat* was ever published.

I would like to add a bit more detail concerning the ceremony of going outdoors to greet Shabbat as bride and queen. The link between reciting the *seder qabbalat shabbat* and going outdoors, and especially the understanding that *Lekha Dodi* was a song specifically to be sung out of doors, was long preserved among Kabbalists. Because those opposed to this innovation had the very considerable authority of R. Moshe Cordovero to call upon, the matter became quite controversial and aroused strong feelings. Here are the words of the *Hemdat Yamim*, a precious description of Kabbalistic practice in Jerusalem and elsewhere in the early eighteenth century:

> In my own house of study, after reading the Song of Songs I was accustomed to delve into the praises[40] of the Matronita together with the companions, may God preserve them. (We would read) the sixth of the Tiqqunim, folio 143a (beginning): "Rabbi Simeon arose and said: 'Assemble, supreme holy forces'" and so forth, to the end of the tiqqun.[41] They then recited *qaddish de-rabbanan*. (Says the editor: I found in the author's writings that this passage should be recited on the eve of Shavu'ot, preceding the Idra.) Then they should join together again in perfect love to go forth and greet the Sabbath queen.[42]

Here follows a lengthy homiletical digression on the description of Shabbat as "bride" and "queen," in which the author suggests that those who say "bride" believe that she is only betrothed to *tiferet* at this moment, while those who call her "queen" believe that the cosmic marriage has already taken place. Further discussion concerns Jacob and Moses who went forth to greet their brides at the well, these passages taken as biblical paradigms for greeting the *shekhinah*. The ritual description then resumes:

> Our holy master the ARIZaL derived from the expression "Let us go forth and greet" (the words of R. Hanina, quoted above) that one should go outdoors, to the field, in the secret meaning of "Jacob sent and called Rachel and Leah to the field" (Gen. 31:4), that of the holy apples (*shekhinah*). This was the master's custom. On each Sabbath eve, he and his disciples would go forth to wander meditatively in the field (*la-suah ba-sadeh*; Gen. 24:63) to greet the Sabbath queen. Beyond the deeper meaning of this matter for those who know it, the clever eye can see it from without as well as from within (cf. Ex. 25:11). When a king of flesh and blood comes to a city, all the townsfolk walk forth several miles to greet him. This is mentioned in the Midrash on *(parashat)* 'Emor: "The leaders of the town praised him as the townsfolk went five miles out in greeting." How much more fitting is it to go forth to greet the Sabbath queen, the holy Matronita, outdoors. The man of perfect faith (*ish ha-tamim*) should not think of this allegorically ('al derekh hash'alah) but indeed as going forth to greet the supreme king

and queen, as we have said. He should rejoice in the coming of Shabbat like one who has gone to greet the king or to greet a bridegroom, as is a well-established custom.

So too in our day, here in Jerusalem, may she be rebuilt and established, many wholehearted people hold firmly to this custom of the ancients and go forth from the city into the field with great joy, there to perform *seder qabbalat shabbat*. They then return and do it again around their tables,[43] with two torches of fire in their hands[44] as they come inside.[45]

The author then tells us of his difficulty in continuing this Jerusalem practice during his times of wandering in other communities:

During my exile, for I am exiled today from dwelling in the inheritance of the Lord, in the places I have passed I was for various reasons not permitted to do these things (*lo hursheyti la-'asot ka-eleh mi-koah kamah sibbot*). I thus became accustomed to go out to the synagogue courtyard, a place of open air that is appropriate for greeting, to recite the *seder qabbalat shabbat*. Then I would reenter the synagogue, circle the *tevah*, and recite *seder qabbalat shabbat* again, as we have written. All the qualities[46] described by the sages are only in accord with each person and his place; a person is obliged (to follow them) only in accord with his own measure (i.e., insofar as he is able). To this day, in all those places they hold to the custom of going out to the courtyard, an open-air place. But they understand the matter quite simply, like going outdoors to greet a bride and groom. Enough said.

It is fitting for every Jew who has it within his power to protest, and whose words are listened to, to address the hearts of the holy people so that they establish this practice in every synagogue and house of study, for the honor and glory of the *shekhinah*. They should not just greet her from their places inside the synagogue, lest this, God forbid, be an insult to the *shekhinah*.

What are we being told in this rather pained personal recollection? Why would the Kabbalist/author not have been permitted to go outdoors for *qabbalat shabbat*? It could be, of course, that Cordovero's opposition to this custom, popularized by its mention in the *Shney Luhot ha-Berit*, had already come to carry the day in the various diaspora communities he visited. But would this lead synagogue leaders to actually forbid a respected Kabbalist from following a well-documented Lurianic practice? The author of *Hemdat Yamim* is terribly insistent about this matter. After commenting on *Lekha Dodi*, he returns to the question of going out to the field and offers still another folio or more (42c–44b) of *kavvanot* to be recited while going forth, of biblical verses associated with fields, and so forth. Here again I think it is appropriate to raise the Sabbatian question. Might it be that the custom of going outside to greet the Sabbath was a bit of enthusiasm that in Sabbatian times came to be linked to the dream of going forth to greet the king messiah? Such a connection was already aroused in the widely known pre-Sabbatian tale told of Luria's calling upon his disciples one Friday evening to continue from this trip out to the field onward to Jerusalem. When some doubted that they could walk so far, or at least said that they would have to go home first to tell their families of their absence, then the master cried out and wept, saying to the companions: "How has Satan's accusation cancelled the redemption of Israel! I call heaven and earth to witness that from the times of Rabbi Simeon ben Yohai until today, there has been no time more proper for redemption than this hour. Had you accepted it, the Temple would have been rebuilt and the dispersed of Israel gathered into Jerusalem. Now the hour has passed, and Israel have returned to exile."[47]

It would seem only likely that this association of *qabbalat shabbat* with the moment of redemption was highlighted in Sabbatian circles and given great importance. This would explain the severity of the argument around it and the great emphasis placed on this practice within the book, though without explicit explanation. It would also account for the forbidding of this practice to a Kabbalistic guest, possibly a suspicious one, as he visited various communities.[48]

Finally, a comment on *Lekha Dodi* and its relationship to the *neshamah yeterah*. Of course I agree with Kimelman and others that the main subject of the song is the *shekhinah*, her arrival on Shabbat, her joy in uniting with both her divine and human spouses, and especially the longing for her complete redemption. But the poem was also written to serve as the climax of *qabbalat shabbat* in the sense of receiving, to be recited at the moment when the *neshamah yeterah* enters the person, immediately before the start of the evening service. The final verse, *bo'i ve-shalom*, "Come in peace," is precisely a celebration of that moment. On it *Hemdat Yamim* says: "Here one should intend to receive the additional *nefesh*, according to the secret of 'Awareness is pleasant for the soul' (Prov. 2:10). And one should prepare also to receive the additional *ruah*."[49] Versions of this understanding of the final verse of *Lekha Dodi* persist even in recently printed prayerbooks. A siddur I own, published in Jerusalem for the Iraqi community in 1960, says just before the final *bo'i kallah*, "come, O bride": *yekhaven le-qabbel tosefet neshamah yeterah*, "one should intend to receive the addition of the extra soul."

If this final verse is indeed the climax of *qabbalat shabbat*, I contend that a purpose of *Lekha Dodi*, along with its other meanings, is to arouse the worshipper to receive this extra soul. Part of the poem's richness lies in the ambiguity of the phrase *lekha dodi liqrat kallah,* "Go forth my beloved to greet the bride." Who is the *dod*/beloved? Whose is the bride? Of course, one is addressing God, and the Sabbath is the bride of both God and Israel. But I propose that there is another level of meaning hidden within the song as well. Here I return to the earlier question of "receiving." What is the nature of this receiving? Where does the extra soul come from at this moment? The Zohar's mythological answer is quite clear: it comes from above, from the upper Garden of Eden. But *Lekha Dodi* addresses itself to another, more naturalistic, answer as well: the *neshamah yeterah* is hidden within the person. During the week it is too frightened and too shy to emerge. As Shabbat begins, we call it forth, telling it that it is now safe to let itself be revealed. *Lekha Dodi* may be read, if you will, as a flirtation or seduction song to the *neshamah yeterah*, seeking to coax her out of hiding. If we look at a number of lines from the poem with this in mind, we will see that they fit this meaning as well as they do the adventures of the *shekhinah*. The gloomy soul, oppressed by the weekday world, is now told: "Enough of dwelling in the vale of tears. . . . Shake yourself off! Arise from the dust. . . . Awake, awake!" Yes, *shekhinah* is described as being "asleep" in exile, but the dormant inner self also needs to be aroused from its slumber. The key verse for this reading is:

lo tevoshi ve-lo' tikalmi, mah tishtohahi u-mah tehemi, "you will not be shamed, not disgraced. Why are you downcast, why disheartened?" The scriptural context for this verse is Psalms 42–43. There the phrase *mah tishtohahi,* a verb form found nowhere else in the Bible, is repeated four times, each with the noun *nafshi,* "my soul."

So the phrase here, too, I suggest, refers to the soul, hesitant to arrive (or "come forth"), too downcast to emerge in this moment of Shabbat joy. This verse is more clearly about the soul than it is about the *shekhinah*. There is not much reason, without forced explanation, that *shekhinah* should be *boshah ve-nikhlemet*, "shy or shamed" to enter her huppah. Here the clearer explanation is that the poet has turned to the *neshamah yeterah*, seeking to convince her, almost to seduce her, to emerge, for the time of her forced hiding has ended.

Here, at least, the *dod* to whom the poem is addressed is the inner self. And indeed Berakhah Zak reminds us, in her reading of *Ayelet Ahavim*, Alkabetz's unique commentary on the Song of Songs:

"The beloved (*dod*) for Alkabetz is the person. . . . When Alkabetz turns to the *dod*, he is turning to himself, his companions, and his disciples."[50]

The self toward which he is turning here, I would add, is the inner self, that which is about to reveal itself in the form of *neshamah yeterah*.

NOTES

1. *Qabbalat shabbat* has been treated by many historians of Jewish liturgy and mysticism. See especially Yizhak Yosef Cohen, "*Seder Qabbalat Shabbat u-Fizmon Lekha Dodi,*" in *Sefer Adam Noah* (Jerusalem: Makhon Fischel, 1970), 321–57 (also published by the author in separate pamphlet form; Jerusalem, 1969); Kimelman, *'Lekha Dodi' ve-'Qabbalat Shabbat': ha-Mashma'ut ha-Mistit* (Jerusalem: Magnes, 2002).
2. On this literature, see Y. D. Wilhelm, "*Sidrey Tiqqunim,*" *'Aley 'Ayin*, the Salman Schocken Jubilee Volume (Jerusalem: Schocken, 1948–52), 125–46.
3. Elliot K. Ginsburg, *Sod ha Shabbat: The Mystery of the Sabbath* (Albany: SUNY Press, 1989), and *The Sabbath in the Classical Kabbalah* (Albany: SUNY Press, 1989).
4. In addition to these, I have been helped by Yehiel Goldhaber's article "*Li-Qerat Shabbat Lekhu ve-Nelkhah*" in *Bet Aharon ve-Yisrael* 64 (1996): 118–39; 66: 91–112; 70: 125–46; 73: 121–34, which he was kind enough to give me. Although this article is organized in nonhistorical fashion, its notes contain a wealth of interesting source materials.
5. B. Shabbat 118b. On the matter of adding to the length of the Sabbath, see the remarks by Y. Ta-Shma in "*Tosefet Shabbat,*" *Tarbiz* 52, no. 2 (1983): 309–23.
6. *Abudraham ha-Shalem* (Jerusalem: Usha, 1959), 144.

7. It is not clear whether this refers to a special ritual garment or simply a warm wrap for going outdoors. R. Hanina and R. Yannai are both *amoraim* of the first generation in Erez Yisra'el, third century.

8. Ketubot 7b; see the parallel idea in Midrash Tehilim 92:3.

9. *Tola'at Ya'aqov* (Cracow, 1581), 41a.

10. This change of language between the two versions of the fourth commandment is widely understood in Kabbalah to refer to the last two of the ten *sefirot*, *yesod*, the "male" potency, and *shekhinah* or *malkhut*, the "female." This linkage is based on the association of *zakhor* ("remember") in the Exodus version with *zakhar*, or "male." See the full treatment by Ginsburg in *Sod ha-Shabbat*, 86n3.

11. B. Bezah 16a. *Va-yinafash* is intentionally misread here as *Vey! nefesh*.

12. Ginsburg, *The Sabbath in the Classical Kabbalah*, 122.

13. Zohar 2:13sa–b. For English translation and commentary, see D. Matt, *Zohar: The Book of Enlightenment* (New York: Paulist Press, 1983), 132ff. It is famous because of the Hasidic custom of reciting it following *qabbalat shabbat*, using it precisely as it was written, to serve as a grand invocation for *barekhu* in the Shabbat eve liturgy.

14. Zohar 3:173a.

15. Zohar 1:48a.

16. On early Jewish practices of crowning bridegrooms, see the discussion in my *Keter: The Crown of God in Early Jewish Mysticism* (Princeton: Princeton University Press, 1997), 78ff.

17. *Sefer ha-Rimmon* 47a, ed. Wolfson (Atlanta: Scholars' Press, 1988), 119. The biblical echo is that of Eldad and Medad receiving the Holy Spirit. Thus *qabbalat shabbat* is depicted as rising to a higher form of consciousness.

18. 2:135b; Zohar Hadash Ruth (Midrash ha-Ne'elam), 79b.

19. Jacob Katz, *Halakhah ve-Qabbalah* (Jerusalem: Magnes, 1986), 44f.; Yisrael Ta-Shma, *Ha-Nigleh sheba-Nistar* (Tel-Aviv: Ha-Kibbutz ha-Me'uhad, 1995), 21.

20. *Tola'at Ya'aqov* (Cracow, 1581), 41b.

21. *Manhig* 1:198; Kimelman, '*Lekha Dodi' ve-'Qabbalat Shabbat*', 11n78.

22. *Igrot Rabbi Ovadiah mi-Bertinoro*, 49; Kimelman, '*Lekha Dodi' ve-'Qabbalat Shabbat*', 13n83.

23. See Kimelman's discussion at n. 69ff.

24. *Sefer ha-Qaneh* (Cracow: S. Diamant, 1894), 65b; Kimelman, '*Lekha Dodi' ve-'Qabbalat Shabbat*', 13n82.

25. First published by Solomon Schechter in the appendix to his *Studies in Judaism* (Philadelphia: Jewish Publication Society, 1908), 2:295. Also available in *Hanhagot Zaddiqim*, a convenient four-volume collection edited by H. S. Rottenberg (Jerusalem, c. 1990), 63.

26. Cordovero's opposition is mentioned in his prayer book commentary *Tefillah le-Moshe* (Prszemysl, 1892), 193a. Although this work was not previously printed,

Cordovero's view was mentioned in the siddur of R. Isaiah Horowitz, *Sha'ar ha-Shamayim* (Amsterdam, 1717), 158a–c. This fact has been discussed by Moshe Halamish in *Ha-Kabbalah ba-Tefilah ba-Halakhah uva-Minhag* (Ramat Gan: Bar Ilan University Press, 2000), 336ff. As will be clear from my remarks below, I do not believe that Cordovero's coolness toward this practice is sufficient explanation for its later decline.

27. A well-known Zoharic symbol-term for *shekhinah*. This line from Vital's description has entered the Hasidic/Sephardic rite, recited immediately before Psalm 29.

28. *Sha'ar ha-Kavvanot*, chap. 6 (Jerusalem, 1873), 64c. This work was first printed in Salonika, 1852, but was well known in manuscript much earlier and influenced other works that were in fact printed earlier. On the traces of this description elsewhere in Lurianic sources, see Goldhaber, *"Li-Qerat Shabbat Lekhu ve-Nelkhah,"* 129n16.

29. *Hekhal ha-Qodesh* (Amsterdam, 1653), 30b.

30. See the extensive treatment of sources on this by Goldhaber, *"Li-Qerat Shabbat Lekhu ve-Nelkhah,"* 123ff.

31. A printing history of *qabbalat shabbat* would be particularly interesting. (Parts of it are to be found in Goldhaber's work.) Was it certain publishers who included the new liturgy in all their prayer books, or did inclusion vary, even at the same press, by liturgical rite? At what point did Ashkenazic prayer books begin to include *qabbalat shabbat*, and how long did it take before the inclusion of it became standard throughout Ashkenaz?

32. See S. Mowinckel, *Psalmenstudien* (Kristiana: J. Dybwad, 1921). For a discussion and evaluation of this controversy, see M. Brettler, *God Is King: Understanding an Israelite Metaphor* (JSOT Supplement Series #76; Sheffield: JSOT, 1989) and the bibliography there.

33. I have discussed the transposition between sacred space and sacred time regarding Shabbat in "Sabbath as Temple: Some Thoughts on Space and Time in Judaism," in *Go and Study: Essays and Studies in Honor of Alfred Jospe* (Washington: Bnai Brith Hillel Foundations, 1980), 287–305 and in this volume.

34. In passages to be quoted and discussed below, the author clearly describes himself as a Jerusalemite. However, Moshe Fogel suggests that his origins were in Izmir. Perhaps we are dealing with more than one author. Identifying the author of this section might be helped by his reference (f.40c) to his own *Sefer Mahamadey 'Ayin*. There is no published book by this title, but a thorough check of manuscripts or cross-references might yield some results. That work extends well beyond the scope of this paper.

There is an extensive scholarly literature on the authorship of *Hemdat Yamim* and its relationship to Sabbatianism, a link that was both suspected and vigorously denied already in the eighteenth century. The most recent contribution to this scholarly debate is Moshe Fogel's "The Sabbatian Character of Hemdat

Yamim: A Re-examination," in *The Sabbatian Movement and Its Aftermath: Messianism, Sabbatianism, and Frankism,* ed. R. Elior (Jerusalem: Institute for Jewish Studies, 2001), 2:365–421. There the reader will find full references to the earlier studies.

35. *Hemdat Yamim* (Venice, 1763), 37–2c. I have not found an earlier Kabbalistic source for this role of Moses in the bestowal of *neshamah yeterah.* The association is explained a bit more in f. 42b. Referring to *yismah Moshe,* "Moses rejoices" from the Shabbat morning liturgy, the author remarks that Moses' joy comes from his weekly act of restoring to Israel all the crowns that were taken from them at Sinai, after they made the Golden Calf, and were given to Moses. The coming of the additional soul is here homologized to the restoration of those crowns.

36. The designation of these six psalms as parallel to the six days of the week is not mentioned by either Machir ben Moshe or Moshe Elbaz. The first source to note it, according to Goldhaber (131f.), is *Tiqquney Shabbat* (Cracow, 1613). (This is the second edition of *Tiqquney Shabbat*; the first is Venice, 1594. I have not had the opportunity to check these works independently.) From there it was copied into various *siddurim.* It reflects the Kabbalistic notion that each of the seven lower *sefirot,* referred to throughout Kabbalistic writings as *shiv'at yeme ha-binyan,* has something of Shabbat within it. As the *sefirot* emerge in order, each one represents the *shevitah* or cessation/completion of the emanatory task of the previous rung: it therefore has about it something of Shabbat. The seventh *sefirah* represents the cessation/completion of the entire system, the closing of what R. Todros Abulafia calls the circle of the seven lower *sefirot.* It therefore is the true Shabbat. But the presence of an element of *shevitah* in each of the sefirot allows the earlier Kabbalists—Todros Abulafia, Recanati, and others—to interpret the old rabbinic dictum: "One who is lost in the wilderness and does not know when Shabbat occurs should count seven days and observe Shabbat" (Shabbat 69b)—to mean that each day has an element of Shabbat within it. See Abulafia's *Ozar ha-Kavod* (Satmar, 1926), 24a–b.

37. He is deriving *mizmor* from *le-zammer 'aritsim* (cf. Is. 25:5), a well-known play on words.

38. *Hemdat Yamim* 1:40d.

39. Ps. 45:3–8. Jewish Publication Society translation.

40. I am emending the Venice edition's *shabta* (?) to *shivha,* based on the Constantinople 1737 edition, f. 44b.

41. I do not have a first edition of the *Tiqquney Zohar.* In the Ortakoy 1719 edition, this passage is on f. 144b in a section of addenda to the Tiqqunim.

42. *Hemdat Yamim* 1:40b–c.

43. The repetition of *qabbalat shabbat* around the table is also mentioned in R. Jacob Zemah's *Nagid u-Mezawweh* (first published in Amsterdam, 1712) (Constantinople, 1726), f. 53a.

44. This surely seems to imply that the whole ritual takes place before sunset and that even the recital of *Lekha Dodi* in the field, with its receiving of the *neshamah yeterah*, has not yet indicated halakhic acceptance of the arrival of Shabbat.
45. The meaning of the following two words *u-fanah le-sovev* is unclear to me. Does he turn around and circle the table in the other direction?
46. Hebrew: *middot*. He seems to mean "special practices."
47. From the letter of R. Shlomo Shlumiel of Dresnitz, first published in *Ta'alumot Hokhmah* by Joseph Solomon Delmedigo (YaSHaR of Candia) in Basel, 1629, f. 46. See Goldhaber, "*Li-Qerat Shabbat Lekhu ve-Nelkhah*," 134n31. For another messianic association with going out to the field, see *Siddur Sha'ar ha-Shamayim* by R. Isaiah Horowitz (SHeLaH) (New York, 1958), f. 157; Kimelman, 'Lekha Dodi' ve-'Qabbalat Shabbat', n. 139.
48. See the corroborating explanation of the *Hemdat Yamim* author's exile from Jerusalem offered by R. Yehudah Moshe Fatayyah, quoted by Goldhaber, "*Li-Qerat Shabbat Lekhu ve-Nelkhah*," 136n41 from a manuscript notation in his copy of *Hemdat Yamim*.
49. *Hemdat Yamim* 1:42b.
50. Berakhah Zak, "The Mystical Theology of Solomon Alkabetz," PhD diss., Brandeis University, 1977 (Ann Arbor: University Microfilms), 188.

4

Judaism and "The Good"

Our Torah begins with goodness. God the Creator speaks the world into existence. Once each day, as being in its infinite variety continues to unfold, God sees that it is good. Six times the narrative of Creation is punctuated with the expression *va-yar' elohim ki tov* ("God saw that it was good"), though this phrase is missing from the second day, when God separated the waters above the firmament from those below. Division is not goodness. More notably, the phrase does not appear after the creation of human beings. God "saw that it was good" after He created the animals on the sixth day, but after the emergence of humans we are only given the summary statement: "God looked upon all that He had made, and behold it was very good." That word "very"—*me'od*—added only here, is debated by the rabbis. Some reverse the consonants and read it as *'adam*—"God looked up all that He had made, and behold man was good." But others somewhat shockingly read it as though it were another word similar in sound: *mot* or "death." "God looked upon all that He had made, and behold death was good."[1]

The latter is, to put it mildly, hardly a "typically Jewish" or rabbinic idea. I suspect someone had to go that far only to counter the other view: that the human was the best of God's creations. The Bible is not particularly impressed with human goodness. It may not be possible, in biblical terms, to characterize human beings as "good" at all. A bit later in Genesis, in connection with the flood, we are told that God sees that "The inclination of the human's heart is only evil, from his youth" (Gen. 8:21; cf. also 6:5). This is the source of the word *yetser*, "inclination" or "tendency." It is only the rabbis who much later soften this biblical judgment on humanity and add a *yetser tov*, a "good inclination" to balance off the will to evil. Both the biblical and rabbinic authors seem to be sufficiently familiar with the endless human capacity to do evil to avoid superficially rosy depictions of human nature.

Perhaps surprisingly, this tendency toward doing evil in no way lessens the Bible's insistence that the human being is created in God's very own image and likeness. I believe this to be the most important moral statement in the Jewish tradition, the basis of our concept of human decency and the clearest guide to proper behavior that Judaism offers. We define human decency as treating the other, every other, as the image of God, and therefore as an embodiment of holiness. All of us, even we winners, bear God's holy presence within us. Our task, as the only ones of God's creatures who are reflections of the divine self in this way, is to increase the image of God in this world. We do so by propagating the species, fulfilling the first commandment, but also by living, acting, and treating one another as images of God's own self.

This belief that the human being is God's own and only image is also the reason for the most basic prohibition or taboo in the Jewish religious consciousness: the forbidding of idolatry. It is not because God has no image that we are not allowed to make depictions of God's likeness. Precisely the opposite! God has but one image and likeness in the world: that of every living human being. We are to fashion an image of God in this world; that is our task. But the medium in which we are to do it is the entirety of our lives. To take anything less than a living person—a canvas, stone sculpture, wooden statue—and to see in it God's image would be to demean our own Godlike humanity and thus to lessen God.

The same connection to faith in the human as God's image is found in the two other absolutes of the Jewish moral code. All commandments may be violated, indeed should be violated, for the saving of even a single human life. All except for these: idolatry, murder, and sexual degradation. Idolatry, because you are and therefore cannot "make" the image of God; murder, because the other is also the image of God; sexual degradation, because you are both the image of God, and you are enjoined not to degrade or diminish that image.

But what does the divine image have to do with *goodness*? The Bible can describe sun and moon, trees, plants, and animals as "good" in its account of Creation. Humans are in the image and likeness of their Creator, but they are not described as good. How can we be in God's image if we are not even good? Here we must recall some of the meanings attached to the divine likeness. We are creatures who bear moral choice, the only ones of God's creatures who were tempted (or some would say: destined) to eat of the Tree of Good and Evil. With moral choice goes responsibility, hence the possibility of being judged either good or evil, according to our deeds. The divine image also means that we are possessed of imagination and the spark of further creativity, the only creatures with the power to continue and participate in God's own creative act. Here too the question of moral culpability will loom large: we humans are responsible for that which we create. We should also recall with some trembling that God's own goodness is not beyond question in our tradition. Isaiah's God is the single source of both good and evil, the One who "forms light and creates darkness, makes peace and creates evil" (45:7). To be a monotheist is to believe that there is a single source for all that comes to pass in this world. Of course we may question the nature of evil, its relationship to God, how the divine creation comes to be evil—and all the rest. But we may not say that there is a second, independent source. The Kabbalists tell us that God too is engaged in an ongoing struggle for self-purification, an attempt to remove the dross that exists near the very highest levels of cosmic existence. *Our human struggle for goodness is thus not ours alone, but our way of participating in God's own search for a perfect universe*, one in which *shalom*, peace and wholeness, will reign throughout. We do this by following the way of Torah. That is the best measure of goodness we have as we are to realize it in ordinary day-to-day human life.

"And now, O Israel, what does the Lord your God demand of you?" (Deut. 10:12) is the root-question posed, and supposedly answered, by religions of revelation. God has spoken. This is the key claim of classical Judaism.[2] Contemporary theologians, among whom I count myself, may offer elaborate theories of what those three words mean. Leaning on the works of Jewish esoteric theologians over a thousand years, we will try to tell you that the *event* of revelation, or revelation as *process*, is what is central and that the contents of revelation are secondary, are unclear, or emerge from human interpretation of a revelation that is in itself beyond content or beyond language. Such notions have taken deep root in the intellectual life of thinking religious Jews, and they are by no means exclusively modern. Both philosophical and mystical theologians, medieval as well as modern,[3] are interested in what they can learn and teach from revelation about the nature of the divine self, the relationship of that self to its creatures, and especially the ways in which divinity is manifest in the human soul and particularly in the soul of the prophet.

But this is not the dominant voice in the Jewish tradition. While philosophers, mystics, and their teachings have come and gone, the Jewish legal tradition, continuing to build and grow with each succeeding generation, has been interested precisely in the *content* of revelation, concerning itself little with exactly what we mean by the terms "reveal," "speak," "hear," or "will of God." It is this tradition, that of *halakhah*, the way or the path, that has shaped the contours of the classical Jewish community, including its ethics ("the commandments between person and person"), its devotional forms ("the commandments between person and God"), the delimiting of its borders, and its ability to confront an ongoing array of new circumstances in every phase of its existence. This has been the tradition of the rabbis and the people, both of whom often show distressingly little interest in the theological implications or deeper meanings of their own actions. They live out their spiritual life by great faithfulness and devotion—occasionally even to the point of martyrdom—to the *halakhah*, which to them is fully identified with faithfulness to Torah as divine word or to the will of God.

As is well known, Torah contains two bodies of teaching: the written law and the oral law. This formulation, probably originating in about the fourth century, embodies a reality that is still older. The written law, given to Moses either on Mount Sinai or over the course of his lifetime (there are differing views on this in the rabbinic sources, though the former view later comes to dominate),[4] consists of the first five books of the Hebrew Bible; the oral law is the interpretive and later codified tradition. The rest of scripture occupies a somewhat intermediary position, but since it contains relatively little by way of specific legislation, determining its place in the system is not a crucial issue. It is quite clear that aspects of the oral tradition, that is, the interpretation of a written code within the community, go back to the biblical period itself, and this process in its early stages is sometimes witnessed in later biblical writings. The written Torah contains, according to a count first found in Talmudic sources, 613 commandments, divided between 248 positive commands and 365 prohibitions.[5] Despite an explicitly stated stricture within the Torah (Deut. 4:2) against adding anything on to the Torah God has given, the earliest rabbis were permitted under very restricted circumstances to add a few actual commandments.

They also asserted the much broader authority to legislate as specific needs arose, occasionally even in contradiction to the agreed-upon meaning of a biblical injunction or prohibition. (Such legislation would be rabbinic dictum—termed *taqqanah, gezerah*, etc.—but not "command of

God," except insofar as Torah enjoins one to listen to "the judge who will exist in those days" [Deut. 17:9].) But by far the greatest portion of their work falls under the category of expansive interpretation, the reading first of sources in the written Torah, but later of authoritative and quasi-canonical rabbinic texts, and their deft manipulation to apply them to an ever-changing and expanding set of circumstances.

As I said above, this has been the Judaism of the people as well as the rabbis. For a very long time the Jews defined themselves as a community of praxis rather than one of particular faith or doctrine. Nowhere is this reality more dramatically indicated than in the Talmudic tale of Rabbi Meir, onetime disciple of Elisha ben Abuya.[6] The latter had become a "heretic" and had left the rabbinic community. The two of them were walking and talking one Sabbath day after Elisha had ceased living in accord with the ways of the rabbis. When they reached the Sabbath-border, that distance outside a town beyond which one is not permitted to walk on the Sabbath, Elisha warned his disciple to go back, lest he violate the prohibition. Taking the opportunity offered by his former teacher's still obvious awareness of the law, Meir responded: "You, too, go back" meaning "recant your heresy." Elisha, however, would not do so, and the one walked on while the other returned, portraying in unusually graphic terms the "border" of life within the classical Jewish community.

The tradition that "membership in good standing" within the community of Israel is defined by religious practice (symbolized particularly by observance of the Sabbath) is still the case within today's observant community. Notice that I use the word "observant" here rather than "ortho-dox." As I have often explained to students in introductory courses on Judaism, there is no word for "orthodoxy" in premodern Hebrew or Yiddish. Jewish courts will accept the word of a witness who is known to be observant of the Sabbath; they will not ask him what he thinks is the nature of God or how he understands revelation. I remember my pious grandmother making discreet inquiries in the community about a certain butcher, trying to find out whether he was a Sabbath-observer before she would trust him to sell her properly prepared kosher meat. Again, the "orthodoxy" of his opinions was not a matter of public interest, but the strictness of his observance surely was. Here is where the line was drawn between a fellow-member of the House of Israel and one who had chosen to become an "outsider."

The careful reader of this paper may note a certain wavering between the past and present tenses in my presentation of this situation. The reason for that is quite simple. The classical Jewish self-definition becomes deeply problematic in the modern world. Today some 85 percent of Jewry lives outside the authority of Jewish law, though a significantly higher proportion are selectively observant of certain traditions. This wholesale abandonment of legal boundaries has been the case increasingly since the beginning of the nineteenth century, with the faithful core shrinking at different times and to various degrees in each of the far-flung Jewish communities. The leadership of those remaining communities (now indeed often defined as "Orthodox") has been at great pains both to sharply denounce the unacceptable behavior of the majority and at the same time to find ways to keep them within the Jewish community. One strategy has been to distinguish between leaders and followers in viewing these "outsiders": it is the wicked "rabbis" and teachers of the nonorthodox who have led the flock astray; the folk themselves are to be considered like "babes captive amid the heathen,"[7] who can hardly be held responsible for their own deeds. Another has been to refer to "the Jewish soul" that still exists among such people, leaders as well as followers, and to try by means of patience and kindness to develop that soul[8]—including elements of remaining religious conscience—in order to lead those Jews to penitence and return to "authentic" (meaning legally bounded) observance of the tradition.

Therefore we ask: "What does the Lord your God demand of you?" The scripture here answers quite clearly: "Only this: to revere the Lord your God, to walk only in his paths, to love him, and to serve the Lord your God with all your heart and soul, keeping the commandments of the Lord which I command you this day, for your good." The "good" here is the reward Israel is to receive in return for living in accord with the divine commandments.[9]

It would appear, then, that classical Judaism's vision of the good life is at once very clear and almost infinitely complex. "To do good" is to live out all the commandments as the sages have interpreted them over the generations, combined with an attitude of piety and a loving acceptance of this rule of law. This is not an entirely inaccurate description, and it should not be dismissed. It is the most ancient and "native" response to this question implanted by the tradition in those who follow its ways, reflecting life as lived by those considered "religious" within the Jewish community. It especially accords with such a well-known dictum as "Be as careful with a minor commandment as a major one, for you do not know the true weight of the commandments" and others in its spirit.[10]

The problem with such a view is that it is entirely dispiriting to discussions such as our own. All it would leave us to do is to wend our way through such a tome as Maimonides's *Book of the Commandments*, or perhaps Joseph Caro's *Set Table*, and only after mastering these (one a listing of the biblical commandments; the other the key code of religious law on a practical basis) would we be empowered to speak of Judaism's vision of the good. But much more seriously, of course, such a view also gives insufficient guidance to the religious Jew who daily has to make choices among the commandments, since no one can observe all the laws of God at the same time. What does God want of me?—to study Torah day and night or to work to support my family? What does God want of me when I see my people desecrating the name of God and Israel? Shall I fulfill "Openly reprove your neighbor" (Lev. 19:17) or shall I say, "All its paths are peace" (Prov. 3:17), and therefore opt for scholarly quiet and noninvolvement?

Fortunately our position is not quite so severe as that. *Halakhah* in Judaism always lives in tandem (and sometimes tension!) with *aggadah*, those narratives and teachings that constitute the nonlegal portion of traditional wisdom. There we have many summary statements, reformulated in almost every generation, of the "values of Judaism." There are numerous statements, and even compendia of statements, that allow one to go beyond the simple enumeration of commandments.

One of the most famous of these from within the very Talmudic passage that first mentions the numbers of 613 commandments, should be quoted here:

> Rabbi Simlai expounded: Six hundred and thirteen commandments were spoken to Moses, three hundred and sixty-five prohibitions, corresponding to the days in the solar year, and two hundred and forty-eight positive precepts, corresponding to the limbs of man's body. . . .
>
> David came and reduced them to eleven, as it is written: "A Psalm of David. Lord, who shall sojourn in Your tabernacle? Who shall dwell in Your holy mountain? (1) He who walks uprightly, (2) works righteousness, (3) speaks truth in his heart; (4) he who has no slander upon his tongue, (5) nor does evil to his fellow, (6) nor takes up reproach against

his neighbor, (7) in whose eyes a vile person is despised. But (8) he honors those who fear the Lord, (9) he swears oaths at his own expense and does not violate them; (10) he does not lend money at interest (11) or take bribes against the innocent. He that does these shall never be moved" (Ps. 15:1–4).

Isaiah came and reduced them to six, as it is written: "(1) He who walks righteously and (2) speaks uprightly, (3) who despises profiting from oppression (4) and shakes his hand loose from holding bribes, (5) who stops his ear from hearing of blood and (6) shuts his eyes from looking upon evil" (Is. 33:15–16).

Micah came and reduced them to three, as it is written: "It has been told to you, O man, what is good and what the Lord requires of you: only to do justice, to love mercy, and to walk humbly before your God" (Mic. 6:8).

Again came Isaiah and reduced them to two, as it is written: "Thus says the Lord: Keep justice and do righteousness" (Is. 56:1).

Amos came and reduced them to one: "For thus says the Lord to the house of Israel: Seek Me and live" (Am. 5:4). But to this Rabbi Nahman ben Isaac raised an objection: [Might this not be taken to mean] Seek me by observing the entire Torah and live? Rather it is Habakkuk who came and [properly] based them all on one, as it is written: "The righteous shall live by his faith" (Hab. 2:4).[11]

The biblical language here is quite lofty in tone, using prophetic phrasing to point to what seems to be the "real meaning" of the religious life. But we should not permit the use of biblical language to divert our attention from the rabbinic origins of this passage. The passage in the Talmud that first codifies the number of 613 commandments is essential for the later development of *halakhah*. The medieval discussions of the list of commandments, hence, of which acts (or non-acts, such as faith in God!) are required by Torah, all depend upon this passage. Yet the Talmud itself responds to this numbering of the commandments by a series of attempts to get at the moral or religious essence of the *mitzvah* system. It is asking not "what are the things commanded?" but "what is the moral essence of the divine command?"

As lawyers, the rabbis were not generally fond of such broad and lofty statements. More typical of rabbinic language is the following formulation of "the highest Jewish values." I juxtapose it to the Makkot passage because it too seems to rise in protest against the quantification of divine command. Here the Mishnah lists those commandments that are without fixed measure ("the more the merrier," in other words). Joined to it is a list of observances so beloved by the human community as well as by God that they are claimed to be double in their form of reward. This passage is quoted in the daily prayer book and thus is familiar to any observant Jew:

These are things which have no [prescribed] limit: the corner of the field [to be left for the poor], the first fruits [brought to the Temple], appearances [at the Temple on pilgrimage], bestowing kindness, and the study of Torah.

These are things the fruits of which a person enjoys in this world while the principal remains for him in the world to come: honoring father and mother, bestowing kindness, coming early to the study-house morning and evening, hospitality to guests, visiting the sick, dowering [poor] brides, attending to the dead, devotion in prayer, and bringing peace between fellow-persons. But the study of Torah surpasses them all.[12]

The first of these two statements (the Makkot passage) clearly belongs to the realm of *aggadah*. While it refers to an ordering of commandments in various prophetic teachings, it does not seem to have any normative function. The second inhabits an intermediate status between *halakhah* and *aggadah*. While its Mishnaic language sounds like that of law, we would be hard pressed to claim it as a truly legal formulation of the highest values within the rabbinic tradition. But within *halakhah* proper there are also necessarily statements that prefer one normative act over another. The well-known use of Lev. 18:5 ("You shall live by them") to indicate that in most circumstances human life takes precedence over other commandments is perhaps the prime example. Halakhic authorities throughout the ages were also well aware that it is possible to be a "knave within the domain of Torah," that is, to technically fulfill all the demands of the law and still be a miserable human being, worthy of condemnation. As detailed as the law seemed to be, in itself it could not fully shape one into being a "good person." Thus the Torah contains certain passages that themselves demand that one go beyond the letter of the law. It is to two of these that I would like to turn our attention.

"Do what is right and good in the sight of the Lord" (Deut. 6:18) is taken as a catch-all to determine behavior that is not specified elsewhere in the law. Here is the comment of Nahmanides, the thirteenth-century Catalonian sage who was certainly one of the most respected Jewish personages in his era and who remains a major figure in any discussion of *halakhah*. Nahmanides is expounding on an earlier rabbinic teaching:

> "What is right and good" refers to compromise and [willingness] to go beyond the letter of the law. The intent of this is as follows. First Moses stated that you are to keep God's statutes and testimonies as commanded you, give thought as well to doing what is right and goodly in God's eyes, for God loves the right and the good. This is a basic rule. It was impossible that the Torah specify all aspects of a person's conduct with neighbors and fellows, all of a person's interactions, and all the ordinances of various countries and societies. But since many of them were mentioned, such as, "You shall not go about telling tales" (Lev. 19:16); "You shall not take vengeance or bear any grudge" (18); "You shall not stand idly by the blood of your neighbor" (16); "You shall not curse the deaf" (15); "You shall stand up in the presence of the white-haired" (32)—and so on, the Torah goes on in a general way to say that in all matters we should do what is right and good, including compromise and going beyond the letter of the law.[13]

Compromise in legal cases, especially within the civil code, is not enjoined by the law itself. If the judges find for me, after all, then the full sum is mine and I have a right to demand it. But the rabbis realized (in days long before insurance) that litigation could ruin individuals and families, and thus they urged compromise in such cases as constituting "the right and the good." The same was true with going beyond the letter or, more literally, staying "within the line" of the law. There are situations when the right thing is for one not to assert one's full legal rights, and the decent person is to know when those times are.

The *hasid*, or lover of God, is defined by the Talmud as one who lives well within that line, doing and giving more than the law demands, both to God and to one's fellow. It is the heart's sensibility, trained, to be sure, by a lifetime of living within the law, that tells such a *hasid* when to do more. Just as the doors of inner prayer come to be more readily opened by a life of regular fixed prayer, so do the inner instincts of caring and generosity of spirit come to be more highly attuned by a life of daily concern for demands of the moral law. The constant training of that moral sensitivity is central to what Judaism views as piety or *hasidut*.

The next passage to which we turn is found a bit farther on in Deuteronomy, amid the prohibitions of divination and augury. There (18:13) the text says "You must be *tamim* with your God." The term *tamim*, sometimes translated here as "wholehearted," is the same word translated as "unblemished" in references to both priests and the animal sacrifices they offered. The verse will offer to Samson Raphael Hirsch, the key figure in nineteenth-century German-Jewish Orthodoxy, a chance to say some important things about the Jewish religious "ethos." The call to be *tamim* is

> a demand for the completeness of our devotion, the devoting of every phase, without exception, of our being to God. This is the most direct result of our consciousness of the "oneness" of God, the realization of the *'am segulah* mission, the mission of a nation belonging exclusively, in every phase, to God. We are not to cut the slightest particle of any phase of our life away from God; we are to be with God with our complete life, with every fibre of it. Thereby the whole of the heathen attitude toward life depicted in the preceding verses is banned from the Jewish sphere. God, the sole Director of our fate and Guide of our deeds, alone decides our future; His satisfaction is the sole criterion by which we are to decide what to do and what to refrain from doing. Not blind chance, the Moloch "luck" rules over our lives or the lives of our children . . . the *tamim* is so completely engrossed in God that he lives entirely in the thought of doing his duty all the time; he leaves the rest, including his own entire future, to God.[14]

While Hirsch does get a bit "preachy" (here as frequently), he shows us another occasion where a verse in the Torah carries us far beyond its seeming intent. *Tamim* here really means "whole" or "unblemished" in the life of faith, going far beyond the specific prohibitions of the immediate context. The knowing reader of scripture in the Hebrew will immediately be carried back to the Bible's first use of *tamim*, that which God says to Abraham in Genesis 17:1: "Walk before me and be *tamim*." The contemporary translators' (JPS, RSV, Jerusalem Bible) "blameless" is inadequate in this case; there is nothing negative about *tamim*. I rather prefer the King James's "perfect." Of course this is the language introducing Abraham to the commandment of circumcision; it is the (paradoxical) perfection of his body that he is about to undertake, as an outward sign of the moral or religious being he is to become. *Tamim* as "perfect" would be rather close to *shalem—shalom* as "whole" or "complete." This is as close as we come to the possibility of a person's "being" as well as "doing" good in the Bible.[15]

But Abraham is very much to the point in this discussion. He lives before the commandments are given and therefore would seemingly have to lead a religious life without them.[16] Might his example then be able to tell us what it means to be a good person without going through the entire list of the commandments? A great deal is made in Christian scripture and tradition, ranging from Paul to Kierkegaard, of Abraham as the ideal figure of faith, living before the law was given. But the rabbis are aware of the Christian claim, and therefore the Talmud insists, based on Genesis 26:5 ("inasmuch as Abraham obeyed Me and kept My charge: My commandments, My laws, and My teachings") that "Abraham our Father observed the entire Torah" even before it was given.[17] They go so far as to say that he knew every detail of the law, even the clearly rabbinic device for preparing Sabbath food on a festival, a matter that admittedly has not a shred of biblical basis. The point is that for the rabbis there is no piety outside the law, and they will not allow our own patriarch to be used to show otherwise.

Despite the rabbis' claim of our ancestor, however, he remains important as a model for the religious life and not just as a faithful follower of the law. Throughout Jewish history Abraham is the ideal type of piety, much as Moses is of learning or Solomon is of wisdom. The less naive among later writers, while not openly challenging the rabbinic claim, set it aside to return to the pastoral image of the patriarch who lived as close to moral and devotional perfection as human life seems to permit. Here is Maimonides in a famous passage from his *Guide for the Perplexed*:

> And there may be a human individual who, through his apprehension of the true realities and his joy in what he has apprehended, achieves a state in which he talks with people and is occupied with his bodily necessities while his intellect is wholly turned toward Him, may He be exalted, so that in his heart he is always in His presence, may He be

exalted, while outwardly he is with people, in the sort of way described by the poetical parables that have been invented for these notions: "I sleep but my heart wakes; the voice of my beloved knocks" (Cant. 5:2) and so on. I do not say that this is the rank of all the prophets; but I do say that this is the rank of Moses our Teacher. . . . This was also the rank of the patriarchs, the result of whose nearness to Him, may He be exalted, was that His name became known to the world through them: "the God of Abraham, the God of Isaac, the God of Jacob . . . this is My name forever" (Ex. 3:15). Because of the union of their intellects through apprehension of Him, it came about that He made a lasting covenant with each of them.

Also the providence of God watching over them and over their posterity was great. Withal they were occupied with governing people, increasing their fortune, and endeavoring to acquire property. Now this is to my mind a proof that they did these actions with their limbs only, while their intellects were constantly in His presence, may He be exalted. It also seems to me that the fact that these four were in a permanent state of extreme perfection in the eyes of God, and that His providence watched over them continually even while they were engaged in increasing their fortune—I mean while they tended their cattle, did agricultural work, and governed their household—was necessarily brought about by the circumstance that in all these actions their end was to come near to Him, may He be exalted, and how near! For the end of their efforts during their life was to bring into being a religious community that would know and worship God.[18]

This of course is the *vita contemplativa*, descriptions of which are to be found in the devotional classics of all our traditions. What is particularly interesting here is the combination of contemplative and active life, or the way in which the patriarchs go on about their this-worldly work while their minds are wholly with God.

The figure of Abraham and his religious life was especially inspiring to the Hasidic masters, who saw in him a model for their own "spiritual" fulfillment of the commandments. In addition to living in accord with the ways of the law, they wanted to find the inner root of each divine command, which they were quite sure also collectively made up the inner root of the human soul. By devotion to the commandments in a spiritually aware way, they would come to do what they saw Abraham as having done. They would discover the entire Torah as it is inscribed within their own souls and would thus come to know the commandments as a deep inner map of the spiritual journey that God has given to those who truly seek. The word *mitzvah* ("commandment"), they taught, is actually the name of God in half-hidden, half-revealed form. It is by turning in to the *mitzvah* (which they sometimes derived from the Aramaic *tsavta* or "togetherness") that one comes to meet God. This emphasis on the "inner commandments," accompanying and enriching their outward fulfillment, is a highly characteristic path within the Jewish mystical tradition.

What kind of person is it the tradition is trying to create? What is its vision of the good life as it is to be lived by Jews who follow it? We have had a glimpse of Abraham, the ideal type of the *hasid*, loving God and always ready to do even more than the law demands. We should join to him the figure of Moses, teacher and prophet, for the rabbis the idea of the original sage and master. If the Abraham-ideal is one of pastoral simplicity, the image of Moses is one of student-scholar-teacher, the *talmid hakham* or wise disciple as leader of the people. It was such scholar-sages of the law whom traditional Jewish society most came to venerate over the centuries, people about whom countless tales were told to show that in every detail of their lives they embodied the way of Torah, especially in its ethical ramifications.[19]

The *hasid* and the sage stand in interesting tension with one another. One is a potentially extreme figure, jumping forward to do more than the law requires. The *hasid* loves God; that love is the single center of his religious life. For the sake of this love he is ever ready for martyrdom; sometimes one has the sense that he even seeks it out. Purity of devotion and boundless giving are his hallmarks. The sage is a figure of significantly greater sobriety. He will not act without consulting the sources, without seeking precedent in the generations that have come before. The sage imitates God in loving both the Torah and the people Israel, carefully balancing these two loves as he tries to show Israel how to live the life of Torah. His own love of God is quiet and understated, realized mostly in this life of *imitatio Dei*, "walking in His ways," as it is said in Hebrew. In a classic moment of confrontation between these two ideals, the Talmudic discussion of Sabbath law notes: "One who kills [life-threatening] snakes or scorpions on the Sabbath, the spirit of the *hasidim* is not pleased with him." The Talmud adds, thanks to an editor with just a bit of a sardonic touch: "The spirit of the sage is not pleased with such *hasidim*."[20]

With room for some notable exceptions, I think it fair to say that the spirit of the sages triumphed in Jewish history. Commitment to the rule of law became a chief virtue within this tradition, one strangely upheld by the large number of Jewish attorneys, legal scholars, and judges throughout the Western world who may not practice our own native legal traditions but nevertheless hold fast to the broader ideal. (In the modern world, of course, it was often the power of law that saved Jews from persecution and upheld the protection of minority rights that were so important to them.) Judiciousness and sobriety, the virtues of the judge, are very much those of the pious Jew. Spontaneity and self-expression are to be held in check until one sees whether the expression is appropriate to the dignity of one who proudly upholds an ancient law, until one knows whether there is any danger of being misunderstood, until one sees whether the expression will help or harm the ever-endangered house of Israel.

There is a stoic influence to be noted in the mores of Judaism, one that comes to penetrate Jewish ethics through both of the two great contacts Judaism had with Greek civilization. In the first two centuries of the Common Era, when the Jewish-Christian sects eventually crystallized into a new religion that was deeply Hellenistic in both mythos and ethos, emerging rabbinic Judaism managed to maintain a relatively more purely Semitic mythic structure, but in ethos it too became a part of the broadly Hellenistic philosophic world. The very figure of the sage himself, and his way of knowing God through an understanding of ancient texts, has been seen as belonging, *mutatis mutandis*, to the intellectual world so extensively developed by Alexandria and all it represented. The moral teachings offered by these sages, recorded in the pages of Mishnah Avot and cognate sources, also reflect a good deal of Hellenistic school wisdom only slightly dressed up in Jewish garb. The second contact of Judaism with the Greeks, mediated chiefly through the philosophy and ethics of Islam in the early Middle Ages, greatly reinforced an already somewhat developed stoic point of view. This will be clear if one opens almost any page of Bahya Ibn Paquda's *Duties of the Hearts*, perhaps the greatest moral treatise of medieval Jewry, written in Arabic in eleventh-century Spain. Patience, equanimity, and self-control are high on the list of virtues in this and the many works that followed it. There is a passion in the love of God (especially in the later and Kabbalah-inspired treatises), but this passion is to be given proper expression by the love of His creatures, by walking in His ways, and by following the counsel of the sages.

A part of this enshrining of sobriety as a virtue is a strong sense of the ongoing battle every person fights with *yetser ha-ra'*, the human inclination toward evil. Even for the rabbis, it appears that the two *yetsarim* (moral inclinations) are not quite balanced in the human being, the negative force naturally having something of the upper hand. The fact that human instincts and passions are both real and powerful is not something that Jewish moralists have sought to deny. But the reality of a drive does not make for its goodness or even its permissibility. *The law is there as God's gift to help one achieve the self-control needed in order to become a more perfect and whole vessel for the service of God.*

In this area, I might add, the traditional ethos of rabbinic and later Judaism is sharply at odds with the contemporary popular post-Freudian tendency (very much not that of Freud himself!) to accept and affirm every aspect of our inner selves. The clearest example that occurs to me is in the treatment of anger and aggression. Our aggressive drives, in the rabbinic view, are part of our *yetser ha-ra'*, that libidinal energy reserve which may be called the "evil" inclination, but which they also knew full well to be vital to our survival and to the propagation of the species. Aggression runs deep in all of human existence; the task with which we are faced is that of finding proper channels for expression of this aggressive drive. Anger, the most ordinary and readily available expression of aggression, is universally recognized by Jewish ethicists as a bad outlet. Anyone who "lets off steam" in an aggressive outburst against another human being is committing the ultimate double sin of "lessening the divine image" in both the receiver and the giver of that anger. Traditional moralists will urge us to convert the energy behind that anger into virtue, perhaps using it to defend the faith or to reprove the wicked. But such reproof, they hasten to add, cannot be offered in anger. There is no greater act of love than that of seeking to bring a fellow human back into relationship with God. One cannot engage in such work until one has "uplifted" rage, or "sweetened it in its root," in the Kabbalistic formulation.

This work, and much of the religious living that goes with it, can only be achieved in humility, a virtue not much spoken of in our contemporary world. Ultimately I believe the prophet Micah was right when he reduced the commandments to three: "Do justice, love mercy, and walk humbly before your God." This statement of virtue is one that preserves the best of the ancient Hebrew moralistic tradition. Its ancient roots in Judaism are widely seen in the Psalter, whence it also came to have a key role in the teachings of Jesus and the Sermon on the Mount. I would like to see it take the place it deserves in the encounter among our three sister-faiths and in the activities undertaken in the spirit of such an encounter. I therefore close by quoting a few words from a lovely essay on humility by our teacher Martin Buber:

> The humble man lives in each being and knows each being's manner and virtue. Since no one is to him "the other," he knows from within that none lacks some hidden value; knows that "there is no man who does not have his hour. . . ."
>
> "God does not look on the evil side," said one zaddik. "How should I dare to do so?"
>
> He who lives with others according to the mystery of humility can condemn no one. "He who passes sentence on a man passes it on himself."
>
> He who separates himself from the sinner departs in guilt. . . . Only living with the other is justice. . . .
>
> He who lives with others in this way realizes with his deed the truth that all souls are one; for each is a spark of the original soul, and the whole of the original soul is in each.[21]

NOTES

1. *Midrash Bereshit Rabbah* 9:5, 12. See further in that chapter for a series of "surprising" readings of *me'od*.
2. See Franz Rosenzweig's letter to Martin Buber, included in Rosenzweig's *On Jewish Learning*. On the Buber-Rosenzweig debate over revelation and law, cf. Paul Mendes-Flohr, in *Jewish Spirituality*, ed. Arthur Green (New York: Crossroad Books, 1987), 2:317ff.
3. On the role of mysticism in the revelation-theology of twentieth-century Jews, cf. Rivka Horwitz in *Jewish Spirituality*, 2:346ff.
4. This debate is the central subject of Abraham J. Heschel's *Torah min ha-shamayim*, vol. 2. This important book, is now available in English as *Heavenly Torah*, most ably translated and interpreted by Gordon Tucker (New York: Continuum, 2005).

5. B. (=Babylonian Talmud) Makkot 23b. The Talmudic sources do not list what the 613 actually are, but only fix the number. Listings of the specific commandments are disputed among the various medieval sages.

6. B. Hagigah 15a.

7. Based on b. Shabbat 68b.

8. On the development of this strategy in later Hasidism, cf. M. Piekarz in *Studies in Jewish Mysticism . . . Presented to Isaiah Tishby* (in Hebrew) (Jerusalem, 1986), 617ff.

9. RASHI, ad loc.

10. M. (=Mishnah) Avot 2:1.

11. B. Makkot 23b–24b.

12. M. Peah 1:1.

13. Translation adapted from that of C. Chavel.

14. Hirsch Humash, vol. 5, ad loc. Minor changes in style are my own.

15. Cf. also Job 1:1, where the hero of that book is described as *tam we-yashar*, "perfect and upright." If we want a biblical description of a "good man," that verse and its parallels in the Psalter and Proverbs are key passages.

16. Cf. my discussion in *Devotion and Commandment: The Faith of Abraham in the Hasidic Imagination* (Cincinnati: Hebrew Union College Press, 1989).

17. B. Yoma 28b.

18. Maimonides 3:54, Pines translation, 623f.

19. Cf. E. Urbach, *The Sages: Their Concepts and Beliefs* (Jerusalem: Magnes, 1975) and Gershom Scholem, "Three Types of Jewish Piety" in *Eranos Jahrbuch* 38 (1969).

20. B. Shabbat 121b.

21. "The Life of the Hasidim," in his *Hasidism and Modern Man* (New York: Harper, 1958).

PART 2

Theology and Mysticism in Classical Sources

5

Bride, Spouse, Daughter

Images of the Feminine in Classical Jewish Sources

For the first time in Jewish history, women are taking a full and equal role in the search for religious meaning in Jewish tradition. This coincides with their admission to positions of religious leadership in the community and with their full involvement in the life, on all levels, of the Jewish people. It seems entirely appropriate, at such a moment in history, that we comb our sources for images of the feminine in Jewish religious literature as they might be of use to such a generation of women. On the face of it, all of this is both obvious and entirely legitimate. As we probe a bit more deeply, however, two questions emerge that must be treated at least briefly as we begin to engage in such a search.

Is it really women who alone are in need of feminine imagery? Do images of the divine feminine belong only to women? Might they not belong to, and respond to, the needs of men as well as women? Or, as a friend posed the question a long time ago with reference to Catholic spiritual literature, does Theresa of Avila need to be the bride of God more than does John of the Cross? Does John need God the Father more than God the Mother? Indeed, is it Mother whom the passionate Theresa seeks so boldly? Might one not argue that men need the feminine, as women would need the masculine, if religious life involves something like what the depth psychologists call a search for polarities? In the course of our intense longing for the divine Other, a longing long depicted as having a strong erotic component, might it not be opposite rather than like that needs first to be sought out? Or might same and opposite both be needed, one for identification and the other for attraction? Or might the nature of gender in symbolic usage be much more complex and subtle than anyone might think at first glance? This moment in history demands a wide-angled look at gender-laden symbols, not a narrowly politicized one. This brings us, automatically, to a second important question in the anomalous situation in which we find ourselves.

As we turn to the tradition to seek out images of the feminine, we will have to admit that all the images we find are those of women as imagined by or created by men. We are not looking at the spiritual life of Glückel of Hameln or the pitifully few other women who have left us anything at all by way of written record in the annals of Jewish history prior to modern times. Rail against this fact as we may, we simply cannot create historical sources that do not exist. Women as created by men, women in the fantasies of men, albeit sacred fantasies, are what we have.[1] Are these the kinds of texts women will need? Will the fact that such images of the feminine are male creations in itself somehow negate their usefulness? Might there emerge a feminist and female-created commentary or literature of commentary on the old male-created series of feminine images? Or need the old be negated altogether in the quest of women of our times?

Both of these questions, that of who needs feminine imagery and that of the usability of feminine imagery as created by a male religious community, will pursue us throughout any such search.

The Jewish religious community, insofar as it existed as a public and corporate body in premodern times, was a male community. Women surely had a place in that community, indeed they had a vital role in Jewish life throughout history, one that need not be defended here. But insofar as that community saw itself as an assembled group, insofar as it came before God in the house of prayer or the house of study, it existed, it wrote for itself, it thought of itself, by and large, as a community of men. What does it mean then to note that this community regularly spoke of itself in the feminine, as *knesset Yisrael*? What does it mean that this primarily male community saw itself as the bride in its commentary on the Song of Songs? What does it mean that this male community saw itself as the female spouse, as it were, of the masculine God? There are some who would turn to the sense of powerlessness and castration in Jewish history in order to answer such a question. It would be argued that it was because the Jewish people had no political independence, because we were not masters of our own lives and of our own historical situation, that we saw ourselves as "mere" powerless women rather than as real men. That works until one notices that the linguistic tradition is much the same in the Church. The Church, too, the all-powerful Church of the Middle Ages, saw itself as the *Ecclesia*, as the bride of God. While women had a more active role in the Church than in the synagogue, surely those images there too reflect the self-description of a male-dominated community.[2]

Why is it that men, in talking about their relationship with God, turned to images of the feminine in order to describe themselves? This seems to be a major issue in understanding the psychology of a religious community. What I want to propose is simply this: in the search for the kind of intimacy, tenderness, and warmth that such people wanted to express in talking about the relationship between God and Israel, they could not remain in the domain of the all-male universe where they lived their public lives. There is no way, without turning to images of the feminine, or without thinking of the relationships between men and women, that most men can express the degree of love, passion, and warmth that the spiritual life may arouse in them.

All this imagery of the feminine still assumes the basic masculinity of God. If we talk about the female community of Israel, or Israel as the bride, in such word pictures we are talking about God, of course, as "man." When the sages spoke of the relationship between God and Israel in "man-to-man" terms, they found themselves limited primarily to two images: Israel (or the individual) as son and Israel as servant. The son, as is said so clearly in the Rosh Hashanah liturgy, may duly expect to be the object of divine loving kindness, while the servant may but turn to his Master in supplication for His pity (or His justice?). There is, of course, a depth of love between Father and son depicted in Jewish sources that is not to be underestimated. Much of the love literature, particularly within the context of liturgy, and in Hasidism as well, speaks about Israel as the son of the king. 'Eved, the servant, brings out more clearly the aspect of yir'ah (the fear of God) and of a sense of complete dependency, while at the same time perhaps pointing to mutual responsibilities in a relationship of fealty.

Neither of these images, however, exhausts the full measure of our capacity for love, surrender, or passion. In a touchingly understated article published some years ago, Judah Goldin indicated that Rabbi Akiva's emphasis on love as the center of the religious life—it was Akiva who said that "all of Scripture is holy, but the Song of Songs is the holy of holies"—had to do with his attitude toward his own marriage and that his marriage was somehow a model for him of the relationship between God and Israel.[3]

The rabbis say that the handmaiden at the crossing of the Red Sea saw more than Ezekiel the prophet. Ezekiel, it will be recalled, was the prophet who spoke in the most bold, open way of what he had seen in a visionary state. Here the handmaiden—not the servant, but the handmaiden—is said to have seen more than Ezekiel. Why the handmaiden? Only in the context of the rabbis' reading of the Song of Songs does the passage make sense. God is Israel's great lover, liberator, bringing her out from Egypt and across the sea. At that moment, the moment when she greets her lover, she sees more than the male Israel, Israel the son or servant, might. This is consistent with the imagery that runs through the entire Midrash on the Song of Songs. Despite a highly conservative and, from our point of view, at times prudish attitude toward the erotic in a religious context—an attitude in part inherited from the old biblical struggle against cultic sexuality—we find in early rabbinic sources a significant strand that recognizes the inevitability of this theme's reappearance as one discusses "matters that touch the human heart."[4]

The imagery of Israel as the bride of God shares its place in this search for feminine metaphors with another interesting and perhaps surprising image, that of Israel as the daughter of God. For this we turn to a text, quoting the Midrash on the Song of Songs (3:7):

"King Solomon made a palanquin for himself" (Cant. 3:9). Rabbi Azariah in the name of Rabbi Judah the son of Simon interpreted this verse as speaking of the Tabernacle.[5] The Palanquin is the Tabernacle. Said Rabbi Judah the son of Ilai. This may be compared to a king who had a young daughter. Before she grew up and the signs of puberty were found in her, the king would see her in the market place and speak to her openly, in the courtyard or in the alleyway. When she grew up, however, and she reached puberty, the king said: "It will not be proper for my daughter that I speak to her in public. Rather make her a pavilion, and when I need to speak to her I will speak to her in the pavilion." Thus scripture says, "When Israel was a lad I loved him" (Hos. 11:1). In Egypt they saw Him in public, as scripture says, "The Lord passed by to smite the Egyptians" (Ex. 12:23). At the sea they saw Him in public, as scripture says, "Israel saw the great hand" (Ex. 14:31). And then the young children pointed to him with their fingers and said, "This is my God and I will glorify Him" (Ex. 15:2). At Sinai they saw Him face to face, as scripture says, "The Lord comes from Sinai" (Deut. 33:2). But once Israel had stood at Mt. Sinai and received the Torah, saying, "All that the Lord has said we shall do and obey" (Ex. 24:7) they became a mature people. Then the Holy One, blessed be He, said: "It is not proper for my children that I speak with them in public, rather let them make a Tabernacle for Me; when I need to speak with them I'll speak to them from within the Tabernacle." Thus scripture says, "When Moses came into the Tent of Meeting to speak with Him" (Ex. 34:34). This palanquin was made by King Solomon; "Solomon" here refers to the King of Peace.

What we see in this text is surely a reflection of proper royal class behavior in Mishnaic times. The daughter has a right to the protection of her modesty, and a casual approach to her on the streets, even by her own father, would demean her. This image is then applied to the relationship of God and Israel, superimposed on the classical period of Israel's sacred history. The truth is that there is something distinctive here in the relationship between father and daughter which is not present in the relationship between father and son. Father and daughter develop a certain shyness with one another as the daughter reaches puberty, a shyness which is not the same between fathers and sons. The daughter now has a right to privacy; the father accepts her as a mature woman and respects, indeed helps to set, the bounds of her contacts with men, including himself. Being the king's daughter is different from being His son; there is a relationship being spoken of here that a male can never fully understand, and that the tradition itself has not been able to fully appreciate until now, because there has never been a commentator on any of this material who was herself a daughter and knew what the relationship between father and daughter was about.

But it is not only Israel who is described as being the king's daughter. We find quite a few sources describing Torah as daughter of God. In this example the reference is again to the building of the Tabernacle:

"Moses has commanded the Torah to us, an inheritance for the house of Israel," read not "inheritance" [*MoRaSHaH*] but rather "betrothal" [*Me'oRaSaH*]. The bridegroom, so long as he has not actually married his bride, becomes a regular visitor in the house of his future father-in-law. From the time they are married, however, her father must come to visit her. Similarly, so long as the Torah had not been given to Israel, scripture tells us, "Moses went up to God" (Ex. 19:3). Once the Torah was there with Israel, God said to Moses, "Make Me a Tabernacle and I will dwell in their midst" (Ex. 25:8).[6]

The image of Torah as feminine is, of course, related to ancient traditions of wisdom, *hokhmah* or *sophia*, which in biblical literature and elsewhere is frequently described in feminine terms. Such description has a long history, first in ancient Wisdom literature, later in both Gnostic and Neo-Platonic sources. A latter day mystical transformation of that symbol lies behind the well-known passage of the Zohar that describes the Torah as a beautiful and stately maiden, hidden away in a castle, who reveals bits of herself only to her lover as he walks by her gate each day to seek her out. It is a passage filled with the imagery of medieval courtly love.[7] These passages demand that we consider seriously the notion that the Torah is woman. This becomes particularly interesting in the context of the current controversy over the ordination of women as rabbis. The rabbi in Judaism, unlike the Christian priest, is in no way the personification of God in the liturgy. If anything, the rabbi is the embodiment of Torah, the one who represents Torah in the midst of the Jewish community. But if the Torah, in a significant part of ancient rabbinic imagery, is described in feminine terms, what inadequacy can one find in its being represented by a woman?

Still, let us not rush to politicize our study of symbols. The question is meant in the first place as a devotional one: What does it feel like to be the king's daughter? What particular devotional content might a woman find in that metaphor of relationship? Might it offer some new/old enrichment to *all* of us who seek, both male and female? What does it feel like for a man to be wedded to the daughter of a king? Have we fully understood both the joy and the awesome responsibility of that self-description?[8] What does it feel like to be an embodiment of Torah, Torah as a feminine presence, perhaps a female wisdom on a deeper, more hidden, or more subtle level than the conventionally "masculine" wisdom of cumulative law and tradition?

There is in the tradition of the rabbis a great love of feminine imagery. Again and again the most poignant passages to be found in rabbinic literature will involve a female voice or image. One need think perhaps only of one of the most famous of rabbinic homilies on the destruction of Jerusalem, in which, after the Patriarchs, Moses, Jeremiah, and the Prophets all stand up to accuse God of His unfaithfulness in allowing His Temple to be destroyed, it is only mother Rachel, in talking about how she set aside her jealousy of Leah, who can shame God into setting aside his jealousy of the petty and foolish idols that Israel had taken to worship.

There is little question that even this wealth of traditional imagery will not suffice for our own day. Many will rightly claim that new kinds of female images are needed and that the multiplicity or variety of female models sought today are not all there in the early sources. There is, however, a body of material to work with, and it is considerably greater than many would first assume when looking at what is frequently dismissed as a male-dominated religious tradition. This material might form the basis of a contemporary commentary—though surely such commentary must go beyond anything found in the prior literature.

All of the above has to do with the situation in which the masculinity of God is still assumed, while that which stands in relation to God may be seen as feminine. We turn now to a new sort of literature, that of the Kabbalah, in which a female component of divinity itself is given place. Here, of course, the roster of sources is somewhat shorter, and we must beware of exaggerated and ahistorical claims that are sometimes made for this material. A new myth of Judaism emerged in the twelfth and thirteenth centuries, hiding behind the word *kabbalah*, which means tradition itself. Here is presented a Judaism of mythic complexity that had been previously unknown, one in which the single, static, and essentially masculine God of biblical-rabbinic monotheism is replaced by a dynamic, multifaceted, ever-flowing, separating and uniting, new kind of ten-in-one monotheistic deity. In that paradigm of the inner life of God, described through so many rich and varied images in the kabbalistic literature, the *Shekhinah* took a major role.

Using an ancient term for the indwelling or presence of God, the Kabbalists now employed *Shekhinah* to symbolize a particular realm within the divine world. Described as daughter, bride, mother, moon, sea, faith, wisdom, speech, and a myriad of other figures, usually but not always feminine by fact or association, the *Shekhinah* is the chief object of both the divine and human search for wholeness and perfection. She is the bride of God within God, mother of the world and feminine side of the divine self, in no way fully separable from the male self of God. Indeed, the root of all evil, both cosmic and human, is the attempt to bring about such a separation. The picture of that feminine aspect of divinity is a complicated one. As the tenth of the *sefirot*, or manifestations of divine self-hood, she is, when facing those above, passive and receptive. She takes all the upper powers into herself; "All the rivers flow into the sea," as the Kabbalists love to quote from the book of Ecclesiastes (1:7). But as the sea transforms all the rivers, gives them new life as a dynamic power all her own, and reaches her destined shores as a new being, so is the *Shekhinah*, when facing the lower worlds, described as giver, provider, ruler, and judge. In a way that cannot be fully understood, she is represented as the mystical embodiment of the Community of Israel: the Kabbalist has transferred the locus of mystical marriage from the relationship of God and the earthly Israel to an entirely divine plane. Rather than seeing himself and his people as the bride of God, he now joins with God above in rejoicing at a sacred marriage that has taken place, as it were, within God. Perhaps most interestingly, *Shekhinah* is the only aspect of divinity that most Kabbalists ever claim really to experience. The *Shekhinah*, the outermost gate to the divine mysteries, is all the Kabbalist dares to say that he has attained. It is through the union of *Shekhinah* with God above that the Kabbalist, too, is bound to those higher forces. He serves as "attendant of the bride," knowing secretly that his soul is born of this union that he has helped to bring about.

We read now of the *Shekhinah* from the earliest text we have in all of Kabbalistic literature, the *Sefer HaBahir*, which appeared in southern France in the latter decades of the twelfth century. The *Bahir* is written in an intentionally mystifying and yet defiantly simple tone, one that does much to set the stage for the later symbolic development within Kabbalah. Here the *Bahir* is commenting on the biblical verse "Blessed be the Glory of God from His place" (Ezek. 3:12). Glory, in Hebrew *kavod*, is the biblical term which the Kabbalists (following the *Targum*) usually took as a code word for the *Shekhinah*.

> This may be compared to a king who had a matron in his chamber. All his hosts took pleasure in her. She had children, and those children came each day to see the king and greet him. They would say to him, "Where is our mother?" And he would answer, "You cannot see her now." To this they would reply, "Blessed be she, in whatever place she is."

Immediately the *Bahir* adds a second parable:

This may be compared to a princess who came from a faraway place. Nobody knew where she came from. Then they saw that she was an upstanding woman, good and proper in all her deeds. They said of her, "This one surely is taken from the place of light, for by her deeds the world is enlightened." They asked her, "Where are you from?" She said, "From my place." They said, "In that case, great are the people of your place. Blessed are you; blessed is she and blessed is her place."[9]

The *Shekhinah*, the mysterious woman, queen or princess, hidden or coming from a place beyond, is the only one we see, the only one we greet. What is her place, what is her origin? These are hidden somewhere in the mysteries of God beyond. All we can say of the God we know, of that feminine God we encounter, is "Blessed is she and blessed is her place." The glory of God is apparent to us, the glory of God lies within the realm of human experience. The *Shekhinah* is the God we know. Surely, that *Shekhinah* stands in relation to a transcendent deity, whether described in male terms or in terms of more pure abstraction, but our knowledge of that is only through her. Blessed is she and blessed is her place.

While the *Shekhinah* plays a central role in all of Kabbalistic literature, it is especially in the Zohar that its feminine character is highlighted. The author of the Zohar was possessed of a seemingly boundless mythic imagination, a great deal of it centering on female figures, both sacred and demonic, as well as on deeply ambivalent fantasies concerning human women in this world.[10] In what is surely one of its most strikingly impassioned passages, the Zohar speaks of the love of God through the symbol of the kisses that Jacob gives to Rachel. From the passage it becomes clear that the experience of the mystic is that of being aroused, drawn into, and kissed by God. As the passage develops, Rachel, the recipient of the kisses, is really related to an entirely hidden and abstract God beyond, a God so abstract and hidden, however, that He cannot be described as one who kisses. How, indeed, can one be loved by a God who is hidden beyond all being? Jacob is the personified manifestation of this hidden God, personified only, as it were, in order that the great mystery be enabled to kiss the bride. The passage reads as follows:

When it (the spirit of love) enters the palace of love, the love of supernal kisses is aroused, those of which scripture says: "Jacob kissed Rachel"

(Gen. 29:11). This arousal brings about the kisses of supernal love, as needs to be. These kisses are the beginning of all love, attachment, and binding above. That is why the Canticle opens its praises with: "Let Him kiss me." Who is to "kiss me"? The one hidden in sublime hiding. But should you ask: "Do kisses apply to the most hidden One? Does that one kiss below?"—come and see: that most hidden of hiddens, no one knows it. It reveals of itself but a slim ray of hidden light, revealed only through a narrow path that proceeds from it. But this is the light that gives light to all. This is the arousal of all the sublime secrets, yet it remains hidden. Sometimes hidden, sometimes revealed. But even when it is not revealed at all, it remains the source of arousal for those ascending kisses. And since it is hidden, the Canticle begins its praises in a hidden (i.e., third-person) way.[11]

But if kisses are from there, what need have we of Jacob here? Do not the kisses proceed from Him? The matter is thus: "Let Him kiss me"— the One who is hidden above. But how? Through that plane in which all the colors are reflected and joined together, and that is Jacob.[12]

So here we are, Israel, male and female, personified together as Rachel, receiving the kisses of God as Jacob. No, we receive the kisses of the God beyond, the God who is neither male nor female, neither here nor there, not this way or that way, the God who is utterly beyond all such duality and polarization. Here it seems that it is only the reality of human life and the gender-defined nature of our passions that cause the mystic to speak, for those of us who cannot follow him utterly into abstraction, in the language of male and female.

This all-too-brief selection from the Kabbalistic sources on *Shekhinah* might best be concluded with a line from another thirteenth-century work, the *Gates of Light* by Joseph Gikatillia. We have seen the *Shekhinah* as locus of the classic symbols of the feminine and as the mystical Community of Israel. Here we see her represented by individual women, an aspect seldom found in the early sources. Gikatillia writes:

"In the time of Abraham our father, of blessed memory, the *Shekhinah* was called Sarah. In the time of Isaac our father, she was called Rebecca. In the time of Jacob our father, she was called Rachel."[13]

The point is clear. The names of the *Shekhinah* change with the genera-tions, as do the names of every other aspect, male and female, of divinity. God is identified with all of the patriarchs, with all of the heroes, whereas *Shekhinah* is identified with all of the mothers, the heroines of the Bible.

Are we the bride of God, the people whom He weds on that Sabbath of revelation? Are we related to God as female to male, seemingly an image so clear in commentary on the Song of Songs? Or are we, as some other imagery suggests, God's son-in-law, wedded to his daughter the Torah or his daughter the Sabbath? Try to sort out the imagery of *lekhah dodi*, "Come, my dear friend to greet the bride." Whose bride is it that we are greeting? Sabbath, *Shekhinah*, the bride of God? Ourselves, collectively Israel, the bride of God? Or Sabbath, the bride of Israel? Or can no such clear or clean distinctions be made? Must we not rather say that we are at once male and female in relating to God, who is Him/Herself at once male and female; both of them inadequate metaphors to describe the mysterious self beyond all gender, indeed, beyond all distinction, but lacking none of the passion we know in our fragile human attempt to unify the polarities?

None of this will probably suffice for a new generation of women, those who are for the first time becoming fully involved in the creative spiritual life of the Jewish people. The foundation for such creativity, however, is here. The situation of women fully entering participation in the Jewish community is entirely anomalous. The new generation should rejoice in that, seeing its holy duty as one of creating an element in our shared myth that has been developed in only a fragmentary way. It will be a tragedy—one of the great Jewish tragedies of our age—if those women who enter roles of leadership in Jewish life become "sons of the King." That will do none of us any good. They will remain awkward in that role, and the Jewish people will remain unenriched. A truly feminine, and truly Jewish, spiri-tuality is one of the urgent tasks of our age. It is a proper point of origin, for it would be the encounter of contemporary Jewish women with those symbols of the sacred feminine given us by our tradition.

NOTES

Adapted from an address given to the Women's Rabbinical Alliance, 1979.

1. A possible exception is provided by some of the literature of *tehinot*: prayers and supplications written specifically for women. Quite a number of these were pub-

lished in various collections, especially in Yiddish, over the past three hundred years. In most cases it is not known, however, whether the authors themselves were women.

2. Of course, the marital motif for the relationship of God and Israel goes back to the Bible; the prophet Hosea makes especially strong use of it in describing Israel's infidelity. Given their early histories of persecution as well as their later competitive claims, it is not hard to see why both the rabbinic and the ecclesiastic authors chose to highlight the faithfulness of God's spouse and the undying affection He has for her.

3. Judah Goldin, "Toward a Profile of the Tanna, Aqiba ben Joseph," *Journal of the American Oriental Society* 96 (1976): 1.

4. I have discussed these sources more fully in "The Children in Egypt and the Theophany at the Sea," *Judaism* 24, no. 4 (1975): 446–56.

5. The portable sanctuary in the form of a tent that was used during the forty years of wandering.

6. Exodus Rabbah 33:7.

7. Zohar 2:99a–b.

8. They are most fully drawn out in the fantasy-creations of Rabbi Nahman of Bratslav. See the first two in his collection of *Tales*, now available in the faithful English rendition of Arnold Band (New York: Paulist Press, 1978). On Nahman's tales, see Appendix II in my *Tormented Master* (Tuscaloosa: University of Alabama Press, 1979) 337-71.

9. *Bahir* (Margaliot ed., 131–32; Scholem ed., 90).

10. The classic essay on feminine symbolism in the Kabbalah is Gershom Scholem's "Shekhinah: The Feminine Element in Divinity," included in his *On the Mystical Shape of the Godhead* (New York: Schocken, 1991). Isaiah Tishby's introduction to *shekhinah* in *The Wisdom of the Zohar* (London: Littman Library, 1989) is also very valuable. Since the original publication of this essay in 1979, a great deal has been published on eros and the feminine in Kabbalah. Among the key studies are Elliot Wolfson's *Circle in the Square: Studies in the Use of Gender in Kabbalistic Symbolism* (Albany: SUNY Press, 1995), as well as other works by Wolfson, and Moshe Isel's *Kabbalah and Eros* (New Haven: Yale University Press, 2005). The reader may also be interested in seeing my own "Shikhinah, the Virgin Mary, and the Song of Songs" in *AJS Review* 26, no. 1 (2002): 1–52.

11. Rachel does not say to Jacob, "Kiss me!" as the Canticle opens, but rather "Let Him kiss me." The hidden God beyond cannot be addressed in the second person of prayer, but can only be hinted at in the more secretive third person manner.

12. Zohar 2:146b.

13. Joseph Gikatillia, *Sha'arey Orah*, ed. Ben-Shlomo (Jerusalem: Bialik Institute, 1981), 230.

6

The Children in Egypt and the Theophany at the Sea

Modern Jewish thinking about God has long suffered from a striking lack of poetic and symbolic imagination. Rooted in the world of German post-Idealism, our theologians chose to write in the language of abstraction and thus produced little which reached into the depths of religious consciousness, a consciousness which is more easily aroused (if all the studies on premodern religion are to be believed) by myth and symbol than by the antiseptic niceties of philosophical theology.

When modern Jewish scholars and theologians did turn to models from the Jewish past, it was most frequently in Maimonides that they found what they had sought. Here was an intellectual elitist in their own image, towering far above all the vulgarisms of popular piety and committed to an idea of God which, for abstraction, could easily vie with their own. If one views the amount of attention to Maimonides and the entire medieval school that was given by late nineteenth- and early twentieth-century Jewish scholarship, as reflected in writing as well as in curricula of Jewish studies at seminaries and universities, it becomes clear that the great model of Jewish thought for those generations was the medieval philosophical sage, one who spent much of his life explaining away those very metaphors and symbols for the divine which earlier figures of piety, the biblical and particularly the aggadic authors, had created.

The existentialist trend in modern Jewish theology has offered but a partial solution to the problem. True, Buber's rediscovery of Hasidism and Rosenzweig's turn to Halevi both represented a search for alternative spiritual ancestors of a more poetic variety. Nevertheless, the language in which these and others who followed them chose to express their own thoughts continued to be one of abstraction; concreteness and unabashed anthropomorphism in religious writing were still the domain of poets, not of theologians. One need only to contrast the Yiddish poetry of such figures as the young A. J. Heschel and Aaron Zeitlin with the theological writings of their Germanophone and Anglophone contemporaries to perceive the ongoing bifurcation of living religious language and religious thought in the modern Jewish consciousness.

The great task of Jewish theology today is the recovery of an authentic Jewish religious language. The dramatic and frightening events of recent Jewish history have lent to the theological enterprise a new and desperate seriousness, revealing a depth of longing that can no longer be sated by the language of abstraction. Our search for authentic religious voices draws us to the writings of Isaac Bashevis Singer and Elie Wiesel; only there do we find a spiritual texture sufficiently rich to encompass our grief and anger, while finding some room (at least in Wiesel) for the exultation of personal and national rebirth. The turn of such a figure as Emil Fackenheim to the search for a new Midrash, and perhaps, above all, the work of Gershom Scholem and his followers in making available to us the great wellsprings of Jewish mystical literature, are guideposts toward the old/new avenues which Jewish religious thought must explore in our age.

It is in this spirit that the present literary/historical study is offered. It is hoped that the rediscovery of this and other long-neglected aspects of Jewish religious language will serve to enrich the discussion of theological matters in contemporary Jewish circles. The new Midrash, while taking its own directions, will become an authentic Jewish voice only insofar as it is nurtured by the old. As is the way of Midrash, readers are left to draw their own conclusions from the complex of images here presented.

Classical Jewish literature may be said to be marked by two opposing tendencies with regard to the question of physical anthropomorphism. Well known is that strain, found in a few Rabbinic texts, the Targumim, and culminating in the classics of medieval Jewish philosophy, which seeks to deny the attribution of any bodily characteristics to the Creator or, at the very least, to deny the possibility that human beings may "see" any physical representation of God during their lifetimes.[1] Beginning with Alexandria,[2] much of Jewish theology has accepted as an essential part of its task the rereading of seemingly anthropomorphic passages in the Bible and, by means of various literary devices or quasi-philosophical machinations, to explain away those claims which seem to run counter to the assumption that God is not possessed of a body and cannot be seen by the human eye.[3]

Surely less well known is the opposing strain, one that is nonetheless equally representative of a major portion of Jewish literature: a tradition of acceptance of anthropomorphism and even of radical anthropomorphization far beyond the rather restrained claims of the Hebrew Bible. This current may also be found in Midrashic literature, particularly in those passages which involve interpretation of the Song of Songs and is traceable through the long-respected literature of *Shi'ur Qomah*,[4] which discusses the dimensions of the mystical body of God, the *Idrot* of the Zohar,[5] which deal in detail with such matters as the difference between the hairs of God's head and those of His beard, and the vast literature of Lurianic Kabbalah, which describes the various states of conjugal union of the male and female aspects of the Deity in strikingly unabashed detail.

Until rather recent times, it was still commonplace to present the former of these two tendencies as that of "normative" Rabbinic Judaism, while the latter was seen as a rather minor aberration of the mystics, surely not rooted in authentic Jewish sources and ways of thinking.[6] The direction of Jewish scholarship in the past few decades, however, has been one which expands the canon of the normative, often to the point where esoteric and exoteric doctrines are used to shed light upon one another.

The examination of a particularly rich complex of legends surrounding the suffering of Israel in Egypt and the crossing of the Sea of Reeds may serve to demonstrate anew the presence of this latter stream within the sources of Rabbinic literature and, indeed, may shed light on certain major theological motifs in Rabbinic Judaism:

We read in Exodus Rabbah 23:8, commenting on the Song of Moses:

Rabbi Judah says: "Who spoke the praise of God? The children whom Pharaoh had sought to cast into the Nile—they are the ones who recognized God. How is this?

When Israel were in Egypt and an Israelite woman felt that she was about to give birth, she would go out to the fields and have her children there. After she had given birth, she would leave the infant there, saying to God: 'Lord of the World! I have done mine, now You do yours!'"

Rabbi Yohanan said: "God Himself[7] would immediately come down to cut the umbilical cord and to wash and anoint the infant. . . . He would place two stones in the child's hands. From one he could suckle oil, and from the other honey . . . and so the children would grow up in the fields. . . . When they were asked: 'Who took care of you?' they replied: 'A certain beautiful and praiseworthy young man came down and took care of all our needs,' as is written: 'My beloved is fair and ruddy, a paragon among ten thousands'" (Cant. 5:10).

When Israel reached the Sea, those same children were among them. They saw God at the Sea, and said to their parents: "This is the one who did all those things for us when we were in Egypt!" Thus scripture says: "This is my God and I will glorify Him!" (Ex. 15:2).

The same legend appears in various forms in a number of Rabbinic sources. The relevant passages have been cited by Ginzberg and Lieberman.[8] It is interesting to note that a number of these versions sought to tell the tale in a theologically more guarded manner: It was the angels, rather than God Himself, who cared for the Israelite children. The price of such theological propriety was, however, the total obfuscation of the point of the legend. If the children had not seen God Himself in their infancy, but only an angel, how would they have been able to recognize the Lord when they saw Him at the Sea? Thus Rabbi Yohanan's account, quoted elsewhere in the name of Rabbi Hiyya,[9] must be an original part of the tale. The children saw God Himself in Egypt, and it was in that same form, as the comely young man described in the Song of Songs, that He appeared at the Sea.

Further examination of the versions of our legend will show that they abound, sometimes gratuitously, in allusions to verses from the Song of Songs. Thus we find in Exodus Rabbah 1:12 that the Israelite women gave birth beneath apple trees in the fields, fulfilling the verse: "Beneath the apple-trees I roused you" (Cant. 8:5).[10] Another version has the mothers in Egypt asking their children, as they entered their parents' homes: "Tell me, my beloved, how did you feed? How did you lie down at midday?" (Cant. 1:7).[11] "The flocks of your companions" in the same verse is also viewed as a reference to the children, who came back to their homes like flocks returning from pasture.

The most complete version of this tale appears in a variant text of Deuteronomy Rabbah.[12] It has a richness of detail lacking in the other sources, which makes it worthy of being quoted in its entirety:

"The Lord your God has caused you to multiply (Deut. 1:10). . . ." When did God cause you to multiply? In Egypt, as scripture says: "I caused you to multiply like plants of the field (Ezek. 16:7)." How did this happen? When Pharaoh decreed that every male child be cast into the Nile, an Israelite woman would go out into the fields when she felt herself ready to give birth. After her child was born, she would turn her eyes heavenward and say: "I have done mine, as You have said: 'Be fruitful and multiply' (Gen. 1:28).¹³ Now You do Yours!"

What would the Egyptians do when they saw the Israelite women going out to the fields to give birth? They would keep watch from some distance, but as soon as the woman got up to return to town, they would take rocks in their hands to kill the infant. As the Egyptians approached, however, the child would be swallowed up by the field. When the attackers moved away again, the child would reappear, but each time they approached, he would again be swallowed up by the field. This went on until the Egyptians tired of it and went away.

How did those children live in the fields? Said Rabbi Levi: "God would send two angels to each of them, one to wash him and one to dress him. They would provide for him to be nursed and anointed with oil, as is said: 'He suckled him with oil from the rock, and honey from the flintstone' (Deut. 32:33). Thus scripture further says, 'I bathed you in water . . . and gave you garments of brocade' (Ezek. 16:10)."¹⁴

Rabbi Hiyya Rabba said: "It was not the angels who did this, but rather God Himself, for scripture says: 'I bathed you.'¹⁵ Had the verse said: 'I caused you to be bathed,' one might think it was done by an angel. But 'I bathed you' means that there was no angel involved. Praised be the name of God! He Himself did this for them!"

The children grew up in the field like plants, and when they were grown they would return in flocks to their homes. . . . But how would a child know the home of his own parents? God would go along with them, and to each child he would point out his father's house. He would tell them: "Your father is to be called thus, and your mother thus." The child would say to his mother: "Do you remember the day you gave birth to me, in such-and-such a field, on such-and-such a day, five months ago?" Then the mother would ask: "Who cared for you?" And the child would answer: "A young man with beautiful curls;¹⁶ there is none like him. He brought me here and is waiting outside." The mother would say: "Show him to me." When they went outside, however, though they would search everywhere, they could never find him.

When they saw Him at the Sea of Reeds, they pointed with their fingers to show their mothers: "This is the one who raised me! 'This is my God and I will glorify Him!'" (Ex. 15:2).

The claims of such an aggadic text are startling to the Jewish reader who has been trained in the later dominant tradition which teaches him that all anthropomorphisms are to be explained away. It is not surprising, therefore, to find a later commentator attempting to apologize for our legend:

> *A Certain Beautiful and Praiseworthy Young Man*: Any bodily attribute is far from being applicable to God, praised be He. The meaning here is rather that they understood that God, as a pure and holy transcendent power, had saved them through His providence . . . and the scriptural passages quoted here are only meant figuratively and to serve as literary adornment.[17]

While it is true that other well-known aggadic motifs speak of God Himself as having been directly present in the redemption from Egypt,[18] those sources do not speak of Israel *seeing* God in Egypt, but only indicate, as does the biblical text itself, that they knew of His presence through His saving deeds. It is the physical manifestation of God in human form in Egypt and at the Sea which lends to this text its unique significance.

The tale of the children in Egypt is always linked to the crossing of the Sea of Reeds. This event seems to take a central role in the speculations of certain of the early Rabbis, a role which goes even beyond those of the plagues in Egypt or the Exodus itself.[19] It is only by understanding the significance of that event to the Midrashic authors that we may come to understand the boldness with which our legend speaks of God's appearance. In order to do so, however, we must turn our attention not to the Song of the Sea, as one might expect, but rather to the Song of Songs.

There is considerable difference of opinion in Rabbinic sources as to the authorship and original setting of this biblical book. While some views unhesitatingly accept the ascription to Solomon, in the first verse, and speak of Canticles as one of the three books which Solomon wrote under the guidance of the holy spirit,[20] others try to trace the origin of the Song of Songs to the generation of the Exodus, claiming that the *Shelomoh* of the superscription refers not to Solomon but to the King of Peace, and thus they claim God Himself as the author of the Song.

Rabbi Akiba, in describing the Song of Songs as the "holy of holies" within Scripture,[21] refers to "the day when the Song of Songs was given to Israel." The term "given" is the same as that consistently applied in Rabbinic literature to the revelation at Sinai; it would not be applied to a work of human authorship, even one written under divine inspiration. Other Midrashic sources discuss quite plainly whether it was God or the angels who first recited the Song of Songs.[22]

What was the "day on which the Song of Songs was given?" "Where was it said?" asks Midrash.[23] Various answers are supplied—at the Sea, at Sinai, in the Tent of Meeting, in the Temple—and appropriate verses are adduced to support each opinion. As Lieberman has shown,[24] each of these opinions has its roots in the Tannaitic schools. Rabbi Eliezer ben Hyrcanus teaches that the Song of Songs was said at the Sea,[25] Rabbi Akiba is the author of the view that it was first recited at Sinai,[26] Rabbi Meir traces it to the Tent of Meeting, and an anonymous Tannaitic source holds that its origin was in the Temple.

The latter three opinions can all be readily explained. That the "holy of holies" was revealed at the holiest of moments, at Sinai,[27] should come as no surprise. The Tent of Meeting is also the site of revelation, a more intimate revelation, as it was apprehended only by Moses. The Temple as the original location of the Song of Songs fits well with the tradition of Solomonic authorship. It is only the suggestion of Rabbi Eliezer that seems in need of further explication. The verse quoted by R. Hanina bar Papa: "I would compare you, my dearest, to Pharaoh's chariot-horses" (Cant. 1:9),[28] hardly seems to provide sufficient justification for such an elaborate claim. Nor does the exegesis of Canticles 2:14, ascribed to Rabbi Eliezer himself,[29] seem particularly convincing. The opinion that the Song of Songs was first said or "given" at the Sea of Reeds must be based on something other than the exegesis of the text itself.

Fortunately, another text is preserved, in the name of Rabbi Eliezer, on the very same verse around which our legend was elaborated:

"This is my God and I will glorify Him (Ex: 15:2)." Rabbi Eliezer comments: "How do we know that a handmaiden at the Sea saw more than

Isaiah or Ezekiel? From the verse 'I [appear] to the prophets in parables'" (Hosea 12:11).[30]

The prophets know God only through *demut*, parables or similitudes, while the handmaiden at the Sea actually *sees* in a way not vouchsafed to prophets! Rabbi Eliezer conceives of the crossing of the Sea as a moment of *seeing*, as an experience of revelation higher than that granted even to the greatest visionaries among the prophets of Israel. We are now dealing not only with a moment of miraculous salvation at the Sea of Reeds but also with a theophany which, as we shall see, is comparable to that of Sinai itself. While such a moment of revelation is not mentioned in the biblical narrative, it seems possible that the verse "Israel saw the great hand" (Ex. 14:31) may have been a point of departure for such speculations.

In the context of Rabbi Eliezer's view of the event at the Sea, the legend with which we began takes on new meaning. It is not accidental that the vision of God as a comely young man was vouchsafed to those children who were to stand at the Sea, nor is it accidental that our legend is replete with references to the Song of Songs. The crossing of the Sea is the moment of a great visionary experience, and it is the day on which the Song of Songs was given. And what is the content of this vision? The God whom the handmaiden sees at the Sea is none other than that black-curled young man whom the children saw in Egypt, the lover of the Song of Songs! Nor is the "handmaiden" herself coincidental. What more appropriate image for Israel than that of the handmaiden, who, at the final moment of her long-awaited liberation, sees her bridegroom and redeemer (think of Boaz and Ruth) coming toward her?

The vision of God as a young man at the Sea is not unknown in other Rabbinic sources. A series of Aggadot which seek to attest to the oneness of God, despite His varied appearances, make reference to God's appearance at the Sea as a young warrior:

> *The Lord Is a Man of War* (Ex. 15:3) Why is this said? Because He was revealed at the Sea as a warrior in battle . . . and at Sinai as an old man full of compassion. . . . Scripture took care not to allow an opening for the nations of the world to say, "They are two domains." "YHWH is a man of war, YHWH is His name." He it was in Egypt; He it was at the Sea. He was in the past and He shall be in the future! He is in this world

and the World to Come! Thus scripture says: "See now that I, I am He" (Deut. 32:39).[31] And it is written: "Unto old age I am He" (Is. 46:4) and further: "Thus says the Lord of Hosts, King and Redeemer of Israel: I am the Lord of Hosts, the first and the last" (Is. 44:6).[32]

This motif of the two theophanies, that of the warrior at the Sea and that of the compassionate elder, sometimes depicted as a judge, entered Jewish liturgy through the *Shir ha-Kavod*, composed in medieval Germany and still recited on Shabbat in the Ashkenazic rite. While some Midrashic sources list three or even four examples of God's varying revealed forms (the revelations to Solomon and Daniel are added),[33] the central place of Sinai and the Sea is maintained.[34] The implications of this motif, namely, that the people of Israel experienced *two* great moments of collective revelation in the great period of their sacred history, have seldom been drawn out in the literature of Jewish theology.

With Sinai and the Sea established as the two great moments of Israel's revelation, we may now proceed one step further in our analysis of Rabbi Eliezer's view that the Song of Songs was "given" at the crossing of the Sea, particularly as contrasted with the view of Rabbi Akiba. He may agree with Akiba that the Song of Songs is "holy of holies," recited at the greatest moment of Israel's revelation. But he chooses to assign that dignity to the Sea, rather than to Sinai. Alternatively, it may be argued that Akiba seeks to identify the lover of Canticles with the God of Sinai, in keeping with the tradition which sees Sinai as the moment of sacred marriage between God and Israel. Eliezer takes the obvious difference between the two moments more seriously; if Sinai is a revelation of God as elderly judge, the Song of Songs is hardly an appropriate metaphor for that particular moment. The Song, in his view, describes not the fatherly compassion of the God of Sinai; its erotic tone is appropriate rather to the handsome young hero of the Sea!

These two images, God as young lover-bridegroom and God as compassionate father-judge, may be seen as the central metaphors in the Rabbinic discussion of the love of God. In the course of later Jewish literature, however, with the notable exception of the Kabbalah, the former image seems to all but disappear. Jewish liturgy, which had a tremendous impact on the imagination of later generations, is almost exclusively a liturgy of the father-king.[35] Where the God of the Sea does appear, He is warrior, but not lover. While this process of literary change is a long and complicated one, a significant clue to one aspect of it may be found in a text we have already examined.

"Y-H-W-H is His name" in Exodus 15:3 was written in order "not to allow an opening for the nations of the world to say: 'They are two domains.'" Who are these "nations of the world" who would distinguish between the young man of the Sea and the elderly father figure of Sinai? It seems most likely that the reference is to Christianity and its distinction between the Father and the Son.[36] In the face of the distinctions made between the two Persons even in pre-trinitarian Christian doctrine, the Rabbis sought to assert in the strongest terms that God as elder and God as young man are one and the same. The verses quoted in the text, particularly Isaiah 44:6, seem clearly suggestive of the early Jewish-Christian polemic.

This understanding of the passage of the Mekhilta is confirmed by another version of the same Aggadah, where its anti-Christian character is still more obvious:

> "Face to face the Lord spoke to you" (Deut. 5:4). Rabbi Levi said: "In many images He appeared to them. To one He appeared standing; to another, seated. To one as an old man; to another as a youth. How is this? When God was revealed at the Sea of Reeds to do battle for His children and to demand of the Egyptians their due, He appeared as a youth, for battle is appropriate only to the young. But when God revealed Himself at Sinai to give Torah to Israel, He appeared as an elder. Why? For it is written: 'Wisdom is with the aged, and length of days is understanding' (Job 12:12). Thus Daniel says: 'I kept looking until the thrones were set in place and the Ancient of Days took His seat' (Dan 7:9)."
>
> Rabbi Hiyya bar Abba said: "If the son of a whore should say to you: 'There are two gods,' answer him: 'I am He at the Sea; I am He at Sinai.'"[37]

The likelihood that *bar zenayta* (son of a whore) here is a Christian was already noted by Meir Friedman in his edition of *Pesikta Rabbati*.

We are now in a position to suggest why it happened that the God of the Sea of Reeds, particularly insofar as He was lover and not just warrior, disappeared from later Jewish literature. The Rabbis could not hold onto this image of God in the face of the Christian usage. Christianity usurped from Judaism the image of the youthful Deity; the archetype of God as young lover-hero became so deeply identified with Jesus in the western world that it lost its place in Judaism. By default, exoteric Judaism was left with the worship of God the Father. True, the Song of Songs was retained as sacred scripture, but it was overlaid with national and historical allegory which left little room for its original passion, and it was linked with Sinai rather than the Sea.[38] Only the Kabbalists, with their reassertion of bold anthropomorphism and religious eroticism, were able to reveal again the God of the children in Egypt and the handmaiden at the Sea.

NOTES

1. Cf., for example, *Yevamot* 49b, where Isaiah is said to have been sentenced to death for having claimed that he saw God, and *Sifrei* Numbers 103 (ed. Friedmann 27b), where it is made clear that Moses himself attained no more than a "vision of the Word" (*mar'eh dibbur*).

2. Rabbinic and Hellenistic sources are quoted in Wolfson's *Philo* (Cambridge: Cambridge University Press, 1947), 1:116, 2:97–98, 127ff. Wolfson claims that Palestinian Judaism contained within it a native discomfort with anthropomorphism, which is not necessarily to be traced to Hellenistic influences through Philo.

3. Of course, from a rigorous philosophical point of view, these are two separate problems. It is perfectly conceivable that God is, indeed, possessed of bodily attributes, but that these cannot be perceived by living humans. In the classical discussions, however, the two issues are generally intertwined.

4. Lieberman, in appendix D, 118–26 , of G. Scholem, *Jewish Gnosticism, Merkabah Mysticis, and Talmudic Tradition* (New York, 1960), has shown that the traditions of *Shi'ur Qomah* are related to ancient Midrashic understandings of the Song of Songs. Many of the sources discussed in this article have been collected and commented upon by Lieberman, though toward a somewhat different purpose.

5. These sections are not included in the five volumes of the Soncino translation of the Zohar, but their publication in English has now been announced by Roy A. Rosenberg, under the title *The Anatomy of God* (New York: Ktav, 1973). I have not yet seen this volume.

6. Discussions of the problem of anthropomorphism in Rabbinic Judaism are to be found in Marmorstein, *The Old Rabbinic Doctrine of God*, vol. 2 (London, 1937); Kadushin, *The Rabbinic Mind* (New York, 1952), chap. 7; and Urbach, *HaZal* (Jerusalem, 1969), 30–35, 75–76, 131–32.

7. Lit.: "in His glory" (*bi-khevodo*), but generally used to indicate God's own presence.

8. Ginzberg, *Legends of the Jews*, 5:394n25; Lieberman, appendix D, 120f.

9. *Deuteronomy Rabbah* (ed. Lieberman), 14f. In the version of this legend that is preserved in *Targum Jonathan* to Exodus 15:2, the angels have become quite superfluous.

10. The verse is also used in this context in b. *Sotah* 11b.

11. *Midrash Shir ha-Shirim* (ed. Grünhut), 10.

12. *Deuteronomy Rabbah* (ed. Lieberman), 14f.

13. An interesting formulation, in view of the fact that Jewish law considers this commandment to be binding only upon men.

14. This chapter is also often quoted in our legend, due to the strikingly direct applicability of Ezekiel 16:4–7.

15. In the *qal* conjugation, rather than the *hif'il*.

16. A reflex of Cant. 5:11.

17. *Yefeh To'ar to Exodus Rabbah* 23:8.

18. The famous passage that appears in the Passover Haggadah and in *Mekhilta Bo.* 7 (ed. Horovitz-Rabin, 23) has been discussed by Judah Goldin in his article "Not by Means of an Angel and Not by Means of a Messenger," in *Studies in the History of Religion, 1968* (Goodenough Memorial Volume), 412ff. The articles by Morton Smith in that volume (315ff.) and in the *Bulletin of the John Rylands Library*, 1958, also have bearing on the subject matter of this paper.

19. A contrary view, according to which the Exodus is given primacy over the splitting of the Sea, is recorded in *Exodus Rabbah* 22:3, couched in halakhic terms. The obligation to make daily mention of the Exodus in the blessing that follows the recitation of the Shema is more stringent than that to recall the events at the Sea. Two reasons are given: the Exodus was the more difficult of the two feats, and it is mentioned in conjunction with God's name in the first commandment, while the splitting of the Sea is not. The discussion concludes with the statement that the crossing of the Sea is worthy of mention in the liturgy only because it brought Israel to have faith (Ex. 14:31). One wonders whether this downplay of the centrality of the events at the Sea is not a direct polemic against those tendencies, discussed below, which saw such great significance in those events.

20. *Canticles Rabbah* 1:1:10.

21. *Mishnah Yadayim* 3.5.

22. *Canticles Rabbah* 1:2; *Shir ha-Shirim Zuta*, beginning. Cf. Lieberman, appendix D, 118f.

23. *Canticles Rabbah* 1:2.

24. Lieberman, appendix D, 119.

25. *Mekhilta de-RaSHBI* (ed. Epstein), 143; *Canticles Rabbah* 2:14.

26. *Mekhilta de-RaSHBI*, 143. In that text, the controversy is presented as one specifically between R. Akiba and R. Eliezer. See Lieberman for the other sources.

27. This interpretation accords particularly well with the interpretation of R. Akiba's view of the unique centrality of Sinai, as propounded by A. J. Heschel in his *Torah Min ha-Shamayim*, vol. 2 (London, 1965).

28. *Canticles Rabbah* 1:2.

29. *Mekhilta de-RaSHbI*.

30. *Mekhilta Shirta* 3 (ed. Horowitz-Rabin), 126. Cf. the translation and commentary by Judah Goldin in *The Song at the Sea* (New Haven: Yale University Press, 1971), 112. The rabbinic understanding of the stem *DMH* as meaning "to make similitudes" is well attested by *Genesis Rabbah* 27:1 and its many parallels. A study of the meaning of various terms derived from this stem could have interesting implications for a better understanding of classical Jewish theology.

31. The continuation of the verse reads: "There is no God beside Me." Isaiah 44:6 continues in similar fashion; a pointed reference to this phrase seems to be clearly indicated.

32. *Mekhilta Shirta* 4, 129f. Translation and commentary by Goldin, *Song at the Sea*, 126ff. The Lauterbach text from which Goldin has translated omits the two verses from Isaiah here quoted and substitutes Isaiah 41:4. Might these verses, particularly 46:4, have been too offensively sharp a reference at some point in the history of Jewish-Christian relations and thus have been replaced by the less pointed verse in the Lauterbach text?

33. *She'iltot, 'eqev* #145 (Jerusalem, 1966/67, 203) and other sources.

34. Note, for example, in the addenda to *Aggadat Shir ha-Shirim* (ed. Shechter, 87), that although God is said to reveal Himself in "many" forms, the only two examples given are those of Sinai and the Sea. In *Mekhilta Shirta* 4, 129–30, the images of God ascribed to Sinai and Daniel seem to be conflated into a single figure of the elderly, throned judge. Cf. also Grünhut's edition of *Midrash Shir ha-Shirim*, 50b–51a.

35. The liturgical exception to this general trend is to be found in the *Piyyutim* for certain occasions. In the Ashkenazic rite, several of the *Yozerot* and *Ofanim* are noteworthy examples of the religious use of the romantic metaphor. It is also interesting to note that later Jewish liturgical practice supports the view of Rabbi Eliezer that the Song of Songs was recited at the Sea, by assigning its place in the liturgical calendar at Passover (and on the seventh day, if there is no intermediate Sabbath). The seventh day of Passover is taken to be the day when the Sea was crossed.

36. Unlike those *shtei reshuyot* passages discussing Creation, there is no sense of demonic force or demiurge implied here. It thus seems unlikely that the reference would be to Gnostic or other dualisms but entirely appropriate that it be to emerging "orthodox" Christianity. It is especially worthy of note that Canticles 5:10, which appears so prominently in this series of legends, is interpreted by the church father Theodoret as referring to Jesus. The relevant passage is quoted by Raphael Loewe in his article "Apologetic Motifs in the Targum to the Song of Songs," in *Biblical Motifs: Originals and Transformations,* ed. A. Altmann (Cambridge: Harvard University Press, 1966), 187.

37. *Pesikta Rabbati* 21:6, ed. Friedmann, 100b–101a, and cf. Friedmann's notes *ad loc*. Recent scholarship confirms Friedmann's suggestion: Cf. *Encyclopedia Judaica*, vol. 10, s.v. "Jesus."
38. On the exoteric and esoteric aspects of Jewish interpretations of the Song of Songs, cf. the comments by Abraham Halkin in the *Alexander Marx Jubilee Volume*, 392ff., and R. Loewe's important article quoted in note 36.

7

The Song of Songs in Early Jewish Mysticism

For my friend Bob Cover: The lecture he never got to hear. *Haval al d'avdin!*

I

Of all the metaphors for the divine/human relationship which the Jewish mystics inherited from the earlier, exoteric Jewish tradition, none was more central to them than that of the Divine Bridegroom and Israel as His beloved spouse. God as lover of Israel had shared center stage in the early rabbinic imagination with God as father and king, the twin images of divine transcendence most generally associated in later times with the religious language of Judaism. With the contraction of midrashic thinking in the Middle Ages and its displacement by philosophical theology as the dominant Jewish way of speaking about God, the traditions of sacred eros, scandalous to the philosophers, became virtually the unique legacy of the mystics.[1] As though to spite their philosophical opponents, the Kabbalists—as Jewish mystics were called from the thirteenth century— developed an erotic mythology that would shock not only the respectable Maimonidean, but even the earlier and more daring midrashic masters themselves.

The biblical basis for talk of a love affair or marriage between the Creator and the people of Israel is in fact rather meager: not a mention in the Torah itself, and a somewhat sparse collection of passages from Hosea, Isaiah and Jeremiah, a good many of which spoke of God's marriage to His people in order to chide Israel for her unfaithfulness rather than to praise her or to extol the match. These passages were enhanced, indeed overwhelmed at a rather early date, by the "evidence" of the biblical book Song of Songs. This witness, however, to the love of God and Israel was not without its problems.

The debate as to the original *Sitz im Leben* of those poems which constitute the biblical Song of Songs is not yet concluded. Some have chosen to read these poems much as the biblical text itself seems to present them: a series of love, courtship, and marriage poems between shepherd and shepherdess. Other, perhaps more penetrating readers see the Canticle as a somewhat more sophisticated and urban literary product rather than as a collection of country folksongs. The references to the tower of David and the daughters of Jerusalem, perhaps even to the Solomonic superscription, are but the beginning points of this reading. The text is seen as too artful, too conscious of its own rhythms, too lavish in its use of metaphor to be a group of traditional songs randomly strung together.

But the real debate over the Canticle's origin is that which concerns its purported cultic background. Love poetry of this sophistication, so the argument goes, could only have existed in a cultic context in the ancient Near East. Shepherd and shepherdess are, in one way or another, god and goddess or deity and consort. Of course, ancient Near Eastern gods do fall in love with human females and vice versa, so one partner or the other in a particular poem may indeed be a mortal, and mortals may have dramatically acted out one or both roles in the cultic performance in which the poems were set. But the poems themselves, so exultant and unabashed in their celebration of eros, could not be other than a part of that erotically charged and fertility-centered Canaanite religion that was such anathema to the prophets of Israel.[2]

Each side in this debate will of course be able to adduce its parallel sources and ancient witnesses. But those who choose to view the song as a cultic product will have on their side, albeit obliquely, the rather surprising support of Rabbi Akiva ben Joseph, the leading rabbinic teacher and theologian of the early second century. The canonicity of the Canticle was still being debated in Akiva's time, and it was he who insisted on its inclusion with the now classical formulation: "The whole world is not worthy of the day the Song of Songs was given to Israel, for all of scripture is (or all the Songs are) holy, but the Song of Songs is the Holy of Holies."[3]

What did Akiva have in mind? Clearly it was not just romance. Love was indeed a supreme value in Akiva's religious worldview, but it was hardly the erotic passions of that country shepherd's existence which he himself had abandoned that he extols here as the "Holy of Holies."[4] For Akiva it was clear that the Song of Songs is a holy book, which is to say that its verses describe a love that involves the Deity. Since Akiva's God is the singular and essentially masculine figure of the biblical and rabbinic traditions, it seems fair to say that the Song, from Akiva's point of view, is about the love between that God and His beloved consort, bride, or spouse, whoever that may be. It is in this sense that Akiva—with the later synagogue and church fully behind him—lends support to the view that the Song of Songs is sacred or cultic in its original or "true" meaning. Unable to retain the old pagan names or references to cultic practice, the shapers of the canon knew, perhaps instinctively, that this was a sacred poem, and as such preserved it, though denuded of such references in the moment it was frozen into the biblical text, it does have a surprisingly "secular" appearance. By Akiva's day, battles with the ancient cults of Palestine long won and forgotten, a new pair of names, *qadosh barukh hu* and *y'israel*, could be assigned to these ancient and properly revered verses of sacred eros.[5]

We all know, of course, that the rabbis read the Song as a love poem between God and the Community of Israel. The best witness to this reading is the Targum, here very much an extended Aramaic paraphrase of the Song—as was required—rather than a translation.[6] The Targumist's reading is primarily a historical one, in which the verses of the Song recount the narrative of Israel's redemption from Egypt, standing before "her" God at Sinai, wandering through the wilderness, coming into the Promised Land, building the Temple, sinning with other gods, being cast out, and again awaiting God's redemption. There is something quite reductive about the spelling out of God and Israel's love in such full historic detail. "Thy two breasts" as "the two tablets of the law" or as "Moses and Aaron" does leave something to be desired in the realm of literary eros.

The late Saul Lieberman has claimed, however, that this historical allegory was, to Akiva and his circle, merely the exoteric reading of the most sacred Song. Noting that Akiva spoke of the day when the Song of Songs was *given* to Israel, a term otherwise applied only to the Torah itself, Lieberman shows the early rabbis to have believed in the revelation of the Song, spoken by the angels or by God Himself and revealed to Israel in a moment of theophany, either at the splitting of the Sea or at the foot of Sinai, one of those two moments when God descended in His chariot and was actually seen by the Community of Israel.[7] Another statement of Akiva's (though preserved in a late source and in somewhat garbled form) says that "had the Torah not been given to Israel, the Song of Songs would have sufficed for the conduct of the world"—indeed a rather intriguing possibility.[8]

Akiva seems to belong to those who see Sinai as the setting of the Song, and the Song itself as the crown of that great apocalyptic moment when the heavens opened and all of Torah—primordial, written, oral, and yet to be developed—was brought forth.[9] Eliezer hen Hyrcanus, a leading scholar of the generation before Akiva, assigned it rather to the Sea. This may be related to the midrashic tradition that sees God as having revealed Himself as a wise and elderly judge at Sinai, but as a young warrior for the defeat of the Egyptians—each according to the moment's needs. Surely the God of Canticles is the youthful figure, not the elder. (Jewish ritual practice, incidentally, follows Eliezer's view, assigning the reading of the Song to the latter days of Passover.) The sages seem to agree, however, that the esoteric meaning of the Song is a description of the body of God as seen by Israel in the moment of revelation: the lover, described so passionately limb by limb, is the Holy One as Israel saw Him. No wonder they forbad the public teaching of this esoteric midrash! The love dialogue between God and Israel, properly understood, was not a recounting of Jewish history, but an erotic hymn in which divine lover and earthly beloved whispered to one another descriptions of secret and intimate beauty.

This midrash, as Lieberman further shows, was the exegetical context for what became known as *shi'ur qomah shel yotzer bereshit*, the measurement of the Creator's form. In a series of fragments preserved amid the Hekhalot sources (early "Palace" mysticism), gigantic measurements of the limbs of the divine body are offered, entirely unaccompanied by explanation. This speculative tradition, so Lieberman claims, grows directly out of that midrash which stated:

His Head is a Gold Diadem (Cant. 5:10)—this is the King of Kings who appeared to Israel in many images. Doing battle with Pharaoh at the Sea He appeared as a youth, because a youth is fitting to battle . . . and just as they saw Him, as it were, so too they saw the *Merkavah* which had come down to the sea.[10]

The *shi'ur qomah* tradition, preserved by the Near Eastern rabbis into the early Middle Ages, was rigorously denounced by the rationalist Maimonides, dismissed as the creation of some Roman (i.e., Byzantine) preacher and surely not of the sages. It was the Kabbalists who were able, in the face of the Maimonidean denunciation, to preserve it. When Maimonides proclaimed in his Code, "One who says that God has a body or a depictable form is a heretic," Rabbi Abraham ben David of Posquiéres, the earliest figure to be associated with Kabbalistic tradition, replied in a gloss, "Greater and better persons than he believed it."[11] This *shi'ur qomah* tradition, however imperfectly preserved or understood by the time of its twelfth-century migration to Languedoc, provided justification (and perhaps impetus as well) for the strong erotic current in the Kabbalists' own theosophical speculations, including a prominent new role they gave to their reading of the Song of Songs.

II

Writing at a very late date in the history of Kabbalistic exegesis, Elisha Gallico of Safed (late sixteenth century) says that he knows of four readings of the Canticle, to which he hopes to add a fifth.[12] The four he knows are:

a first reading in which "the Community of Israel longs for and seeks out her lover and He responds in kind"—presumably the midrashic reading;

a second one relating to "the Torah and its students," where the Song concerns "the desire of students to attain to Torah, both hidden and revealed." This he rightly ascribes to a recent innovation, the commentary *Ayelet Ahavim* by his compatriot Solomon Alqabets;

a third in which "intellect and matter" are the loving pair, or an Aristotelian reading; and

a fourth in which "the soul, drawn from beneath the throne of God, longs to return to the spiritual delights of her master's home, in which she delighted before her descent into this world," or the Neoplatonic.

What then has become of Kabbalistic exegesis? Can it be that this latter-day Kabbalist ignores the contribution of that tradition in which he stands? Did the Kabbalists add nothing to the interpretation of the Canticle? Far from it. As they did in many areas, the Kabbalists entered into the mainstream of rabbinic exegesis and proclaimed it their own. Like the early rabbis, the Kabbalists claimed that the Song was about the love between the Blessed Holy One and *Knesset Yisra'el*, the Community of Israel—but with a difference. For the Kabbalist, the "Community of Israel" no longer designates a human group in its primary meaning, but refers to the *Shekhinah*, the feminine-receptive element within the Godhead, designated elsewhere as Kingdom, Jerusalem, Temple, Sabbath; Moon, Sea, Bride, Glory, and other symbolic terms. To say it in a nutshell (a well-known Kabbalistic appellation for the guarding of mystery), medieval Jewish esotericism sees the *hieros gamos* (divine coupling) taking place *within* God, rather than between God and Israel. This development is made possible by the major innovation in Kabbalistic thought, the *sefirot*, symbol-laden stages in the divine self-revelation.[13] The static unity of God, a cornerstone of Jewish philosophy, is converted by the Kabbalists into a dynamic unity of one-in-ten. The ten *sefirot* are bound to and leap forth from the One, in the words of a widely used image, "like a flame attached to a coal," having all the irregularity and yet the unity of the multiple darting tongues of a single fire.

The essential subject matter of all Kabbalistic teaching is an account of this pulsating inner life of divinity: how the hidden One, beyond all description, takes on the multiple garments of God as we know Him—and in this case we do well to add—and Her. God the lover, warrior, judge, king, father, mother, son, daughter: all have particular loci in the sefirotic system. As already indicated, personal metaphors by no means exhaust the Kabbalists' store: the Zohar, the greatest work of Spanish Kabbalah, seems to give as much play to images of light and water as it does to those of person. To use the water imagery for a moment, we may say that the most hidden levels of divinity are described as "the depths of the well." At the surface of this well there bubbles forth a spring, and thence there proceed six intertwining rivers, all of which ultimately flow into the sea, or the *Shekhinah*. The tenth *sefirah* thus represents the divine fullness, the energy of God at the crest of its flow, ready to spill over into the lower worlds.

But the *sefirot* are used not only to describe the orderly and uninterrupted flow of divine energy into the world. The myth of evil, that which causes the flow to cease, is an essential part of the Kabbalistic system; through it elements of alienation, emptiness, and longing are added to the picture of divinity. The link between the *Shekhinah* and the upper nine stages of divinity is broken by the power of human sin, the this-worldly embodiment of cosmic evil. Only human goodness in the form of fulfillment of God's commandments can reestablish the broken connection, bringing the *Shekhinah* back into the good graces of her spouse and restoring some measure of divine presence to the lower worlds as well. In this drama of alternating longing and fulfillment within God, it is easy to see that the Canticle will have a major role to play.

Upon my couch at night I sought the one I love–
I sought, but found him not.
"I must rise and roam the town,
Through the streets and through the squares; I must seek the one I
    love."
I sought but found him not. I met the watchmen
Who patrol the town.
"Have you seen the one I love?" Scarcely had I passed them
When I found the one I love.
I held him fast. I would not let him go
Till I brought him to my mother's house.
To the chamber of her who conceived me.

(CANTICLE 3:1–4; JPS translation)

Who are we latter-day readers to tell the Kabbalist that the real subject of this passage is some obscure shepherd girl who has stumbled into Solomon's Jerusalem, rather than the eternal mythic female ever longing for the renewed espousals of her youth?

The first Kabbalist to comment on the Song of Songs, Rabbi Ezra ben Solomon of Gerona, composed in about 1250 a commentary often ascribed to his more famous contemporary, Moses Nahmanides.[14] He prefaces his commentary with a brief lexicon, a list of terms which, as he tells the reader, you will find in no dictionary. "Lebanon," "wine," and "spice," he tells us, all refer to *Hokhmah*, the second of the ten *sefirot* and the most recondite of which we may speak. "Apple" and "garden" both refer to the Glory or *Shekhinah*, while "lily," with its six petals, refers to the six intermediary channels. He also warns us—perhaps because he knew our generation was to come—against over-interpretation: many verses in the Song, he says, are there simply to carry out the imagery begun elsewhere and for no other purpose. This rather conservative exegetical declaration was ignored by most of Rabbi Ezra's Kabbalistic successors.

The work is called "Song of Songs," he tells us, because in the words of Psalm 19, "Day unto day utters speech"; this Song is sung by each of the divine "days" or *sefirot*, beginning with the lowest, Throne of Glory, and culminating with *Hokhmah* above. Thus the sages have described the Canticle as "that song which God sings each day." As an example of

Rabbi Ezra's exegesis, we may quote his reading of the opening verse, "Let Him kiss me":

> The words of the Glory, desiring longingly to ascend, to cleave to that sublime and unequalled light. The ascent is one of mind and thought, and thus is spoken of in a hidden manner (i.e., in the third person). The kiss symbolizes the joy of the soul's attachment to the source of life . . . "for your kisses are sweeter than wine": read: are sweet when from wine, and emanated light increases when it comes from wine, the wisdom of God's "I," the rung of sublime light (*Hokhmah*), to which all desire to cleave and ascend. "Are good" (in the plural) refers to the abundance of sublime light that is divided and sparkles forth in every direction, as scripture says, "When he kindles (*be'hetivo*) the light" and "God saw the light, that it was good."

The association here of devotional and sefirotic mysticism is typical of Ezra's work. The "Glory" here is the devoted bride whose longings for union with her spouse also represent the longing of the worshipper's soul for reunion with God.

Ezra's immediate successor in the Kabbalistic exegesis of Canticles was Isaac lbn Sahula, who lived in the Castilian town of Guadalajara and wrote during the 1280s. Ibn Sahula is primarily known to the student of Hebrew literature as the author of *Meshal haKadmoni,* an erudite and witty collection of fables and morality tales that achieved considerable popularity in the later Middle Ages. He lived in the same town as the author of the Zohar, whom we shall discuss presently, and his works contain the earliest known quotations from the Zohar literature, an important link in Gershom Scholem's masterful detective work a generation ago in conclusively assigning that work's authorship. Sahula's only other preserved work, surprisingly unpublished until now, is his commentary on Canticles, which survives in but a single Oxford manuscript.

Sahula's approach to the text is a two-pronged one; he uses the by now widely accepted notion that a text may be—nay, must be—read on both hidden and revealed levels. His esoteric commentary remains just that, even after careful reading. Believing that the mysteries of the *sefirot* should not be revealed to the uninitiated, Sahula's references are short, elliptical, and often obscure. He will interpret one verse simply by quoting another, leaving it to the experienced reader of Kabbalistic lore to put the two together and come out with some—hopefully the intended—referent to esoteric teaching.

On "the kisses of his mouth," he says, in a lovely rhymed Hebrew couplet: "I have heard that there is an awesome secret to the word 'His mouth,' a powerful staff, a rod of beauty. And who knows whether His mouth and His heart are in accord, encouraging the humble?" From parallel comments elsewhere, especially in the Zohar, and from a general familiarity with Kabbalistic rhetoric, we can make an educated guess that "mouth" here is being read as the *Shekhinah*, a "powerful staff" because of her associations with the left (or judging) side of God, but here held in the hand of *Tiferet* or Beauty, the essential masculine principle within divinity. *Tiferet*, located at the center of the Kabbalistic diagram, is also often called "Heart," so that the accord of mouth and heart probably refers to the union of these two, or at least to the uplifting of the *Shekhinah* so that she can be on the same rung as her spouse. All of this involves a certain amount of guesswork on the part of the reader. This may be why, after all, Sahula's manuscript never found a publisher.[15]

If the esoteric commentary is hard to decipher, however, the exoteric interpretation is a source of real delight. Here Sahula makes generous use of his considerable urbanity and literary skill. For him, the "plain" meaning of the Song of Songs is what can best be characterized as devotional: it is an allegory of the eternal human striving for perfection, identical, in his reading, with the longing of the ideal soul for the blessed presence or *Shekhinah* of God. On this level he is willing to speak quite openly about "the kisses of his mouth":

Our sages have already informed us about the rung of the "kiss" in telling us concerning the verse "Moses the servant of the Lord died there by the mouth of God" (Deut. 34:5) that he died by a kiss.[16] This being the case, we know what a high rung the kiss must be, that by which Moses our master passed from this transitory and fleeting life into life eternal. Then too there is a tradition claiming that Moses did not die at all, but ascended and serves in heaven."[17] This kiss would be a flowing forth of spirit from its source. . . . Even speaking in a revealed manner we may say that the kiss represents the beginning of thought and the end of deed. The sage mentions it as he opens his book so that the reader may be aroused to long for this high rung . . . the entire verse, then, is about the quest of the perfected person to attain this precious rung in the circle of the upright community. "Let Him kiss me" means "May He help me to cleave to Him!" speaking the language of those lovers who cling to one another in the intensity of their love and kiss with the kisses of their mouths.

While this exoteric commentary is formally Kabbalistic (it still makes mention of the *sefirot*), in Elisha Gallico's categories it should clearly be listed among the Neoplatonic, concerned as it is throughout with the individual soul and its longing to return to God. Rather obviously missing from Sahula's commentary is the national-collectivist allegory which had featured so prominently in the reading of the early sages. The "Community of Israel" has on the one hand been hypostatized to the point of inclusion within the Deity, and on the other it has been atomized into an aggregate of individuals, each on a different rung in the striving for God. Lip service is paid here to "the circle of the upright community," but little more. Even in medieval Judaism, with all its deeply collectivist tendencies, the struggle for spiritual attainment was ultimately a lone one.

III

Finally we come to consideration of the Zohar itself. Suffice it to say, by way of introduction, that the Zohar makes all other users of Kabbalistic symbolism look like amateurs. Moses De Leon and his circle, in those years of inspiration when they wrote in the name of the ancient Rabbi Simeon, raised the literary instrument of Kabbalah to dazzling new heights. The Zohar's bold style is utterly enthralling; the reader is convinced that the writer has succeeded in conveying within the language and style of the text itself something of the intensity of his own inner experience. Surely the language of the Zohar, which was to become an essential part of the vocabulary of Jewish spiritual expression for the next five centuries and beyond, has within it something of transcendence.

There is no consecutive commentary of the Zohar on the Song of Songs. The section of *Zohar Hadash*[18] that begins to comment on the Song never goes beyond the first few verses. That text and the six-page section in volume 2 of the Zohar—a digression, as the Zohar comments on the building of the tabernacle[19]—form the most concentrated treatments. But the fact is that there exists hardly a page in the entire Zohar in which the Canticle is not discussed in a broader sense. Quotations from this relatively brief biblical book are everywhere, and even where it is not quoted, its theme remains central to the author's consciousness. The Canticle's "perfumed garden" wafts through the entire work.

The Zohar takes the Solomonic superscription of the Song more seriously than had most prior Jewish commentators. While all agreed that Solomon was the author, we have already seen that the "true" origin of the Canticle was both higher and earlier; to those rabbis Solomon was presumably recorder or perhaps final editor of a text that had been passed down from the day it had been "given" until his generation. The name *Shlomo* had also, since early rabbinic times, been read supraliterally as "the king of peace," meaning God Himself, and the rabbis had established that all references in the Song to Solomon, but for one, were to God.[20]

Basing itself on a divergent rabbinic tradition,[21] the Zohar asserts that the "day the Song was given" was in fact the day that Solomon completed his building of the Temple, and that there is an utter convergence between the King of Peace above and His earthly counterpart beneath.

Rabbi Yosi opened with the verse "The Song of Songs which is Solomon's." King Solomon composed this song when the Temple was built, when all the worlds, above and below, were perfected into a single wholeness. Even though the companions have some dispute about this, the Canticle was spoken only in this wholeness, when the moon was full and the Temple was built, just as it is above.[22]

From the day this world was created there was no hour of joy before God like that in which the Temple was erected. The tabernacle that Moses had put up in the desert in order to bring the *Shekhinah* down to earth—on the day it was erected another tabernacle went up above.[23] Thus scripture says *the* tabernacle was erected. *The* tabernacle refers to that other one that went up with it. This was the tabernacle of the angel Metatron, no more. But when the first Temple was erected, another first Temple was erected with it. It existed in all the worlds. Its light shone through them all and the cosmos was perfumed; all the upper windows were opened for the light to shine. There was no joy in all the worlds like the joy of that day. Then those above and those below proclaimed the song, and that is the "Song of Songs"—the song of those musicians who play before the blessed Holy One.

King David composed "A Song of Ascents," and Solomon composed the "Song of Songs," the song of those musicians. What is the difference between them? They seem to be one, and indeed they are. But in the days of David the musicians had not yet taken their proper places, for the Temple was not yet built. . . . On the day the Temple was erected all of them were established in their places and the candle that had not shone began to shine. The Song was created for the supreme king, the king of peace; it is more exalted than any praise which had yet existed. The day when that song of praise was revealed in the world was a day of perfection throughout, and that is why it *is* the Holy of Holies.[24]

It was not out of special devotion to Solomon that the Zohar chose to credit him so firmly with the Song. The Zohar was much involved with its own reconstruction—on a purely theoretical and contemplative plane—of Temple piety and the cult of sacrifice. This in turn has to do with its tremendous emphasis on mythical cosmology and the vision of cosmic wholeness. Its author saw himself living in a blemished universe, one in which the full flow of *Shekhinah* blessing into the world could not be fully experienced. He longed frequently for the great time of wholeness, that period when the smoke of the earthly altar would rise into the heavens and arouse the altar in the Temple above, causing divine radiance to shine throughout the cosmos and the world to be filled with grace. Even the mystic, living as he does in an exiled cosmos, can have but a taste of what all Israel had known fully in the days when the Temple had stood. That the most perfect of songs should have been spoken on that most perfect of days in the most perfect of places should not surprise us when we hear it from the Zohar's author.

Still, this passage has gotten our author into a bit of trouble. He seems to be placing Solomon on a higher level than Moses, the one who is clearly "lord of all prophets" and whose encounter with God was never to be equaled. Elsewhere in the Zohar, as throughout Jewish literature, it is Moses who embodies the sublime vision, and the Zohar is sensitive to the unspoken criticism. In prophecy, De Leon admits, Moses knows no equal. But when it comes to the poetic muse, matters are somewhat different. Moses' song—that of the sea—was still attached to matters of this world; he was thanking God for Israel's deliverance and singing praises of His miraculous deeds.

But King David and his son Solomon spoke a different sort of Song. David sought to arrange the maidens and to adorn them along with the Queen, to show the Queen and her maidens in all their beauty. This is his concern in his Psalms and praises; it was they, Queen and maidens, he was seeking to adorn. When Solomon arrived he found the Queen adorned and her maidens decked out in beauty. He then sought to bring her to her bridegroom and to bring him under the canopy with his bride. He spoke words of love between them so that they be joined as one, so that the two of them form a single one in the wholeness of love.

In this did Solomon rise high in praises above all other humans. Moses was wedded to the Queen in this world below so that there be a whole union among the lower creatures. Solomon brought about the complete union of the Queen above, first bringing the bridegroom under the canopy and only afterwards joyously inviting both of them into the Temple which he had built. . . .

Blessed are David and Solomon his son for having brought about the union above. From the day God had said to the moon "Go and diminish yourself"[25] she had not been fully coupled with the sun until King Solomon came forth.[26]

Moses the prophet still needs to bring the *Shekhinah* into the lower world. He has a people to worry about, a people wandering in the wilderness who need assurance that God is indeed in their midst. The prophet's concern is his flock. Solomon, the mystic hierophant, can afford to be utterly selfless: it is not of his own love that he speaks or even the love of earthly Israel for their God. He is the attendant, or perhaps the officiant, at the union of bridegroom and bride: offering his song as an epithalamium, a gift to the sacred couple, intending nothing more and nothing less than to fill all the universe with his freely given words of love. Here indeed the Song is cultic in the full sense of the term. But now the cult is that of the mystic, in whose loving heart bride and bridegroom are joined as one.

1. See my earlier discussion in "The Children in Egypt and the Theophany at the Sea," *Judaism* 24, no. 4 (1975): 446–56.
2. The scholarly discussion on the origins of the Canticle is summarized by Marvin Pope in his Anchor Bible edition of the Song of Songs (Garden City NY: Anchor, 1977); see especially the extensive annotated bibliography, 252ff.
3. *Mishnah Yadayim* 3:5.
4. Cf. Judah Goldin, "Towards a Profile of the Tanna, Aqiba ben Joseph," in *Studies in Midrash and Related Literature,* ed. Barry Eichler and Jeffrey Tigay (Philadelphia: JPS, 1988).
5. The rabbinic reading of the Song of Songs has been discussed by Gerson D. Cohen in "The Song of Songs and the Jewish Religious Mentality," *Samuel Friedland Lectures, 1960–1966* (New York: Jewish Theological Seminary, 1966).
6. Cf. Raphael Loewe, "Apologetic Motifs in the Targum to the Song of Songs," in *Biblical Motifs: Originals and Transformations,* ed. A. Altmann (Cambridge: Harvard University Press, 1966), 159–96.
7. Saul Lieberman, *"Mishnal Shir ha-Shirim,"* published as appendix D to Gershom Scholem's *Jewish Gnosticism, Merkabah Mysticism, and Talmudic Tradition* (New York: Jewish Theological Seminary of America, 1960).
8. *Agadath Shir Hashirim,* ed. Solomon Schechter (Cambridge, 1896), line 22. I suggest that the line, which is incomprehensible in its present form, be emended to read *ilu lo nittenah torah, kedai hayyetah [=hayah] shir hashirim linhog et ha'olam.*
9. *Mekilta de-RaSHBI,* ed. Y. N. Epstein, 143; Lieberman, *"Mishnal Shir ha-Shirim,"* 119. Compare with Akiva's view of the Sinaitic revelation as discussed by A. J. Heschel in *Torah min haShamayim,* vol. 2 (London, 1965).
10. Lieberman, *"Mishnal Shir ha-Shirim,"* 121; also see 122n24.
11. *Mishneh Torah,* Teshuvah 3:7, and cf. I. Twersky, *Rabad of Posquiéres* (Philadelphia, 1980), 282f.
12. For a complete introduction to Kabbalistic thought, and sefirotic symbolism in particular, see the sections on *sefirot* and *Shekhinah* in Isaiah Tishby's *Wisdom of the Zohar* (New York: Published for the Littman Library by Oxford University Press, 1989). A brief and necessarily much more general introduction to the subject is to be found in my essay "The Zohar: Jewish Mysticism in Medieval Spain," in *An Introduction to the Medieval Mystics of Europe,* ed. Paul Szarmach (Albany: SUNY Press, 1984), 97ff., and now in my *Guide to the Zohar* (Stanford: Stanford University Press, 2004). On the symbolism of the *Shekhinah,* see also the more analytic treatment by Gershom Scholem in "*Shekhinah*: The Feminine Element in Kabbalah," in his *On the Mystical Shape of the Godhead* (New York: Schocken, 1991).

13. On the myth of evil in Kabbalah, see the appropriate chapters in Tishby, *Mishnat haZohar* and Scholem's chapter 11, "Sitra Achra: Good and Evil in Kabbalah," in *On the Mystical Shape of the Godhead*.

14. The most accessible edition of the Hebrew is that published by Hayyim Dov Chavel in *Kitvey RaMBaN* (Jerusalem, 1963), 473ff. The French translation by Georges Vajda (Paris, 1969) is accompanied by valuable introductions and notes.

15. MS Oxford, Neubauer 343. This writer has prepared a critical edition of that manuscript, published in *Jerusalem Studies in Jewish Thought* 6 (1987). Fragments of a Psalms commentary by Sahula are also extant.

16. Rashi, *ad loc*; cf. *Baba Batra* 17a.

17. Cf. *Sotah* 13b and the discussion by L. Ginzberg, *Legends of the Jews* (Baltimore: Johns Hopkins University Press, 1998), 6:161n951.

18. A collection of passages from the Zohar corpus that were omitted from that work's first editions. They were published as a separate work under that title in Salonika, 1597. Scholem has determined that these passages are authentic to the original body of Zohar writings, being the work of Moses De Leon. Cf. *Major Trends in Jewish Mysticism* (New York: Schocken, 1941), 159ff.

19. Zohar 2:143a–145b,

20. *Shevu'ot* 35b.

21. *Shir haShirim Rabbah* 1:2; cf. Lieberman, "*Mishnal Shir ha-Shirim*," 119.

22. The earthly Temple parallel to the heavenly Temple.

23. Cf. *BeMidbar Rabbah* 12:11.

24. Zohar 2:143a–b.

25. The reference is to the well-known legend in *Hullin* 60b, where the moon is told to diminish herself because of her unwillingness to share her rule with the sun. For the Kabbalist, "moon" is an alternate symbol for *Shekhinah*.

26. Zohar 2:144b–145a.

PART 3

Hasidism

Mysticism for the Masses

8

Around the Maggid's Table

Tsaddik, Leadership, and Popularization in the Circle of Dov Baer of Miedzyrzecz

I

Hasidism represents one of the great success stories in the history of religious movements. When Israel Ba'al Shem Tov, the figure around whose image the movement was to coalesce, died in 1760, we know of no more than twenty or thirty people who can be identified as associated with him or laying claim to his spiritual heritage. These were all within Podolia, a somewhat remote corner of southeastern Poland, up against the Russian and Turkish borders. Although his reputation as a clairvoyant and wonder-worker was beginning to grow, we have little specific knowledge of influence the BeSHT had beyond this group and his own town of Miedzhybozh. Half a century later and beyond, large swaths of eastern European Jewry, majorities in some areas, considered themselves followers of the movement that carried his banner.

Hasidism as a mass movement was created by the disciples of the Great Maggid, Dov Baer of Miedzyrzecz (1704–1772). They belong to what is conventionally called the third generation of Hasidic leadership, though they were in fact the movement's founders. It was members of this circle who brought Hasidism into the public arena as a distinctive and to a degree separatist religious phenomenon, arousing both avid support and bitter denunciation.[1] In the extensive anti-Hasidic polemical literature of 1772–1800, it is almost always members of the Maggid's circle who stand at the center of controversy.[2] It was they who sought to "conquer" new communities for the movement, to introduce Hasidic practices and customs over wide geographical realms, and when necessary to take on opponents in public disputation and response to controversy. While there were indeed contemporary Hasidic authors writing and devotional circles flourishing outside the Maggid's domain,[3] we almost never find them embroiled in the great Hasidic-Mitnaggedic confrontation.[4]

Because of this, it seems correct to assume that a decision was taken by this group, surely with the agreement (though reluctant, as I hope to show) of its leader, sometime in the 1760s, to "go public" with Hasidic teachings and to offer them as an alternative vision of Jewish religious life intended to have mass appeal. It may have seen an opportunity after 1764, when the Polish authorities abolished the Council of Four Lands, ending even a shadow of regional rabbinic hegemony. Members of the circle spread outward, especially to the north, taking Hasidic ideas from the two Ukrainian provinces of Podolia and Volhyn across the vast distances of Polesia and Belorussia, even to the gates of Lithuania, where they were to meet strong opposition, as well as west to Galicia. Within the original Hasidic heartland there seems to have been rather limited controversy regarding the Maggid's disciples and their teachings, possibly because of relatively weak rabbinic leadership.[5] But as their influence spread, rumors of a new "sect" and its dangerous heresies went with it, culminating in a single semi-formal meeting of the disciples in 1772 in response to the publication of the first bans against them.

From within the list of those whom Hasidic memory records as disciples of the Maggid, special credit for the spread of Hasidism has to go to seven of the closer disciples. Four of these carried the message northward, thus particularly running into difficulty with the rabbinate and communal authorities: R. Menahem Mendel of Vitebsk (c. 1730–1788),[6] R. Abraham of Kalisk (1741–1810),[7] R. Shne'ur Zalman of Liadi (c. 1745–1813),[8] and R. Aaron of Karlin (1736–1772).[9] In Poland and the entire southern tier, only one man is named as the object of the anti-Hasidic bans: R. Levi Yizhak of Berdyczow (c. 1740–1809).[10] It seems highly likely that he was a key figure in both the decision to disseminate Hasidic teaching and the actual carrying out of that task. Two other disciples are added to this list, although they were not centrally involved in the Hasidic-Mitnaggedic controversy. These are R. Menahem Nahum of Chernobyl (1730–1797),[11] listed in part because of the activity of his son, Mordecai, who still in his father's lifetime was an active propagandist for the movement.[12] R. Elimelech of Lezajsk (c. 1717–1787) carried on leadership of an intimate disciple circle after the Maggid's death and, largely through his students, brought about the spread of Hasidism through Poland and Galicia.[13]

The Miedzyrzecz years represent the formation of a close spiritual/intellectual circle, a group of young men intensely devoted to a set of ideals, to the task of spreading religious revival, to their master, and (for the most part) to one another. Members of the circle continued in their work for decades after the master's death, into the early years of the nineteenth century. The end of this "third generation" of Hasidic leadership and the waning of its influence is generally depicted as taking place between 1809 and 1815, with the deaths of Levi Yizhak and Shne'ur Zalman, but also the passing of several key disciples of Elimelech of Lezajsk.

As Hasidism began to spread and gain a mass following, veneration of the *tsaddikim*, as the leaders of the new movement were being called, and faith in their supernatural powers became defining hallmarks of the movement.[14] But who was a *tsaddik*, and how could one attain this status? Was not aspiring toward such a claim of righteousness in itself a violation of the virtue of modesty and hence a paradoxical impediment to one's path? Were *tsaddikim* predestined to be such, chosen by God and "emplanted in each generation"?[15] Or was such righteousness something one could earn by virtue of spiritual struggle and growth? What did discipleship have to do with becoming a *tsaddik*? Were only those who had served apprenticeship under the BeSHT, and then under his immediate followers, to be called *tsaddikim*? Surely it is hard to imagine anyone calling *himself* by the name *tsaddik*; it was up to others to do that.[16] But even to this there are exceptions. Then did being a *tsaddik* result from achieving a following? Could *anyone*—without pedigree of either discipleship or rabbinic learning—who reputedly worked wonders, prayed with great intensity, and looked the part be set up by himself or by followers as a "holy man?" All of these questions swirled about the emergence of Hasidism as a historical force in the last quarter of the eighteenth century. The phenomenon called Hasidism (a name derided in documents penned by its opponents, therefore clearly in use by the *hasidim* themselves)[17] grew in spontaneous and uncontrolled ways, without social controls or rigorous standards of any sort. One might say that it created a situation ripe for abuse, and the many reports of such abuses were surely not only the product of the anti-Hasidic imagination.

But what of the inner circle that created Hasidism and made the decision to take it public? I am not of the view that the founders of Hasidism from the start set out to create an elite who would have exclusive control of the levers to divine access, chiefly as a way of asserting its own power.[18] Surely the followers of the BeSHT and the Maggid were serious religious people, out to create a great religious revival, not simply looking for power, money, and control over the masses, as their enemies, both early and late, depicted them. How did they view the figure of the *tsaddik*, his powers, and how such personalities might come to be? A close reading of the sources reveals that there was a good deal of divergence on these questions, even within the circles that took them most seriously. These differences surely were in part determined by the various personalities involved and questions of faith, but they also reflect diverse positions regarding the spread and popularization of Hasidism. Indeed one of the most difficult issues to determine is the balance between personal belief and strategy in their varying portrayals of the *tsaddik*. Do more extravagant claims for the *tsaddik's* powers, or for the necessity to attach oneself to the *tsaddik*, reflect the authentic spiritual/intellectual position of a particular author, perhaps based upon his relationship with his own teacher, or were these views elaborated in order to gain more followers?

What follows will be a series of such close readings, particularly from within the Maggid's circle. But first we will turn our attention to the writings of the first published and most prolific of early Hasidic authors, R. Jacob Joseph of Polonnoye (d. 1783), and to a few other general remarks that will proceed from them.

R. Jacob Joseph was the leading disciple of the Ba'al Shem Tov who did not become a member of the circle in Miedzyrzecz, perhaps even resenting the Maggid's growing authority. He had been rabbi of Szarogrod, one of the largest Podolian Jewish communities, when in the 1740s he became attracted to Hasidism of the pre-BeSHTian type, including both self-isolation for meditative prayer and a rigorous pattern of ascetic self-mortification. His community was not pleased with this turn and he was deposed from his rabbinic post. One of his guides in the ascetic life, a figure known as Aryeh Leib the "reprover" of Polonnoye, introduced him to the Ba'al Shem Tov, who had begun making a name for himself in these proto-Hasidic circles. Their meeting apparently changed Jacob Joseph's life. For the next thirty-some years, he humbly referred to Israel ben Eliezer as "my teacher," even though he was the far greater scholar by any conventional measure of rabbinic knowledge.[19] R. Jacob Joseph was author of four volumes of collected sermons, three of which stand among the first printed works of Hasidism, beginning in 1780. In hundreds of places, his long and erudite homilies, often quite difficult to follow, are dotted with brief quotations that "I heard from my teacher" or "I heard in my teacher's name." These are accepted by scholars as among the most reliable evidence of the BeSHT's transmitted teachings.[20]

A preacher of the old school, Jacob Joseph's conversion by the Ba'al Shem Tov did not change him completely. We have preserved an important (and apparently authentic) letter in which the BeSHT chides him for not following his advice and clinging stubbornly to the old ascetic path.[21] His writings reflect him as a crusty and sharp-tongued polemicist. Religious leadership is the central question dealt with in his sermons. He fulminates endlessly against both the aloofness and the corruption of the rabbinate and the irresponsibility and greed of the lay oligarchy that runs the communities hand in hand with their own chosen rabbinic appointees.

In contrast to these "Jewish Demons"[22] (and a host of other nasty epithets by which he calls them), Jacob Joseph holds out an ideal of the true *talmid hakham* (he generally prefers this term over *tsaddik*), the proper spiritual and temporal/legal leader of the Jewish people. He knows no distinction yet between *rav* and *rebbe,* but he expects the former to embrace many of the characteristics we associate with the latter. The *Toledot* (as he is often called, after the title of his first book) is clearly an elitist who sees Jewish spiritual life in rigidly stratified terms. Using terminology rooted in ancient Platonic tradition, he defines the truly and selflessly pious scholars/sages as "men of form," while the masses of ordinary Jews, sunk in corporeal concerns, are "men of matter." The former are destined to serve as leaders, exemplifying the life of holiness and uplifting the spiritual lives of the communities they serve. The latter are to serve as *tamkhin de- oraita,* "sustainers of Torah," attaching themselves to the leaders by means of material support and loyal obedience. He does not give the impression of any flexibility in the social structure as he imagines it, of "men of matter" growing in such a way that they might enter the category of "men of form." While indeed the purpose of leadership is to help people turn from pursuit of matter to that of form, he does not speak in terms of transformations in which the line between leaders and followers is crossed. He exhibits little patience either for hypocritical or badly motivated scholars or for the sinfulness, and especially the excessive materialism, of ordinary Jews. One of the great questions of his writings, on which he vacillates frequently, is whether bad leaders have corrupted the folk or a lowly populace has dragged its well-meaning leaders downward to its level.

Through his contact with the BeSHT, Jacob Joseph has come to appreciate the pious innocence that is sometimes found among simple people. There are passages in his writings representing the once much touted "democratizing" side of Hasidism, that which elevates the holiness potentially to be found in ordinary Jews, and not just in the learned.[23] Nevertheless, when he describes the ideal leader, he thinks in terms of a refined spiritual/intellectual elite, learned scholars who will also embody the level of wholeness and innocence that his teacher so personified. The *tsaddik*, in an old phrase widely quoted by the *Toledot* as well as other Hasidic sources, is one who "holds fast to both heaven and earth,"[24] becoming a personified link between them. His task is not only to teach the people and to serve as a moral exemplar but actually to become a personal link between the "upper" and "lower" worlds. A Talmudic *aggadah*[25] much beloved by Jacob Joseph[26] describes Rabbi Hanina ben Dosa, a renowned first-century wonder-worker, about whom God is heard to say, "The entire world existed for the sake of Hanina, My son." The words "for the sake of" in Hebrew are *bi-shevil*, which can supraliterally be read as "by the path of." The *Toledot* insists in the name of the BeSHT (repeatedly but not originally) that this teaches that the *tsaddik* himself becomes a pathway or channel through which divine blessing flows into the world. Elsewhere the *tsaddik* is an earthly container or throne where the divine presence might alight.[27] This claim will become a great opening point for popular Hasidism, which called upon the masses to attach themselves to *tsaddikim*, with the promise that through them they could come to share in that blessing. In the *Toledot* this dependence is not yet categorical. Indeed "men of matter" or weekday Jews need to attach themselves to the proper sage, the personification of the Sabbath among humans.[28] But we also find warnings against excessive reliance on the spiritual elite. On the battlefield, if all soldiers were to rely on a single hero, once he is disarmed the entire battle is lost. Better to build up one's own spiritual weaponry in the great struggle against the enemy, the evil urge.[29] The *Toledot* also makes it clear that the dependence between the two categories of Jew is mutual; the otherworldly "men of form" are to depend on the ordinary folk for support and physical sustenance just as the others rely upon them to keep open the font of divine blessing.[30]

The man of form lives on a plane that transcends the ordinary course of nature. It is because of this that he has the powers long attributed to the *tsad-*

dik in certain biblical and rabbinic passages that are often quoted throughout Hasidic writings, beginning with the *Toledot*. These begin with the biblical *tsaddik moshel be-yir'at elohim* (2 Sam. 23:2), which, when taken totally out of context, can be rendered either as "The *tsaddik* rules by means of fearing God" or "The *tsaddik* rules [over] the fear of God." That verse itself is quoted by the sages to defend their view that "The blessed Holy One issues a decree, but the *tsaddik* may negate it."[31] The activity of seeking to nullify divine decrees is already evidenced in the Ba'al Shem Tov's famous letter to his brother-in-law Gershon Kitover, the last part of which is devoted to such efforts. It should be recalled, of course, that a *ba'al shem* as shamanic healer is engaged in precisely that work, since illness as well as oppression by either pogroms or governmental edicts were seen as reflecting the will of heaven or the power of demonic forces.[32] A powerful intercessor could affect that will. It was for this that a *ba'al shem* earned his livelihood.

What was a Jew to do in times of trouble, in the era prior to Hasidism? To whom could one turn for help if one's ill fate seemed to be decreed from above? One could go to the graves of the righteous, especially one's own pious ancestors, and ask them to intercede, to "go before the Throne of Glory" and seek mercy for those still on earth. But the living *tsaddikim*, like the famous thirty-six, in pre-Hasidic times were supposed to keep hidden and were not in the habit of giving out blessings. One might turn to a famous rabbi, of course, but the rabbinate did not recognize this as part of its role. A wide discrepancy existed between the needs the community and the willingness of its leaders to fulfill those needs. The highly intellectualized world of rabbinic learning in Eastern Europe did little to support the people's desire for a "holy man." The typical *rav* was not taught to give out blessings or even to reassure those wavering in their faith because of personal troubles. Training in "spiritual leadership," one might say, was not part of the curriculum that led to the rabbinate. A *ba'al shem* stood in this breach, having the professional role of healer, which also meant intercessor.[33] He was the one who might be able to offer what it would take to make your prayers more effective. The *ba'al shem* could offer you an amulet or teach you a formula of holy names to recite that might ward off those evil spirits that were beleaguering you. (Of course an effective *ba'al shem* knew herbs and natural medicines as well as names; these certainly added to the likelihood of his cures.) There were *ba'aley shem* before the BeSHT who were also shamans in the fullest sense, partaking of out-of-the-body experiences, having revelations, etc., but this was not essential to the fulfillment of their professional role. Significantly, the *ba'al shem* was able to function as a healer not because of claims of special righteousness or moral fitness. Nowhere are we told that *ba'aley shem* in general were great *tsaddikim*; they were plying a holy trade, comparable to that of *mohel* or *shohet*. Nor did a *ba'al shem* need to be a person of especially venerated ancestry. Subject, of course, to the generally expected norms of piety, he was a man possessed of esoteric knowledge, especially that of divine names bearing supernatural powers. A *ba'al shem* is, in short, a magician, one particularly devoted to the arts of healing, or a folk doctor possessed of esoteric knowledge.

What happens in Hasidism is that the roles of *tsaddik* and *ba'al shem* come to be amalgamated. Once Hasidism proclaims that there are indeed living *tsaddikim* who can be found, revered, and followed, the functions served by *ba'al shem* very quickly migrate to these *tsaddikim*. Tellingly, there is no other *ba'al shem* prominently associated with the Hasidic movement after the Ba'al Shem Tov. There is no longer a need for one; the Hasidic *tsaddik* has taken his place.[34] The *tsaddik* is the channel of divine bounty flowing into the world. Surely he can pray for your sick child, your barren wife, or your failing business. He is also the one who can ward off the broader evils that may be affecting the Jewish community as a whole. He may still use some of the old magical devices, which surely did not disappear with the advent of Hasidism. Eastern European Jewish life, especially in the Ukrainian/Moldavian regions, was immersed in magical beliefs and practices right down to modern times, many of them practiced alongside and intertwined with faith in the *tsaddik*. But in Hasidism a very important difference struggles against this background. In the emerging Hasidic hierarchy of values, personal piety and intensity of prayer take precedence over a body of esoteric knowledge about holy names and how to write or pronounce them. At least as reflected in the theoretical writings of the Maggid's school, it is the former that now make the *tsaddik* a capable intercessor and worker of wonders. It is God's love for the *tsaddik* and his exceptional devotion that causes him to be endowed with these powers. Even though some Hasidic *tsaddikim* continued to use holy names and amulets, these devices themselves were increasingly seen as powered by the piety of the one who prescribed or wrote them, rather than as being independently potent.[35]

Not only is there no *ba'al shem* in Hasidism after the BeSHT; no one in the circles that created the Hasidic movement is prominently described as a "Kabbalist."[36] Although many, including the Maggid and Shne'ur Zalman of Lyady, were highly learned in the mystical tradition, that term had come to imply either a recondite and other-worldly ascetic or someone capable of performing in the realm of "practical Kabbalah" or magic. These people were choosing a different path, one in which their healing abilities, though not denied, had more to do with personal righteousness than with technical skill. For some, the claim of power to heal or intercede would come to be seen as secondary, or even atrophy almost completely, overwhelmed by their role as teachers and personal exemplars, as we shall see below.[37]

The shift from *ba'al shem* or Kabbalist to *tsaddik* takes place in the teachings of both of the BeSHT's most important disciples, the *Toledot* and the Maggid. In a sense it reflects a reintegration of the supernatural powers of the magician into the normative religious traditions of Judaism. In providing the living and identified *tsaddik* as an accessible model, these successors to the BeSHT were themselves opening a channel that would allow the religious worldview of the post-Safed mystical revival to extend to a much wider audience within Jewry and even beyond. Knowledge of magical secrets was no longer required, either by the individual or (in some cases) by those to whom one turned. Faith in the notion that there are indeed living *tsaddikim* in the world and that they bear divine grace and render it accessible was now sufficient. Finding such a true *tsaddik* and attaching yourself to him was now at least the proper first step for living a life blessed by God's presence.

II

We turn now to Dov Baer of Miedzyrzecz, and then to his circle, to see the issues that emerged around the proclamation and definition of this old/new role. We should always bear in mind that while Hasidism was in some ways a revolutionary movement in both the spiritual and social spheres, its rhetoric was always traditionally rooted, dependent entirely on creative exegesis of ancient sources within the Jewish canon. Determining what the authors of Hasidic homilies sought to teach, how they differed from one another, and how they may have been arguing or responding to one another's views always depends upon subtle readings of difficult texts (usually Hebrew-written synopses of much longer oral talks delivered in

Yiddish), the meaning of which is often not entirely clear. A sense of both dignity and of the timeless and transcendent nature of Torah interpretation did not permit specific reference to contemporary events or controversies. Instead, the scholar has to ferret them out from extended discussions of Abraham's encounter with the angels, Moses' confrontation with Pharaoh, the many leadership conflict stories in the biblical book of Numbers, and lots more. For this reason, certainty with regard to the contemporary "address" of such sermons is always hard to achieve.

The first and most important collection of the Maggid's teachings is found in his *Maggid Devarav le-Ya'akov*. Published in 1781 (making it the third Hasidic book printed), it was (quite poorly) edited by his disciple Shelomo of Lutsk. Many additional teachings were preserved in recensions copied from a manuscript by Levi Yizhak of Berdyczow, published later in fragmentary form. Especially useful among these is *Or Torah* (1804), the only version of the Maggid's teachings that follows the weekly Torah cycle.[38]

The most obvious divergence between Jacob Joseph and Dov Baer's view of the ideal leader has to do with the absence of rigid categorizations in the latter's writings. Gone is the distinction between "men of matter" and "men of form;" these terms are completely absent from the Maggid's corpus. The polemical tone of lambasting improper leaders is also missing. Dov Baer is not interested in preaching *against*, but rather in building *toward*. Tellingly, this difference in their writings confirms descriptions of their distinct personalities as recorded in the legendary sources. Jacob Joseph is said to have been angry and short-tempered. For this reason he did not succeed in developing either a popular following or a coterie of students, a matter that he did not accept quietly.[39] Dov Baer seems to have been more of a teacher. Although a powerful mystical presence, he was more a contemplative than an ecstatic type.[40] He seems to have possessed a charisma of a quieter and less obvious sort than his master. He was able to imbue his disciples with a deepened commitment to his mystical view of existence and his psychologized rereading of key symbolic terms of Kabbalah. At the same time, his less buoyant personality allowed room for those around his table to cultivate their own distinctive religious personae and to feel empowered by him to begin to spread the teaching.

Even a casual reader of the Maggid's teachings will be struck immediately by the prevalence of loving and psychologically sensitive parental metaphors throughout his writings. The love between God and Israel or the *tsaddikim* is always that of father and son, even if he is expounding a passage in the Song of Songs where another sort of love is the obvious subject. Rivka Schatz-Uffenheimer's index to her edition of *Maggid Devarav le-Ya'akov* offers long lists of father/son and king/prince parables, often repeated throughout the text. This motif has a long history, as we know from reading Moshe Idel,[41] but I hope to show that it is also anchored in a real-life emotional context. Dov Baer had only one son, Abraham "the Angel" (1740–76), born after a significant period of barrenness in his marriage.[42] He must have been an exceptionally loving father. It seems likely as well that he had fatherly feelings toward his younger disciples. For this reason I choose to open this discussion of the Maggid's views on the *tsaddik* with a reading of the following text:

> "May the glory of Y-H-W-H be for the world" (Ps. 104:31.)[43] All the worlds cannot bear the brilliance of the blessed Holy One, but He has wrought multiple reductions of it (*tsimtsumim*) so that they might be able to do so.
>
> But this seems problematic. Wouldn't the inaccessibility of God bespeak greater glory [Then why should He reduce it?]? But [the verse continues] "Y-H-W-H delights in that which He makes," God wants to rejoice in His creatures.
>
> This is like a father who has a young child. The little child wants to take a stick and ride about on it as though it were a horse. But a real horse leads its rider; this child is just leading the stick! Still, he has fun with it. The father helps by giving him the stick, to fulfill his son's desire.
>
> Such are the *tsaddikim*, who want to lead the world. God created the worlds so that they would enjoy leading them. God's essential glory remains beyond our grasp, but we can grasp His glory as it exists within the worlds. This is why God reduced Himself into the worlds, so that He derive pleasure from the joy that the *tsaddikim* find [in leading] the worlds.
>
> This is the meaning of "Those who fear Him bring about will" (Ps. 145:19).[44] In the Infinite (*eyn sof*) "will" does not apply; it is brought about by those who fear God, the *tsaddikim*. This is the meaning of "He consulted the souls of the *tsaddikim*" (in creating the world).[45]

This is a truly astonishing text, one that needs to be read on multiple levels. Its obvious meaning is theological. God is indeed utterly transcendent and unknowable. At the same time, He loves His creatures (especially the righteous), having created them in order to derive pleasure from that love. These intelligent human seekers want to stretch their minds to conceive God's glory, which will give them the power to "lead the world." But that glory by definition remains beyond them. What does the loving Father do? He lets them have a stick, a toy glory, as it were, the reduced form of glory found within the worlds, and lets them "play horsey" with it, pretending that they really have some influence in conducting the worlds. Because He loves them so much, He takes great parental pleasure in watching this game, while being fully aware that it is just child's play. The point is that humans can't really "rule the universe" by perceiving the bit of divine glory that He allows to seep into "the worlds." But *tsimtsum*, the illusion that we are doing so, is good for us and gives our Creator pleasure.

The parable has another unspoken level of meaning. The phrase *ha-tsaddikim rotsim le-hanhig et ha-'olam* would clearly be heard by a contemporary reader to mean "the *tsaddikim* want to lead the community."[46] We have here the Maggid's comment on the desire of his disciples, the newborn *tsaddikim*, whom he also sees as his spiritual "children," to go forth and become leaders, spreading his teachings widely. He considers this childish. How much of his profound mystical teachings could be contained in the vessels they will design to reach the public? They will be fooling themselves, thinking they are "riding the horse" of true spiritual teaching, bringing the *oylem* or community to perceive God's glory, when they are really just riding about on a stick, having no real effect on the world around them! Nevertheless, the loving father will give them the stick. Their efforts will still bring him pleasure. In this reading, the Maggid himself is that "father." The *tsaddikim* have brought about the will within their earthly teacher-father, and perhaps also their Father in heaven, to let them "lead the world" in this way.

Barely hidden within this text is a statement of the master's ambivalence regarding his disciples' desire to become leaders, to spread the teaching forward in such a way that they would take on roles of communal responsibility. This was not what he originally had in mind. In welcoming these young men to his table in Miedzyrzecz, he was creating a mystical brotherhood, a *kloiz* where his own approach to spiritual questions would be cultivated.[47] His intent was no different than that of the BeSHT and quite consistent with the other Hasidic circles that existed in and before his day, a group of master and disciples, cultivating their own spiritual lives, and perhaps influencing a few around them. But he sees the impatience of his young followers: "*tsaddikim* want to lead the community." In his fatherly love for them, he cannot refuse them, and here he is announcing his willingness to support their desire. We are being told in this text that the decision to spread the teachings and essentially create the Hasidic movement was not Dov Baer's but that of his disciples, for which they achieved his somewhat reluctant support. I am suggesting that this text should cause us to revise the way we think about the original spread and popularization of Hasidism. Rather than the Maggid's "sending forth" disciples to build the movement, we might think about young disciples bursting at the seams to go forth and teach, finally receiving their master's blessing to do so. The Maggid's reaction (as recorded in later tradition) when the hammer of opposition came down in 1772 would tend to confirm this view. His *hasidim* considered turning the *herem* around and excommunicating their opponents. "You have lost your head," he told them, a statement taken as predicting his imminent demise later that year. It was *their* fault, their decision, which had wrought the controversy and the *herem*, not his.[48]

This is not to say that the Maggid is a nonbeliever in the real powers of the *tsaddikim*. The ability to "bring about will" in God (his reading of Ps. 145:19) is no small matter. The transcendent God allows Himself to follow the lead of His earthly elect. In a well-known homily on Numbers 10:12,[49] "Make yourself two silver trumpets," the Maggid reads the word *hatsotserot* (trumpets) as *hatsi tsurot* (half forms), saying that God and the *tsaddik* are each incomplete without the other. Daringly reinterpreting Ezekiel 1:26's *demut ke-mareh adam* to mean "an image reflected in a mirror," he suggests that God's worldly actions follow where the *tsaddik* leads. "If love is awakened in the *tsaddik*, love is awakened in all the worlds." The *tsaddik* thus rules "like a king in his troop." According to multiple texts in the Maggid's writings,[50] changing the will of heaven as it affects the world is very much within the *tsaddik's* grasp. God is exceptionally generous with those who accept His rule.

"Yours O Y-H-W-H is loving kindness, for You repay a man according to his deeds" (Ps. 62:13). We may understand this by a parable. If an artisan fashions a vessel for a householder, what reward does he give him?

Only that which is appropriate to the effort he put in. Does he really give him full exchange of value? Or consider a country where people accepted a certain person to be their king.[51] The king will be good to those noblemen and reward each of them appropriately to his own station. But it would be impossible for him to return to each of them a royal crown, parallel to the one they gave to him.

But the blessed Holy One rewards with full value. Whoever makes God King, God makes into ruler over all the worlds. God issues decrees and he cancels them. "The *tsaddik* rules (over) the fear of God." The *tsaddikim* create worlds, resurrect the dead, and make fruitful the barren. Such is their this-worldly reward. This is "You repay a man according to his deeds—the reward You pay is up to the full value of his actions."[52]

This indeed sounds very much like something Joseph Weiss once described as "The Great Maggid's Theory of Contemplative Magic."[53] In exchange for his loyal submission to divine authority, the *tsaddik* is given the ability to change the decrees of heaven. In fact God as *eyn sof*, the endless Source of existence, or as *ayin*, the Nothingness behind all being, is indifferent to the fate of individuals or the outcome of historical events. But God loves the *tsaddik*, who then can take advantage of this relationship to implant concern for human affairs in God. This radically anthropocentric theology is complicated by the fact that it is sometimes "Israel" rather than *tsaddik* that appears in these sources, since "God created the world for the sake of Israel," etc. That would seem to make the fate of Israel an essential divine concern rather than a human-generated afterthought. But such inconsistencies abound in these sources. The grandest inconsistency of all, that of God as *ayin* or primal Nothingness, in the very radical mystical formulations that lie at the heart of the Maggid's theology, and the loving parent-God of his favorite metaphors, also remains essentially unresolved. Of course he has the old distinction of *eyn sof* versus *sefirot* to rely on, except that he has converted the *sefirot* into mostly psychological categories. Therefore the mirror image quoted above may be particularly important in a theology that he realizes needs to be left partly unspoken. The God of his abstract theology has no specific will beyond the rushing flow of being or light issuing from the great and endless font of *eyn sof*. Only we humans have will. But because that divine energy flow can also be described as love (*hesed*, the creative/procreative *eros* of existence), it allows itself to be shaped by the desire of its love objects, Israel or the *tsaddikim*.[54]

Yet a certain ambiguity remains in the Maggid's teachings about just how real the powers of the *tsaddikim* are. Listen to him again in another typically affectionate paternal description of the relationship between God and the *tsaddik*:

> Our master and teacher the holy lamp Dov Baer offered the following parable:
>
> A father is teaching his son and he wants the boy himself to speak forth the objection in an argument or the solution to it. He wants it to be considered the child's own question or answer, so the child will take pleasure in having mastered it, even if it is something too deep for him to truly understand. The father explains it fully, enough to make the child understand it [on a superficial level] and say it back to him. Even though he really comprehends nothing of it, and it's all due to his father's willing explanation of the matter, the child takes pleasure in having spoken the question or its answer. They then call it "his."
>
> The same is true when the *tsaddik* nullifies the decrees of the Blessed One. The *tsaddik*'s thought to pray about this matter itself came from God! Nevertheless, since the nullification came about through the *tsaddik*'s words and the intensity of his prayer, this negation of decree is called by his name. This is so even though both the thought and the words were sent by God.[55]

Both the Maggid and his disciples were aware of the problematic nature of extravagant claims for the *tsaddik*. While the shift from Ba'al Shem as purveyor of wonders to *tsaddik* as deserving grantee of divine blessing was a return to the few well-known and oft-quoted scriptural and rabbinic sources, the granting of heavenly powers to the righteous was enough to create some nervousness. It was not difficult to foresee the abuses that could emerge from such claims. Here it is again dismissed as a sort of child's play. All the powers really belong to God, not to the *tsaddik*. These may also have been attempts to forestall the emerging anti-Hasidic critique. They were reason enough for the Maggid to have originally wanted to be quiet and cautious about what he understood to be very radical ideas, potentially dangerous in the wrong hands. Here is a passage where R. Menahem Nahum of Chernobyl presents and defends the Maggid's view, one that seems to have the emerging critique of Hasidism clearly in mind:

Our sages taught: "What is Hanukkah? On the twenty-fifth day of Kislev . . . as the Greeks [i.e., the Seleucid army] entered the sanctuary . . . (b. Shabbat 21b)." It would seem that the sages are asking why these days are called by the name Hanukkah. If so, what answer is here offered? In fact the word Hanukkah is composed of *hanu koh*, "they dwelt in 'thus.'"

There is an aspect of divinity that is called "thus"; this is *malkhut,* the seat of divine rule. The king commands "Thus will it be! Thus will it be!" It is this aspect that issues commands through all the worlds, by which the universe is ruled. This is why the *tsaddikim* have within their power dominion over all the worlds: they bear within themselves this aspect of divine kingship (i.e., they are *hanu koh*; they dwell in 'thus'). So the rabbis (b. Mo'ed Katan 16b) have taught us on the verse "The righteous one rules the fear of God (2 Sam. 23:3)." On this verse they said, "Who rules over Me? The *tsaddik*. The blessed Holy One issues a decree, but the righteous one may cancel it."

The Zohar (1:45b) objected: "Does the *tsaddik* then control God?" In fact it is God Himself who cancels the decree. Several times we have taught that "In all their suffering, He suffers" (Is. 63:9), referring to the *shekhinah* in exile. *Shekhinah*—so called because She dwells (*shokhenet*) everywhere—is identical with this aspect of divine rule. She is also called *kenesset yisra'el*, "Assemblage of Israel," gathering all of Israel within Her, since all of them come from Her.

Thus our sages (b. Shabbat 128a) taught: "All Israel are children of kings" (i.e., of *malkhut*). All sufferings that Israel undergoes, God forbid, secretly belong to the fall of *shekhinah*. Scripture refers to this in "You weaken the Rock that bore you" (Deut. 32:18). The righteous, by their good deeds, raise up the *shekhinah,* as it were, as in "Give strength to God! (Ps. 68:35). The rabbis (Ekhah Rabbah 1:33) add: "Israel add power to the upper 'family.'" *Malkhut* is called "family" because She gathers into Herself all the divine potencies that stand above Her. All of their powers flow into *shekhinah*. As She is uplifted, all decrees and judgments are negated.[56]

We see here the awkwardness felt by the Hasidic author about a claim that would limit divine authority and make the *tsaddik* look too much like a magician bearing somehow independent powers. Relying first on a Zohar passage (which actually goes in a somewhat different direction), Menahem Nahum attributes the power to the *shekhinah*, within which Israel dwell. God as *shekhinah* (=*kenesset yisra'el*) identifies fully with human (i.e., Israel's) suffering; this is the nature of Her exile. If a Jew acts for the sake of *shekhinah*, that authority within Her embraces his intent and causes it to be fulfilled. But this pious idea is being used here to interpret the statement "Who rules over Me? The *tsaddik*," and that usage demands explanation. The answer is that the *tsaddik* is not magician, as it might appear, but devotee. It is his submission to God and devotion to the *shekhinah*'s need, to the point of his own nothingness, that brings God to do his bidding.[57] Note how different this is from the classical *ba'al shem*, where the issue of selfless acting for the *shekhinah* is not part of the rhetoric.

This change in the language by which the holy man's power is described has everything to do with the Maggid's school's well-known dropping of interest in the complex system of Lurianic *kavvanot* or mystical intentions, the renewed preference for *kavvanah* over *kavvanot*.[58] The latter have to do with the realm of esoteric knowledge, very much like the *ba'al shem*'s knowledge of holy names and amulet writing. The Lurianic intentions are of course more respectable than "practical Kabbalah" or magic, but they are similarly technical in their highly detailed apparatus. There is no longer a need for any of these; all that matters is selfless devotional intent. The receptiveness is there within God for the *tsaddik* to have his will reflected in the divine Self, so long as that will really is for the sake of heaven. Nothing more is needed, either for the great task of uplifting the *shekhinah* and mitigating Her exile, or for the ancillary task of bringing blessing forth into this world. Elsewhere the Maggid tells us that even the forces of nature recognize and are awed by the *tsaddik*'s righteousness. The Reed Sea fled when it saw that the Israelites were bearing Joseph's coffin (cf. Ex. 13:19), so powerful was even the memory of that original *tsaddik* who "fled outside" (*va-yanos ha-hutsah*) to escape the wiles of Potiphar's wife (Gen. 39:12). His denial of natural impulses took him "outside" the power of nature, allowing him to dwell in a supernatural state, one that remained present in his bones even as they were brought forth from Egypt. "The Sea saw it and fled" (Ps. 114:3) means that the Sea saw the *va-yanos* of Genesis 39:12! He may also have in mind reading *va-yanos* as derived from *nes*, rendering "The Sea saw it and became a miracle."[59]

But just how much is the *tsaddik* allowed to have an interest in the latter function, that of bringing blessings into this world, and especially to the *oylem* of his own disciples? His potential capability for doing so is unquestioned by the Maggid, but he is no advocate of wholesale usage or "marketing" of such powers.[60] In fact we see in the Maggid's writings almost none of the admonitions to believe in the *tsaddik*, or the insistence that God can be approached *only* through the *tsaddik*, that we will find so much of later on in Hasidism. Truth to be told, the task of 'avodah is really the duty of every Jew. Frequently his teachings go back and forth among *adam*, *yisra'el*, and *tsaddik* as the subject of their discourse. God created the world so that humans, or Israel, or the *tsaddikim*, might serve Him. The *tsaddik* is just a Jew who has managed the task better than most and thus serves as a beacon to others.

Here we see the great divergence that emerges within the Maggid's school, one that stands in direct relation to the popularization of the Hasidic message. The great advocates of the *tsaddik*'s worldly powers are the key figures in urging that the nascent movement burst forth from Miedzyrzecz and "lead the world." These are R. Aaron and Shelomo of Karlin and R. Levi Yizhak of Berdyczow.

The key role of Karlin as an early center of Hasidism is well known, documented especially by Wolf Rabinowitsch in his *Lithuanian Hasidism*,[61] based on important discoveries he made in the archive of the Karlin/Stolin *tsaddikim* in the 1930s. *Hasidim* in the north (including Vilna) were originally referred to as "Karliner" in many of the bans and other anti-Hasidic sources throughout the 1770s and 1780s.[62] R. Aaron was an active missionary for the movement already in the late 1760s, not only in Karlin, essentially a suburb of Pinsk in Polesia, but daring to wander far north into the Lithuanian heartland of rabbinic authority itself. Salomon Maimon's diary mentions "K" along with "M," clearly Karlin and Miedzyrzecz, as the two centers of the new sect.[63] Unfortunately, we know rather little of R. Aaron's own teachings. He died young and very early in the process of

Hasidism's spread (during Pesah of 1772, several months before the Maggid).[64] His disciple R. Shelomo, who took his place in Karlin, however, carried forward the twin emphases that he learned from his master.[65] Karlin was famous for loud, prolonged, and highly demonstrative prayer and for faith in the dependence of the *hasid* on his master for prayer and support, including prayers for matters of this world. The Hasidism of Karlin (the source also first of Amdur and later of Lachowicze, thence Kobryn, Novominsk, and Slonim) was hardy and enduring. R. Shelomo left Karlin around 1784, due to a combination of persecution by the Pinsk rabbinate and the difficulty of competing with the growing influence of R. Shne'ur Zalman.[66] He migrated to the Ukraine, settling in Ludmir (or Wladimyr-Volynsk), an area more receptive to their brand of Hasidism. However, his follower R. Asher, the son of R. Aaron, returned to Polesia and reestablished the court in nearby Stolin. They and their offshoots remained the only significant alternative to HaBaD in the entire Polesian, White Russian, and Lithuanian region.

The Maggid's disciples' venture northward was continued by R. Menahem Mendel of Vitebsk, who had established a center in Minsk by 1770. He was the chief object of the 1772 bans against Hasidism, considered the most significant leader of this northern branch.[67] His disciple R. Abraham of Kalisk had by the same time, or perhaps even earlier, created a small following in his own town. The Kalisker, among the youngest of the disciples, seemed to have played the role of *enfant terrible* in the Maggid's circle. The first bans against Hasidism, those of Shklov in 1771, which led to the great *haramot* of 1772, may have been directed against him. In a letter describing the events as they unfolded, R. Shne'ur Zalman describes the excesses of *hasidey TaLK*, the extreme pietists of 1770. The Kalisker and his disciples are accused of *kulyen zikh*, turning somersaults, in front of the *aron kodesh* as expressions of their ecstatic devotion and in general of *harbeh yaldut*, "much childish behavior."[68] They were also known for excessive mockery of scholarly rabbis. The letter suggests that responsibility for the entire campaign against Hasidism should be laid at the feet of the Kalisker, obviously an exaggeration, perhaps exacerbated by the fierce struggle over both ideology and money in which the two were engaged in the late 1790s and beyond. But it does supply the interesting memory that in 1772, when the disciples gathered in Rovno to take counsel after the first *haramot*, the Kalisker was afraid to face his master, and both R.

Mendel Vitebsker and R. Shelomo of Karlin had to speak up for him before he dared to enter the room.

Outside the northern territories, where hostility was more consistent, the battle against Hasidism may be seen as having been directed almost exclusively at R. Levi Yizhak. Unlike either Karlin *tsaddik*, Levi Yizhak was an ordained rabbi and an acknowledged *talmid hakham*. He had been brought to Miedzyrzecz by R. Shmelka Horowitz, whom he succeeded as rabbi of Ryczywol when R. Shmelka moved on to Sieniewa and later to the very distinguished rabbinate of Nikolsburg (Mikoluv) in Moravia, well outside the pale of Hasidic influence. Levi Yizhak then became rabbi of Zelechow, southeast of Warsaw, the first of the disciples in central Poland, well before Hasidism's spread there. He was active enough in preaching the Hasidic doctrine to arouse the enmity of the community's leaders and was forced out of his post, probably in 1771 or 2. From there he went to Pinsk, a community that at first welcomed him and seems to have had a significant pro-Hasidic population.[69] But eventually (c. 1784) he was forced to resign that position as well, possibly as a result of outside pressure from the Vilna Gaon and others. He was then invited to assume the rabbinate of Berdyczow, the largest Jewish community in Volhyn, in 1785.[70]

Kedushat Levi, the compilation of R. Levi Yizhak's teaching published after his death (Berdyczow, 1811),[71] is replete with claims for the *tsaddik*'s powers, repeating over and over various versions of the Talmudic (b. Mo'ed Katan 16b) "the *tsaddik* ordains and the blessed Holy One fulfills" or "The blessed Holy One issues a decree, but the *tsaddik* nullifies it."[72] More than any other single work of Hasidic teaching, the *Kedushat Levi* reveals its author as a popular propagandist for Hasidism. His sermons are addressed to the needs and beliefs of ordinary Jews. Levi Yizhak was, of course, famous for caring about ordinary people and their concerns, and he believed in a God who did so as well. While he shares the abstract notions of the Maggid's mystical theology, he is more attracted to the parental side of his master's God, and he tends to focus repeatedly on real human beings (always Jews, of course) and their needs. The earthiness of the BeSHT's message is fulfilled for Levi Yizhak in his touching expressions of human concern. The following is an indication of his distinctive approach to leadership.

"May Y-H-W-H the God of the spirits of all flesh set forth a man over the community . . . and may the community of Y-H-W-H not be like a flock that has no shepherd" (Num. 27:16–17).

The principle is that one has to speak out in defense (*li-lemod* [!] *zekhut*) of Israel, who do not constantly fulfill God's will as do the angels, since they are burdened by earning a living. Thus Abraham, the man of *hesed*, sought to speak in Israel's defense. That was why he brought the angels food to eat, to show them about human needs, so they would not speak accusingly against Israel.[73]

This is why Moses refers to Y-H-W-H as "God of the spirits of all flesh." A person of flesh and blood needs to earn a livelihood. Because of this, he cannot serve God constantly. "God of the spirits of all *flesh*" means that You are a Judge and Leader who ever seeks to defend Israel. Just as You defend human beings who do not always serve You, Moses asks that You set forth over Israel a [human] leader who will do the same.[74]

The text of *Kedushat Levi*, here and elsewhere, supports the image of its author depicted in the later hagiographical literature. But it also completely dovetails with the anti-Hasidic emphasis on him as the central figure of the movement's spread. He is a preacher willing to give the people what they need, the constant reassurance that the *tsaddik* has heavenly powers and will seek to wield them for their benefit, relieving their burdens of daily life. This point of view is by no means uncontested in the Maggid's circle. The master's own preference is for service dedicated to the *shekhinah*, not to the needs of the human community. That more elitist and limiting view is given a significant barb in the following teaching by Levi Yizhak, one that I would suggest may be directed against the master himself, a part of the inner debate within Miedzyrzecz about whether to step forth into the public arena:

"Moses went up to God" (Ex. 19:3). . . . Moses our Teacher, of blessed memory, prepared himself in very intense and powerful ways to have God speak to him on a high level, one that no other person could understand. God said to him: "Do not prepare so much as you want to do. [If I address you on such a high level,] you will not be able to teach the Children of Israel."

This is the meaning of "Moses went up to God"—he was preparing for this high level, that of going up to God, to speak on God's level. But the blessed Holy One did not want that, for He wanted to teach Israel. That is why "God called him from the mountain" (19:3), on a lower level. God's intent was "to say" to Israel, the people that were near to Him.[75]

What God wants of his leaders, Levi Yizhak is arguing here, is not that they strive to reach the contemplative heavens, but that they bring heaven down to earth.[76] This means a *tsaddik* who sees himself deeply committed to helping with real human needs, rather than getting lost in his own strivings to achieve oneness with divine abstraction.

But it is not only the Maggid who needs to be convinced. There are other voices around the table in Miedzyrzec who express (perhaps in teachings only articulated later, but formed by this debate) much more hesitancy about the popularizing push. Chief among these is the *Or ha-Me'ir*, R. Ze'ev Wolf of Zhitomyr.[77] His work, while on the radical edge of the circle in some theological ideas, is marked by sharp criticism of popular Hasidism as it is beginning to emerge. He is concerned both with the emergence of false leaders, would-be *tsaddikim* who are themselves profit-seeking ignoramuses, and shallow followers of *tsaddikim* who pretentiously imitate their behavior. Following are brief examples of each:

Not like what has become so widespread in this generation, when ignorant people burst forth and raise themselves up. They claim that they too deserve a place among the great, saying Torah filled with plays on numbers and letters. They imagine they have influence for good, offering advice on the service of God. But truly they are wise [only] in their own eyes. Their wisdom amounts to nothing, since they are filled with improper and deceptive motives, ruled by desire.[78] "The feeble sheep (*'atufim*) belonged to Laban, but the robust ones were Jacob's" (Gen. 30:42).

There are some people who, even in the course of walking the royal path and doing God's commandments, including study of Torah and prayer, are really doing so for purposes of their own self-glorification and pleasure. They think "How nicely I speak! How nicely I act!"

Our eyes see this in our own generation, when so many burst forth to wrap themselves up in a *tallit* that is not really theirs. As soon as they see a *tsaddik* or an enlightened person act in a certain way, they try to clothe themselves in the very same actions. Those fools do not understand that even if they lived a thousand years they would not attain such a rung! "How can the fool have the price in his hand to attain wisdom, when he has no heart?" (Prov. 17:16). He can't even see to the task of setting right his own seven personal qualities,[79] keeping away from their negative sides, but he peers into the actions of others, the pure and enlightened, without any understanding of their secret meaning as a way to pursue the path of truth.

The Torah hints at this by saying that the feeble sheep (*ha-'atufim*, also meaning "wrapped up") belonged to Laban, but the robust ones (*ha-keshurim*) were Jacob's.

This verse provides a sign. Those who wrap themselves up in a *tallit* not their own, looking to what others do when they don't yet properly see themselves, still belong to Laban. They have false weights in their hands, and do everything by cheating. These are the qualities of Laban the cheat. But the *keshurim* (also "attached"), those who do all their deeds in a bound up or attached way, belong to Jacob. They have conceived how exalted God is, and they take no part of practices that belong to others . . . their spirit keeps faith with God; they belong to Jacob our Father, whose quality is truth.[80]

Here and in several other places R. Ze'ev Wolf seems to anticipate the dangers in a spreading of Hasidism that will come up so sharply a half-century later in the caustic views of R. Mendel of Kotsk. Levi Yizhak would be considerably more forgiving of such people, viewing the task of the *tsaddik* as seeing the good in people and pleading their cause, rather than condemning them for trying to imitate the *tsaddik*'s behavior![81]

III

An interesting lens on this debate within the Maggid's circle may be seen in a series of homilies around Numbers 20, the account of Moses striking the rock, the Torah's *locus classicus* for discussion of errant leadership. Levi Yizhak has a predictable comment on this passage. The reason Moses was led to sin by striking the rock was his lack of patience with the people. He ties the Numbers text into a well-known Hasidic typology of two sorts of preachers:

> "Speak to the rock before their eyes . . . because you did not have faith in Me, to sanctify Me in the eyes of the Children of Israel" (Num. 20:8, 12).
>
> RaSHI and RaMBaN are divided as to the sin of Moses. One says it is that of saying "Listen, O you rebels!" (vs. 10) and the other defines it as striking the rock. But they really are the same, for one led to the other.
>
> There are two sorts of preachers who address Israel to get them to do the Creator's will. One speaks to them in a positive tone, telling each one of Israel what a high rung is his, how the souls of Israel are truly hewn from beneath the Throne of Glory. [He reminds them] of the Creator's great pleasure in a *mitsvah* performed by any Jew, how all the worlds are joyous at seeing God's command fulfilled. This kind of preaching bends the heart of Jews to do God's bidding and to accept the yoke of God's kingdom. But other preachers reprove Israel with tough language, shaming them until they are forced to do God's will.
>
> The difference is that the one who approaches them with goodness, uplifting their souls to such great heights . . . is a fitting leader for Israel. Not so the one who speaks harshly. When a preacher speaks so well of Israel . . . all the world's creatures necessarily turn of their own accord to doing Israel's will, since it was for Israel's sake that they were created. But if one doesn't speak well and uplift Israel's righteousness, each creature will have to be forced to do their bidding, that for which they were created.
>
> When Moses said, "Listen, O you rebels!" he was reproving Israel with harsh words. That was why he had to strike the rock in order to force it to fulfill its created purpose. Had he uplifted Israel as the blessed Holy One intended by saying, "Speak to the rock," he would have been saying, "You, O rock, who were created for the sake of Israel! They are on such a high rung that you have to do that for which you were created,

to bring forth water for Israel!" But now that he had reproved Israel harshly, he needed to strike the rock. . . .

"Because you did not have faith in Me, to sanctify Me in the eyes of the Children of Israel." The one who approaches Israel through goodness can pass this understanding on to them, "sanctifying Me in the eyes." . . . Our sages (Shir ha-Shirim Rabbah 1:23) say that "eyes" refers to the wise within the community. They too would be able to attain this understanding.[82]

Although the concluding line is a bit unclear, it seems he is suggesting that Israel too (not just a specific group of "leaders") could have gained the wisdom that all nature is there to serve them, had Moses addressed them with proper respect and affection. Then the rock would have gushed forth on its own, just as the Reed Sea had been so transformed at the sight of Joseph's bones! The message, in other words, is to have great faith in Israel and patience with them, even in hard times, always defending them and thus raising them up to their true high level. This is Levi Yizhak's essential teaching.

A similar view to that of Levi Yizhak is taken by his colleague and supporter R. Elimelech of Lezajsk.[83] Moses felt he needed to do the sort of deed that would impress the people, even if it was somewhat contrary to God's instruction:

It is the way of the *tsaddik* to constantly seek out what is good for Israel, even if doing so appears to contain some bit of transgression. If it is for Israel's good, he will do it, even accepting that he might have to suffer Hell for their sake. His entire desire is to do what is good for them. The *tsaddik* could in fact bring forth the flow of blessing just by his word, without any physical act at all, but sometimes he has to do it . . . for those who do not believe.[84]

The words of the *tsaddik* will affect only those who already believe in him, but a "physical act"—a miracle—will convince everyone. R. Elimelech of Lezajsk is in fact a very prominent figure in the Maggid's circle. His book *Noa'm Elimelech* (Lvov, 1788) stands alongside the *Kedushat Levi* as one of the best-known works of early Hasidism. Like Levi Yizhak, he devotes much attention to the *tsaddik* and is often portrayed as the key figure in developing this aspect of Hasidism.[85] But there is an important difference between the treatment of *tsaddik* in these two works.[86] Unlike Levi Yizhak, Elimelech maintained a close circle of disciples, essentially carrying on for another generation what had existed in Miedzyrzec. Most of the leadership of Hasidism in the next generation, both in Poland and Galicia, emerged from the *bet midrash* of R. Elimelech (and his own successor, R. Ya'akov Yizhak, the *Hozeh* of Lublin). The *No'am Elimelech* is addressed primarily to this circle. It is a series of homiletically formed instructions on how to become and behave as a *tsaddik*.[87] He understands his own role as that of cultivating an elite group of future *tsaddikim*, who in turn would lead the people.[88] Elimelech is a tough master, one who (like the Maggid) never fully gave up the old pre-BeSHTian ascetic path.[89] Although fully a believer in the *tsaddik* and his powers, he does not tout them as does Levi Yizhak. Here he is telling his would-be *tsaddikim* how much courage the role will demand of them, even the sort of courage that might put at risk their own future other-worldly reward. The *tsaddik* is very much there "for others," even at the cost of his own self-interest. This is R. Elimelech at his best.[90]

But now we turn to another homily on this same text, leading to a very different conclusion. R. Issachar Dov, rabbi of Zloczow, is the author of *Mevasser Tsedek* (Dubno, 1798), one of the lesser known works of the Maggid's circle. He and Levi Yizhak were in-laws, having known each other at a young age. Both of them spent some time in the *bet midrash* of the town of Lubartow (Levi Yizhak's wife's home town) in the Lublin district, where they were married to the daughters of two brothers prominent in the town. In fact it was from there that they were both attracted to the Hasidic path[91] and found their way together to Miedzyrzec.[92] Here is his reading of Moses' striking the rock:

> A *tsaddik* who wants to bring about some change in the order of creation needs to go to the root of the thing that is to be changed. Suppose someone made a vessel out of clay. If you wanted to change its function, you would go back to its maker and ask him to change it to suit your purpose.[93]

When Moses wanted to get water for the people to flow miraculously from that rock, he had to raise the people up to the rock's own Source. This is what the blessed Holy One intended, that Moses uplift the people; then speaking would have been sufficient. Moses did so. But the ordinary folk also needed water [immediately], and he was unable to raise them up to that high level, the Source above. Thus he did not succeed and was forced to strike the rock, representing a lower level [of religious action], as is spelled out in the *Likkutey Torah* of Rabbi Isaac Luria.[94]

The *tsaddik* was punished for this. Even though it was impossible to raise up the masses, he should have elevated the *tsaddikim*, who are called "the eyes of the community," so that Y-H-W-H would be sanctified in their sight. Thus the verse says, "Moses and Aaron assembled the congregation," including the ordinary masses. "Facing the rock": having them look into the rock, toward its Source. In this lay their failure; the ordinary folk were just not able to rise up that high. Once Moses saw that they were unable to concentrate on the Source, but only on the rock below, he said to them, "Listen, you rebels! Shall we bring you water out of *this* rock," meaning the rock that you see. This is indeed impossible. And since you are incapable of rising to the Root, it will not bring water forth for you. Therefore, "he struck the rock," acting at a lower level. Then "the community drank," including the masses.

Y-H-W-H said to Moses and Aaron: "Because you did not have the faith in Me to sanctify Me before the eyes of the Children of Israel." These are the community's "eyes," the *tsaddikim*. Even though you couldn't succeed with the ordinary people, you needed to "sanctify Me before the eyes," the proper leaders. Because of this, "you will not bring."[95]

What was Moses' sin? He stooped too low, going down to the level of ordinary Jews. Their thirst did not let them rise to the level of "Speak to the rock." They were desperate for a miracle, something they could *see*. Moses responded too readily to that, reaching down to the lowest common denominator among his flock, and struck the rock. Instead, he might have spoken to it, done something that reached only ʿeyney ha-ʿedah, the "eyes" of the community, but raising them up to the heights. They then could have taken it to the next level forward, reaching down toward the common folk. The sin, in other words, was too much of a rush toward popularization, giving the people what they need rather than raising them up. I read this text as a critique of emerging popular Hasidism and probably one directed squarely at his old friend and relative Levi Yizhak.[96]

The position taken by R. Issachar Dov would have been shared by several other members of the Maggid's circle, those who felt more nervous about the pace and measures taken for the sake of convincing the masses. The Berdyczower is a popularizer, ready to reach out and down to the level of the folk. "Isn't that the Ba'al Shem Tov's message?" he would argue. "What's wrong with the level where the people stand? They are all holy Jews, after all, and their needs are all holy needs. Who are we to dare judge them otherwise?" The *Mevasser Tsedek*, the *Or ha-Me'ir*, and others[97] are much less convinced of this and may even have been horrified by what they saw emerging. The *No'am Elimelech*, despite his agreement in this specific instance, was somewhat more cautious.

But let us return once more to Moses and the rock. It turns out that this series of interpretations was not initiated by Levi Yizhak or Issachar Dov but by the Maggid himself. In a passage published in both *Maggid Davaraw le-Ya'akov* and *Or Torah*, he says the following:

The Zohar (1:28b) teaches that "had Moses spoken to the rock, there would have been no forgetting [i.e., Torah would never be forgotten]."[98] The reason is that all the miracles Moses performed were accomplished by speech alone; he did not belong to the realm of action. He was told to lift up his staff (Ex. 14:16), but the Sea was subdued by the word alone, [with no need to strike it]. This was not the case with Joshua. Moses represents the category of mind or awareness; as such he was drawn toward speech. His generation was also called "the generation of awareness." For this reason they are referred to as *dor ha-midbar*, which can mean "the generation of speech" (b. Sanhedrin 108a). Speech is drawn forth from the mind. Hence they received the Torah in speech. . . .

When this first generation was dying out and another was coming along, Moses perceived that they were people more related to action. They were going to inherit the land [i.e., earthiness; *erets/artsiyyut*]. That was why he struck the rock. But the blessed Holy One in fact said just the opposite: his task was to *uplift* that second generation, to raise them higher.

"They were to inherit it in the name of their fathers" (Gen. 48:6), the generation of the wilderness/speech. Speech alone would have brought water out of that rock. In this way they too would have become a generation of awareness. By hitting the rock he brought about forgetfulness, a fall from speech to action.

The Maggid is accusing Moses of an excessive willingness to popularize, descending to the level of *artsiyyut*-focused deed rather than raising the people up to the rung of speech. But here a new element is added: that of generational divide. The generation of Moses is, ingeniously, *dor ha-midbar*, "the generation of speech." That of Joshua is *dor ha-arets*, "the generation of earth[iness]."

But these are *derashot*, sermons, not texts of biblical interpretation! Their real focus is the present, not the ancient past, as these authors themselves so frequently remind us. When reading a sermon one has to ask why the preacher chose to say these things, *toward whom his words were directed.* In this case, who was "sitting on the other side of the table"? The Levi Yizhak camp in this inner-group argument was saying: "But we need to reach out *to the young people,* the next generation that will follow us. Profound teachings (i.e., "speech") are not enough for them. The masses we are trying to reach did not sit at the Maggid's table, drawn by the power of the word. They need some *action,* something they can see. We need to offer them faith in a *tsaddik* who can *do* something about their worldly woes. A *tsaddik* who dwells in the upper worlds, praying for the *shekhinah*, is not enough." This is the master's answer to his impatient disciple. The Maggid and others with him are responding to the radical popularizer: "No, that's just the point. Our job is *to raise them up,* not to go down to where they are. We should not be in the business of providing a *tsaddik* as miracle-worker, but should be leading the people to think of the *shekhinah* rather than themselves. Profound and convincing teachings are *precisely* what they need."

The presence of this text within the Maggid's own written corpus, in print by 1781 and also present in prior manuscript versions,[99] makes it completely clear that the debate about popularization and its price had begun already in the Maggid's lifetime. Levi Yizhak was among the great agitators for moving forward. The Maggid, we see here once again, is more hesitant, worried about corrupting the purity of his teaching. He had permitted his "sons," the *tsaddikim*, to ride about on that stick and thus "lead the world," but he was very worried about the results.

In fact we have a passage by Levi Yizhak, in the Torah portion immediately preceding this one (though we know nothing of the year in which he said it), where he takes up the same question of generational difference, the time of Moses being that of speech and the time of Joshua demanding action. Speech is adequate, but it needs to be clothed in the "world of action." It is our *middot*, meaning our moral/emotional character, that allow us to do so.

> "Korah took..." (Num. 16:1). . . . There are the generation of the wilderness and the generation that entered the Land of Israel. *Dor ha-Midbar* refers to speech; they accomplished everything by speaking. There are *tsaddikim* who accomplish everything by speaking and do not need to perform any deed. "The generation that entered the land of Israel" refers to action; they needed to do some deed. That is why Joshua, when doing battle with the thirty-one kings, had to perform some act with the javelin and the ambush (Josh. 8:18–19). Moses, who lived in the generation of *midbar*, needed no such act; he did it all through speech. . . .
>
> The Torah of Moses is parallel to speech, since he accomplished all by speaking. But it becomes garbed through the *middot* in the world of action as well. Of this scripture says: "I am first and I am last" (Is. 44:6) [meaning that God is present on the highest and lowest levels].
>
> When Korah saw that this generation would not enter the Land of Israel, he had no faith that Moses' Torah could become garbed in action. . . . Korah believed only in the world of speech . . . and not that it could be garbed in the world of action.[100]

This passage is of course squarely based on the Maggid's teaching just quoted. The *tsaddik* who can do everything with speech (Moses in the homily) is none other than the Maggid himself. Unlike his master the BeSHT, the Maggid was not known for performing miracles. He had assembled his remarkable circle of followers by the word, by the power of his teachings alone. But now that we are entering "the land," the realm of ordinary Jews who dwell in *artsiyyut*, those verbal teachings need to be garbed in action.[101] We need to give them actions they can see! Here with remarkable daring Levi Yitzhak identifies the refusal to garb speech in action with none other than Korah! Although he says this with less direct dichotomization than the Maggid himself employed, the audacity is hard to avoid. Quite clearly the two of them are on opposite sides of a great debate. Levi Yizhak wants to break forth out of the small circle that will be attracted by words alone. He wants to give the people a *tsaddik* who can act, who can reshape the will of heaven in response to their needs. But other voices, including that of the Master himself, say back to him: Your love for the people is leading you to excess. Beware lest you reach out so generously that you debase our precious words and thoughts, making us into wonder-workers rather than profound teachers. Levi Yizhak's reply? "Do not be like Korah, believing only in the word. We are entering the land now (i.e., "we are dealing with an earthy generation"); you have to dress the master's verbal Torah in clothing they can see and touch."[102]

IV

Not everyone in the Maggid's circle took an active position in this debate. If we look at the *M'eor 'Eynayim* of Menahem Nahum of Chernobyl, we find relatively less interest in the question of the *tsaddik* than we do in Levi Yizhak or in R. Elimelech. Of all the Maggid's circle, he is the one who stays closest to the essential message of the Ba'al Shem Tov: the divine presence is everywhere, needing to be served in every way, and our job is to cultivate awareness (*da'at*) and to uplift the fallen sparks. The task belongs to all Israel, and the *tsaddik*'s role is not easily distinguished from that of all Jews.[103] R. Nahum's son Mordecai of Chernobyl (1770–1837) did make much of the *tsaddik*, particular of the emerging dynastic model, but there is much less of that in the father. Other authors within the Maggid's circle who did not become *rebbes* with a following, including B. Benjamin of Zalozce, R. Joseph Bloch, and R. Uziel Meisels, have rather little to say about the *tsaddik* and the need for faith in his powers. The *Or ha-Me'ir* occupies a middle position on this question. There are places where *tsaddik* is the vehicle for the renewed receiving of Torah in each generation; it is specifically the *tsaddikim* of each generation to whom Torah is revealed.[104] But in other places *tsaddik* seems virtually interchangeable with *mi she-yesh bo mi-da'at kono*, "anyone with a bit of spiritual awareness."[105]

The writings of R. Menahem Mendel of Vitebsk and especially of R. Abraham Kalisker play a special role here, reflecting some delicate balance of the question of the *tsaddik* and his role. They left Russia for Erets Yisra'el in 1777, surely in part because of the severe persecution they had encountered.[106] Once in Tiberias, they had to give up on their original intent of spreading Hasidism far and wide. In effect they too had created, by force of geography, a small, intense hothouse of Hasidic piety. The question of the pace of popularization was no longer theirs. In his letters back to Russia, R. Mendel does ask for the continuing loyalty of his own disciples, though he seems to know that the next generation will turn elsewhere.[107] But in a letter to a *hasid* who asks him for a blessing to cure barrenness (a very common request for the prayers of *tsaddikim*), he demurs, making a very interesting distinction between the Ba'al Shem Tov, who could successfully intercede for such matters, and all other *tsaddikim*. Then he adds, very caustically: "There are some big-time *tsaddikim* in our generation who open their mouths and promise such things, but I am not one of them."[108] Whom might he have had in mind in that nasty remark? Perhaps R. Shelomo of Karlin, who was "eating his lunch" back home in Belorussia? In the writings of the Kalisker, there is a unique emphasis on *dibbuk haverim*,[109] the intimacy of spiritual peers, a phenomenon growing directly out of life in that sheltered but constricted community in the Holy Land. With no broader *oylem* to lead, the *tsaddik* was indeed teacher/exemplar to an intimate circle, perhaps in some ways parallel to that of R. Elimelech among his disciples.

The one key figure of the Maggid's circle with whom we have not yet dealt is their successor in the leadership of Hasidism in Belorussia, R. Shne'ur Zalman of Lyady.[110] As indicated above, he and Levi Yizhak were friends, both deeply committed to the spread of the Maggid's teachings and the creation of a popular movement. In fact it is fair to say that with the death of R. Aaron Karliner and the emigration of the Vitebsker and the Kalisker, they became the two key figures in Hasidism's spread. Their prominence in the anti-Hasidic polemics certainly gives the impression that it appeared that way to Hasidism's enemies throughout the 1780s and 1790s. But on the issues of the *tsaddik*, his nature and function, and the methods of popularization, there is a very deep divide between them.

R. Shne'ur Zalman's original published work, the *Tanya* or *Likkutey Amarim* (Slavuta, 1797),[111] differs from all other writings to emerge from the Maggid's circle. Neither a collection of Torah-cycle homilies nor a random collection of moral instructions (*hanhagot*), it is written as a systematic treatise. Its language is one of personal instruction, but its tone is also clear and categorical, laying out a position in a definitive manner. Its main section is a presentation of religious psychology, in the sense of *psyche* as "soul." Its primary subject matter includes the origins and parts of the soul and the nature and various aspects of worship and religious devotion. This treatise is subtitled *Sefer shel Beynonim*, The Book of Intermediates, meaning Jews who fit neither the category of *tsaddik* or *rasha'*, "wicked one." In expanding this category, those to whom the treatise is addressed, R. Shne'ur Zalman is quite restrictive in his definition of *tsaddik*.

There are two types of *tsaddikim*, according to the opening chapter of the Tanya, following an old Talmudic paradigm.[112] These are the complete or perfect *tsaddik (gamur)* and the imperfect one. The former is a person who has completely uprooted the evil urge from within himself, taking no pleasure whatever in material things, committed to the love of God alone. He has thus transformed the evil urge into good. The incomplete *tsaddik* has not yet achieved this sort of perfection, still retaining some degree of attraction to worldly things, while being completely without actual sin. R. Shne'ur Zalman's language is quite intense and graphic:

> The complete *tsaddik*, in whom evil has been transformed entirely into good, is therefore called "the *tsaddik* who bears goodness."[113] He has entirely removed the filth-soiled garments of evil. He deeply reviles the pleasures of this world, those things in which people take pleasure in fulfillment of their bodily desires alone, rather than for God's service.[114] They do so because they are attracted and influenced by the "shells" and the "other side."[115] The complete *tsaddik* absolutely despises all that derives from the "other side" because of his great love for God and the pleasure he takes in the holiness of that passionate "great love." "One opposite the other has God made" (Eccles. 7:14). "I despise them with utter hatred; they are become my enemies. Search me and know my heart" (Ps. 139:12–13). The greater one's love of God, the more utterly does one despise the "other side" and revile evil, since revulsion, like hatred, is the opposite of love.

> The incomplete *tsaddik*, who does not despise the "other side" entirely, does not feel utter revulsion toward evil. But if one's hatred and revul-

sion are not utter, some bit of love and pleasure [for evil] must remain. The filthy garments have not been entirely removed. . . . Therefore he is called an incomplete *tsaddik*.[116]

How far we are here from the forgiving and accepting world of Levi Yizhak! In a formal sense, of course, they could be reconciled. Levi Yizhak indeed "loves the sinner, not the sin." But the tone is entirely different. It is presumed that no reader of such a text could dare think of himself as a *tsaddik*, not even aspiring toward that goal. The purpose of the treatise is not to cultivate future *tsaddikim*, as we have read both the Maggid and R. Elimelech, but to allow the reader to strive toward the high goal of being a proper *beynoni*.[117] Presumably only the group's single leader would be described by the *hasidim* as a *tsaddik*. R. Shne'ur Zalman articulates a position that is surprisingly close to that of R. Jacob Joseph of Polonnoye's elitism of the *tsaddikim* as *anshey tsurah* (without his terminology), people of an essentially different nature than those around them.[118]

The *Tanya*, as is well known, was a great vehicle for the popularization of the Hasidic message. Its publication became a focal point during the third round of anti-Hasidic agitation, leading to the arrest of its author in 1798. But this is popularization of an entirely different sort. One cannot imagine Shne'ur Zalman's *tsaddik* reaching down to experience life on the level of the ordinary Jew in order to raise him up. If he did, such an act would bear no edge of dangerous spiritual adventurism, such as one might see in the writings of several of the Ukrainian masters. It could only be an act of *lèse majesté* on the part of a perfected being, a kind of Jewish *boddhisatva* coming down to help those in need. In setting forth what was to become the organizational structure of HaBaD, the *Tanya* is interested in cultivating serious *beynonim*. The average reader begins as much less than a *beynoni*, a *rasha' ve- tov lo*, a wicked person containing some bit of good. The leading disciples of Shne'ur Zalman were put forth as *beynonim*. These were to become the teachers and personal exemplars— indeed accessible models demonstrating an attainable spirituality—who were to spread the doctrine and build the movement. They represented the intermediate rung that we have seen described by R. Issachar Dov of Zloczow as "the eyes of the community." But in his view, along with that of R. Elimelech, these are "*tsaddikim*-in-training," the disciples who will eventually "graduate" and become *tsaddikim* in their own right, as indeed was to become the Galician model. Shne'ur Zalman does not seek this. He wants a doctrine that will work to transform the lives of *beynonim*, without allowing them to aspire to a higher status. But he also does not want to have them attached to *tsaddikim* simply by fealty, which becomes the HaBaD critique of most other Hasidism. Something has to be done for their own spiritual lives, but such a path needs to be taught by fellow *beynonim*. They now have in their hands a *Sefer shel Beynonim*, which is to be taught, recited, and imbibed—a sort of Hasidic catechism—in the spreading forth of what are to become the "wellsprings" of HaBaD Hasidism. For this purpose an exalted and uncompromising view of the *tsaddik* is well suited.[119]

Shne'ur Zalman would agree with the critics of Levi Yizhak that one should work to raise the masses upward rather than reach down to their level. Thus there is no proclamation at all in the *Tanya* of the *tsaddik*'s special powers or his ability to intervene for his followers' needs. He offers no miraculous "deeds" to attract the masses. In fact we are told[120] that R. Shne'ur Zalman disdained such an approach and refused to entertain requests for prayer regarding worldly matters.

The method of "uplifting" proposed by this highly educated and refined author, clearly a member of the Lithuanian-Jewish intellectual elite while at the same time a disciple of the Maggid, was by systematic inculcation of value-laden teachings. Intense study and recapitulation of large parts of the *Tanya*, along with instruction for meditation on its key themes, became the path of HaBaD.[121] In the context of the highly educated Lithuanian-style community of northern Belorussia, this method was highly successful in creating its own sort of mass movement. For those in the early years who were not attracted to, or satisfied by, this intellectual/contemplative approach, other alternatives such as the Hasidism of Karlin or Amdur, remained available. With the passage of time, HaBaD became so pervasive in the areas it dominated that it found room for Jews with a wide variety of intellectual abilities and aspirations.

The wide-ranging discussion of the *tsaddik*'s nature and powers that characterizes the writings of the Maggid's circle took place over a period of forty years, extending several decades beyond R. Dov Baer's departure from this world. Varied paths were chosen by the disciples, determined by factors of personality, cultural geography, and historical circumstance, including the effects of persecution. But the essential questions surrounding the identity of the *tsaddik*, the old-new holy man they first saw in the person of their master, and what his role was to be in the growth and popularization of the as yet undefined movement were first thrashed out "around the Maggid's table" during those formative years in Miedzyrzecz and Rovno. Reflections of that debate, which must have continued in the minds of those present for decades onward, are to be found throughout their writings, if one has the patience to read them with care and discernment.

NOTES

A Hebrew version of this essay appears in *Zion* 78, no. 1 (2013): 73–106. I am grateful to my research assistant, Ariel Mayse, for his help with footnoting this article.

1. The key study of this period is Ada Rapoport-Albert's "Hasidism after 1772: Structural Continuity and Change," in her edited volume *Hasidism Reappraised* (London: Littman Library, 1996), 76–140. Much that is said below agrees with and builds on her conclusions, although some demurrals will be noted.

2. This emerges clearly from a reading of the anti-Hasidic polemics and bans collected by Mordecai Wilensky in his two-volume *Hasidim u-Mitnaggedim* (Jerusalem: Mossad Bialik, 1970).

3. This, as Rapoport-Albert points out, was directly continuous from the situation during the BeSHT's lifetime and even before he was recognized as a key figure in the emerging proto-Hasidic movement. Important individuals, including Jacob Joseph of Polonnoye and the BeSHT's grandsons Ephraim of Sudylkow and Barukh of Miedzybozh, did not accept the Maggid as their master. Independent Hasidic circles also existed around Pinhas of Korzec and Yehiel Mikhl of Zloczow. I disagree with the extravagant claims made for Yehiel Mikhl of Zloczow and his circle in Mor Altschuler's *The Messianic Secret of Hasidism* (Leiden: Brill, 2005), a book that reads more like an advocacy brief for Yehiel Mikhl than a work of scholarship. Regarding the Pinhas of Korzec circle, see most recently Ron Margolin, *Mikdash Adam* (Jerusalem: Magnes, 2005), especially 409ff. and the classic treatment by my teacher A. J. Heschel in *'Aley 'Ayin, Sefer ha-Yovel le-Zalman Schocken* (Jerusalem, 1948–52), 213–44, translated in Heschel's *The Circle of the Ba'al Shem Tov* (Chicago: University of Chicago Press, 1985), 1–43.

4. The *books* of R. Jacob Joseph of Polonnoye were condemned and even burned in the second round of anti-Hasidic bans, but he personally does not seem to have been denounced or to have taken an active role in the disputes. This is the case, I am suggesting, because the move toward actively seeking to expand the movement came entirely from the Miedzyrzecz circle, of which he was not a part.

5. See Simon Dubnow, *Toledot ha-Hasidut* (Tel Aviv: Dvir, 1930–31), 165–69. Yochanan Petrovsky-Shtern suggests to me that these two provinces of Volhyn and Podolia were dominated by the Orthodox Church, unlike Eastern Galicia and Polesia, which were largely Catholic and Uniate. In the Uniate areas, the Jesuits were active, making for higher levels of literacy among townsmen. It would be interesting if the nature of Jewish intellectual life somehow reflected that of the general society. (I am grateful to Petrovsky-Shtern for several other notes as well.) Of course this was also an era when these regions were exporting the best of their rabbinic talent westward to communities including Frankfurt, Prague, and Mikoluv. A *herem* was issued in Brody as part of the 1772 bans, and copies of the *Toledot Ya'akov Yosef* were burned there after it appeared in 1780. However, Brody (technically across the border in Eastern Galicia) and Ostrog (where there was also a well-known Christian seminary) were towns with stronger rabbinates than most of the region, and perhaps that made the difference. It is noteworthy that the rabbi of Brody, R. Zvi Hirsch Bosko, did not sign the anti-Hasidic ban.

6. See Moshe Hallamish, "The Teachings of R. Menahem Mendel of Vitebsk," in *Hasidism Reappraised*, ed. Ada Rapoport-Albert (London: Vallentine Mitchell, 1997), 268–87; Mendel Piekarz, *Ha-Hanhagah ha-Hasidit* (Jerusalem: Mossad Bialik, 1999), 192–94, esp. n. 10; Rapoport-Albert, "Hasidism after 1772," 98–100.

7. For a foundational study of R. Abraham, see Ze'ev Gries, in his article "From Mythos to Ethos: Toward a Portrait of R. Abraham of Kalisk," *Umah ve-Toldoteyha* 2 (Jerusalem: Merkaz Zalman Shazar, 1984): 117–46 [Hebrew]. Further discussion of this important figure will continue below.

8. For the most recent study of this leader, see Immanuel Etkes, *Ba'al ha-Tanya: Rabbi Shne'ur Zalman mi-Li'ady ve-Reyshitah shel Hasidut Habad* (Jerusalem: Merkaz Zalman Shazar, 2011), and especially his extensive bibliography. Naftali Loewenthal's *Communicating the Infinite: The Emergence of the Habad School* (Chicago: University of Chicago Press, 1990) also remains central.

9. See Wolf Z. Rabinowitsch, *Ha-Hasidut ha-Lita'it me-Reshitah ve-ad Yameynu* (Jerusalem: Mossad Bialik, 1961). Reprinted in English as *Lithuanian Hasidism*, trans. M. B. Dagut (New York: Schocken, 1971).

10. In 1781 Rabbi Avraham Katzenellenbogen of Brest-Litovsk referred to Levi Yizhak as *resh biryoney shelahem*, "their chief thug." A critical study of Levi Yizhak and his role in the dissemination of Hasidism is a desideratum of Hasidic scholarship. Samuel Dresner's *Levi Yitzhak of Berdichev: Portrait of a Hasidic Master* (New York: Hartmore House, 1974) has some important footnotes but hovers too much between biography and hagiography. My student Or N. Rose is writing a doctoral dissertation on the theme of leadership in Kedushat Levi. See also my entry "Levi Yitshak of Barditshev" in the YIVO *Encyclopedia* (2009). In saying that he is uniquely the object of the bans, I do not mean to ignore the attacks on others in the works of David of Makow, for example. But

these were more after-the-fact denunciations than testimony of outright persecutions.

11. On Chernobyl, see my introduction to Menahem Nahum of Chernobyl, *Upright Practices: The Light of the Eyes* (New York: Paulist Press, 1982), and Gad Sagiv, "The Chernobyl Hasidic Dynasty: Its History and Thought from the Beginning till the Eve of the First World War" (PhD diss., Tel Aviv University, 2009) [Hebrew]. Full discussion of the emergence of dynastic leadership in Hasidism goes beyond the scope of this essay. I would suggest, however, that the role of Barukh of Miedzybozh in creating that pattern has to be underscored. By the mid-1790s his own nephew Nahman of Bratslav saw Barukh as embodying the corruption of Hasidism, proclaiming himself a *tsaddik* primarily because of family descent. He sought to assert singular leadership of the movement as *tsaddik ha-dor*, a claim at leadership based on heredity, probably (and appropriately) the first such claim within the Hasidic camp. See the sources, oral as well as written, assembled by R. Margaliot in *Makor Barukh* (Zamoszcz, 1931), chaps. 1, 5, and 9. It is likely that this scion of the BeSHT inspired the Chernobyler's son and others to do the same. See the discussion by Rapoport-Albert, "Hasidism after 1772," 109ff. While it is true that we do not have an early or authentic collection of teachings by R. Barukh, the accounts of his self-aggrandizing behavior totally fit the personality type described in the sources, a prototype for the later R. Israel of Ruzhin, ironically a descendent of the Maggid.

12. His is the only name of a son listed along with his father's (indicating that both are alive and active) in R. Aaron Auerbach's list of Hasidic leaders, printed in R. David of Makow's *Shever Posh'im*. See Wilensky, *Hasidim u-Mitnaggedim*, 2:101 and Sagiv, "The Chernobyl Hasidic Dynasty," 175.

13. For an analysis of R. Elimelech's life and teachings, see Gedalya Nig'al's excellent introduction to his edition of *No'am Elimelech* (Jerusalem, 1978). See also Louis Jacobs, "The Doctrine of the Zaddik in Elimelech of Lizansk" in his *Their Heads in Heaven: Unfamiliar Aspects of Hasidism* (London: Vallentine Mitchell, 2005), 73–89, and Rivka Schatz-Uffenheimer, "On the Essence of the Zaddik in Hasidism," *Molad* 144–45 (1960): 365–68 [Hebrew].

14. Arthur Green, "Typologies of Leadership and the Hasidic Zaddiq," *Jewish Spirituality: From the Sixteenth-Century Revival to the Present* (New York: Crossroad, 1987), 2:127–56; reprinted in Hebrew in *Tsadik va-Edah* (Jerusalem: Merkaz Zalman Shazar, 2001), 422–44; Arthur Green, "The *Zaddiq* as *Axis Mundi* in Later Judaism," *Journal of the American Academy of Religion* 45, no. 3 (1977): 327–47. [Both of these essays are included in the present volume.]

15. B. Yoma 38b.

16. For some exceptions to this seemingly obvious limitation, see sources quoted by Piekarz, *Ha-Hanhagah ha-Hasidit*, 41f. Of course, Rabbi Simeon ben Yohai had already described himself in this way in the second century: Genesis Rabbah 35:2, quoted in Green, "*Zaddiq* as *Axis Mundi*," 332. An interesting justifica-

tion for self-praise by the *tsaddik* is found in a passage attributed to R. Nahum of Chernobyl in *Siftey Tsaddikim*, 62d–63a. He is like a peddler calling his wares— "Perfume! Needles! Pins!" etc. The *tsaddik* offers the opportunity to return from sin, but sinners will be embarrassed to come to him, thus publicly admitting their guilt. He therefore calls out a variety of wares—"I heal illness! I cure barrenness! I can improve your love life! I can make your plants grow!"—so that sinners can come to the *tsaddik* without others knowing that they are really coming to repent. *Siftey Tsaddikim* is a late-published work (Lviv, 1864), but seems to have been composed in the 1820s and includes much interesting early material.

17. Including a play on *hasidim* and *hashudim*, one that works especially well for *Litvak* Hebrew pronunciation.

18. This is the general impression one takes away from Ada Rapoport-Albert's early essay "God and the Zaddik as Two Focal Points of Hasidic Worship," *History of Religions* 18:4 (1979): 296–325. Reprinted in G. Hundert, ed., *Essential Papers on Hasidism* (New York: New York University Press, 1991), 299–329. See esp. 314–16 in the Hundert edition.

19. For a fine summary of the ways in which the BeSHT was "my teacher" to both the *Toledot* and the Maggid, see Haviva Pedaya, "The Ba'al Shem Tov, R. Jacob Joseph of Polonoy, and the Maggid of Miedzyrzecz: Guidelines toward a Religious Typology," *Da'at* 45 (2000): 25–27 [Hebrew]. Aspects of her views will be discussed below.

20. R. Jacob Joseph's memory was not perfect, however. Scholars have shown that he sometimes attributes the same sayings to the BeSHT and to other figures.

21. For a translation, see Moshe Rosman, *The Founder of Hasidism: A Quest for the Historical Ba'al Shem Tov* (Berkeley: University of California Press, 1996), 114–15.

22. *Toledot, va-ethanan* (Korzec, 1780), 169c; the term is based on Zohar 3:253a.

23. See *Toledot, va-yakhel*, 67b (commenting on Num. 11:29): "It was Moses' intent that all Israel attain the same rung he had reached. This is not impossible, since a person has the free choice to purify his corporeal self until he reaches the rung and status of Moses." Also quoted in Dresner, *The Zaddik: The Doctrine of the Zaddik According to the Writings of Rabbi Yaakov Yosef of Polnoy* (New York: Schocken Books, 1974), 276n23.

24. Zohar 1:31a, based on an alleged (but unknown) Targum to 1 Chron. 29:12. Cf. Green, "*Zaddiq* as *Axis Mundi*," 338n14.

25. B. Ta'anit 10a; Zohar 3:216b.

26. See, inter alia, *Ben Porat Yosef* (Warsaw, 1883; henceforth, BPY), *Va-Yehi* 63b, 80b, etc.; Green, "Typologies," 131–32. See discussion by Moshe Idel in his *Ben: Sonship and Jewish Mysticism* (New York: Continuum, 2007), 531–39.

27. On the earlier history of *tsaddik* as both "vessel" and "pipe," see Idel, *Hasidism: Between Ecstasy and Magic* (Albany: SUNY Press, 1995), 189–207. The metaphor of *tsaddik* as throne immediately calls to mind the old rabbinic saying, "The patriarchs themselves are the [divine] chariot" (Bereshit Rabbah 82:7) as well

as Idel's discussion of the "Hermetic" model of spiritual influence in the world, first in *Kabbalah: New Perspectives* (New Haven: Yale University Press, 1988), 40, and frequently in his later writings.

28. *Ben Porat Yosef, va-yigash*; also cited in Dresner, 280n73.

29. *Toledot, emor*, 104b/c; Dresner, 280n73.

30. *Toledot, va-yetse*, 22c–d. Ron Margolin discusses this mutuality at some length in *Mikdash Adam*, 398ff.

31. B. Mo'ed Katan 16b; cited in *Toledot, mishpatim* 56b–c.

32. Immanuel Etkes has emphasized that R. Israel BeSHT was known as a *ba'al shem* who took great interest in the fate of Jewish communities and of Jewry altogether, not just in the affairs of specific "clients." See Etkes, *The Besht: Magician, Mystic, and Leader*, trans. Saadya Sternberg (Waltham MA: Brandeis University Press, 2005), 97–112. Ze'ev Gries has rightly questioned the centrality of the BeSHT's letter in the historical development of Hasidism, compared to the very central role given to it in modern scholarship. See his "The Historic Image of the BeSHT," *Kabbalah* 5 (2000): 411–46, 420 [Hebrew].

33. On *ba'aley shem* and their role, see Etkes, "The Place of Magic and Ba'aley Shem in Ashkenazic Society in the Seventeenth and Eighteenth Centuries" [Hebrew], *Zion* 60 (1995): 69–104 (mostly translated as chapter 1 of his book cited in the preceding note) and the article by Pedaya mentioned in n. 19 above.

34. A keen observer of Polish Jewish life like Dov Baer Birkenthal of Bolechow already noted that "the *ba'aley shem* have changed their name to *hasidim*." See Gershon Hundert in *AJS Review* 33:2 (2009): 258. My thanks to Dr. Hundert for this reference.

35. A special place in this transition may belong to the story of the BeSHT's use of amulets containing only his own name. See the tale connected with R. Isaac of Drohobycz in *Zikkaron la-Rishonim* (Piotrkow, 1912), cited by Abraham Joshua Heschel, *The Circle of the Ba'al Shem Tov*, 167–70. Another example of the BeSHT's own name bearing magical power is found in *Shivhey ha-BeSHT*, ed. Avraham Rubenstein (Jerusalem: Rubin Mass, 1991), 232–34; translated in Dan Ben-Amos and Jerome R. Mintz, *In Praise of the Ba'al Shem Tov* (Bloomington: Indiana University Press, 1970), 180–81. It may be, however, that these accounts are there to indicate the BeSHT's power as a magician rather than a transition from magician to *tsaddik*.

36. This term had been used to identify the BeSHT in the Polish tax records in Miedzybozh. See Rosman, *Founder of Hasidism*, 159–70. Of course, some early Hasidic figures may have been called *mekubbal* on title pages or in *haskamot*, but such designations are not to be taken too seriously.

37. Of course, such transitions do not take place overnight. In the Maggid himself one can still see some elements of the *ba'al shem*'s impersonal magic present in the *tsaddik*. See, for example, *Maggid Devarav Le-Ya'akov* (Jerusalem: Magnes Press, 1976; henceforth, MDL), 30–31. For a Kabbalist close to the Maggid's cir-

cle, see the *Seraf Peri 'Ets Hayyim* by R. Moshe of Dolina (Chernovtsy, 1866). Though printed relatively late, some of the *haskamot* seem to indicate that the book was prepared for publication much earlier. This work stands directly within the Lurianic tradition, unlike the author's briefer *Divrey Moshe*, a more typically Hasidic volume, showing that the two genres were clearly distinguishable, even by a single author.

38. Others include *Likkutim Yekarim*, edited by R. Meshullam Feibush Heller of Zbarasz (1796), *Kitvey Kodesh* (1862), and *Shemu'ah Tovah* (1938). See the discussion by Rivka Schatz-Uffenheimer in the introduction to her edition of *Maggid Devarav le-Ya'akov*. Exactly what in these later collections represents the thought of Dov Baer and what is drawn from other sources is exceedingly difficult to determine. There are many parallels between *Likkutim Yekarim*, a work that really belongs to the literature of *hanhagot*, and *Tsava'at RYVaSH*, where the teachings are attributed to the BeSHT. This is only one of many complexities examined by Ze'ev Gries in his *Sifrut ha-Hanhagot* (Jerusalem: Mossad Bialik, 1990), esp. 103–230. Levi Yizhak's precise role in editing the Maggid's writings is less than fully established.

39. See Ben-Amos and Mintz, *In Praise of the Baal Shem Tov*, 61–70, 81–84. For Dresner's slightly different accounting of this rivalry and transition, see *The Zaddik*, 59–62. See also the memoir of Shelomo of Sadegora quoted from manuscript by Heschel in *The Circle of the Ba'al Shem Tov*, 79–80n72.

40. Haviva Pedaya has made an important contribution to understanding the relationship between the BeSHT and his disciples. See n. 19 above. She suggests that aspects of the mystical/ecstatic model of leadership that were essential and natural parts of the BeSHT's personality were imitated by his disciples as a program toward which they aspired but which they did not necessarily fulfill. While we are told in Shelomo Lutzker's introduction to *Maggid Devaraw le-Ya'akov* that the BeSHT taught the Maggid certain secrets of his own supernatural praxis, it seems clear that these were not the heart of the Maggid's teaching and were not what he chose to pass on to his own disciples. I am suggesting that this divergence in spiritual temperaments asserted itself, especially after the master's death, and that the Maggid forged his own path. Hasidism as it emerged afterward is very much an amalgam of the two.

41. As quoted above in n. 26.

42. This seems to be the case based on the early sources. David Assaf, *Derekh ha-Malkhut* (Jerusalem: Shazar Centre, 1997), 49, agrees. I am thus surprised to note that Israel Berger's *'Eser Orot* (n.p., 1907), 25, quotes the *Igra de-Pirka* of Zevi Elimelech of Dynow as referring to the Maggid's children, in the plural.

43. Of course the *peshat* meaning of *le-'olam* is "forever." All following translations of biblical verses are contextual.

44. Again, a total distortion of the verse's original meaning, ignoring the construct state of *retson* and reading it as the object of the sentence.

45. MDL #7; the final line is from Bereshit Rabbah 8:7.

46. The singular form *'olam* here, instead of the plural *'olamot*, better fitting the theological reading, makes that entirely clear. *Oylem* in Yiddish means "the public" or "the community," and *di tsadikim viln firn dem oylem* was surely the Yiddish original as spoken. This text also appears at the beginning of Ron Margolin's very important chapter on "The Zaddik in Early Hasidism," in *Mikdash Adam,* 382. Unfortunately, he too quickly accepts Rivka Schatz-Uffenheimer's conclusion that the text is to be read on a metaphysical, not a social, level. These preachers were masters of making their point on more than one level at once.

47. A late-recorded tradition reports that the Maggid regretted having become a public figure and was told that it was a punishment for a transgression he had committed. See Berger, *'Eser Orot,* 25, #10.

48. Y. Berger, *'Eser Orot,* 35. Berger's account of the meeting, including the attempted counter-*herem*, and Levi Yizhak's central role in it, is most interesting. He does not offer a source for it. I am reading the Maggid's words as applying more broadly than is reported by Berger. Of course, *ibbadetem et ha-rosh shelakhem* is also a translation of the oral Yiddish *ir hot farloiren eyer kop!* or "you've gone mad!" That might support the narrower reading.

49. MDL #24.

50. See MDL #26, 60, 127. See also MDL #1, quoted by Margolin, *Mikdash Adam,* 383. This seems to follow what is reported to be the BeSHT's reading of Psalm 121:5: "Y-H-W-H is your shadow." Cf. Ephraim of Sudylkow, *Degel Mahaneh Ephraim, Shabbat Shuva* (Jerusalem, 1963), 267b.

51. He has in mind the elected Polish monarchy, where kings were chosen by the powerful nobility.

52. MDL #185, following the manuscript version in Schatz-Uffenheimer's edition.

53. See Joseph Weiss, "The Great Maggid's Theory of Contemplative Magic," *Hebrew Union College Annual* 31 (1960): 137–47; Joseph Weiss, "The Saddik—Altering the Divine Will," *Studies in Eastern European Jewish Mysticism and Hasidism* (London: Littman Library of Jewish Civilization, 1997), 183–93. Weiss's views on this subject are taken up in a new and richly comparative context by Jonathan Garb in his *Shamanic Trance in Modern Kabbalah* (Chicago: University of Chicago Press, 2011). I am generally sympathetic to his approach, which sees the *tsaddik's* ascent to the state of *gadlut* as a power-bearing shamanic experience.

54. There is precedent in pre-Hasidic sources for the notion that the recipients of divine bounty may shape and direct divine blessing. However, the statement that divine will *itself* is created by humans seems to step beyond what had been claimed previously.

55. *Kedushat Levi, kedushat Purim* 5, ed. Michael Aryeh Rand (Ashdod, 2005), 366. This text would fit well into what R. Schatz-Uffenheimer defined as "quietism." But it may in fact be just the opposite, where attributing the power to heaven in fact masks an extreme theurgic activism.

56. *Me'or 'Eynayim, derush le-hanukkah* (Ashdod, 2008), 109.

57. See Margolin's perceptive note on this in *Mikdash Adam,* 388n45.

58. See Joseph Weiss, "The Kavvanoth of Prayer in Early Hasidism," in *Studies,* 69–94; Schatz-Uffenheimer, *Hasidism as Mysticism* (Princeton: Princeton University Press, 1993), 215–41. For a different perspective on this question, see Menachem Kallus, "The Relation of the Baal Shem Tov to the Practice of Lurianic Kavvanot in Light of His Comments on the Siddur Rashkov," *Kabbalah* 2 (1997), 151–68. Rapoport-Albert uses the rejection of *kavvanot* as evidence of the new charismatic elite that Hasidism sought to put in place of the former rabbinic and Kabbalistic elites. See "God and the Zaddik" in Hundert, *Essential Papers,* 316. But the very text she quotes, the Maggid's well-known admonition that "breaking the heart opens [the door] to everything" proves just the opposite. Surely the ability to "break the heart" does not belong only to a charismatic elite! Again, I am not claiming that either magical or Lurianic praxis disappears entirely or overnight. Nothing could be further from the truth. But within this circle, especially for its key authors, a new ideal is being forged that structurally diminishes the importance of both.

59. MDL #183, based on Bereshit Rabbah 87:8.

60. This distinction between belief in the *tsaddik's* powers and the active "marketing" of such belief is not made by Margolin (*Mikdash Adam,* 381) and should not be overlooked.

61. See note 9 above.

62. See Wilensky, *Hasidim u-Mitnaggedim,* 1:64–65; Rabinowitsch, *Lithuanian Hasidism,* 14–15.

63. For Maimon's report on his visit to a Hasidic "sect," see *Solomon Maimon: An Autobiography,* trans. J. Clark Murray (Urbana: University of Illinois Press, 2001), 151–75. See also David Assaf's discussion in "The Teachings of Dov Ber the Maggid of Mezritch in Solomon Maimon's Autobiography," *Zion* 71 (2006): 99–101 [Hebrew].

64. The volume called *Bet Aharon* (Brody, 1875) is made mostly of teachings by his grandson, Aaron II of Karlin-Stolin; only occasionally is a fragment quoted in the name of Aaron I (*ha-gadol*).

65. Sayings, teachings, and tales of R. Shelomo were collected in *Shema' Shelomo* (1928; Jerusalem, 1974).

66. See the discussion by M. Nadav, "Pinsk and Karlin between Hasidism and Its Opposition," *Zion* 34 (1969): 98–108.

67. Wilensky, *Hasidim u-Mitnaggedim,* 1:40–41, 63–65.

68. The letter was written in 1805 or 1806. See Tsevi Hillman, *Igrot Ba'al ha-Tanya* (Jerusalem, 1953), #103, 175, and 177, and discussion by Rapoport-Albert, *Hasidism after 1772,* 119, as well as by Ze'ev Gries, "From Mythos to Ethos," 117–46. The practice of performing headstands before the ark is already mentioned in the *haramot* of 1772, though without linkage to any particular per-

son. In some of the *haramot* the somersaults were interpreted as a form of idolatrous practice derived from the worship of Pe'or, whose service, according to the Talmud, included defecating in his presence! Ze'ev Gries has argued that since Shne'ur Zalman is the only source linking the Kalisker with this behavior and that the document doing so was a letter written in the heat of their conflict, the linkage should be considered suspect. I tend to doubt that Shne'ur Zalman would have dared to make up this accusation entirely, including the account of the Kalisker's fear of being in the Maggid's presence at the Rovno meeting, while there were still others alive (including Levi Yizhak) who had been there and knew the truth. Of course, there may be exaggeration, but not fabrication, as in some of the later HaBaD accounts discussed by Rapoport-Albert and other.

69. See Rabinowitsch, *Lithuanian Hasidism*, 14 and note ad loc., as well as Hayyim Lieberman, "The Rabbinical Positions of R. Levi Yitzhak of Berditchev," *Ohel RaHeL* (Brooklyn: Empire Press, 1980), 66–69 (Hebrew). Although Pinsk is in Polesia, adjacent to northern Ukraine, politically and culturally it was identified as part of greater "Lithuania." Pinsk was one of the five major communities to receive the original documents of the Vilna *herem* in 1772, but its rabbinate did not sign on to them. On the complicated history of the Pinsk community's changing attitudes toward Hasidism, see M. Nadav, as cited in note 66 above.

70. Yohanan Petrovsky-Shtern, "The Drama of Berdichev: Levi Yitshak and His Town," *Polin* 17 (Oxford: Littman Library of Jewish Civilization, 2004), 83–95.

71. *Kedushat Levi* on Hanukkah and Purim was published during the author's lifetime in Slawuta, 1798.

72. For a few examples, see *Kedushat Levi ha-Shalem* (Jerusalem, 1973; henceforth KLS), 9b, 39b, 131a, 134a, 151a, 306b. The index in the new Rand edition points out that this passage is his single most quoted text from all of rabbinic literature!

73. Of course, the angels were on their way to destroy Sodom, not "Israel." The biblical Abraham does not speak to God in defense of *Israel*, who do not yet exist in his day, but rather of *anshey Sedom* (Might we dare call them "Palestinians?"). Levi Yizhak conveniently ignores this fact.

74. KLS, 237b. See also the teaching quoted from "the rabbi of Zelechow" by R. Uziel Meisels in *Tif'eret Uziel* (Brooklyn: Imrey Shefer, 2003), *Yitro*. RLY was called "Rabbi of Zelechow" through his Pinsk period, but after 1785 he was generally known as rabbi of Berdyczow. R. Uziel is thus likely quoting an early teaching, but one in which this focus on humanity and its needs is already fully developed. On RLY's attraction to the parental metaphor, see inter alia KLS 269a, the call to be judged on Rosh ha-Shanah by God only in His role as parent.

75. KLS, 129b. Cf. Levi Yizhak's very important discussion of Abraham and Melchizedek, KLS, 15b ff.

76. For a parallel view by R. Elimelech, see *No'am Elimelekh* on Num. 7:9 (ed. Nig'al, p. 376). Saul is not fit to remain king over Israel because he is "from shoulder up above all the people" (1 Sam. 9:2), too much a moral perfectionist to be a leader.

77. See the discussion of R. Ze'ev Wolf by M. Piekarz in *Ha-Hanhagah ha-Hasidit*, 94ff. and sources quoted in n. 44a.

78. *Or ha-Meir* (Jerualem, 1995), *bereshit*, 6b. See also *Hukkat* 111b and 115b. It is worth noting here that the phrase *lomar Torah (zogn toire)* seems to be a unique Hasidic expression. See two other places where the *Or ha-Me'ir* uses it, quoted by Piekarz, *Ha-Hanhagah ha-Hasidit*, 95. I am suggesting that *a rebbe zogt toire; a rov zogt a vort oder a dvar toire;* I do not know whether Yiddish philologists have noted this distinction.

79. The *middot* are the seven lower *sefirot*, reread in Hasidism as the essential moral qualities that need to be uplifted. This is an especially predominant theme in the *Or ha-Me'ir* and the *Me'or 'Eynayim,* as it is in the writings of R. Pinhas of Korzec and his circle.

80. *Or ha-Me'ir, va-yetse,* 51b–52a.

81. He is forgiving toward the *tsaddikim* as well. See his striking comment on *homer ba-kodesh* in KLS, 306, where he justifies the *tsaddik*'s attraction to money. In the course of uplifting ordinary Jews, some of their material thoughts cleave to the *tsaddik*, who is himself *kodesh*.

82. KLS, 344b–345b. On these particular "two types of *tsaddikim*," see also KLS, 304b.

83. R. Elimelech's most serious involvement in the battle with the *mitnaggedim* comes in the form of an impassioned defense of Levi Yizhak in a letter signed by his son but extensively quoting the father. See the text in Wilensky, *Hasidim u-Mitnaggedim,* 1:169–76.

84. *No'am Elimelech, Balak,* ed. Nig'al, 447f.

85. See Rivka Schatz-Uffenheimer, "On the Essence of the Zaddik in Hasidism," *Molad* 144–45 (1960): 365–68 [Hebrew].

86. It is worth recalling that Elimelech was considerably older than Levi Yizhak. If we assume a debate about how or whether to expand the movement that took place in c. 1765, Levi Yizhak was twenty-five years old and Elimelech was forty-eight; this difference may explain a lot.

87. For this understanding of the *No'am Elimelech* I am indebted to conversations with my student Rabbi Ebn Leader. This reading diverges from the usual understandings of the *No'am Elimelech,* including those of Schatz-Uffenheimer and Piekarz, *Ha-Hanhagah ha-Hasidit,* 148.

88. See, for example, *No'am Elimelech va-yera* to Genesis18:4 (ed. Nig'al 44–45), where he refers to the disciples around his table as *tsaddikim*. This continues the view of the Maggid, seen above, demonstrating clearly that R. Elimelech is training them for that role and, in good educational fashion, is already treating them as "colleagues."

89. A good selection of teachings on the tsaddik, his prayer, and his powers, can be found in *Noʼam Elimelech, va-yehi*. In order to pray effectively for worldly blessings for his flock, he needs to be completely detached from worldly things. See Nigʼal, 151.

90. When I say "at his best," I leave room for the fact that there are passages in the book, especially when read outside the disciples' circle, that may have led in a different direction. Certainly in later Hasidism R. Elimelech was read, as suggested by n. 82 above.

91. Via R. Shmelke. He seems to have played an important intermediary role in constituting the Miedzyrzec circle. R. Jacob Isaac, the future seer of Lublin, also came through him.

92. See the biographical note *Toledot Rabbenu* on 145–46 of the Jerusalem 1970 edition of *Mevasser Tsedek*.

93. He has in mind the ayin teachings of the Maggid, taking everything back to its roots in God prior to individuation, in order to effect change.

94. See *Likkutey Torah* (Jerusalem, 1988), hukkat, 220. Cf. *Ets Hayyim*, II 32:6.

95. *Mevasser Tsedek* (Jerusalem, 1970), 112b–113a.

96. Juxtapose this text especially with Levi Yizhak on Korah, to be quoted below.

97. See, for example, the fierce comment of R. Benjamin of Zalosce: "The flatterers among the *tsaddikim* who do not reprove people should tremble, more than just fearing, for they will be punished first . . . the *tsaddik* who does not reprove will not only be caught up in the sins of the generation, but will be punished in Hell for them." *Torey Zahav*, 155a–b, as quoted by Piekarz, *Ha-Hanhagah ha-Hasidit*, 107. What would he say to Levi Yizhak?

98. The dangers of forgetting Torah and aids to prevent such forgetting are an ancient part of Jewish esoteric lore, reaching back into the *merkavah* era.

99. It is quoted by R. Zvi Hirsch of Nadworno in his *Tsemah ha-Shem Li-Tsevi* ad loc, from the *haʼatakot*, pre-publication manuscripts of the Maggid's writings that were in his possession.

100. KLS, 341.

101. In fact this discussion of *artsiyyut* and *dor ha-arets* may be hiding another Hebrew/Yiddish locution that could not be spoken here. ʻAm ha-arets in both languages means "an ignorant person," in somewhat insulting terms. "What do we need to do to convince these *amaratsim* of our message?" may be the unuttered question here.

102. For another example of the Maggid's position with regard to leadership and outreach, see *Or Torah, shemot* on Ex. 4:27 (=mdl, ed. Schatz #62). Moses is unable to redeem Israel from Egypt on his own because he is all hesed, drawn from the water (=hesed), as his name indicates. He needs the *tsimtsum* of Aaron to balance him. The Maggid is saying something about leadership here, probably addressed to Levi Yizhak or the "Levi Yizhak faction" among his disciples. "If you want to redeem people from the Egypt of *galut ha-daʼat* and

galut ha-middot in which Jews are now exiled, you can't do it by love alone."
We have already seen how Levi Yizhak would disagree with such an approach.

103. Gad Sagiv agrees with this view. See Sagiv, "The Chernobyl Hasidic Dynasty," 375.

104. Piekarz, *Ha-Hanhagah ha-Hasidit*, 100.

105. Piekarz, *Ha-Hanhagah ha-Hasidit*, 31.

106. The 1777 ʿaliyah has been extensively treated by scholars. For bibliography, see David Assaf in "The Rumor was Spread that the Messiah has Already Come," *Zion* 61 (1996): 318ff. The decision to emigrate and settle in the Holy Land was seen by earlier scholars of Hasidism as a response to the resistance to Hasidism in Lithuania and Belorussia. See Dubnov, *Toledot ha-Hasidut* (Tel Aviv: Dvir, 1931), 133–37; Rabinowitsch, Lithuanian Hasidism, 26. More recent discussion by Raya Haran and David Assaf has focused on the positive reasons for their decision, rather than the rather obvious reality that they were in flight from severe persecution. Raya Haran ascribes the ʿaliyah as a quest for attainment of higher spiritual status in the Holy Land. She bases her view on the letters sent home by both R. Mendel and R. Abraham. Such documents, however, cannot be taken entirely at face value. They would naturally choose to highlight the positive and spiritual, rather than admitting to their followers that they had fled their enemies. Assaf, while offering a nod to a more balanced view, deals primarily with the possible influence of a messianic prediction as a motivator of their ʿaliyah. But surely the difficult decision to emigrate was motivated by a push as well as a pull, something one would hardly expect to find detailed in the documents. See Haran in *Cathedra* 76 (1995): 77–95 and Assaf in *Zion* 62, no. 3 (1997): 283–88.

107. See his letters, collected by Y. Barnai in *Igrot Hasidim me-Erets Yisraʾel* (Jerusalem, 1980), 92ff., 108. This whole school is newly discussed in the opening section of Immanuel Etkes's *Baʾal ha-Tanya*.

108. *Avot ha-Hasidut be-Erets Yisraʾel* (Jerusalem, 1987), letter 7, 13a.

109. See Joseph Weiss, "R. Abraham Kalisker's Concept of Communion with God and Men," in Studies, 155–69; Raya Haran, "The Teachings of R. Abraham of Kalisk: The Path of Devekut as an Inheritance of Those Who Immigrated to Israel," Tarbiz 65, no. 4 (1996/97), 517–41.

110. I am grateful to Naftali Loewenthal for several suggestions regarding the following paragraphs.

111. There is a vast literature, both by HaBaD devotees and by critical scholars, around the Tanya. See sources cited by *Etkes in Baʾal ha-Tanya*. On the specific theme of leadership, see M. Hallamish, "*Yahasey Tsaddik ve-ʿEdah be-Mishnat R. Shneʾr Zalman me-Liadi*," in Hevrah ve-Historiyyah, ed. Y. Cohen (Jerusalem, 1980), and E. Etkes, "Rabbi Shneʾr Zalman of Lyady as a Hassidic Leader," Zion 50 (1985): 321–54.

112. B. Berakhot 7a.

113. This is a complete distortion of the passage's original meaning, which has to do with theodicy. Cf. ibid.

114. That is, he recognizes that the ideal is not celibacy, but engagement in physical—notably sexual—activity exclusively as an act of devotion to God.

115. Kabbalistic terms for the cosmic forces of evil.

116. *Likkutey Amarim—Tanya* (Brooklyn: Kehot Publication Society, 1983), chap. 10.

117. I could thus not imagine Shne'ur Zalman making a statement like that quoted from R. Elimelech in n. 83 above.

118. I would thus restrict Margolin's comment (*Mikdash Adam*, 390) that the Maggid's disciples followed R. Jacob Joseph toward an elistist view of the tsaddik, rather than the Maggid's more "egalitarian" model. I find this most applicable to R. Shne'ur Zalman. At least Levi Yizhak and Elimelech believe that one may strive successfully to become a tsaddik, something I do not see in R. Jacob Joseph or R. Shne'ur Zalman. A very slight possible bridge between *beynoni* and *tsaddik* is found in *Tanya*, chap. 14. A *beynoni* who turns utterly from evil and learns to despise the things of this world quite thoroughly might attract the soul of a departed tsaddik to "impregnate" him, that is, to dwell within him, giving him some glimmer of the *tsaddik's* light.

119. Of course one may also say that this was the appropriate strategy for establishing and preserving a single vast HaBaD "empire," rather than a welter of new spiritual fiefdoms, as happened in the Ukraine and Galicia. Could it be that R. Shne'ur Zalman was noticing the parallel between the failed Polish state, crippled by too many independent authorities, and the pattern that was emerging in Ukrainian and Galician Hasidism? He and his descendants became well-known admirers of the unified and bureaucratized Russian autocracy. Was the centralization of power somehow a part of what he learned from the czar's conduct of his empire?

120. Etkes, *Ba'al ha-Tanya*, 48–56. quoting from R. Shne'ur Zalman's extant letters and Heilman's Bet Rabbi.

121. See Loewenthal, Communicating the Infinite, esp. 47–51.

9

Typologies of Leadership and the Hasidic *Zaddiq*

The Question of Leadership

No issue was more central to the emerging Hasidic communities of the late eighteenth century than that of leadership.[1] Conceived in the midst of both a Jewish community and a larger Polish society beset by crises of public office, the phenomenon that was to be called Hasidism bore at its very heart an image of master and disciples, bound together by bonds at once esoteric and personal, an image that stood out in relief against those corruptions of leadership that many had come to revile. It was in fact participation in such a relationship that defined one's sense of belonging to the Hasidic movement, at least in its heyday. For that movement the term *hasid* (unlike all of its many previous usages) implies the question: "*Hasid* of whom?" The term here functionally means "disciple" in addition to the usual and literal "pious one" or "lover of God." The disciple stood in relation to the rebbe, or master, a relationship that is the subject of much discussion in both the early theoretical literature of Hasidism and the later tales.[2]

The complex of ideas, distinctive religious practices, and patterns of lifestyle that were to make up the nascent movement was first taught by a generation of rabbis and preachers in the Ukraine, a group much influenced by earlier mystical (including messianic) teachings and marked by a strong sense of alienation from the contemporary leadership of the Jewish communities. That leadership is frequently caricatured in the preaching of the age, Hasidic and non-Hasidic alike. Both rabbis and lay leaders were held up to derision, the former for the twin sins of pride and self-distancing from the community, the latter for their high-handedness in the conduct of community affairs. These same homilists, especially those outside the Hasidic camp, also viewed the common folk of their times as extraordinarily sinful, a generation appropriate to, if not responsible for, its woeful leadership. Accurate or not, it was the perception of many thinking Jews in mid-eighteenth-century Poland that they lived in the most awfully sin-ridden of times, a time when extremes of purgation were required to return Israel to the pious norms of old.[3]

The first published work of Hasidism, the *Toledot Ya'aqov Yosef*, is much concerned with these questions.[4] Alternatively blaming flock and shepherds for leading one another down the path toward sin, it is Jacob Joseph of Polonnoye who first crystallizes the question of leadership as a central preoccupation of Hasidic thought. Though himself a rabbi serving in various distinguished communities,[5] he viewed himself as a disciple of one who had no rabbinic title or ordination, a rather unusual situation in so authority-centered a tradition as premodern Judaism. His "teacher," as he generally calls him, Israel Ba'al Shem Tov, was a sage of a rather different sort from the normative rabbinic figure.[6] Though sharing most of the values of the latter, including dedication to both Torah study and life within the tradition, the Ba'al Shem saw himself generally as a teacher of "the fear of heaven" and spiritual wakefulness rather than of the tradition itself. The numerous quips and epigrams that the *Toledot* quotes from him uniformly point in this direction; he is the teacher who can *use* the language of tradition to point to a religious consciousness of a depth beyond that which the ordinary talmudist is called upon to see.[7] Accompanying this, he has the power to look into human souls and call forth their healing in a way that goes beyond the stock-in-trade of the usual Ba'al Shem, purveyor of both amulets and herbs, folk doctor, and expert on the names of God and angels. The BeSHT as depicted in the sources is a charismatic holy man; it was this figure (rather than the *Toledot* himself, a rather retiring scholarly type) who was to provide the model for leadership in the new movement. While operating wholly within the context of tradition, Hasidism was to call for a major transformation of values: simple devotion was to be placed over abstruse learning, the joy of service over penitential brooding, and the rediscovery of God's all-pervasive presence over the sense of longing and exile. The transformation was to be effected by a new sort of leader, himself the personal embodiment of the movement's teachings. The image of this leader is colorfully presented in the descriptions of the Ba'al Shem Tov himself as recorded in the popular hagiographic work *Shivhey ha-BeSHT*.[8]

Hasidism must be viewed as both a religious and a social movement.[9] Innovations in spiritual teaching or devotional practice offered by its teachers functioned also as guideposts toward the establishment of a new community, an alternative form of social organization that stood over against the much-troubled traditional *kahal*. Rather than owing primary loyalty to the geographically defined corporate body of Jewry, Hasidism in practice suggested that truly pious Jews might constitute themselves in disciple groups around a particular master, these translocal loyalties to be represented in each town by a conventicle of *hasidim* who espoused a particular path.[10] These *kloizlekh* or *minyanim*, first of *hasidim* in general and later of particular Hasidic groups, would, by the very nature of things, be more closely related to one another than they would to the community at large, an institution that early Hasidism did not deem much worthy of support. Unlike earlier pietistic conventicles, these Hasidic groups saw the expansion of their own circles as an essential part of their mission. The Hasidic *minyan* in a town could not simply be left alone to worship God and glory in its master. It strove—and in the long run often successfully—to dominate the entire Jewish community, at least in matters of the spirit.

Whence the authority for such innovation? Here was, in the circles around both the BeSHT and his successor the Maggid of Miedzyrzec, a group of ready leaders with a message that was soon to show itself of tremendous power to attract a following. But in what terms might the role claimed by such figures, termed by their opponents "recently arrived newcomers," be legitimated?[11] Authority to lead the community has, by all the canons of Jewish tradition, only one legitimate source: the word of God. That source, in turn, might be invoked in one of two ways: through a claim of direct revelation of God's will or by means of the normative chain of tradition, the legitimacy of rabbinic interpretation. Neither of these, however, could the early leaders of Hasidism invoke with full force.

The Ba'al Shem Tov and others in the early circles were surely motivated, in fact, by some sense of divine call. The religion of spiritual revival that they taught is by its very nature one in which the devotee is likely to have a deep sense of personally appointed mission. The BeSHT spoke rather openly about experiences of transcendence and messages from heavenly sources: we need only refer to his well-known letter to R. Gershon of Kuty to see that this is the case. But to claim legitimacy on the basis of heavenly journeys alone was a highly dubious business. Formally speaking, prophecy had ended with the destruction of the Temple; prophetic voice had been "taken from the prophets and given" either to the sages or to "fools and children"—depending on which version of the ancient saying one chooses. Since then, again in a formal sense, we "pay no attention to heavenly voices."[12] Of course, we know that such pronouncements were often observed in the breach and that especially in the sorts of popular mystical circles from which Hasidism sprang there was always much attention paid to dreams, "ascents of the soul," and various other personal illuminations. The real reason why authority could not be based on such claims lay much closer to home. Such dreams and "prophecies" were the stuff of which the recent and well-remembered Sabbatian claims had been made; they had a dangerous association with the very sort of mystical heresy from which Hasidism was at pains to dissociate itself.[13] While the early leadership of Hasidism fully believed in the reality of heavenly voices and angelic messengers (as did its most trenchant opponent!), it saw good reason not to locate the source of its authority in these. There were those who claimed, as we shall see later, a degree of prophetic mantle for the new movement, but this was done in a cautious and somewhat secondary way.

The normative claim to authority already belonged to the rabbinate, the very sort of rabbinate against whom Hasidism was set in opposition. No one could claim, on purely Talmudic/halakhic grounds, that the rabbis loyal to Hasidism in the early days were the leading luminaries of their time. Though Hasidism was far from being the movement of the unlettered masses that later romantics made it out to be, its leadership surely was not prepared to battle the rabbinate on the latter's own turf. Those with the finest pedigrees of learning and family—from Elijah Gaon in Vilna to Rabbi Ezekiel Landau in Prague—were known to be unsympathetic to the new movement and its leaders.

The Zaddiq

Hasidism found its way out of this dilemma by proposing another sort of claim for its leaders, one that was highly innovative in its usage here though having the needed venerable associations in the earlier history of Judaism. It was not as bearer of either revelation or tradition, but rather as *zaddiq*, that the Hasidic leader was to claim his mantle. His authority was of a different order, one that bypassed the controversial matter of the word of God and went directly to another cosmological line, one that had ever existed in Judaism side by side with the centrality of Torah, though previously always in a somewhat secondary way. The *zaddiq*, "righteous one" or holy man, was known to the Talmudic sources as one who stood at the very center of the cosmos and could, by virtue of his meritorious deeds, intervene to reverse the decrees of heaven.[14] For such figures (often called both *hasid* and *zaddiq* in the early sources) it had always been the virtue of meritorious action rather than learning or traditional authority that had lain at the core of their powers to attract a following. The *zaddiq*'s merit sustains the universe: what greater claim than this need be made for the leadership of a religious community? The authority of the *zaddiq* was not opposed to that of Torah either in earlier or in Hasidic times, but rather stood side by side with it, exemplifying another aspect of Jewish religious ideology. While not in conflict with the values of Torah, the *zaddiq*'s authority was of a different order and of different historic lineage as well. Since the Middle Ages, this ancient figure of piety and power (for the *zaddiq*'s power was said to be able to annul a divine decree) was associated with the aspect of divinity called *yesod* by the adherents of Kabbalah. *Yesod* (lit.: "foundation") is the ninth of the ten *sefirot* or aspects of the divine self, the one that gathers together all the forces from above and causes them to flow into the feminine *Shekhinah* or "Community of Israel." As such, *yesod* is identified with the male procreative organ, with the "covenant" of sexual purity, and with Joseph, the original *zaddiq* who became such by resisting Madame Potiphar's wiles. The deeds of the earthly *zaddiqim*, or kabbalists, are essential in aiding the *zaddiq* above to continue that flow of life that sustains the universe. This kabbalistic association tended to highlight the term *zaddiq* among the various appellations of the pious and probably indirectly affected the use of this term to designate the Hasidic master.

Well known and almost archetypically Hasidic is the interpretation offered in several of the movement's early sources of a Talmudic passage in praise of Rabbi Hanina ben Dosa, a famous wonder-worker and *hasid* of the first century:

The Talmud says that "a heavenly voice came forth and said: The whole earth is sustained for the sake of (*bi-shevil*) Hanina My son, but Hanina My son has to do with only a ration of carob from one Sabbath eve to the next." See the second chapter of Berakhot. A famous question is asked on this text: Why is the latter part of it needed? [Why bother to mention what Hanina ate?] I have seen an answer in the book *Yad Yosef* which says that this latter phrase offers a reason for the former:

the whole world is sustained for the sake of Hanina *because* he makes do with but a ration of carob. It is because of this that his merit suffices to sustain the entire world.

But in the name of my teacher: Hanina My son forged a path (*shevil*) or a pipeline to draw divine bounty into the world. This is the meaning of "the world is sustained by the *shevil* of Hanina My son." The words of the wise are gracious. To me it appears that he not only made such a pathway or pipeline, but that he himself was called *shevil* or channel, since the bounty flowed through him. This would be an esoteric reading for "Blessings to the head of the *zaddiq*" (Prov 10:6). (*Ben Porat Yosef* 80b; ed. Warsaw 1883; based on *Berakhot* 17b)[15]

The *Toledot* first quotes a non-Hasidic reading of the Talmudic passage, one that suggests the ascetic feat as the reason for Hanina's world-sustaining merit.[16] He then offers the BeSHT's reading of the passage as a contrast, one that emphasizes the charismatic side of Hanina's deed. The question as to the latter phrase has not really been answered by the new interpretation but the focus has been shifted: Hanina *is* the path by which the cosmos is sustained. It turns out that the BeSHT's reading too is not original; recent scholarship has shown that it is already to be found in the *Two Tablets of the Covenant,* an early seventeenth-century work by Isaiah Horowitz that enjoyed immense popularity in later pietistic circles.[17] But no matter: our interest is in the *use* made of such a reading in Hasidism, not in its originality. In the Hasidic context the reading is no longer abstract: its frequent repetition serves to underscore a claim made by a known and specific group of people to be the successors of Hanina, the *zaddiqim* who will sustain the world in this time. In the following text R. Menahem Nahum of Chernobyl makes a similar claim, here referring to a Talmudic parallel in which Hanina is not mentioned:

The fact is that "*zaddiq* is the foundation of the world" (Prov 10:25). He is the foundation and the channel through which divine bounty and life flow down into the world and to all creatures. It is all by his *shevil,* for he sets out the pathway and road which this life-flow will follow. By means of his constant attachment to the Creator he becomes a dwelling for the letter Aleph, the cosmic Aleph that lives within him. Thus Scripture says: "I shall dwell in their midst" (Exod. 25:8). Thus he is truly a part of God, and has a place, as it were, with Him. This is the portion of his soul, a part of the Aleph. He also has a place among created beings, since he shares with them the letters *Dalet Mem* (=*DaM*, blood); the animal soul is contained in his blood just as it is in all creatures. How right and proper, then, that he be the intermediary between the blessed Creator and the full world, binding all to Him so that bounty flows to His creatures along the path that he, the *zaddiq*, has set out by his devotion and attachment. Thus did the rabbis say of the verse, "For this is the whole of man (*'aDaM*—Eccl. 12:13)—the entire world is created by the *shevil* of this one." They said it in the present tense . . . for Creation is constant. "He renews each day the work of Creation." By the constant flow of His life into His creatures the act of Creation is ever taking place. This is the meaning of "this is the whole of *'aDaM*—it refers to the *zaddiq*, who unites in himself Aleph with *DaM*. Constant Creation happens only through his path. . . . Thus Onkelos translated "He holds fast to heaven and earth" he binds the whole world to its Creator. (*Me'or 'Eynayim, Yitro* [Jerusalem 1966], 109; quoting *Yoma* 38b)

The figure described in these texts is one familiar to the students of "holy man" traditions in the most diverse religious contexts. He is a figure at once human and mythic, a spiritualized Hercules, if you will, holding the world aloft by his own inner strength and ever renewing creation's bond to its source. Such a being, in some traditions identified with God more fully as Avatar or Incarnation, elsewhere as the prophet reborn or the first man *redivivus*, is indeed hinted at from the very earliest sources of Jewish esotericism. Elements of it are found in aggadic discussions of Abraham, Jacob, David, Elijah, and especially Moses. He is given prominence in the medieval Kabbalah, particularly through the protomessianic figure of Rabbi Simeon ben Yohai as described in the Zohar.[18] In the popular religious culture of the later Middle Ages, these ancient holy man traditions developed in two directions at once. One of these emphasizes the hidden and therefore potentially ubiquitous presence of such figures. A folk tradition reaching back to Talmudic times speaks of a certain number of *hidden zaddiqim* (usually thirty-six) for whose sake the world is sustained. But here their anonymity is essential to the legend: not only does it protect the virtue of humility, but its very point seems to be that you never know if the stranger before you might not be such a one, and you are to treat him accordingly. The *zaddiq* tradition in this sense is parallel to that of Elijah, the mysterious and virtuous stranger ever in your midst.[19] Another offshoot of this tradition points to well-known individuals of the present or the recent past as possessors of the holy spirit or of some special "influence" in the upper realms. Such tales were told of many great rabbis; the veneration of holy men's graves, widely attested in Jewish popular religion at least from the late Middle Ages, is an outgrowth of belief in the dead *zaddiq*'s power to intervene on high for the faithful he has left behind. The Zohar, which is to be seen in its narrative portions as an artful usage of these popular traditions, spurs their development further. Here the two lines meet, as such well-known figures as Rabbi Simeon and his friends encounter anonymous elders, children, and donkey drivers who turn out to be hidden saints and revealers of secrets. In the later Kabbalah as well, especially after the Safed revival, legends about the *zaddiqim* and their powers were widespread, some of these entering that genre of hagiography (*shevahim*) that so influenced Hasidism.[20] In the esoteric literature of the Sabbatian movement; the term is used as a cipher for the Messiah, but again in veiled ways. Other Sabbatian charismatics are referred to rather openly and daringly as prophets (*navi'*) and are frequently designated by the term *hasid*, but it appears that there *zaddiq* was generally reserved for the Messiah himself.[21]

The figure of the Hasidic *zaddiq* emerged most specifically out of the homiletical and moralistic literature of the seventeenth and eighteenth centuries, a body of writings often influenced by Sabbatianism but not wholly dependent on it, Much scholarly attention has been focused on this literature in recent times, and there is no need here to repeat, other than in brief summary, what has been said elsewhere. The homiletic literature of the age, obsessed as it was with sin and its corrosive effect on both soul and cosmos, was concerned largely with the question of penitence. The moralizing preacher, himself a penitent, to be sure, saw himself as extending a helping, even saving, hand to those who heard his sermons or read his books. The very nature of this position made him an intermediary between the sin-ridden public and the will of heaven contained in the message that he bore. This image of self held great fascination for the preachers of the age, especially insofar as they saw themselves as not living utterly beyond the temptation toward sin in their own lives. (Think of the fascination with self-image in the psychotherapeutic community of our own day and of the problematic of the therapist's own healing and its relationship to his or her abilities as a professional.) In the course of such discussions, older images were evoked of the *zaddiq* descending into hell to redeem the souls of those who suffered there: thus were the preachers depicted as rescuing their hearers from the pit of damnation that was sure to await them upon their deaths. Such a preacher was frequently a tormented figure, seeing himself as his community's last or best hope for reconciliation with God and yet at the same time ever aware of his own inadequacy to the task.[22] Though such preachers were not called *zaddiqim* and no miracles were ascribed to them, they saw themselves as linking heaven and earth, moral intermediaries between God and his people.

Speaking out of this tradition, the early teachers of Hasidism forged some essential final links. Charged with a new sense of religious optimism, they spoke against excessive brooding over one's sins and largely set aside the penitential/ascetic rigors of the earlier preachers' worldview. This lessened the sense of inadequacy inherent in the leader's self-identification as *zaddiq*, or in his claim to provide the link between his people and the God whom they sought to serve. The preacher linking the sinner to God, identified already with the *zaddiq* saving the souls of the wicked, could now be identified as well with another aspect of the *zaddiq*, the pillar on whom the earth is set or the forger of that *shevil* by which God's grace comes down to save the world.

The term *zaddiq*, as found in Hasidic writings of the movement's first three generations (until about 1800), by no means uniformly designates the leader of a Hasidic community. On the contrary, the term is generally used in its earlier sense—one that combines a normative notion of moral righteousness (*zaddiq* as opposed to *rasha'*) with an overtone of that mythic/mystic figure to whom we have alluded. As such, *zaddiq* may remain that hidden one of the folk tradition and also be a normal model toward which all should aspire. The *Toledot* belongs essentially to the earlier homiletic tradition in the ways it speaks of *zaddiq*. Rebbe as well as rabbi are generally designated by R. Jacob Joseph by the normative *talmid hakham*. In the writings of the Maggid's school, even in the very *zaddiq*-centered *No'am Elimelekh*, the term still usually has a general, or at least ambiguous, sense; the reader frequently is given the impression that he too, with the proper awareness and behavior, might reach that state. It is in that school, however, that a new dimension is added to the term *zaddiq*. In a sense, it is the preacher who now comes back to haunt the Hasidic *zaddiq*. It is somehow wrong, or at least inadequate, for the righteous one to live alone in his righteousness, even if that righteousness bears the merit that sustains the world. A new typology is developed in these writings (though it too has earlier precedents),[23] one that pits the *zaddiq* "who is only for himself" against the one who serves as "*zaddiq* for himself and for others."

"The *zaddiq* blossoms like a palm tree, tall as a cedar in Lebanon" (Ps. 92:1). There are two types of *zaddiqim*, both of them completely righteous. The difference between them is as follows: One is ever attached to God, blessed be He, doing the task that has been placed upon him. He is the *zaddiq* only for himself, but for no other. He does not cause his righteousness to flow forth to others. Thus he is compared to the cedar which, as our sages noted, does not bear fruit. He is a *zaddiq* only within himself, not bearing the fruit of bringing others back to the good, so that *zaddiqim* might multiply in the world. This one does only for himself, reaching high and adding to his reward. The second *zaddiq* is rather likened to the palm tree, one that bears fruit or "blossoms." He brings forth the precious from the cheap, causing good to blossom and increase in the world. Of this our sages spoke when they said: "In the place where penitents (*ba'aley teshuvah*, lit., 'masters of penitence') stand, absolute *zaddiqim* cannot stand." They meant to speak of the second *zaddiq*, the one who is called "master of penitence," for he is master and lord over repentance as he brings others back to the good. "He brings many back from sin" (Mal 2:6) as he makes for penitence in the world. Surely his reward is greatly redoubled over that of the first *zaddiq*, even though he too is completely righteous. (Dov Baer, *Or Torah*, Psalms [Jerusalem, 1968], 119)[24]

"But My servant Caleb, because he was of another spirit, and he followed Me wholly" (Num. 14:24). There are two kinds of *zaddiqim*. There are some who need to be set aside and separated from people, for when they are among people [or in public situations] they might fall from their proper rung. Then there are *zaddiqim* who mingle pleasantly among people and converse with them, not falling from their own rung and in fact bringing others back to the good. Thus have I heard from my

master and teacher . . . Dov Baer. . . . "Holy flesh has never turned rot-
ten" (Avot 5:5)—he interpreted as "whoever is holy flesh"—a complete
zaddiq—"never rots, even when he is among people and speaks with
them." This is "My servant Caleb, because he was of another spirit"—
even when speaking with them, but did not fall from his rung, "he followed Me wholly." (*No'am Elimelech, shelah*; ed. Nig'al, 403f.)[25]

Many elements of the tradition have converged in the making of these
statements. The ancient belief that the *zaddiq* sustains the "world" is now
given a social context; it is the very particular "*oilem*," in the Yiddish usage,
of his community that he sustains and justifies before God, as well as the
cosmos as a whole. As heir to the *mokhiah* of the immediately preceding
generations he is teacher and spiritual healer, binding himself to God and
humanity and holding them together. But as heir to the Talmudic *zaddiq*
he is also a supernatural intercessor: his merit bears within it the power
to negate the divine decree. The responsibility of bearing such power calls
forth in him a quality antithetical to that usually found in the psyche of
moralizing preachers: like the prophets of old, he becomes *defender* of
Israel as they are judged by God. The intense devotion of the *hasid* to
his master stems in part from the confidence that this master, who has
high standing in the heavenly realms because of his own righteousness
or that of his ancestors, stands ready to sacrifice all for the sake of his
disciples. In psychological terms it may be said that the rebbe is thus a
true father figure, both in embodying the values of tradition and in his
willingness without limit to defend his "children" from divine judgment
or demonic threat.

So much for the hidden *zaddiq*. If he is to help others along the path,
it becomes fully legitimate for him to reveal himself to them. True, it is
theoretically possible to combine both virtues: to keep one's own constant
attachment to God a secret and, posing as a poor sinner among others, to
preach the word of God to them. But if the preacher/*zaddiq*'s work is to
be done effectively, better that he discard his mask and set himself to the
social and religious task in earnest. For *zaddiq* to serve a social function,
as leader and rallying point for a spiritual community, he must also be
identified. There thus emerges in Hasidism a remarkable group of religious
teachers and charismatic figures who are identified by their followers and
(though only obliquely) by themselves as *zaddiqim*. The meaning attrib-

uted to this term here and in later common speech—*zaddiq* as leader of a community of *hasidim*—is entirely original to Hasidism.

The Search for Paradigms

The preoccupation with leadership brought about in Hasidism a new reading of the earlier tradition, one in which diverse sources were combed for the light they could shed on the question of *zaddiq* and his relationship to community. Precisely because the term did not have a tradition of public leadership associated with it, models of leadership that would serve as paradigms for his proper role were to be sought elsewhere. It is not surprising that, for a community in which preaching took so central a role, it was to scripture that Hasidic authors most frequently turned for guidance in the ways of proper leadership. In fact, the writings of more immediately past generations had rather little to offer on this question that had now become so crucial. It is hard to find postbiblical, or at least post-Talmudic, sources in which the nature of proper leadership is a central topic of Jewish intellectual concern. In the medieval and later communities, proper leaders for the Jewish community were judged by standards essentially extrinsic to the question of leadership itself. The most defined leader role was that of rabbi. The rabbi, however, was trained and evaluated primarily in relationship to Torah; his "pastoral" skills were quite secondary to his learning and mastery of Talmudic law. The *hasid* of medieval Germany and later Safed was such by virtue of his extraordinary acts of piety. While these frequently had to do with the realm of the interpersonal, they did not necessarily show the skills and responsibilities appropriate to leadership. On the contrary, the humility appropriate to such an ideal type might well keep him from seeking out such a role. Communal lay leaders were judged for honesty, in accord with the rigorous standards of the Talmudic civil code. It was taken for granted, apparently, that such virtues as learning, piety, and integrity would make for fitting leadership. These were, after all, the values that the community was to hold in high regard, and they could best be supported if exemplified in its leaders. Such barely self-conscious notions of leadership seem to have generally sufficed, despite periodic complaints and reports of abuses.

If later Jewish history was lacking in treatments of this leader theme, however, the pages of scripture were a virtual textbook on the question. From Moses and Aaron in the wilderness to David in battle and the prophets of calamity and consolation in Jerusalem and in exile, the Bible is filled with concern over the issue of proper and responsible leadership and the relationship between God's people and those He has appointed to minister to them. The three figures of prophet, priest, and king immediately come to mind; the proper role of each of these three and the not infrequent clashes between them bespeak the very essence of ancient Israel's unique religious situation.

The same is true, though to a lesser extent, of late Second Temple and early rabbinic times. There too were new religious leader ideals in the making, not least because all three of the biblical models had run their course. Once prophecy was deemed at an end, it was only the interpretive authority of scribe or sage that could claim access to the divine word. Kingship and priesthood were identified wholly with the houses of David and Aaron, respectively, the one consigned to the messianic future and the other, much discredited after Hasmonean times, about to become vestigial with the Temple's destruction. The new types that emerged in their stead, the scholar/sage and the wonder-working *hasid*, were both reflections of types to be found elsewhere in the Hellenistic world. The unceasing attempts of the Midrash to convert Moses into rabbi and David into leader of the Sanhedrin reflect a pseudohistory that seeks to legitimate the rabbi by proclaiming him a biblical type.[26] The *hasid* had a greater chance of identifying with such a model of Elijah or Elisha, but he too was essentially a creation of the new era, searching the tradition for ancestors of his spirit.

A similar process now took place in Hasidism, an age of renewed creativity in leadership types, again born of the collapse of previously available models. And again the earlier tradition is combed in search of precedent or archetype with whom the present leader might identify. All of the biblical models—priest, king, prophet, as well as the rabbinic *hasid* and sage—are to be found in early BeSHTian Hasidism's descriptions of its *zaddiq*. The wide range of earlier models accessible to Hasidic preachers gives to their discussions of *zaddiq* a rich and varied texture. The interplay between the literary figures of these texts and the actual social institution is a complex one: the theoretical literature of Hasidism (almost all of it, we must remember, originally delivered as oral sermons)[27] both reflected and created the *zaddiq* as a living figure. Here as in other areas we see a dialectical relationship between Hasidic theory and social form.

In examining the various models to which the literature appeals, we seek to cast our net wide and examine such paradigms of leadership as they are found throughout the writings of early Hasidism, not limited to any single author or school. We should at the same time note, however, that here as in most things it is the *Toledot* and the Maggid who appear as "original" sources and upon whom most other Hasidic preachers draw.

The Zaddiq *as Priest*

The figure of priest is widespread in Hasidic discussions of the *zaddiq*. It is hard to find a collection of Hasidic homilies arranged according to the weekly Torah-reading cycle that does not, somewhere in Exodus or Leviticus, apply biblical mention of the *kohen* to the leader of its own day. In one place the *zaddiq*/priest may be offering the inward sacrifice on the altar of the heart; elsewhere he may be robed in the spiritual equivalent of the priestly garments, purifying the defiled of soul; or calling forth the divine bounty by the power of his blessing. All of these are priestly functions that go to the very heart of the *zaddiq*'s function in the Hasidic community. The following source, an unusually extended treatment of this subject, takes the form of a running comment on the opening Mishnah of *Berakhot* and a portion of the Gemara's discussion of it. We shall be well advised (unlike the original) to begin by quoting those Talmudic texts in full:

> Mishnah: From what time does one recite the *Shema'* in the evening? From the hour the priests come in to eat of their heave-offering, until the end of the first watch. These are the words of Rabbi Eliezer. But the sages say: until midnight.

> Gemara: From when do the priests eat of the heave-offering? From the time when the stars come out. Then teach [that *Shema'* be recited] from when the stars come out! We are being taught something by the way [in the present formulation, namely] that the priests eat of the heave-offering from the time the stars come out.

> Comment: This is the meaning of "From when does one recite the *Shema'* in the evening": When will we be able to call out to God so that He will hear all our prayers, "in the evening" in this bitter exile which is the dark of night? "From the hour when the priests come in to eat of their

TeRuMaH (heave-offering)." The priests are the *zaddiqim*; they draw forth holiness and *devequt*. "Their *TeRuMaH* refers to the raising up of the *shekhinah*, *TaRuM He*" [Uplift the letter *He=shekhinah*]. This is their "eating," as is said of Abraham "He stood over them beneath the tree and they ate" (Gen. 18:8). Torah was not given to the angels: when they came to Abraham they heard words of Torah, the Tree of Life, from his mouth. The holiness they drew forth in this manner was their "eating." The Gemara asks on this: "From what time do the priests eat of the heave-offering? From the time when the stars come out. When will this level be attained, that from which such holiness and *devequt* can be drawn forth? "When the stars come out"—when our righteous messiah arrives, as in "a star courses forth from Jacob" (Num. 24:17). . . . "Then teach: From when the stars come out" for the "priests" will "eat" at the same time that the "stars" appear! The Gemara answers that the text "taught us something by the way": the Tanna teaches us that in walking "by the way" of God's path and His holy Torah, by following in the paths of the *zaddiqim*, one can attain to great holiness, even to the holy spirit, now too, in the exile. (*No'am Elimelech, wa-yiggash*; ed. Nig'al, 139f.)

The *zaddiqim* are today's priests, "eating" of holiness as the Temple priests ate of the heave offering. It is interesting that the spiritualization of the sacrifice suggested in this comment brings together *zaddiqim* and angels, both of them (though for different reasons) unable to partake of the offering in its corporeal form. At the same time, here even the supposedly most *zaddiq*-centered *No'am Elimelech* insists that such a path is open to anyone who follows it and that its rewards may even include attainment of the holy spirit, a degree of prophetic revelation. This is typical of the early literature of Hasidism, where the identification of *zaddiq* with a specified elite has not yet become clear. In the following passage, his identity as leader is clearer, though it has to be reinforced by joining the "new" term to a more conventional one (*ha-zaddiqim ha-hakhamim*).

"The Lord spoke to Moses saying: 'Command Aaron and his sons thus. This is the teaching concerning the burnt offering (*'olah*): it is that which ascends on its firewood all the night until morning . . .' (Lev. 6:1–2)."

RaSHI comments that "command" implies urgency, both immediate and for later generations. . . . Now surely the Torah is eternal and applies in each generation. These holy scriptures (in my humble opinion) show the way of God to the wise righteous ones (*ha-zaddiqim ha-hakhamim*), the way to draw the souls of oppressed Israel (God save us!) to the blessed and exalted God. This was the deed of Aaron and his sons as well, as they offered the sacrifices of Israel, sin and guilt offerings or wholly burnt sacrifices, each as appropriate to him and in accord with his own needs. In doing so they would uplift and draw near the souls of Israel, each according to his needs and character. In this way is the passage one of "urgency, both immediate and for later generations"—even though there are no sacrifices in these times, the *zaddiqim* of each generation draw near [to God] the souls of Israel by means of their pure worship and the teachings (*torah*) they offer in truth and wholeness, with inner direction of the heart and in fear and love [of God]. Thus scripture afterwards says: *zot torat ha-'olah* (lit., this is the teaching concerning the burnt offering) *hi ha-'olah* [i.e., it is the teaching that ascends as an offering]. (*Degel Mahaneh Ephraim, zaw* [Jerusalem, 1963], 152a)[28]

Such passages from the homiletic sources are reminiscent of the tale later told of Abraham Joshua Heschel of Apt, who so clearly "recalled" his prior incarnation as high priest in the Temple that he was drawn to reciting the Yom Kippur account of that service in the first person: "Thus did I count . . ." and so forth.

The image of prayer or inward devotion as a spiritual sacrifice is an ancient one, originating in the earliest Jewish sources and a favorite of Jewish moralists throughout the ages.[29] But the notion that there is an officiant at such sacrifice, be he called *zaddiq*, *hakham*, or any other name, is new in Hasidism. He is the one through whom, in some readings, such devotion must be directed to reach its source; for others he is the instructor in this cult of the inner temple or the model of its ideal fulfillment. All these have to do with the essential model we have already seen, that of *zaddiq* as source of blessing or as channel for the flow of divine life into the world. He draws Israel near to God as he draws divine blessing down to his people. Although such descriptions do not accompany the delineations of priestly function in the biblical text itself, which are deliberately this-worldly, there is, in a broader sense, something priestly about them—a sense that the Hasidic authors (greatly aided by the Zohar's freely mythic depictions of the cult) have no difficulty in perceiving.[30]

Another area in which priesthood is important in the *zaddiq*'s image has to do with healing, again relating to his position as the arouser of God's mercies and the bearer of His life-flow into the world. In functional terms, a major part of the *zaddiq*'s role in Hasidic society was that of healer; it was particularly in times of illness or medically dangerous situations such as childbirth that disciples—and other ordinary folk—came to seek out the *zaddiq*'s blessing. Here he was acting as a priestly holy man in a way that probably would have been quite familiar to the Orthodox clergy just across the town square. Quite naturally, it is in homilies on the Torah portions *tazri'a* and *mezora'*, ever the bane of Jewish preachers' lives, that one is likely to find comments on the *zaddiq* in the role of priestly healer.

> "The priest will go outside the camp and see that the leprous sore has healed from the leper" (Lev. 14:3). "From the leper" appears to be redundant. It seems, however, that the *zaddiq* has to come to the lower rungs in order to raise up souls from there. Those souls who desire to cleave to him he will be able to raise up with him, but not so with those that do not want to attach themselves to him. . . . "The priest will go outside the camp"—coming to the lower rungs, to raise up the "leper." The priest "sees"—he draws forth wisdom, which is identical to "sight" and allows for transformation. "And the leprous sore has healed"—but Scripture adds "from the leper," for the will to cleave to the priest must come from the leper himself. Only then can the priest raise him up to wisdom, effecting that transformation which cures his sore. (*Orah le-Hayyim, mezora'* [Jerusalem, 1960], 238)
>
> "When a man has in his skin . . . a leprous sore, he shall be brought to Aaron the priest or to one of his sons the priests, and the priest shall look at the sore . . . and if the hair in the sore be turned white or the sore appears to be deeper than the skin, it is leprosy. The priest shall look at it and proclaim him unclean" (Lev. 13:2–3). The letters of *NeGa'* ("sore") are the same as those of *'oNeG* ("joy"); if one does not take care, however, this sore becomes "leprous." Scripture then speaks of what one should do to set one's deeds aright. *He shall be brought to the priest*—the perfect *zaddiq* is called a priest; he should attach himself to

the *zaddiqim. The priest shall look and if the hair in the sore be turned white*—the *zaddiq* must see the condition of the sore. He must determine whether the white divine fluid [of compassion] has been turned "by a hair," by one of those minor sins which are like "mountains hanging by a hair" or whether the *sore appears to be deeper than the skin,* the affliction, heaven forfend, be more than skin deep. In either case, it is a *leprous sore; the priest shall look at it and proclaim him unclean;* he must show him to understand the great damage he has wrought in all this, teaching him the ways of return and true penitence so that he make good all those bad and shameful qualities that he bears. (*No'am Elimelech, tazri'a,* ed. Nig'al, 309)[31]

The powers of priesthood, including the ability to bless, to heal by the conferral of divine blessing, and to discern—intuitively or by secret sign—the "clean" from the "unclean" in the moral domain, have now all been "naturally" assumed by the *zaddiq.* The use of exegesis as an instrument of social change is particularly striking in these passages. This identification with the ancient priest allows the rebbe to assert the sort of claim that had been defined as outside the purview of the "normative" rabbinate for many centuries. The charismatic leader has now found a locus of authority more venerable, certainly more mysterious, than that of the rabbi himself. Priesthood (a religious institution in full vigor among the surrounding Eastern Orthodox population), with all its mysterious power to bless and transform, was a notion that called forth memories of ancient grandeur but was now represented, in the persons of *kohanim,* by only a pitiable vestige. The *zaddiq* as priest—even a priest who could arouse a degree of awe among non-Jews—was for the *hasid* a living religious symbol that combined grandeur, the warmth of pastoral care, and true magic.

The Zaddiq *as King*

Although the priesthood continued to exist in Israel, if only in vestigial form, the figure of king was one that had long been relegated to historical memory. Royal imagery continued to exist in postexilic Judaism only with regard to the kingship of God, expressed mostly in a liturgical context. The figure of king remained alive, however, partly through this sacred usage and partly because of the influence of the surrounding culture: Hasidism was created in a period when the doings of kings and their courts were very much present in the public mind, from the failure and dissolution of the Polish kingdom to the awesome pomp of the Romanovs and, if one includes the opening decades of the nineteenth century, through the period of Napoleonic adventure and the restoration of royal legitimacy. No wonder that a tradition in search of authority would seek to partake of the symbols of royalty, indicating power and legitimacy at once.

There were various aids in the sources of tradition that made this usage, audacious on the face of things, somewhat more accessible. While the widely quoted "*Man malkhey? Rabbanan*" ("Who are kings? The rabbis") does not seem to be an authentic quotation from the Talmud, the gist of the idea that rabbis have quasi-royal authority is to be found.[32] In recounting the power of true *zaddiqim* to affect the will of heaven, God himself is quoted by one well-known rabbinic source as saying: "Who rules over Me? The *zaddiq*, for I issue a decree and he nullifies it" (*Mo'ed Qatan* 16b). It was also considered perfectly proper, in the formal Hebrew of the Middle Ages and later, to speak of a rabbi in terms echoing those of royalty. Thus a chronicler telling of a rabbi's tenure in a particular town might readily say, "His reign began in year so-and-so, and he occupied the rabbinic throne, judging the people in equity."

The Hasidic sources use this metaphor in their own way, again rather casually allowing the homiletic mode to carry over "naturally" the earlier image into their own circumstances.

"Set a king over yourself, as the Lord your God chooses. From among your brethren take a king. . . . As he sits upon his throne he shall write out this second Torah in a book, before the Levitical priests" (Deut. 17:15, 18). RaSHI comments on "this second Torah" that the king is to write two Torah scrolls, one to remain in his treasury and the other to be carried with him to and fro. This comment, the original source of which is in the Talmud (Sanhedrin 21b), makes no sense. Of what value to him is the scroll that just lies in his treasury?

We know, however, the statement "Who are kings? The rabbis." The sages are truly kings, as scripture says: "Through me [wisdom or Torah] do kings rule" (Prov. 8:15). But the fact is that even if a person learns the whole Torah and all the holy volumes and teachings of the sages, this still will not bring him to repentance or remove the curtain that separates him from God, not until he cleaves to God's holy ones, the *zaddiqim* of the generation. Thus have I heard from my master and teacher, the man of God Elimelech, of blessed and sainted memory; a person must choose one *zaddiq* in his generation to be his master. And who is the one he should choose as master, teacher, and intimate? When he sees a *zaddiq* all of whose comings and goings are conducted in accord with the holy Torah, who is lax neither in the Torah's own commands nor in matters ordained by the rabbis, while in his heart there burns a pillar of fire as he performs the unifications, this thought being visible in his deeds—such a one should he choose as master.

This is the meaning of "set a king over yourself"; "king" here refers to rabbis. "As the Lord your God chooses"—whom should you choose? Scripture goes on to answer this by the words "he shall write this second Torah," according to RaSHI's interpretation. He should have two scrolls, the one that is "carried with him to and fro" refers to the justice of his deeds and the way he conducts himself. The "treasury" in which the other scroll remains refers to his heart, burning with the fire of Torah, proclaiming God's unity in love and fear. Such a "king" whose thought is to be seen also in his deeds, is the one whom you should choose. All this belongs to that *zaddiq* as tradition received from those sublime holy men who were his own masters; these are the "levitical priests" of whom the verse speaks. (*Ma'or wa-Shemesh, shoftim* [Tel Aviv, 1964], 219d–220a)[33]

To this rather typical set of criteria for choosing a rebbe, we may add a Hasidic insistence on the need for a relationship that bears this kingship within it; the *hasid* cannot exist in purely egalitarian circumstances.

"From among your brethren take a king" (Deut. 17:15). The sages add that his fear should be upon you. Now it sometimes happens that you meet a man who treats you as his friend and equal, acting as though you were two brothers, with no difference of rank. In fact, however, this person stands on a higher rung [of spiritual attainment] than you, and it would be fitting for him to hold the ruler's scepter over you. It is because he is so humble that he sees himself as being just like you, relating to you as brother and equal. Of this situation I warn you: "From among your *brothers* take a king." Even if he acts as though he were just your brother, you must make him king, until his fear is upon you like the fear of the kingdom. Now this can be a terrific struggle, that of taking one who is acting as brother and making him into awesome king. That is why scripture chose the word *mi-qerev* ("from among") for use in this verse; Q-R-V also refers to battle. Enough said. (*Ahavat Shalom, shoftim* [Lvov, 1850], 76a)[34]

There are other places in the literature where the specific language of royalty is avoided but where something of the king-subject relationship is bespoken nonetheless. In HaBaD circles the term *nasi'*, or prince, was chosen to refer to the rebbe, and these sources will speak of a particular event as having taken place during the *nesi'ut* of one occupant or another of that dynastic throne. Approbations and introductions to books, hotbeds of hyperbole in any case, will commonly contain some element of regal language. Appropriation of a degree of royal style happened rather early in the history of Hasidism and was widespread. It was Barukh of Miedzybozh (ca. 1750–1812), the BeSHT's grandson, and Mordecai of Chernobyl (1770–1837) who first established "courts" in which it was expected that the rebbe live in a grand manner. Already in 1798 the bitter anti-Hasidic polemicist David of Makov described the Hasidic masters as "seated each upon his throne, with royal crowns on their heads."[35] This and other anti-Hasidic descriptions, including those of Abraham Baer Gottlober, while poisoned with a hatred of their subject, surely have some basis on which to build their mockeries, or else their claims would have been of little power. The very notion of inherited dynasty, the right to authority in the Hasidic community by virtue of birth, smacked of royalism. This claim, loudly proffered by Barukh of Miedzybozh in justifying his prerogative over against those of all his rivals, became normative early on in Hasidism's history. By the second decade of the nineteenth century, most Hasidic communities were led by sons or grandsons of the original group around the BeSHT and the Maggid.

Chief heir to the royal lifestyle of the earlier Ukrainian courts was Israel of Ruzhyn (1796–1850), great-grandson of the Maggid. The luxury in which he and his household lived was legendary and aroused opposition both within and without the Hasidic community. Accompanying the life of pomp and great wealth in the Ruzhyner's "court" was a trumpeting of the claim of Davidic descent that had been a tradition in the Maggid's family. Here the style and traditional symbols of kingship came together, and the evocation of royal language in description of the Hasidic master would forever afterward call forth the image of this most controversial figure. Of course Ruzhyn and its defenders had a series of responses to all the charges laid against them, including the assertion that the rebbe derived no pleasure from the great wealth and power that were amassed in his hands or that his grand manner of living was but a ruse to keep the accuser from discovering his true humility.

> "He is the trustee over all My household" (Num. 12:7). The *zaddiq* is a channel of flow. A pipeline, through which water is to be carried, must be kept clean, no mud or refuse from within the water being allowed to stick to it. If mud does accumulate within the pipe, the water will cease its flow. So it is with the *zaddiq*: he has to keep himself from enjoying any benefit from that which flows through his pipeline. He concerns himself with all these worldly matters but profits from them not at all. Thus he becomes "the trustee over all My household." All of the rich man's fortune passes through the hands of the trustee, but he takes not a cent of his master's hoard. That is why he is so trusted. The *zaddiq* is like Moses [of whom scripture here speaks] in his own generation: all matters of this world pass through his hands, but he derives no benefit from them.[36]

Such a defense is, to say the least, difficult to document, and Rabbi Hayyim of Sanz spoke for many, both *hasidim* and *maskilim*, when he declared "war" on the Ruzhyn-Sadegora dynasty and its way of life.

But the utility and positive value of the royal claim should not be dismissed too quickly. One still can sense even in those groups that stood far from Ruzhyn and its abuses a measure of royalty in the way rebbes of contemporary Hasidic courts conduct themselves and in the manner of the *hasidim* when in their presence. If description in royal terms had served to strengthen the claims made for Hasidic leadership, it also supplied to that leadership the texture of pastoral concern and deeply personal *noblesse oblige* that it sought. Jewish images of sacred kingship, we should recall, had long been colored with the sort of compassionate and warm hues that typify the aggadic descriptions of God's loving relationship with His children, the house of Israel. The sense of Israel as "children of the King" was underscored in Hasidism, where the disciple could also feel himself belonging to the "palace" of a beloved earthly father figure who was revered in the royal manner. "The greatest evil," according to an old Hasidic saying attributed to R. Aaron of Karlin, "is when the king's son forgets who he is." The sharp contrasts between the loving descriptions of God's kingship that filled Jewish literature and the harsh and frightening earthly kingship of the nations as it related to its Jewish subjects were mitigated for the *hasid* by the presence of holy royalty or at least a representative of God's kingship on earth—a psychological factor that should by no means be dismissed. The rebbe's *tisch* or Sabbath meal table, usually the setting where Hasidic teachings were offered, typifies a peculiar combination of priestly and royal elements. That table was, for the *hasid*, a true altar; *shulhan domeh la-mizbeah* ("the table is like an altar") in Hasidism came to bear particular reference to this holy table. Here was the earthly priest performing the mysterious sacraments of which all would take part. This table is at the same time that of a great Polish lord, one at which he and his men joined in feasting and singing. In that "palace," as it is frequently described by visitors and later writers, the *hasid* could forget for a while his Jewish disenfranchisement from the world of royalty and pomp. He was indeed seated at the earthly embodiment of the *shulhan shel ma'alah*, at once the heavenly table, at which the divine king partook of spiritual repast with the souls of the righteous, and the sacred altar of the ideal temple.

The Zaddiq *as Prophet*

We have already indicated that the third type of biblical leader, the prophet, could be invoked by Hasidism only with some difficulty. It would seem at first glance that this should be the most accessible of the models for postbiblical Jews: one need claim neither Davidic nor Aaronic lineage to be a prophet. But the discrediting of prophecy in the age of apocalypse, the association of further claims to revelation with faiths that established themselves as being other than Judaism, and the defined and closed canon of scriptural authority allowed Judaism, at least formally, to declare that it was done with prophecy. "Better sage than prophet," counsels one rabbinic saying (*Baba Batra* 12a),[37] and another, in a legal context: "We pay no attention to heavenly voices." This rather rigid and monolithic view of the Jewish tradition, although important in establishing the rule of law in the postbiblical Jewish community, has been shown to be lacking as a complete description of Jewish spiritual activity for almost every period of Jewish history. Something like the religion of apocalypse continued to thrive among the early rabbis despite their formal rejection of "prophecy" in their time. A historical line may be traced from near-prophetic apocalypse into the heavenly "voyaging" that took the form preserved in the sources of *merkavah* literature.[38] These later journeys lack prophetic message, to be sure, but they contain elements that clearly link them to prophetic vision on the one hand and rabbinic aggadah and liturgy on the other. Medieval Jewry, even before the emergence of Kabbalah, was dotted occasionally with various figures who claimed one degree or another of direct access to heavenly truth. The term "prophet" was mostly (though not universally) taboo, but there were "lesser" and more legitimate sources of revelation that could be claimed: the "holy spirit," the "revelation of Elijah," prophetic dreams, and so forth.[39] From the thirteenth century, these were very much in vogue among writers of the kabbalistic tradition, including some who provided actual instructions for the attainment of the holy spirit. This is especially true of that school within medieval and later Jewish mysticism known as "prophetic kabbalah." Recent historical research has shown that this strand of mystical praxis, long intentionally hidden by the self-censorship of the mystics and the reluctance of printers, played a major role in the new growth of Kabbalah in the sixteenth century and had not a little influence on certain aspects of Hasidism. In these sources, most of which are preserved only in manuscript, the prophetic claim is made quite openly.[40]

The revival of prophecy that both heralded and characterized the Sabbatian movement, highly reminiscent of that which accompanied the early church, was both culmination and negation of all the above. Here the would-be prophets violated the tradition's univocal definition of prophetic legitimacy: they spoke against the law, favoring abrogation of the commandments, at first selectively and later en masse. The radical wing of the Sabbatian movement, that which represented conversion to Islam in the Ottoman lands and gave birth to the well-remembered and much-hated Frankist sect in Poland, had made ample use of the charismatic vehicle, a use that could not but bring such phenomena into disrepute for the much more conservative Hasidic circles. For all their brashness in tone, even the most outspoken of the Hasidic leaders sought to maintain a position within the general Jewish community and to answer their critics and persecutors within the theological language that both held in common.

Nevertheless, there is talk of prophetic revelation in some Hasidic circles; certainly the possibility of attaining prophetic states in our day is not denied. Well known is the claim of the Maggid that prophecy might in fact be more easily attainable to us than it was in the days of the Temple, a claim that stands in direct, if gentle, contradiction to the rabbinic sources quoted earlier. When the king is on the road, says the Maggid, he is more easily approachable for a commoner than when he is protected by all the royal claptrap of his life in the capital. So it is easier to attain to the "holy spirit" in our own day than it was in the times of the prophets, who required "oaths and periods of aloneness" before the spirit would come upon them (*No'am Elimelech, wa-yeshev*, ed. Nig'al, 109f.).[41] Such a distinction makes it clear that the Maggid lives in a world where possession by the holy spirit is a not uncommon occurrence and one that does not require a great deal of rigorous preparation.

Of the Maggid's circle, it was particularly the well-known preacher Wolf of Zhitomir who nurtured this openness to prophetic experience. In his *Or ha-Me'ir*, one of the longer and more profound collections of Hasidic homilies, the distinction between mystical religion and prophecy seems to break down altogether. The true *hasid* in the intensity of his prayers as well as the *zaddiq* while preaching can reach a state in which "the *Shekhinah* speaks from within his mouth."[42] In these discussions, it is the act of prophetic inspiration that interests the Hasidic authors rather than the figure of the prophet himself. There are passages, however, in which it is precisely on prophetic authority that the Hasidic leader draws, despite all the difficulties inherent in such a usage. In the homilies, this claim will typically take the form of identification with Moses, sometimes also making for the association of those who oppose the *zaddiq* with the classic enemies of prophetic authority. In the following passage R. Benjamin of Zalozhtsy proceeds from a discussion of Korah's rebellion against the seemingly arbitrary character of purification through the ritual of the red heifer:

In our generation as well we may see one who serves God in great love, pure of body and whole of mind, worshiping by means of some form that no one else can understand. . . . The *zaddiq* is like Moses; he is "mind" [*da'at*] as Moses was the mind of all Israel. Whoever opposes

him is like Korah. This is why the rabbis asked, "What did Korah see . . ."
meaning "What does the one who is like Korah see in the *zaddiq* who is
like Moses [that leads him to rebel]?" They answered: "He saw the red
heifer," meaning that he saw some practice he could not comprehend.
But just as in the case of the red heifer, the one who is "mind" understands its meaning, and only to others is it [an incomprehensible] stat-
ute. (*Torey Zahav, qorah* 83d–84a)

This identification of the *zaddiq* with Moses as the collective mind of
Israel also places him in a kabbalistic realm significantly beyond that which
is ordinarily claimed. Here the *zaddiq* has "risen" from association with
yesod, the ninth in the sefirotic decade, to *da'at*, third by the usual Hasidic
count. The authority of such a figure is indeed absolute, for he "knows"
by a connection to the inward roots of knowledge that which others may
never hope to comprehend. No wonder then that the enemies of such a
figure can be identified with the classic rebel of the Mosaic tale, long seen
by rabbinic tradition as one who had refused to accept Moses' divinely
authorized interpretation of the law.

There was yet another aspect of the prophetic role, specifically that of
Moses, that was assigned to the *zaddiq*: the role of intercessor or defender
of Israel before the divine throne. Although the term "prophet" is not used
in the Hasidic sources that discuss this function, the model is clearly that
of Moses standing before God following the incident of the golden calf,
pleading with, cajoling, and demanding of God that He not destroy His
people. This ability to argue with God and to demand of Him a standard of
justice or loyalty to His covenant higher than that which appears to rule in
His world is a central part of the prophetic legacy. Abraham at Sodom and
Moses on Sinai serve as models for a rule assumed both by biblical prophet
and by later *zaddiq* or *hasid*. This sense of the ability to speak frankly and
harshly to God (*le-hatiah devarim kelapey ma'alah*)[43] and to achieve the
desired end of course again depends on the righteousness, courage, and
utter unselfishness of the one who does so. In this it is not entirely separable in the mind of the tradition from the power of *zaddiqim* to nullify
the divine decree, though here the distance from magic is even greater.

We shall not deal further here with the influence of the rabbinic and
medieval figures of *hasid* and *zaddiq* on the *zaddiq* of BeSHTian Hasi-

dism. These, along with their development through the twin channels of Safed and ongoing Ashkenazic folk pietism, formed the basis for the newly emerging leader, to which all the biblical imagery of which we have spoken was added. The collections of Hasidic tales frequently contain accounts of miracles wrought by such earlier *zaddiq* types, bearing testimony to the fact that their intended readers saw a continuity between the *zaddiqim* or *hasidim* of prior ages and those who followed the path of the Ba'al Shem Tov.

The Zaddiq *as Rabbi*

Perhaps the strangest employment of an earlier leadership mode among the Hasidim was that of conventional rabbi: *zaddiq* in the garb of *talmid hakham*. Here the very form that had been seen as abused and debased in the times of Hasidism's origin, and the office of those who in so many cases led the opposition to the new movement, is itself claimed as the mantle of the Hasidic leaders. We must be particularly cautious here, because of the misleading possibilities of terminological confusion. In the writings of the *Toledot* and some others, as we have noted, the emerging Hasidic leader is in fact regularly referred to as *talmid hakham*, the *true* scholar/sage as distinct from those who had let this mantle become soiled. Such passages cannot really be used to claim the use of rabbinic justification for the *zaddiq*. But there are others where the matter goes beyond that of terms.

> It is known that the written Torah and the oral Torah are all one, not to be separated from one another at all. Neither can exist without the other; the secrets of the written Torah are revealed only through the oral, without which it would be but half a book. In interpreting the Torah and revealing its secrets, the sages at times even uprooted something from the text, as in the case of the prescribed forty lashes for punishment, of which they permitted only thirty-nine. All this they did by the power of the Holy Spirit that appeared in their midst, so that the very wholeness of the written Torah depends upon the oral tradition. That is why "he who says that a certain inference [as derived by the rabbis] is not from the Torah" or that "a single statement of the rabbis" is not Torah, is as one who denied the Torah of Moses our Teacher. Everything depends upon the interpretation of the rabbis. . . .

Until they had interpreted it, the Torah was not considered complete, but only half-finished; it was the rabbis, through their interpretations, who made the Torah whole. *Such is the case for each generation and its leaders; they complete the Torah. The Torah is interpreted in each generation according to that generation's needs, and according to the soul-root of those who live at that time. God thus enlightens the sages of the generation in [the interpretation of] His holy Torah. He who denies this is as one who denies the Torah itself, God forbid.* (*Degel Mahaneh Ephraim, bereshit* [Jerusalem, 1963], 6a [emphasis added])

Here the Hasidic reading has done precisely that which it would seem is most difficult for it: the new leadership has usurped the rabbinic role precisely in the place where it originated and where its power most critically lies—in the interpretive function. The lineage of rabbinic authority has been wordlessly transferred to the Hasidic master; it is entirely clear to the reader of this passage that R. Ephraim, the grandson of the Ba'al Shem Tov, refers to the Hasidic master/leader rather than to the duly appointed local rabbi (*mara de-atra*, in the traditional parlance) when he speaks of "the sages of the generation." Of course we should recall that R. Ephraim, like a number of other Hasidic leaders, served as both *rav* and *rebbe* in Sudilkov, so for him the distinction may not have been a live issue. The same may be said of Levi Yizhak, author of this very striking parallel to the passage we have just read.

A basic principle in the service of God: We Israelites are obliged to believe in two Torahs, one written and the other oral, both given by a single shepherd. The meaning is as follows: the written Torah was given us by Moses, God's faithful servant, in writing etched on the tablets, black fire on white fire. The oral Torah given to Moses is its interpretation, including "everything a faithful student was ever to discover." This means that the oral Torah as it was given to us essentially follows the interpretation offered by the *zaddiqim* of the generation. *As they interpret the Torah, so it is.* This great power has been given us by the Creator out of love for Israel, His chosen people. All the worlds follow their will [as manifest] in Torah. Thus did the sages say: "The blessed Holy One issues a decree, but the *zaddiq* may nullify it." (*Qedushat Levi, yitro* [Jerusalem, 1958], 134 [emphasis added])

Here rav and *zaddiq* are a single figure, the interpretive function and the righteous power to negate a heavenly decree fully identified with each other! The interpretation *becomes* that which the sage says because of his power to effect change in the uppermost realms, which is where the true Torah dwells. The hermeneutical function reveals itself to be a magical one, as the text changes itself to conform with the interpretation offered by the true *zaddiq*. Here we have something that goes beyond the ongoing presence of the heavenly voice in the deliberations of the rabbis, as documented in the teachings of kabbalists in an earlier age.[44] It is neither the learning of the rabbi nor his role as an authorized interpreter in the chain of tradition that makes him a spokesman for the word of God. It is rather his power, the power of his righteousness, if you will, as *zaddiq*, that makes him the vehicle for revelation in his day. Here the secondary tradition within Judaism, as we have described it above, has indeed become dominant, as the *zaddiq* becomes master over Torah itself.

Thus far the claims for *zaddiq* as the true interpreter of Torah remain within the aggadic realm. There, it may be argued, the claim is a relatively safe one. Medieval kabbalists had already called for complete freedom of interpretation so long as no matter of law is to be affected. This claim is found echoed in Hasidism and explicitly so in the literature of Bratslav.[45] We see in Hasidism a sort of compromise: homiletic license has indeed been given to the *rebbe,* while legal authority is to remain in the hands of the *rav.* In fact, this is the way Hasidism has functioned through much of its history, careful traditionalism in legal matters providing a safe context for theological radicalism and spiritual boldness. The final text we record here is not intended to show the breakdown of traditional legal authority among the Hasidim—not even in the unique sect called Bratslav. It does, however, demonstrate in theory the final handing over of authority, halakhic authority, to the *zaddiq*, and for that reason it is worthy of note. The speaker is R. Nathan of Nemirov, the famous disciple of R. Nahman. His *Liqqutey Halakhot* is an extension of R. Nahman's teachings to cover the institutions of Jewish life, through the form of a series of homilies following the order of the *Shulhan 'Arukh.* Here he deals with the laws of clean and unclean birds, which, it will be recalled, are listed in the Torah but not given any defining characteristics:

"The signs of permitted fowl are not made explicit in the Torah, and the sages say that permitted fowl is eaten only by tradition. . . ." The "fowl" or "bird" here is Metatron, who is of the tree of knowledge of good and evil, which is also the permitted and the forbidden, the pure and the defiled. Scripture says: "Of the tree of knowledge of good and evil you shall not eat" (Gen 2:17). It is forbidden to us to partake of anything in which good and evil are combined, as in the tree. Our eating is uplifted essentially through the oral Torah, the six orders of the Mishnah. These are given over to the *zaddiqim*, those who separate the good from the evil, the permitted from the forbidden. That is why we are told to follow all that the true *zaddiqim* and sages of each generation teach us, as scripture says: "You shall not turn aside from them, right or left" (Deut. 17:8.2), and the sages add "even if they tell you that right is left or that left is right." Purifications are required in each generation, to uplift good from that evil with which it was comingled through Adam's sin of eating of that tree. Not everyone can perform such purifications, however, but only the true *zaddiq* of each generation. Ordinary people, those who have not fully and wholly repented, are not yet at rest. They themselves are like the tree of knowledge of good and evil, sometimes doing what is proper, and sometimes otherwise. Surely then they do not have the power to separate the evil from the good. The true *zaddiq* of each generation is one who has already pushed evil aside altogether; he is like a Sabbath, and he has the strength to effect those purifications, uplifting the sparks that dwell within each thing. He can distinguish good from evil, permitted from forbidden.

The oral Torah was given only to the *zaddiqim*, who are the sages of the generation; since they have set evil aside so fully, the power of purification lies in their hands alone. The rabbis chose this commandment of the pure fowl to indicate this fact: permitted fowl is eaten only by tradition. The fowl is Metatron, the one who represents the tree. Since good and evil are combined in him, it cannot be eaten. Were it not for the *zaddiqim* and sages of the generation, to whom the oral Torah has been given, we would not be able to eat of it at all; it is "eaten only by tradition." The same is true of other eating; it too is possible only through the generation's sages. It is only that the rabbis revealed this more clearly here, since the bird itself is a symbol of that tree. We have only the wise men of our time on whom we can rely; the Torah chose not to offer signs for the pure fowl in order to teach us that we must depend on them, for they alone have the power to transform that tree of knowledge. (*Liqqutey Halakhot, yoreh deʾah, simmaney ʿof tahor* 1 [Jerusalem, 1950], 68)

The *zaddiq* has come full circle: the new leader who stands in the place of the normative rabbinic figure has now become the voice of tradition itself. In this final claim we see Hasidism at its boldest and most audacious stage. That most essentially halakhic area, the realm of *issur we-hetter* (the forbidden and the permitted), has now been transformed and removed from the hands of the *rav* to those of the *rebbe*. No wonder that the rabbinic establishment fought so hard to squelch such a movement! At the same time, however, we see here the conservative streak in Hasidism that was to determine its later character. For as tradition is given over into the hands of the *zaddiq*, he himself takes on the mantle of spokesman for that tradition and becomes its greatest defender. The history of Hasidism bears witness to the fact that in this wedding of normative authority to the charismatic spokesman, it is chiefly the charismatic who is transformed as he feels the mantle of tradition and the responsibility for its maintenance bear down weightily upon him.

NOTES

1. There has not yet been a full treatment of the leadership motif in the literature on Hasidism. The matter has been touched on, however, in the writings of many scholars. See especially B. Z. Dinur, *Be-Mifneh ha-Dorot* (Jerusalem: Bialik, 1955), 83–227; J. Weiss, "Reshit Zemihatah shel ha-Derekh ha-Hasidit," *Zion* 16 (1951); J. Weiss, *Studies in Eastern European Jewish Mysticism* (Oxford: Oxford University Press, 1985), 183–93; M. Buber, *The Origin and Meaning of Hasidism* (New York: Harper & Row, 1960), 128–49; S. Dresner, *The Zaddik* (London: Abelard-Schuman, 1960), 75–141; M. Piekarz, *Bi-Yemey Zemihat ha-Hasidut* (Jerusalem: Bialik, 1978), 280–302; S. Ettinger, "The Hasidic Movement: Reality and Ideals," *Social Life and Social Values of the Jewish People* (=*Journal of World History*) 11, nos. 1–2 (1968): 251–66.

2. The ancient term *hasidim* was used to describe the BeSHT and his followers from the very beginning of the movement. In this usage they were seen as part of a broader phenomenon of pietists who had been on the increase since the end of the sixteenth century when the term was given new life by the Safed revival. In the early anti-Hasidic polemics (1772), the term is widely used and

is the object of wordplays (*hasidim*/*hashudim*, "suspect ones") in such a way as to make it clear that this is the regular designation of the group. See M. Wilensky, *Hasidim u-Mitnaggedim* (Jerusalem: Bialik, 1970), 1:59 (*kat hashudim*, the suspect sect) and 62 (*u-mekhanim shemam hasidim*, self-proclaimed pietists). None of this, however, implies the specific meaning of *hasid* as "disciple," coming in place of the expected *talmid*, as in the phrase *hasid shel mi*. This usage is documented only much later and seems to originate in common speech rather than in the literary sources. *Shivhey ha-BeSHT* (1815; Jerusalem: B. Mintz, 1969) does not yet know this usage, referring to the BeSHT's disciples as *anashav* (143), *anshey segulah de-BeSHT* (75), *anshey havurta qadisha* (144), *ha-sarim le-mishmaʾato* (147), or simply *talmidim* (53), but not *hasidim*. The same is true in the Yiddish version of this text, first published in 1816: *zayne layt* (12b), *zayne hekhste layt* (23a), *mekurovim* (25a), etc. The usage is found only in the later (post-1864) tale literature.

The master of this *hasid* is referred to by a number of terms in the literature, a matter that sometimes leads to misunderstandings or imprecision. His main title in the homiletical literature is *zaddiq* (lit., "righteous one"), but most usages of this term in the early Hasidic sources do not refer exclusively to the leader of a Hasidic disciple group. He is also called *rav* (rabbi), *talmid hakham* (scholar), *mokhiah* (preacher), etc., but none of these is a specific term restricted only to this usage. The Hasidic master was a new institution, for which a precise term did not exist in the vocabularies of those who wrought it. The term *rebbe* in the specifically Hasidic sense does seem to occur in the Yiddish version of *Shivhey ha-BeSHT*: "*un zol im on nemen far eyn rebbe*" (21c).

3. The homiletical literature of the period has been extensively studied, especially for questions of class attitude, social protest, and in an attempt to distinguish both Sabbatian and Hasidic preaching from that of others. See especially the works by Dinur, Weiss, and Piekarz cited in n. 1.

4. See Dresner, *The Zaddik*; G. Nigʾal, *Torot Baʾal ha- toledot* (Jerusalem: Mossad haRav Kook, 1974).

5. Jacob Joseph was rabbi in Shargorod, Rashkov, Nemirov, and Polonnoye. See Dresner, *The Zaddik*, 256n4, based on S. Dubnov, *Toledot ha-Hasidut* (Tel Aviv: Dvir, 1930–31), 94.

6. See G. Scholem, "Demuto ha-Historit shel Rabbi Yisraʾel Baʾal Shem Tov," *Molad* 18 (1961): 335–56.

7. Determining the teachings of the BeSHT is one of the great difficulties in research on Hasidism, since R. Israel left no book of his own and all the later Hasidic masters, despite their highly divergent views, sought to claim the original master as their own. Of first rank in any attempt to characterize the BeSHT's teachings are those few writings which he did leave. To date there are only a few letters that are regarded by most scholars as unimpeachably his, most prominently the letter he sent to his brother-in-law Gershon of Kuty, first published

by Jacob Joseph of Polonnoye in 1781 (translation in L. Jacobs, *Jewish Mystical Testimonies* [New York: Schocken, 1977], 148–55). Second in importance are the many quotations in the name of "my teacher" in the works of Rabbi Jacob Joseph himself. These were later combined with some other materials to form the *Keter Shem Tov* (Zolkeiv, 1794–95); they have yet to be the subject of thorough scholarly examination in their own right. Attention should also be paid, though with greater caution, to the direct heirs of the BeSHT in the Ukraine and especially to his two grandsons, Moses Hayyim Ephraim of Sudilkov (*Degel Mahaneh Ephraim* [n.p., 1808?]) and Baruch of Miedzybozh. Still further caution is needed with regard to quotations from the BeSHT in the writings of Dov Baer of Miedzyrzec and his disciples, who clearly used the authority of the BeSHT for teachings that took a somewhat different direction. An uncritical but most important collection of materials attributed to the BeSHT is *Sefer Ba'al Shem Tov*, ed. Simeon Mendel of Gavartchov (Lodz, 1938). That work is somewhat marred by excessive dependency on writings from the Zydachov/Komarna dynasty. It is clear from all the above that the BeSHT was not a "Kabbalist" as the term was generally used in the eighteenth century (this despite the reported designation as such in the Polish document mentioned in n. 2); he refers only seldom to the symbolic language of contemporary Kabbalists. He does, however, frequently quote and comment on passages from the Zohar. It is also hard to characterize him as a "preacher"; his teachings as reported are short and aphoristic rather than homiletical in the typical lengthy style of the day. He seems to have been especially fond of the pungent play on words, as frequently reported by Jacob Joseph.

8. There is an extensive scholarly literature on *Shivhey ha-BeSHT* and its various recensions. See especially the treatments by C. Shmeruk in *Zion* 28 (1963): 86–105; A. Ya'ari in *Kirjath Sefer* 39 (1964): 249–72, 394–407, 552–61; A. Rubenstein in *Tarbiz* 35 (1966): 174–91, in *'Aley Sefer* 6/7 (1979): 157–86, and in *Sinai* 86 (1980): 62–71, 89 (1981): 59–68, 90 (1982): 269–79. Y. Mondschein has published a full introduction to his facsimile edition of a *Shivhey ha-BeSHT* manuscript (Jerusalem, 1982) containing important material of a textual nature. Mondschein has also replied to one of Rubenstein's articles in *Tarbiz* 51 (1982): 673–80. A literary-structuralist approach to the *Shivhey ha-BeSHT* has been developed by Y. Elstein in his article in *Jerusalem Studies in Jewish Folklore* 2 (1982): 66–79, and in his book *Pa'amey Bet Melekh* (Ramat Gan: Bar Ilan University, 1984). *Shivhey ha-BeSHT* unquestionably contains materials that faithfully reflect the period of the BeSHt's lifetime and information about him and his circle. The historian who makes use of this work has to learn to distinguish the purely legendary material that has been included within it from those passages that contain a grain of historical fact. These distinctions are not made easily and do not depend on the question of the various separate strands from which the work was woven and their editing, to which so much scholarly attention has been

devoted. The specific content of each individual tale must be weighed carefully, compared to what is known from nonlegendary sources, held up against historical realia, etc.

9. See the sources cited in n. 1 and add to them the work of Jacob Katz in *Tradition and Crisis* (New York: Schocken, 1971), 231–44.

10. On the separatist self-perception of medieval German-Jewish *hasidim*, see I. Marcus, *Piety and Society* (Leiden: Brill, 1981).

11. The phrase is found in the epistle sent by the Vilna community to that of Brest-Litovsk, based on Deuteronomy 32:17. The document was part of *Zemir 'Arizim we-Harvot Zurim* (Aleksnits, 1772). It was republished in Wilensky, *Hasidim*, 1:59. The accusation that the *hasidim* are spiritual "newcomers" or innovators is widespread in the bans.

12. *Baba Batra* 12a; *Eruvin* 7a. See N. N. Glatzer, "A Study of the Talmudic-Midrashic Interpretation of Prophecy" (1946), reprinted in his *Essays in Jewish Thought* (Tuscaloosa: University of Alabama Press, 1978), 16–35, as well as E. Urbach, "When Did Prophecy Cease?" *Tarbiz* 17 (1946): 1–11; E. Urbach, "Halachah and Prophecy," *Tarbiz* 18 (1947): 1–27.

13. References, mostly in the form of veiled hints, that the accusation of Sabbatianism was made against the early *hasidim* are widely found in the anti-Hasidic polemical literature. See Wilensky, *Hasidim*, index s.v.v. "Shabbatai Zevi," "Shabtaut," "Shabta'im."

14. See *Hagigah* 12b: "Zaddiq is the foundation of the world," quoting Proverb 10:25. I have discussed this matter in "The *Zaddiq* as *Axis Mundi* in Later Judaism," *Journal of the American Academy of Religion* 45 (1977): 327–47. See also the various treatments of the *zaddiq* by G. Scholem: the chapter "Tsaddik" in his *On the Mystical Shape of the Godhead*. Hebrew version in *Pirkey Yesod be-Havanat ha-Qabbalah u-Semaleha* (Jerusalem: Bialik, 1976); "Three Types of Jewish Piety," *Eranos Jahrbuch* 38 (1969): 323–40; "The Thirty-Six Hidden Tsadikim in Jewish Legends," in *The Messianic Idea in Judaism and Other Essays on Jewish Spirituality* (New York: Schocken, 1971). On *zaddiq* in the rabbinic sources, see R. Mach, *Der Zaddik in Talmud und Midrasch* (Leiden: Brill, 1957).

15. For other references to Hanina in the writings of Rabbi Jacob Joseph, see Dresner, *The Zaddik*, 277n33. This teaching of the BeSHT is also quoted at the beginning of *Keter Shem Tov* #3. See also *No'am Elimelech*, ed. G. Nig'al (Jerusalem: Mossad Harav Kook, 1978), 11a (56).

16. *Yad Yosef* by Joseph Zarfati, printed in Venice in 1616 and in Amsterdam in 1700. The passage quoted is found at the beginning of *lekh lekha* (Amsterdam ed., 12b): "They mean that because he made do with the bare necessities, a high moral rung, the whole world was sustained 'for the sake of Hanina my son'; the reason for this was that 'Hanina was satisfied with a measure of carobs from one Sabbath to the next.'"

17. M. Piekarz, *Bi-Yemey Zemihat haHasidut*, 16ff. It is noteworthy that this state-ment is one of the very few rabbinic-type *divrey Torah* that the *Shivhey ha-BeSHT* (Jerusalem, 1969, 149) also attributes to the Ba'al Shem Tov.

18. See Y. Liebes, "The Messiah of the Zohar," in *Ha-Ra'ayon ha-Meshihi be-Yisra'el* (Jerusalem: Israel Academy of Sciences, 1982), 87–236.

19. On Elijah the prophet, see the psychological study by Aharon Wiener, *The Prophet Elijah in the Development of Judaism* (London: Routledge and Kegan Paul, 1978) and the works quoted in Wiener's bibliography (225ff.).

20. See J. Dan, "On the History of the Hagiographic Literature," *Jerusalem Studies in Jewish Folklore* 1 (1981): 82–100.

21. *Zaddiq* as a designation for Sabbatai Sevi is found in a source included in A. Freimann's *'Inyeney Shabbatai Zevi* (Berlin: Mekizzey Nirdamim, 1912), 54. This passage is discussed by Y. Liebes in the important treatment of the *zaddiq* theme in his "*Zaddiq*, the Foundation of the World: A Sabbatian Mythos," *Da'at* 2 (1978): 37ff.; see esp. nn. 29–31. Cf. Liebes's comments in "The Messiah of the Zohar," 114n118.

22. See J. Weiss, "*Reshit Zemihatah.*" Despite a certain tendency on Weiss's part to exaggerate in the psychological analysis of these materials, I agree with his claim that evidence can be found in the sources of guilt over the (perhaps inevitable) failure of the preachers' mission.

23. Cf. Piekarz, *Bi-Yemey Zemihat ha-Hasidut*, 107ff.

24. Parallels to this text, connecting the distinction made here to that between Noah and Abraham as leaders of their respective generations, are found in the writings of Rabbi Jacob Joseph. See Dresner, *The Zaddik*, 152ff., 284n23.

25. In the previous passage, the Maggid had referred to both types as "complete *zaddiqim*," though this is promptly undercut by the ensuing discussion. The sharp language in which the dichotomy is expressed by Elimelech leaves no doubt that only one of the two is worthy of respect.

26. This is the essential insight of I. Heinemann's *Darkhey ha-Aggadah* (Jerusa-lem: Hebrew University, 1954). On the Hellenistic background of the rabbi as wisdom teacher, see H. Fischel, *Rabbinic Literature and Greco-Roman Philoso-phy* (Leiden: Brill, 1973). On the rabbi in the broader religious context of late antiquity, especially Babylonia, see J. Neusner, "The Phenomenon of the Rabbi in Late Antiquity," *Numen* 16 (1969): 1–20, 17 (1970): 1–18. See also Neusner's "Rabbis and Community in Third-Century Babylonia," in *Religions in Antiquity* (Leiden: Brill, 1970).

27. See my "On Translating Hasidic Homilies," *Prooftexts* 3 (1983): 63–72.

28. In the continuation of the same passage, however, it turns out that the indi-vidual worshiper is to see himself as *kohen*. This shift is a good example of the ambivalent relationship between the democratization of Jewish spiritual life and the promulgation of a new charismatic elite, both of which are typical of early

Hasidism. The passage quoted here contains plays on the words *qorban* (QRV, "draw near") and *'olah* (I.H., "raise up").

29. The idea of prayer as spiritual sacrifice is quite ancient. It may be traced to scripture itself (Hos. 14:3) and is found in the Qumran literature (IQS 9:4, 10:6), A more radical expression of this idea, in which the worshiper places himself on the metaphoric altar, is found in Romans 12:1. S. M. Newton, *Concept of Purity at Qumran in the Letters of Paul* (Cambridge: Cambridge University Press, 1985). Compare with Philo, *On the Special Laws* 1.270 and *Who Is the Heir* 184. Rabbinic sources also see prayer as spiritual sacrifice, *avodah shebalev* (*Ta'anit* 2a). *Numbers Rabbah* 18:21 attributes to Rabbi Simon the view that the worshiper at prayer sacrifices his own fat, blood, and soul. This motif becomes a favorite of later Jewish moralists; see I. Tishby, *Mishnat ha-Zohar* (Jerusalem: Bialik, 1982), 2:183–246.

30. For the Zohar's treatment of the Temple cult, see Tishby's *Mishnat ha-Zohar*, 2:183–246. The Zohar's views on this topic are the subject of a doctoral dissertation by the late and much lamented Rabbi Seth Brody at the University of Pennsylvania.

31. Cf. the discussion of *zaddiqim* and preachers as healers in Piekarz, *Bi-Yemey Zemihat haHasidut*, 120ff.

32. *Gittin* 62a, *rabbanan iqeru melakhim* ("rabbis are called kings"), apparently often confused in later quotation with Nedarim 20b, *man mal'akhey ha-sharet, rabbanan* ("Who are the angels? Rabbis.").

33. Kalonymos Kalman Epstein of Cracow (d. 1823), author of this work, was a leading disciple of Elimelech of Lezajsk.

34. *Ahavat Shalom* contains the sermons of Menahem Mendel of Kossov (1768–1826), progenitor of the Kossov/Vyznitsa dynasty.

35. Wilensky, *Hasidim*, 2:210.

36. Quoted in *Orot Yisra'el* (Jerusalem: n.p., n.d.), a collection of Ruzhyn teachings, p. 152.

37. See n. 12 above.

38. See M. Himmelfarb, "From Prophecy to Apocalypse: *The Book of the Watchers* and Tours of Heaven," in *Jewish Spirituality: From Bible through the Middle Ages*, ed. A. Green (New York: Crossroad, 1986), 145–65. On the prophetic links of the early Enoch literature, sec G. W. E. Nickelsburg, "Enoch, Levi, and Peter: Recipients of Revelation in Upper Galilee," *Journal of Biblical Literature* 100 (1981): 575–600. M. E. Stone has a very interesting note on prophetic models for Enoch in his "Lists of Revealed Things," in *Magnalia Dei: The Mighty Acts of God: Essays on the Bible and Archaeology in Memory of G. Ernest Wright*, ed. F. M. Cross et al. (Garden City NY: Doubleday, 1976). My thanks to M. Himmelfarb for her help with this note.

39. S. A. J. Heschel, "Inspiration in the Middle Ages," in *Alexander Marx Jubilee Volume*, Hebrew Section (New York: Jewish Theological Seminary, 1950).

40. See the discussion by M. Idel in his *Religious Experience in the Thought of Abraham Abulafia* (Albany: State University of New York Press, 1988).

41. Cf. the parallel sources quoted by R. Schatz-Uffenheimer in *Quietistic Elements in Eighteenth-Century Hasidic Thought* (Jerusalem: Magnes Press, 1968), 175lf.

42. See the discussion in Idel, *Religious Experience*, which serves to update the treatment in Schatz-Uffenheimer, *Quietistic Elements*.

43. M. W. Levinsohn-Loewy, *Sefer Hashanah: The American Hebrew Yearbook* (1938): 113–27.

44. See Scholem, *Messianic Idea in Judaism*, 300ff., quoting the kabbalists R. Meir Ibn Gabbai and R. Isaiah Horowitz.

45. See the sources quoted in my *Tormented Master* (Tuscaloosa: University of Alabama Press, 1978), 330n5.

10

The *Zaddiq* as *Axis Mundi* in Later Judaism

The history of Judaism as presented to us by the *Wissenschaft des Juden-tums* of the nineteenth and early twentieth centuries depicted a religious civilization that seemed to have little in common with those societies to which the emerging methodology of the history of religions was first being applied in that same period. With the exception of certain minor "fringe" phenomena, Judaism comprised a world of sober theology, law, and ethics. The battle with myth had been won once and for all in the biblical period, and thus the comparative method of myth, ritual, and symbol studies could contribute little to an understanding of the main lines in postbiblical Jewish thought. This image of Judaism has now been laid to rest, at least in most scholarly circles if not in popular preaching, by the work of Erwin Goodenough, Gershom Scholem, Jacob Neusner, and many others. The present paper, resting particularly on Scholem's conclusions concerning the ongoing presence of mythical motifs in medieval Judaism, particularly as crystallized in Kabbalah, seeks to examine the holy man traditions in medieval and postmedieval Jewish sources, and to demonstrate the perseverance with which myths of sacred person survived and developed in the literature of later Judaism.

One of the most precious notions of modern Jewish apologetics has been the idea that in Judaism there are no uniquely holy persons. Both prophecy and priesthood had ceased to function in postbiblical Israel. The rabbi, working as scholar, teacher, and legal authority, claimed for himself neither the personal charisma of the prophet nor the sacerdotal role of the priest; every Jew had equal and direct access to God through Torah and prayer. The recent work of Jacob Neusner and his school has done much to rectify this one-sided presentation insofar as the Talmudic rabbi is concerned (Neusner: 1969, 1970). Outside of the rabbinate per se, such terms as *zaddiq* and *hasid* were taken by apologists to be embodiments of moral or pious perfection in the language of Jewish authors, but were not to represent what are seen in studies of India, tribal Africa, or Siberia as holy man traditions. If all of Israel is holy and chosen, a "kingdom of priests," so the argument would go, there is no need for the holy man in his classic roles as intercessor, as administrator of sacraments, or as source of blessing. Of course any student of the history of religions, particularly in noting the minority status Jews held in the Hellenistic, Iranian, Christian, and Muslim realms, all of them replete with cults of saints and holy men, must have raised an eyebrow at the ability of such a religious society as a whole to remain faithful to so lofty and rarified a position.

Another "sacred cow" of that view of Judaism, reinforced more recently by the Zionist influence on Jewish historiosophy, concerns the relationship of classical Judaism to its notions of sacred space. While Judaism after the destruction and dispersion was forced, so it is claimed, to reduce its dependency upon the Temple Mount and other loci of mythic or cosmological significance, the nexus of relationship between the Jew and the Holy Land was never compromised or weakened either by the full symbolization of sacred space (i.e., Jerusalem becoming the heavenly Jerusalem alone) or by the transference of that sacrality to any other place.

In applying Mircea Eliade's insights around the symbol of *axis mundi* to the holy man traditions of later Judaism, both of these notions will of necessity be challenged. While neither is by any means being called into question here for the first time, some will still be surprised to discover in Jewish mysticism, particularly after the sixteenth century, a highly developed theory of sacred person, standing at the center of the cosmos and having about him a clearly articulated aura of a new Jerusalem. The fact is that postexilic Jews maintained a highly complex and ambivalent attitude toward their traditions of sacred space (cf. Goldenberg). While longing for a return to the Holy Land continued unabated, the dispersed community of necessity had to have within it various means of more ready access to the sacrality which its great shrine had once provided; Israel wandering through the wilderness of exile was to find that it still had need of a portable Ark of the Covenant. One of the ways in which this was provided was by a transference of *axis mundi* symbolism from a particular place to a particular person: the *zaddiq* or holy man as the center of the world.

It should be noted at the outset that such a transference of sacred space symbolism to that of sacred person takes place in Christianity from the very beginning. When the author of John 2:19–20 has Jesus speak of his own body as the Temple, the stage has been set for the assertion that Christ himself is the *axis mundi* upon which the new edifice of Christianity is to be erected. Sacred person has become the new sacred center. Indeed, if there remains a geographical point which serves as *axis mundi* for classical Christianity, it has moved a very significant few hundred yards from the Temple Mount to the Mount of Calvary. In Islam also, though in rather different form, there exists an association of holy man and *axis mundi*. While the rigors of Muslim orthodoxy and anti-Christian reaction did not allow that the prophet himself be described in such terms, Sufi masters from the eighth century onward speak of the *qotb*, a single holy man who is the "pole," standing at the height of the world's spiritual hierarchy. In later Shi'ite and Isma'ili conceptions of the Imam and his role in the cosmos, the matter is even more clearly articulated.

I

In beginning our examination of this motif in the history of Judaism, we turn first to certain phenomena of popular Hasidism, that eastern European pietistic revival which may be said to have been the last development within classical Judaism before the advent of modernity. Among the disciples of Rabbi Menahem Mendel of Kotzk, one of the great Hasidic masters of nineteenth-century Poland, a song was current that reflects the attitude of a disciple to a visit at the master's court. The chorus of that song runs as follows:

> Keyn Kotzk furt men nisht;
> Keyn Kotzk geyt men.
> Veyl Kotzk iz dokh bimkoim ha-mikdesh,
> Kotzk iz dokh bimkoim ha-mikdesh.
> Keyn Kotzk darf men oyleh regel zeyn.[1]

> To Kotzk one doesn't "travel";[2]
> To Kotzk one may only walk.
> For Kotzk stands in the place of the Temple,
> Kotzk is in the Temple's place.
> To Kotzk one must walk as does a pilgrim.

The place where the *zaddiq* dwells, be it the miserable Polish town that it is, becomes the new Temple, the place of pilgrimage. A generation or two before Kotzk, we are told that the disciples of Rabbi Nahman of Bratslav, of whom we shall have more to say later, were heard running through the streets of that town shouting: "Rejoice and exult, thou who dwellest in Bratslav!" in an ecstatic outburst following the *zaddiq's* establishment of his "court" in that place (*Avaneha Barzel* 13). Of course *zahali wa-roni yoshevet Bratslav* is a play on Isaiah 12:6, except that Bratslav has replaced the "Zion" of the biblical source. Nahman has come to Bratslav; a new Zion has been proclaimed. The town of Sadegora, the later dwelling place of Rabbi Israel of Ruzhin, was described as "the place of the Temple" and the verse "They shall make me a sanctuary and I will dwell in their midst" (Exod. 25:8) was applied to it (Nisensohn: 93).[3] To provide a more contemporary example, I am told that the Jerusalem meeting place of the Lubavitch *hasidim* contains within it a scale model of the Lubavitcher rebbe's headquarters at 770 Eastern Parkway in Brooklyn! Where, indeed, is the true Jerusalem?

It will be noted that the sources thus far quoted are hardly the theoretical writings of the great Hasidic masters, let alone the classics of Judaism. We shall come to these later. But it is just these epiphenomena of popular religion, so often ignored by traditional Jewish scholarship, that the student of the history of religions is learning to take seriously.

We will also note that the claim made in these reports is in a certain way a conservative one. In all of them it is not the *zaddiq* himself as person who seems to have become the *axis mundi* or new Jerusalem, but rather the place where the *zaddiq* dwells. Our contention is, however, that this can only be the very latest stage of development, one which already assumes the notion of the *zaddiq* himself as sacred center. We should also make it clear that we are not claiming by way of these examples that Jewish mysticism or Hasidism abandoned its awareness of or commitment to Jerusalem as the center of the universe. As Eliade has amply shown us, the peculiar logic of *homo religiosus* has no difficulty in absorbing the notion that the cosmos may have more than one center.

II

This image of the *zaddiq* as one who stands at the center of the cosmos will not come as a complete surprise to anyone familiar with the rabbinic sources in this area. A particularly oft-quoted dictum (Hag. 12b) immediately comes to mind: Upon what does the earth stand? R. Eleazar ben Shamu'a says:

Upon a single pillar, and *zaddiq* is its name. Thus scripture says: "*Zaddiq* is the foundation of the world." (Prov. 10:25)

In order to understand the later developments in the Kabbalistic/Hasidic tradition, it is indeed to the rabbinic sources, and particularly to their uses of the term *zaddiq*, that we must first turn our attention. Our best guide in this matter is Rudolph Mach, whose monograph on the subject offers both an exhaustive collection and a perceptive analysis of the materials.

The problem in the rabbinic literature is that the term is both very widely and loosely used; there are many cases where it is applied so generally that a specific meaning can hardly be assigned to it. It does seem possible, however, to delineate two general strands in the material. First, *zaddiq* is used in the forensic sense: "righteous" as what our legal nomenclature would term "innocent." The world is divided between *zaddiqim* and *resha'im*, those found righteous and those found wicked by the standards of heavenly judgment. This sort of righteousness is acquired by proper behavior, especially by conquest of the passions. Minimally, one may be a *zaddiq* in this sense simply by belonging to the better half of humanity or by being more possessed of merits than burdened by sins.

The second usage of the term *zaddiq*, however, is a much more exacting one, and it is that which will prove of interest to us here. This usage takes the *zaddiq* to be a unique individual, a wonder-worker from birth, heir to the biblical traditions of charismatic prophecy as embodied in Moses and Elijah, and at the same time the rabbinic version of the Hellenistic god-man or quasi-divine hero.[4] It is in the former sense primarily that Joseph is the archetypical *zaddiq*: his righteousness is acquired through suffering and passes its greatest test in his conquest of passion when confronting the advances of Potiphar's wife. In the latter sense, it is rather Moses who is the ideal type, recognized from birth as containing the hidden light of creation or as being the bearer of the divine presence in the world.[5]

Both of these uses of the term *zaddiq* have their place in the rabbinic legends on the creation of Adam, and this leads to some confusion. When we are told that God saw both *zaddiqim* and *resha'im* proceeding from Adam's descendants, and that He turned to look only at the deeds of the *zaddiqim* so that the sight of the wicked would not dissuade Him from man's creation, we are seemingly dealing with the former, the forensic use of the word *zaddiq* (*Gen. Rab.* 8:4). When the Aggadah says, however, that

God took counsel with the souls of the *zaddiqim* for advice concerning the future of this humanity He was creating, the same aggadic motif seems to have slipped into the second usage. God would hardly be consulting all those who are to be found more righteous than wicked among Adam's offspring; He is rather seeking out the counsel of those unique individuals scattered through history whose task it will be to sustain the world.

This is indeed the function of the *zaddiq* in that second sense of the term: he is the sustainer of the world. A great number of rabbinic dicta attest to this function in one way or another. Of Hanina ben Dosa, a disciple of Yohanan ben Zakkai and an ideal type of rabbinic folk piety, we are told: "The entire world is sustained for the sake of Hanina My son." Or, more generally, "The entire world is sustained by the merits of the *zaddiqim*" (Ber. 17b). "God saw that the *zaddiqim* were few; He rose up and planted them in each generation" (Yoma 38b). "As long as there are *zaddiqim* in the world, there is blessing in the world; when the *zaddiqim* die, blessings vanish" (Sifre Deut. 38). It is in this sense also that our original passage is to be taken: the *zaddiq* is the pillar upon whom the world rests in the sense that he is the one through whose merits the world is sustained. The cosmological background of this figure of speech, however, should not be ignored. It may not be in a purely metaphoric sense that the rabbis are speaking here.

There are recorded several discussions among the rabbis as to the number of *zaddiqim* whose presence is required in a given generation to offset the world's wickedness and to allow for its continued existence. The Palestinian sources prefer the numbers thirty and forty-five (Mach, 135f.), both of which are as yet unexplained. It is the Babylonian tradition, quoted in the name of Abaye, that fixes on the number thirty-six, a figure which becomes so important in later Jewish folklore. Both Mach and Scholem have indicated the source of this number in Egyptian astrological traditions (Mach, 137ff.; Scholem, 1971:251ff.). At the same time, there seems to be a notion of singular spiritual leadership in a generation among the Palestinian rabbis. Both the *tanna* R. Eleazar and the *amora* R. Yohanan proclaim that the world was created, or is sustained, for the sake of a single *zaddiq* (Yoma 38b). R. Simeon ben Yohai, who will be of great importance to us a bit later, seems to shock us with his immodesty when he says: "If there are thirty, twenty, ten or five *zaddiqim* in the world, my son and I are among them. If there are two, we are they, and if one, it is I" (Gen. Rab. 35:2).

The notion of singular leadership in a generation also exists in rabbinic sources outside the specific *zaddiq* terminology. God takes care, we are told, not to dim the light of one generation's leader until the sun of the next has begun to shine in the world (Qidd. 72b).[6] Both in the generation of Hillel and in the days of Yavneh, it is reported, a heavenly voice was heard by the assembled sages to proclaim: "There is one among you who is fit to receive the holy spirit, except that the generation is not worthy" (Yerushalmi Sotah 9; 24b; Buchler 8f.). This seems to point to a single charismatic leader of Israel, one who may be revealed as such only in a deserving generation. While the term *zaddiq ha-dor* (the *zaddiq* of the generation) does not appear in the old rabbinic sources, it seems clear that such a notion is not entirely foreign to the rabbis' thinking.[7]

III

As we turn our attention from the early rabbinic materials to the speculative universe of thirteenth-century Kabbalah, particularly as manifest in the Zohar, a number of new factors enter to complicate our discussion. Here *zaddiq* has become a conventional term for the ninth of the ten divine emanations (*sefirot*): the same word thus designates an aspect of the divine Self and a particular group of humans. This ninth level of divinity is otherwise commonly referred to as *yesod* ("foundation"), as Joseph, as the phallus of *Adam Qadmon*, or, in better Kabbalistic language, as "the sign of the holy covenant." This complex of associations is hardly accidental. Joseph is the *zaddiq* by virtue of *shemirat ha-berit*, sexual purity in the face of temptation. *Zaddiq* is the foundation of the world based on the verse in Proverbs and on the rabbinic reading we have mentioned, as the reproductive organ is the foundation of the human body. It is this ninth emanation, standing in the central sefirotic column, which serves as the vehicle through which divine life flows into the feminine *malkhut* or *shekhinah*, the last of the *sefirot*, and thence into the corporeal world. One will therefore find in Kabbalistic literature abundant references to *zaddiq* as pillar, foundation, and so forth, including all the expected phallic associations of such terms. The earthly *zaddiqim* are those who stand in particular relation to that element of divinity, arousing the upper flow by virtue of their deeds below.

There is a single pillar that reaches from earth to heaven, and *zaddiq* is its name. It is named for the *zaddiqim*. When there are *zaddiqim* in the world, it is strengthened; when there are not, it becomes weak. It bears the entire world, as Scripture says: "*Zaddiq* is the foundation of the world" (Prov. 10:25). If it is weakened, the world cannot exist. For that reason, the world is sustained even by the presence of a single *zaddiq* within it. (Bahir, ed. Margaliot 102)

It is probably because of this association of the human *zaddiq* with the *zaddiq* figure in God that the early Kabbalists of Provence and Gerona tended to employ the term *zaddiq* as the embodiment of their pietistic ideal, rather than *hasid*, the term more usual to other medieval sources (Tishby 1961: 659, 667).[8] There is an implication, though hidden in the subtleties of symbolic language, that the earthly *zaddiq* is to be seen as the phallus of the human community, i.e., the channel of influx for divine blessing, allowed to be such because of extreme purity of both thought and deed. The frequent associations of *zaddiq* with pillar, foundation, etc., which we could easily be tempted to seize upon in our search for *axis mundi*, refer almost always to God as *zaddiq*. Our primary interest here is in his human counterpart, of whom the Zohar but rarely says:

He who knows these secrets and serves with wholeness, cleaving to his Lord ... draws blessing into the world. Such a man is called *zaddiq*, the pillar of the cosmos. (Zohar 1:43a)

We should also call attention to the belief of the Zohar and of nearly all Kabbalists in metempsychosis. When such authors speak of one *zaddiq* standing in the place of another, they may often (though not always) be claiming that the latter-day leader is none other than his predecessor reincarnate.

The central figure of the mystical dialogues that are the large part of the Zohar is R. Simeon ben Yohai, that same Simeon ben Yohai who had proclaimed the possibility that he might be the single leader of his generation back in second-century Palestine, here re-created in the imagination of a thirteenth-century Spanish Kabbalist. Now that briefly recorded claim has been expanded into a much fuller narrative, in which God Himself is forced to recognize R. Simeon's unique status.

"Abraham will surely be" (Gen. 18:18); YiHYeH (= will be) has a numerical equivalent of thirty.

One day Rabbi Simeon went out and saw that the world was completely dark, that its light was hidden. Said Rabbi Eleazar to him: Come, let us see what it is that the Lord desires. They went and found an angel in the form of a great mountain with thirty lashes of fire issuing from its mouth.

"What are you planning to do?" Rabbi Simeon asked the angel.

"I seek to destroy the world, for there are not thirty *zaddiqim* in this generation. Thus the Holy One, blessed be He, said concerning Abraham: "He will surely be," meaning that Abraham was equivalent to thirty.

Said Rabbi Simeon: "I beg of you, go before the Holy One and tell Him that I, the son of Yohai, am to be found in the world."

The angel went to God and said: "Master of the World, surely that which ben Yohai has said is known to You."

God answered: "Go and destroy the world. Pay no heed to ben Yohai."

When the angel returned to earth, ben Yohai saw him and said: "If you do not leave, I decree that you will not be able to return to heaven, but will be in the place of 'Aza and 'Aza'el [the fallen angels]. When you again come before God, say to Him: 'If there are not thirty righteous ones in the world, let it be twenty, as is written: "I shall not do it for the sake of the twenty" (Gen. 18:31). And if not twenty, then ten, for it says further: "I shall not destroy for the sake of the ten" (Gen. 18:32), and if there are not ten, let it be two—my son and I—as Scripture says: "The matter (*davar*) will be upheld according to two witnesses" (Deut. 19:15). Now *davar* refers to the world, as scripture says: "By the word (*davar*) of God the heavens were made" (Ps. 33:6). If there are not two, there is one, and I am he, as it is written: "*Zaddiq* [in the singular] is the foundation of the world."

In that hour a voice went forth from heaven saying: "Blessed is your lot, Rabbi Simeon, for God issues a decree above and you nullify it below! Surely of you it was written: 'He does the will of them that fear Him'" (Ps. 145:19). (Zohar Hadash, *wa-yera*, 33a)

The second-century Rabbi Simeon, according to an old aggadic source, had also claimed that he, with the help of the prophet Ahijah of Shilo, could sustain Israel until the advent of the messiah (Gen. Rab. 35:2).[9] Now the author of the Zohar has its central character announce that "through this book Israel will come forth from exile" (Zohar 3:124b). The Zohar abounds with praises of R. Simeon, who is commonly referred to in that work as "the holy lamp." He is described as the new Moses and the new Solomon (Zohar 2:148b–149a). A pillar of cloud hovers over him, as it did over the desert tabernacle when God spoke with Moses. As all the sages of the world once turned to Solomon to reveal his wise secrets, now they turn to R. Simeon. While there are other sages and *zaddiqim* present in the pages of the Zohar, it is completely clear to the author that none of them approaches the singular role of this figure. In both name and function, he is the single leader of his generation.

> Blessed is that generation in which R. Simeon ben Yohai lives. Blessed is its lot both above and below. Of it scripture says: "Blessed are you, O land whose king is free" (Eccles. 10:17). What is the meaning of "free"? He lifts up his head to offer revelations and is not afraid. And what is the meaning of "your king"? This refers to R. Simeon, master of Torah, master of wisdom.
>
> When R. Abba and the companions saw R. Simeon, they would run after him saying: "They walk behind the Lord; He roars like a lion" (Hos. 11:10; Zohar 3:79b; cf. also 2:15a)

The association of *zaddiq* of the generation with "king of the land" should already raise our antennae to the possibility of *axis mundi* symbolism here. Certainly there is something of sacral kingship in the air. When R. Simeon is referred to as *qayyema de-'alma*, pillar of the cosmos (Zohar Hadash 24a; Tishby 1957, 31), we are yet closer to a notion of holy man as sacred center. But we need not rely upon any passages of dubious intent. The Zohar finally tells us explicitly that R. Simeon is to be viewed in light of Israel's ancient traditions of sacred space:

> R. Simeon went out to the countryside, and there he ran into R. Abba, R. Hiyya, and R. Yose. When he saw them he said: "This place is in need of the joy of Torah." They spent three days there, and when he was about to depart each of them expounded upon a verse of Scripture.
>
> R. Abba began: "The Lord said to Abram after Lot had departed from him . . . raise up your eyes and see . . . all the land which you see I will give to you and your seed forever" (Gen. 13:14–15). Was Abraham to inherit all that he saw and no more? How far can a man see? Three,

four, perhaps five miles. And He said "All the land which you see"? But once Abraham had looked in the four directions, he had seen the entire land. Further, God lifted him up over the Land of Israel and showed him how it was the connecting point of the four directions, and thus he saw it all. *In the same way, he who sees Rabbi Simeon sees the entire world*; he is the joy of those above and below.

R. Hiyya began: "The land upon which you are lying I will give to you and to your offspring" (Gen. 28:13). Was it only that place which God promised him, no more than four or five ells? Rather at that time God folded the entire Land of Israel into those four ells, and thus that place included the entire land. If that place included the whole land, how much clearer it is *that Rabbi Simeon, lamp of the world, is equal to the entire world!*" (Zohar 1. 155b–156a, based on sources in Gen. Rab. 44:12 and Hul. 91b)

Seeing R. Simeon is parallel to Abraham's vision of the Holy Land. R. Simeon contains the entire world as Jacob's rock at Bethel contained the entire Land of Israel. The *zaddiq* stands at the center of the cosmos, the place where the four directions meet. He is thus the earthly extension of that element within the Deity which is called *zaddiq*, a this-worldly continuation of the Kabbalistic *'amuda de-emza' ita*, the central pillar of the universe. He is in a highly spatial sense the earthly counterpart to the pillar of the sefirotic world.

We should take special note of the Zohar's claim that R. Simeon's generation is unique in having such a leader. While some of the later Kabbalistic sources will claim that such a soul is necessarily present in every generation (Zohar 3:273a, R.M.; *Sha'ar ha-Gilgulim* 29b; *Sha'ar ha-Pesuqim, wa-ethanan,* perhaps based on Gen. Rab. 56:7), others seem to agree that the appearance of such a soul is a rare event in human history and that very few such *zaddiqey ha-dor* exist, each serving to sustain the world for a number of generations that come in his wake. Nathan of Nemirov, the leading disciple of Nahman of Bratslav, claimed in the early nineteenth century that this soul had appeared but five times in Israel's history: it was present in Moses, R. Simeon, Isaac Luria, the great sixteenth-century Kabbalist, Israel Ba'al Shem Tov, the first central figure of Hasidism, and in his own master. It will next appear in the person of the messiah (*Hayyey MoHaRaN* 11, *gedulat hassagato* 39).

But we are running a bit ahead of ourselves. We have made passing reference earlier to the Zohar's R. Simeon as a figure of Moses *redivivus* (*'Emeq ha-Melekh* 4b, 33b).[10] In order to understand the spatial centrality assigned to R. Simeon, we shall first have to turn our attention to the Kabbalistic Moses.

It is now well known through Scholem's monumental interpretations of Lurianic Kabbalah and Sabbatianism that the Kabbalists saw the soul of Adam as containing within it all those souls that were to be born in all future generations (Scholem 1973, 36ff., 302ff.). In this way Kabbalah comes much closer to containing a notion of original sin than most writers on Judaism have been willing to ascribe to the Jewish tradition. A less well known but perhaps equally significant part of the Kabbalistic myth is the notion that the soul of Moses contained within it the souls of all Israel. Each Jewish soul, according to Luria, is related to one of the six hundred thousand mystical letters of the Torah. Each Israelite has a particular soul root that is also manifest in a letter of Scripture. The soul of Moses, however, contains *all* of these; it is called the *neshamah kelalit*, the general or all-inclusive soul. It is because Moses' soul contains both the entire Torah and the entire people that he becomes the instrument of revelation. The structural parallel to classical Christianity is obvious here; revelation is being depicted in nearly incarnational terms. Moses receives the Torah as an outward sign that his own soul is the full embodiment of Torah.[11] According to another formulation, Moses is related to Israel as the soul is related to the body; the leader is his people's soul (*Sefer ha-Gilgulim* 63a).[12]

We now understand the centrality of Moses and the Mosaic revelation in the salvific scheme of Kabbalah. The old rabbinic sources had already seen Sinai as the event which redeemed Israel from the curse of Eden (*Shabbat* 146a). If all souls were tainted by the sin of Adam, the Kabbalists now claim, all the souls of Israel are redeemed by their presence in the soul of Moses as he ascends the mountain. Alas, the sin of the Golden Calf interrupts this moment, and Sinai does not become the final redemption. But Israel's access to this great purification continues to be through Moses. Primarily, of course, the way to achieve this access is through Moses' Torah; in this sense Kabbalah remains faithfully rabbinic. (Otherwise, it would be precisely that Christian faith garbed in the symbols of Jewish esoterica which some Renaissance humanists hoped it to be!)

Nevertheless, the figure of Moses himself remains important here, and the fact that R. Simeon is believed to be Moses' soul reincarnate, an old/new leader who can bring all the souls of Israel to God and compose a book which now *will* effect the final redemption, is what makes him so essential to the mythic structure of the Kabbalah. No wonder that he stands at the center of the world![13]

IV

We now turn to the further development of this motif in eastern European Hasidism, where it was to receive its fullest and most radical treatment. Here a new type of charismatic leader had taken central stage in the Jewish community; claims are made both for his spiritual powers and for his temporal authority, which seem to go far beyond anything previously articulated in Jewish sources. Of the rich legacy of holy men and religious leaders from Israel's past, various paradigmatic figures are brought forth to justify the emphasis placed on the centrality of the rebbe and his boundless powers. Elements of both sacral kingship and cultic priesthood are drawn out of biblical sources in defense of the Hasidic master. Several dynasties within the movement claimed descent from the House of David; particularly in the traditions of the Ruzhin/Sadegora dynasty, the motif of kingship was treated with great seriousness, including an assumed right to regal lifestyle (Nisensohn). It is told that R. Abraham Joshua Heschel of Apt, in leading that portion of the Yom Kippur liturgy in which the words of the ancient high priest are recounted, changed the text from the third to the first person ("Thus did I say . . ."), for he recalled that he had filled that office in a prior incarnation (*'Eser Orot* 114). Many a collection of Hasidic homilies, in dealing with the Torah portions of Leviticus, will make a complete transference from priest to rebbe in verse after verse, almost as a matter of course.

It is the model of *zaddiq*, however, that is most prevalent in the Hasidic discussions of leadership; by the second generation of the movement this term was well on its way to becoming the universally recognized appellation for a Hasidic master. As popularly conceived, it is through this *zaddiq* that the devotee must turn to God; being at once bound to both heaven and earth,[14] the *zaddiq* becomes a channel through which others may ascend to God and by means of which blessing comes down into the world (*Degel Mahaneh Ephraim, be-ha'alotekha* 199b; *Maggid Devaraw le-*

Ya'aqov 64b). As is the way of Hasidic literature, the discussion here draws on the whole of the earlier tradition, but focuses the materials in such a way as to emphasize the values of the new movement. This is most strikingly seen in the following passage from the writings of the Ba'al Shem Tov's successor, the Maggid of Miedzyrzec:

> We begin with the Zohar's interpretation of "One generation passes and another comes" (Eccles. 1:4). There is no generation which does not have a *zaddiq* like Moses (Zohar 1:25a; Gen. Rab. 56:7). This means that Moses included the entire six hundred thousand of the generation. Thus the rabbis said: a woman in Egypt gave birth to six hundred thousand from one womb.[15] This is why "One generation passes and another comes" is said in the singular and not the plural: it refers to the *zaddiq* of the generation. Thus the rabbis say: "Before the sun of Moses set" (Qiddushin 72b), etc., as scripture tells us that "*Zaddiq* is the foundation of the world." Now it is known that *yesod* [the ninth *sefirah* = *zaddiq*] has the power to ascend and draw the divine abundance forth from above because it includes all.[16] The same is true of the earthly *zaddiq*: he is the channel who allows the abundance to flow down for his entire generation. Thus the rabbis said: "The whole world is sustained for the sake of Hanina My son." This means that Hanina brought the divine flow forth for all of them, like a pathway through which all can pass; R. Hanina himself became the channel for that flow [a supraliteral reading of Ber. 17b]. In the same was he [the *zaddiq*] the ladder of which it is said: "They go up and down on it" (Gen. 28:12). Just as he has the power to cause the downward flow of divine bounty, so can his entire generation rise upward through him. (*Or Torah, noah*)

Every generation has a *zaddiq* like Moses or like R. Hanina ben Dosa; he is the channel of flow in both directions between the upper and lower worlds. Here the *axis mundi* symbolism regarding the *zaddiq* is quite fully developed; he is the all-inclusive central pillar linking heaven and earth. Jacob's ladder, perhaps the oldest and best-known *axis mundi* symbol of Jewish literature, has undergone a far-reaching transformation. The *zaddiq* is no longer the dreaming observer of the angels who go up and down the ladder's rungs, as was the biblical Jacob. Nor is he a participant in the constant movement along the ladder, a reading which is found in various other Hasidic comments on this passage. Here the *zaddiq* himself *is* the ladder; it is through him that others may ascend to God.

It is not clear whether the Maggid believed in a *single zaddiq* who was the pillar of a given generation, or whether he accepted the notion that there might be more than one such figure in the world at a given time. While this passage seems to point to a singular figure, and such a claim was later made concerning the Maggid himself (*'Eser Orot* 24),[17] many other passages in his writings and those of his disciples seem to point in the other direction. Even in such a work as the *No'am Elimelekh*, where the emphasis placed upon the *zaddiq*'s powers and the importance of his role in the devotional life of the devotee seems utterly boundless, the idea of a single *zaddiq ha-dor* is not prominent. In the writings of Shne'ur Zalman of Liadi, founder of the HaBaD/Lubavitch school, the phrase "the spreading forth of Moses in each generation" is quoted (e.g., *Torah Or* 68c), but here as earlier it seems to refer more to the presence of Moses in every Jew, or at least in every *zaddiq*, than it does to a single figure. The same is true in the writings of Menahem Nahum of Chernobyl, yet another disciple of the Maggid and a major theoretician of early Hasidism (*Me'or Eynayim, bereshit* 11a). The reality of Hasidic life, which saw many contemporary figures revered as *zaddiqim*, tended to encourage the notion that each *hasid* would have to seek out his own master, the one whose soul root was closest to his own, that *zaddiq* then becoming for him the center of his own subjective cosmos. It should be noted that even in circles where the legitimacy of many *zaddiqim* was recognized, the followers of a particular master would show no hesitation in ascribing symbols of the sacred center to their own leader. Again, the world can have more than one center. Thus R. Uri of Strelisk, a disciple of Jacob Isaac of Lublin around the turn of the nineteenth century, is supposed to have said:

> He who comes here is to imagine that Lublin is the Land of Israel, that the master's court is Jerusalem, his room is the Holy of Holies, and that the *shekhinah* speaks through his mouth. (*Nifle'ot ha-Rabbi* 202)[18]

After his master's death, R. Uri himself was regarded as a *zaddiq*, and presumably he would have expected his disciples to relate to his court in the same way. Nor would he have wanted the disciples of any other master to treat that *zaddiq* with any less "respect."

With regard to the Ba'al Shem Tov himself, however, the situation was somewhat different. There is some reason to believe that the BeSHT, unlike the circle of preachers from whose midst he and the Hasidic movement emerged in the fourth and fifth decades of the eighteenth century, did believe in a single *zaddiq ha-dor* and perhaps that he saw himself in this way (Weiss: 85f.). Since we have virtually no access to the BeSHT's life or teachings except as filtered through the writings of adulating disciples and descendants, the truth of his own belief on such a matter is difficult to determine. It is quite clear, however, that long after the Ba'al Shem's death the claim that he had been *zaddiq ha-dor*, in the fullest sense of that term, was widespread among the *hasidim*. Here was the one figure whose memory was most universally revered in Hasidic circles; devotion to the BeSHT and his teaching was taken as a defining characteristic of adherence to the movement. It should not surprise us then, that the editor of *Shivhey ha-BeSHT*, the legendary biography of the master first published in 1815, makes the claim that the Ba'al Shem Tov's soul was that of Moses and Rabbi Simeon reincarnate (*Shivhey ha-BeSHT* 8)!

The Ba'al Shem Tov had two grandsons who became important figures in the history of Hasidism. The elder of these two brothers, Moses Hayyim Ephraim of Sudilkov, was the author of *Degel Mahaneh Ephraim*, a collection of homilies that is an important source for his grandfather's teachings. R. Ephraim, as he is called, does mention the belief that his grandfather possessed the soul of R. Simeon ben Yohai (*Degel, be-shalah* 101a).[19] When it comes to the question of singular versus collective leadership in his own time, however, the author clearly opts for the latter; he speaks rather frequently of the *zaddiqim*, in the plural, of a given generation (*Degel, zaw* 156b, *emor* 181b). Like other writers on the subject, he seems to accept the reality of his times. His younger brother Barukh, however, was of a different mind. Barukh of Miedzybozh became embroiled in public controversies with nearly all the *zaddiqim* of his day. While both power politics and differences in religious attitudes contributed to these conflicts, underlying both lay the fact that Barukh considered himself to be the sole legitimate heir to his grandfather's mantle of leadership and, as the reigning *zaddiq* in the BeSHT's town of Miedzybozh, viewed all other claimants as usurpers.

It was only the nephew of Ephraim and Barukh who took up the notion of singular leadership and gave it a truly central place in his reading of

Judaism. We refer to Rabbi Nahman of Bratslav (1772–1810), the problematic and tormented great-grandson of the BeSHT and one of the great religious geniuses of Israel's history.[20] Influenced alike by the rich rabbinic/Kabbalistic legacy in this realm and by his own family's personal claims with regard to it, *zaddiq ha-dor* became a major motif in Nahman's writings; it is in large part through his often unacknowledged influence that the term came to be present in other latter-day Hasidic parlance as well.

Nahman sought to bring about a new revival within Hasidism. He felt that the *hasidim* had, in his words, "grown cold" since the time of the Ba'al Shem Tov (*Hayyey MoHaRaN, sihot ha-shayakhim la-sippurim* 19) and that a new spark needed to be kindled. The great enemy of true Hasidism, as far as he was concerned, was popular *zaddiq*ism, in part as personified by his own uncle Barukh. Nahman sought to elevate and purify the *zaddiq* figure far beyond anything that was known elsewhere in Hasidism. The chief vehicle of this new revival from within was to be the notion of *zaddiq ha-dor*, with Nahman himself as its standard-bearer. If there is only one true *zaddiq* at the center of his generation, the misdeeds of lesser figures are of no importance, except insofar as they verify that *zaddiq*'s claim to singular leadership. Though recognized in this role only by a small band of disciples, Nahman maintained that recognition was not at first essential to his role. "There is one," he writes, "who has no apparent authority at all, but nevertheless in a deeply hidden way he rules over his entire generation, even over the *zaddiqim*" (*Liqq.* 56:1).

It was widely whispered in early Bratslav circles that Nahman was a reincarnation of R. Simeon; it has been shown that the figure of R. Simeon as portrayed prominently even in some of Nahman's own teachings is nothing but a thinly veiled reference to the author himself (*Liqq.* 29; *Sippurim Nifla'im* 166; Piekarz: 13ff.). He refers to the *zaddiq* of the generation as the Holy of Holies and also as the *even shetiyah*, the mythical rock at the center of the world from which Creation originated and upon which the Temple was built (*Liqq.* 61:7). He is the true source of insight, needed for all proper interpretation of Torah in his time:

> Know that there is a soul in the world through which the meaning and interpretation of Torah is revealed. This is a suffering soul, eating bread and salt and drinking measured bits of water, for such is the way of Torah. All interpreters of Torah receive from this soul. (*Liqq.* 20:1)

How characteristically Jewish a way to speak of *axis mundi*! The spatial imagery is there, to be sure; as readers of Eliade we could ask for nothing better than the sacred rock at the center of the world. But here *zaddiq* as *axis mundi* is also the channel of interpretive power through which Israel has access to the Torah. The primal energy that radiates from the center now manifests itself as literary creativity through the ongoing promulgation of the oral Torah. This soul *is* in effect the oral Torah for its time, the bearer of the ongoing Mosaic revelation.

When Nahman moved his court to the Ukrainian town of Bratslav in 1802, he quoted in his initiatory sermon a passage from the Zohar in which God shows Abraham the way to the Land of Israel. That sermon is shot through with images of the Holy Land, a point which could hardly be lost on its hearers (*Liqq.* 44). Bratslav is here being proclaimed a new center, the residence of the single true *zaddiq*. Now we understand why it was that the disciples ran through the streets shouting cries of exultation as though to the dwellers in Zion. The single *zaddiq*, the portable ark or Holy of Holies, has found a new resting place. The shouting Hasidim must have seen in themselves a reflex of the dancing David, exulting as the ark of the Lord was brought into their city and a new cosmic center was proclaimed.

It will come as no surprise to the reader of Eliade to discover that the *zaddiq* in Bratslav is also described as a great tree, of which the disciples are leaves and branches (*Liqq.* 66:1, 176).[21] In one brief passage among the several that employ this metaphor, however, Nahman breaks new ground in the notion of *axis mundi*. He lends to the tree imagery a doubly ironic twist, a twist that thoroughly summarizes this uniquely complex figure's view of himself in this regard. Nathan, the faithful disciple, recalls that his master once said: "You see in me a great and wondrous tree with beautiful branches and roots. But at bottom I lie truly in the earth" (*Hayyey MoHaRaN* II, *gedulat hassagato* 5).

In the Hebrew in which it is recorded, the statement has little impact. What does it mean here to "lie in the earth"? Translate the phrase back into the Yiddish in which it was originally spoken, however (published Hasidic texts are most often Hebrew summary translations of oral Yiddish), and its meaning is obvious. "You see in me a great and wondrous tree . . . *ober fun unten lig ikh take in dr'erd*—at bottom I am rotting in hell!" The statement is a confession of all Nahman's well-documented torments and inner doubts about himself and his worthiness for the role that he had chosen.

Nahman, however, is more complex than this. Translate the same Hebrew phrase not into Yiddish but into the other language of Jewish mystical piety, Aramaic, and you come up with a precise paraphrase of Daniel 4:11–12: *ilana . . . be-ram shorshohi be-are'a shevuqu*. But why should this seemingly obscure verse have a place in Nahman's self-description? The fact is that these words in Daniel follow immediately upon a verse that has major importance in Bratslav. Daniel 4:10 contains the phrase *'ir we-qadish min shemaya nehit*, "a holy angel come down from heaven." This phrase is well known in Bratslav and in Nahman's own writings as an acronym for SHiMe'oN (Simeon), Nahman's mystic alter ego (Nathan's introduction to *Liqq.*, cf. Piekarz: 14f.). Nahman was a master of literary form and was one who had wide experience in disguising and yet revealing himself through many masks. Here, in the double pun, he is at once presenting himself as the great tree, the holy angel on earth, the new Rabbi Simeon, and a miserable sinner who is rotting in hell. The *zaddiq* has indeed become the *axis mundi*, here in a unique blending of sacral persona and real person; he is the great tree who in an entirely new way unites the three-tiered cosmos in his own person.

NOTES

1. First recorded by Ruth Rubin among her *Yiddish Folksongs*, Prestige International 13019. Her informant for the song was a former resident of Tyszowce (Tishevits), Poland, a town where there were Kotzker *hasidim*. Such Yiddish songs, intended in a humorous vein, are not unknown among the *hasidim*: witness the highly ambiguous *Brider, Brider*, recorded by the Bobover group on CCL 636. It is possible, however, that this song was a *maskil's* parody of the journey to Kotzk.

2. The phrase "to travel (*furen*) to a *zaddiq*" means "to be the disciple of a master." In Hasidic circles the question "*tsu vemen furt ir*" ("to whom do you travel?") would mean: "To which *zaddiq* do you owe your loyalty?"

3. The description here is attributed to R. Hayyim of Nowy Sacz (Sandz), an opponent of the Sadegora dynasty.

4. Mach 53ff. In his two treatments of the term *zaddiq* and its history (1962, 1969), Gershom Scholem seems to ignore the second rabbinic usage of the term. In seeking to make the point that throughout pre-BeSHTian Hasidic literature, *hasid* is always a more extreme category of description than the relatively nor-

mative *zaddiq*, he has selected the rabbinic *zaddiq* usages only from the former of the two categories here outlined. He is then able to find in Hasidism "a complete turnabout of terminology" (Scholem 1962, 114). Might one not better speak of a second rabbinic usage of the term *zaddiq* described in some detail by Mach, a usage that is picked up by the early Kabbalah and much emphasized in the Zohar, thence passing on into Hasidism, where the terminology of the Zohar as well as that of the early rabbis becomes essential in the formulation of the new ideal type? Isaiah Tishby has already disagreed with Scholem on his treatment of the term *zaddiq* (cf. 1961, 663ff.).

5. On Joseph's conquest of his passions, cf. *Ruth Rab.* 6:4 and *Pirke Rabbi Eliezer* 39. This aspect of *zaddiq* is discussed by Mach (26ff.). The association between Joseph as the prototypical *zaddiq* and this event is only made explicit, however, in Zohar l:59b and 1:153b–154a. Cf. also the passage from Moses De Leon's responsa quoted by Tishby (1961: 664). On Moses as *zaddiq*, cf. Sotah 12a, Exod. Rab. 1:20, 24.

6. But see also *Tanhuma lekh lekhah* 5, which seems to disagree.

7. I have not been able to pinpoint the first usage of *zaddiq ha-dor* as a technical term. It is not to be found in early rabbinic sources, and it was probably born of the medieval exegesis of Genesis 6:9. Parallel terms (*gedol ha-dor, hasid sheba-dor*) are early but do not necessarily indicate a belief in singular leadership.

8. Kabbalists did not develop a notion of earthly *hasid* parallel to *hesed* in the sefirotic world. Such a claim is made for Abraham alone in *Bahir* 191(132), but it is not developed. Of course, the whole mythicosexual quality of the energizing of the upper world would have been thrown off balance by such a notion. For an example of the term *zaddiq* specifically referring to a person who has powers above, cf. Recanati, *qedoshim* 26d (based on the usage in *Mo'ed Qatan* 16b), where the term is almost translatable as "sorcerer."

9. This is the most likely source of the notion that Ahijah was the teacher of the Ba'al Shem Tov.

10. In *Sha'ar ha-Gilgulim* 2:8a–10a Luria is seen as such a figure. *Tiqquney Zohar* 69 (ed. Margaliot. 111b) claims that Moses will return at the end of days to reveal the meaning of the Zohar! This already seems to assume the identity of Moses and Rabbi Simeon.

11. The Zohar (2:11b and Zohar Hadash *yitro* 35a) compares the *tevah* in which the infant Moses floated on the Nile to the *tevah* in which Torah scrolls are kept in the synagogue. (Cf. also *Qaneh* 12a–b; *Sha'ar ha-Pesuqim* 56a, 98a; *Megalleh 'Amuqot ofan* 113.) This claim is later repeated in *Degel Mahaneh Ephraim, wa-yiqra* 148.

12. This is the proper *Sefer ha-Gilgulim*; the work to which we have referred earlier is a version of *Sha'ar ha-Gilgulim*, misnamed *Sefer* by the Przemysl publisher. Although these formulations are original in Kabbalistic thinking, they hark back to that strand of old rabbinic tradition that saw Moses in nearly divine

terms, a tendency largely eliminated in medieval Judaism outside of Kabbalah. On the rabbinic material, cf. Meeks. While the parallels to Christianity and even more directly to Samaritanism are noteworthy, the development here is not necessarily influenced by non-Jewish sources.

13. Certain Kabbalists believe that Moses is present in every generation. The idea is first expressed in the later portions of the Zohar literature. Cf. Zohar 3:216b and 273a (both *Ra'aya Mehemna*) and *Tiqquney Zohar* 69 (112a, 114a); Tishby (1961:688). When spelled out, however, these sources seem to refer more to the presence of Moses in *every* Jewish soul than to the existence of an individual Moses figure in each generation. The Hasidic sources refer this tradition to the *zaddiq*.

14. Hasidic authors tirelessly quote with regard to the *zaddiq* a passage in Zohar 1:31a, *de-ahid bi-shemaya we-are'a* ("who holds fast to heaven and earth"). The reference in that source, however, is to *zaddiq* as an aspect of God, not to the earthly *zaddiq*. On the human *zaddiq*, cf. Zohar 1:43a and 2:15a.

15. The Zohar is quoting *Cant. Rab.* 1:15:3. The Midrashic context makes it clear that R. Judah ha-Nasi is merely making a startling assertion to awaken a sleepy audience; he goes on to explain that Moses is as important as the entire generation. The Kabbalists read his assertion literally to support their assertion that the soul of Moses contained all the others.

16. *Yesod*, often referred to by the name *kol* ("all"), includes the flow of all eight upper *sefirot*.

17. The statement is in the name of Israel of Ruzhin, the Maggid's great-grandson. Of course, in such a statement, the Ruzhiner was making a similar claim for himself as the Maggid's heir.

18. Quoted in Heschel (291). Cf. also *Or ha-Nifla'ot* 22b for a lengthy comparison of the death of a *zaddiq* with the destruction of the Temple. Some of this is the eulogist's hyperbole, but the choice is interesting. It is also told with regard to the BeSHT that one of his disciples, R. Wolf Kutzis, sought to undertake a pilgrimage to the Holy Land. When he went to a ritual bath to prepare for his journey, he was told in a vision that the ark and the tablets of the law were to be found, respectively, right there in Miedzybozh and in the Ba'al Shem's heart. Recorded at Lubavitch in the 1940s. I have not found this tale in any printed collection, although Wolf Kutzis's intended journey is the object of another legend in *Ohaley Zaddiq* 8a.

19. He quotes this in the name of R. Lipa of Khmelnik and seemingly with a certain hesitation.

20. Cf. my book *Tormented Master: A Life of Rabbi Nahman of Bratslav* (Tuscaloosa: University of Alabama Press, 1980).

21. The tree image for master and disciple is already found in Vital's *Sha'ar ha-Gilgulim* 1b.

WORKS CONSULTED

Traditional Hebrew Sources

Avaneha Barzel. Abraham Hazan. Jerusalem, 1961.

Bahir. Ed. R. Margaliot. Jerusalem, 1951.

Degel Mahaneh Ephraim. Moses Hayyim Ephraim of Sudilkov. Jerusalem, 1963.

Emeq ha-Melekh. Naftali Bachrach. Amsterdam, 1648.

'Eser Orot. Israel Berger. Israel, 1973.

Gilgulim (Sefer ha-Gilgulim). Hayyim Vital. Vilna, 1886.

Hayyey MoHaRaN. Nathan of Nemirov. New York, 1965.

Liqqutey MoHaRaN (Liqq.). Nahman of Bratslav. Jerusalem, 1969.

Maggid Devaraw le-Ya'aqov. Dov Baer of Miedzyrzec. Jerusalem, 1962.

Megalleh 'Amuqot. Nathan Spira of Cracow. Lvov, 1858.

Me'or 'Eynayim. Menahem Nahum of Chernobyl. Jerusalem, 1966.

Nifle'ot ha-Rabbi. Moses Walden. Piotrkow, 1912 (?).

No'am Elimelekh. EliMelekh of Lezajsk. Warsaw, 1908.

Or ha-Nifla'ot. Moses Walden. Piotrkow, 1913

Or Torah. Dov Baer of Miedzyrzec. Jerusalem, 1968.

Qaneh (Peli'ah). Anonymous. Korzec, 1784

Recanati 'al ha- torah. Menahem Recanati. Lvov, 1880.

Sha'ar ha-Gilgulim. Hayyim Vital. Przemysl, 1875.

Sha'ar ha-Pesuqim. Hayyim Vital. Jerusalem, 1868.

Shivhey ha-BeSHT. Dov Baer of Linitz. Berlin, 1922.

Sippurim Nifla'im. Samuel Horowitz. Jerusalem, 1961.

Tiqquney Zohar. Ed. R. Margaliot. Jerusalem, 1948.

Torah Or. Shne'ur Zalman of Liadi. New York, 1954.

MODERN WORKS

Brown, Norman O.
    1966, *Love's Body.* New York: Random House.
Buchler, Adolf
    1922, *Types of Palestinian-Jewish Piety.* London: Jews' College.
Dresner, Samuel
    1960, *The Zaddik.* London: Abelard-Schumann.
Eliade, Mircea
    1954, *The Myth of the Eternal Return.* New York: Bollingen.
    1959, *The Sacred and the Profane.* New York: Harcourt, Brace.
    1963, *Patterns in Comparative Religion.* New York: Meridian.
Goldenberg, Robert
    1975, "The Broken Axis." *Journal of the American Academy of Religion* 45, no. 3
    Sup. (September 1977): 869–82.

Heschel, Abraham Joshua
   1973, *Kotzk: In Gerangel far Emesdikeyt*. Tel-Aviv: Ha-Menorah.
Mach, Rudolph
   1957, *Der Zaddik in Talmud und Midrasch*. Leiden: Brill.
Meeks, Wayne
   1968, "Moses as God and King." *Religion in Antiquity*. Ed. Jacob Neusner.
   Leiden: Brill, 354–71.
Neusner, Jacob
   1969–70, "The Phenomenon of the Rabbi in Late Antiquity." *Numen* 16: 1–20; 17:
   1–18.
Nisensohn, S.
   1937, *Dos Malkhusdige Khsides*. Warsaw: Khsides.
Piekarz, Mendel
   1972, *Hasidut Braslav*. Jerusalem: Mossad Bialik.
Scholem, Gershom
   1962, *Von der mystischen Gestalt der Gottheit*. Zurich: Rhein.
   1969, "Three Types of Jewish Piety." *Eranos Jahrbuch* 38: 331–47.
   1971, *The Messianic Idea in Judaism*. New York: Schocken.
   1973, *Sabbatai Sevi: The Mystical Messiah*. Princeton: Bollingen.
Tishby, Isaiah
   1957, *Mishnat ha-Zohar*. Vol. 1. Jerusalem: Mossad Bialik.
   1961, *Mishnat ha-Zohar*. Vol. 2. Jerusalem: Mossad Bialik.
Weiss, Joseph
   1951, "Reshit Zemiatah shel ha-Derekh ha-Hasidit." *Zion* 16: 46–105.

11

Hasidism

Discovery and Retreat

The image of Judaism among the world's religions is one of proclaimer of divine transcendence *par excellence*. The personified God of the Hebrew Bible, alone and bound by no order except that of his own making, stands supreme over all his creation. He is Father (occasionally even Mother) and Judge, King, and Lover. He has chosen Israel and entered into a covenant of intimacy with her. However close he is to his loved ones, indeed however much he is to be found in their very midst, his transcendence remains uncompromised; God stands over against man and world, in love as he does in judgment.

This view of Judaism, recently restated with such elegance in the 1975 Vatican guidelines for interfaith contact with Jews ("the Jewish soul—rightly imbued with an extremely high, pure notion of divine transcendence"), is of course not completely lacking in foundation. It is largely true for the Bible itself and even may be said to characterize the dominant strand in Jewish religion down through the ages. The fact that we shall here study, within the very heart of a group that saw itself as completely faithful to that heritage, formulations of experience that seem entirely contradictory to whatever we think of as biblical western understandings of God, should teach us as much about the history of religions altogether as it does about the particular case of Judaism.

Hasidism is a very late movement within the history of European Judaism; its first central figure, the Ba'al Shem Tov, died in 1760, and most of the literature we are to study comes from the late eighteenth century. Much has been made recently of the fact that socially Hasidism must be seen as an early modern movement, a reaction from within to the breakdown of the long-established social order. Be this as it may, Hasidism *religiously* must be viewed as a late postmedieval phenomenon. Its theological assumptions and limitations are unapologetically (for the last time in

Jewish history) those of the classic rabbinic-medieval world: the authority of Scripture, the inviolability of *halakhah*, the mysterious truth hidden in the teachings and parables of the Talmudic sages. The entire burden of tradition is to be borne with joy, and nothing in human experience may exist that will declare any part of it invalid.

Hasidism may be characterized as a movement of mystical revival; it was a popular phenomenon, embracing the lower classes and rapidly capturing the loyalty of vast numbers of Jews throughout Eastern Europe. As will be expected in such a movement, its leaders were not primarily formally trained theologians but preachers, its doctrinal formulations were loose and easily swayed by the situation in which they were uttered, and passion readily carried the day over caution in the ways one spoke of God. In good Jewish fashion, absolute "orthopraxy" was maintained (only the fixed hours and some textual details of prayer were loosened), though this failed to stave off the rabbinic critics of the movement who raged relentless war against it for the first thirty years of its existence, and whose latter-day followers continue to sneer at Hasidism even to this day.

The main body of Hasidic literature, homiletical, devotional, and legendary (the oral tale was a classic Hasidic form), does not show an essential change in the typology of religious experience as recorded in the earlier Jewish tradition. Yes, there is much made of informal Yiddish conversation with the Master of the Universe, as well as of argument and even occasional chiding, but none of this was entirely new and should not concern us here. Our interest is in the exception rather than the rule in Hasidic literature, in expressions of religious experience that seem utterly alien to the spirit of the tradition out of which they emerge. A number of figures in the early days of Hasidism flirted seriously with such expressions, left striking record of them here and there, and then retreated from them. Our interest is in the inner movement in the history of Judaism to which such seeming anomalies attest, in their appearance and the reaction it caused, and in understanding the rapid retreat from them. Our contention is that Hasidism came to the threshold of a major breakthrough in religious consciousness, but one that at the same time threatened to destroy all that its Western legacy thought was required for the preservation of the religio-social order. At the edge of this abyss, it retreated into safer expressions of traditional Jewish piety.

The sort of material that we seek, formulations of experience that cross the bounds into the realms of pantheism, acosmicism, or mystical union, are not to be found in the literature of Hasidic tales. There the religious expressions are more of the orthodox variety: the tales were frozen into writing only later and were intended for mass consumption. The rabbis appear in the tales generally as loving children of the Father or as loyal, if familiar, servants of the King. It is to the homiletic literature of Hasidism, and then chiefly to that of its first few generations, that we must turn for the more unusual formulations. Even there, it should be emphasized, they are often only half expressed or combined with metaphors more to be expected in Jewish sources.

The Ba'al Shem Tov himself left almost nothing by way of written record. All that can be authenticated as coming from the pen of the first great master himself seems to be a few letters (including a very revealing one). There are, however, a great many quotations from the Ba'al Shem Tov contained in the writings of his various disciples. Most prominent among these sources are the works of Jacob Joseph of Polonnoye (d. 1784). We begin with one of these quotations, couched in the seemingly "harmless" language of the king and his son:

I heard from my teacher, of blessed memory, a parable that he spoke before the blowing of the *shofar*. There was a very wise king who, by means of optical illusion, made walls, towers, and gates. He commanded that he be approached through these gates and towers, and he ordered that the royal treasury be scattered at each gate. One went up to the first gate and returned, another, etc. Finally his loving son struggled hard to reach his father the king. Then he saw that there was no separation between them, that it had all been optical illusion. The meaning is understood, and "the words of a wise man's mouth are gracious." (Eccles. 10:12)[1]

Minimally, the parable (recorded in typically clumsy and elliptical fashion) speaks of the dangers of being led astray in the course of mystical ascent. Some are so lured by the glitter of transcendental experience that they forget what the ascent was all about, returning to the world with mere illusory treasure. The truly faithful son does not have his head turned by riches; he thus comes to know that there is no real content to religious experience but the encounter with God himself.

That the Ba'al Shem was a person of such ecstatic "journeys" we know from the letter that has been mentioned: most of it is a description of just such an ascent. Here he seems to place himself over against a great deal of Kabbalistic tradition, heavily laden with detailed descriptions of the worlds above and the particular meaning of each stage of the journey.

Does the parable tell us more? Is the son also to realize that the world from which he has come is one of illusion? Is he to see that he too is naught and that there is nothing but the king? I think not, or not yet. The phrase that would indicate the latter would be "there was no separation between them," and the Hebrew seems to suggest that intimacy is thus permitted, but not that they are actually one.

The existence of the phenomenal world is probably not at issue here, as it usually is not in the rather practically and devotionally oriented teachings of the Ba'al Shem Tov. His concern is rather that of constructing a sort of mental monism, showing the disciple that in all his *thoughts*, wherever they may stray, there is nothing real but God. This teaching itself has rather far-reaching and potentially dangerous implications, especially since the Ba'al Shem was wont to apply it to thoughts of evil as well as to the meaningless glitter of spiritual titillations. An understanding of this will be our reward for following closely a typically abstruse bit of homiletics, the opening passage in his disciple's *Toledot Ya'aqov Yosef*, in which the teacher referred to is the Ba'al Shem Tov himself:

> It is said in the Talmud that Joseph was liberated from prison on the New Year, as scripture says: "He set it as witness in Joseph when he went forth upon the Land of Egypt" (Ps. 81:6).
>
> To understand this we must recall the Tiqquney Zohar's comment on: "I the Lord have not changed" (Mal. 3:6)—In relation to the wicked God does change and hide Himself . . . in various garbs, veils, and shells . . . these are chaos, void, darkness, etc. Of these scripture says: "I shall hide My face from them" (Deut. 32:20). But for those who are bound to Him and His *shekhinah*, He never changes." So there are various garbs and veils in which the Holy One, blessed be He, is hidden.
>
> I heard from my teacher, of blessed memory, that where a person knows that God is hiding, there is no hiding. . . . All the workers of

iniquity split apart" (Ps. 92:10). This is the meaning of: "I shall hide, hide My face from them" (Deut. 31:18); the verse means to say that He will be hidden from them in such a way that they will not know that God is there in hiding. I have also heard from him that the five words *'amar 'oyev 'erdof 'assig 'ahaleq* ["The enemy said: I shall pursue, catch, divide"—Ex. 15:9] begin with five 'alephs: the Aleph of the universe is hidden here, just as in the name SamaEL . . .

Once a person knows this great principle, that there is no curtain separating him from his God, then even if distracting thoughts come before him while he is at study or prayer, being the garb and veils in which God is hiding—since he knows God is hiding in them, there is no hiding.

This is why *ha-shanah* ("the year") is numerically one more than Satan: add the one of the universal Aleph, for there too is He hiding. Now we understand why it was on the New Year that Joseph came out of prison. Once Joseph knew the *New Year* (lit.: "Head of the Year"), namely that Satan plus the One who stands at the head make the New Year, for He of whom scripture says: "His kingdom rules over all" (Ps. 103:19) is hidden even within the Satanic shells—then the shells are defeated and the year is renewed. When a person knows this, "all the workers of iniquity split apart"; they were the shells that formed the prison for the *shekhinah*. Thus was Joseph, now also in the corporeal world, freed from prison: through this knowledge he had broken the bonds.[2]

Translation: True liberation comes about through the realization that God is hidden even in the seeming forces of evil. Here the Ba'al Shem Tov goes much farther than he had in our earlier parable. Not only is it the illusory beauty of heavenly ascent that may keep one from God; it is also wayward and seemingly demonic thoughts that in fact may contain him! The references to Samael and Satan are crucial here. They remind us that Hasidism emerged from circles that had only of late cut away the demonic elements in their mystical theology. We also see the intellectual-spiritual means by which this cutoff had been effected. Here the archons of the demonic universe, usually treated with such utter seriousness by the Kabbalistic sources, have no power over the one who sees through them, and perhaps have no existence at all outside the unliberated mind. More significantly, such liberation happens not only through ecstatic or transcendent experience. *Awareness* itself seems to suffice: once you *know* that God is hidden in evil, you have in fact found him. A kind of abbreviated hide-and-seek, if you will, in which you don't actually have to touch the quarry to declare him found. In the heights and in the depths of man's inner universe, the Ba'al Shem tells us, there is naught but God.

What then of the phenomenal world? The earliest sources of Hasidism, as we have noted, seem concerned less with questioning its existence than with assuring the possibility of its conversion. The old Kabbalistic image of "the uplifting of sparks" became central here: wherever a person turns, whatever he may encounter, contains sparks of divinity that seek to rise to God through him. "Know Him in all your ways" (Prov. 3:6) became a kind of watchword in early Hasidism, as did the Zohar's "There is no place devoid of Him." All, however, depended on awareness. There is no place devoid of Him" really meant "There is no place or situation that cannot bring a person of awareness back to the presence of God." Hasidism had a penchant for extreme examples:

> Through everything you see, become aware of the divine. If you encounter love, remember the love of God. If you experience fear, think of the fear of God. Even when in the toilet you should think: "here I am separating bad from good, and the good will remain for His service!"[3]

At this point we should stop to ask what it is in these Hasidic sources that makes them surprising to the western religious frame of mind. The notion that God is to be found everywhere? Surely the author of Psalm 139 would not be shocked. That the glories of the upper worlds and the terrors of death and the netherworld are nothing when seen from the perspective of one who has true faith in God? Again, one could find support for such a view in scripture and tradition. No wonder that it has more than once been said of Hasidism that from a doctrinal point of view there is virtually nothing new in the movement. The Hasidim, of course, would be the first to support this reading.

Not so quickly, however, shall we accept this point of view. Given the historical context of Jewish mystical thought, something important has already happened here. The reality of the Kabbalistic universe has begun to be called into question. The outer phenomenal world may remain relatively untouched by the earliest teachings of Hasidism, but the inner "world of truth," as the Kabbalists called it, had started to crumble. Seeking a religion in which personal piety and enthusiasm would be the highest values, the popularizing tendencies of early Hasidism found no room for the heavily arcane quality of the old Kabbalistic worldview. Having turned against the aloofness of the rabbis for their Talmudic mental gymnastics, seemingly without value and beyond the reach of the common Jew, they could not help but feel the same way about the infinitely complex structuring of the cosmos and the meditations on each and every one of the countless spheres that had been promulgated by the post-Lurianic Kabbalists. Simplicity, wholeness of heart, personal awareness of the constant presence of God—these were to carry the day in the new movement, and intellectual mysticism would have to bow before them.

> The mystics have discovered many meanings in each word of prayer. No one person can know them all. One who tries to meditate on the hidden meaning of the prayers can only perform those meditations that are known to him. But if a person joins his entire self to a word, all the hidden meanings enter of their own accord.[4]

Unable to openly deny the world of Kabbalistic gnosis (for this too had become orthodoxy), Hasidism here simply undercuts its value. The same will happen to other areas of Kabbalistic doctrine; it is through the simplification and veiled destruction of the typically medieval multitiered universe of Kabbalah that Hasidism creates a cosmology of its own and enunciates precisely those formulations that are of interest to us here.

This step is taken in the second and third generations of Hasidic development, most particularly in the school of Dov Baer the Maggid ("preacher") of Miedzyrzec. The Maggid was the second great leader of the Hasidic community and the last single figure who commanded the loyalty of even most of the Hasidic groups. By both temperament and education a very different man from his predecessor, the Maggid brought to Hasidism an intellectual-theological sophistication that the movement had not known in its earliest days. An avid student of Kabbalah long before he met and was "converted" by the Ba'al Shem Tov, he in effect sought to offer a rereading of various key terms and symbols in that tradition in light of the new ecstatic devotion by which he was so attracted. He built around himself a school of young followers, several among them major religious *illumi-*

nati in their own right; almost all of the major works of Hasidic thought and schools of interpretation within the movement are somehow rooted in this circle around the Maggid.

We turn our attention first to the *sefirot*, the graded series of ten divine emanations that form the core of all Kabbalistic expression since the thirteenth century. These serve, it will be recalled, both as the stages through which the hidden God comes to be manifest in the revealed creation and as the steps the adept must follow in his journey toward God. They represent an inner structure of the universe believed to be repeated at every level of existence, including within the soul of man as microcosm. This latter fact allowed room for the emergence of a specifically Kabbalistic psychology, usually presented in a moralizing context. This psychology, a view of the inner life of man in terms of the sefirotic structure, gained importance from the sixteenth century, especially through the influence of Moses Cordovero's popular treatise *The Palm Tree of Deborah* (*Tomer Devorah*). It is always understood in these works, however, that the psychological import of the ten rungs is but a reflex of their role in cosmology.

In Hasidism, the *sefirot* have largely been relegated to the world of psychology alone.[5] The Maggid uses the old terms frequently, but almost always in discussions of the inner life of the Hasid: *hesed* and *din*, the right and left sides of the cosmic balance in the Kabbalah, have now become love and fear in the life of the worshiper. The "seven structuring days" in sefirotic cosmology now usually refer to the range of human emotions or moral qualities that must be perfected. In fact the old Kabbalistic cosmology has been vitiated, and only the *first* and *last* of the *sefirot* remain significant in the Maggid's view of the universe. The first is *hokhmah* ("wisdom"), also called by the name *'ayin* ("nothing"); the last is *malkhut* or *shekhinah*, taken here (as in rabbinic sources but not in classical Kabbalah) to refer to the indwelling presence of God in the world.

What follows is one of the many statements in which this "abbreviated" Kabbalah appears in the writings of the Maggid's school. Using the genre of the Kabbalistic tradition itself, and piecing together a number of symbols that are taken from the medieval sources, here Menahem Nahum of Chernobyl has turned Kabbalah against itself. He speaks of the two divine names, YHWH and *'Adonay*, one representing the God beyond and the other God inherent in all things:

All the worlds depend on this—the unification of the God beyond and the God below. Now when these two names are joined together with their letters interspersed in this way (YAHDWNHY), the combined name both begins and ends with the letter *yod*. "You have made them all in wisdom" (Ps. 104:24), and *yod* represents *hokhmah*, the primal source of all the letters. . . . *Hokhmah* is the ultimate prime matter; it is called by the sages *hyle*, from the words *hayah li* ("I had it"). All things were in it; from it they emerged from potential into real existence.

Even though the *'aleph* is the first of the letters (and thus one might expect that it should be used to designate this primal substance), the *'aleph* itself is constructed of two *yods* with a diagonal *waw* between them. The first *yod* refers to primal *hokhmah*, the prime matter in which all the worlds were included. The *waw* (shaped like an elongated *yod*) represents a drawing forth and descent, the bringing forth of that potential. Thus were all the worlds created, finally forming the second *yod*, called the lower *hokhmah* or the Wisdom of Solomon [*shekhinah*], the aspect of *'Adonay*, divinity as garbed in all things and filling the world.

When a person does all his deeds for the sake of God, he draws all things in the lower world near to the upper fount of *shekhinah*, the Creator Himself who calls all the worlds into being. By means of his awareness he fulfills "Know Him in all your ways" (Prov. 3:6). This "knowing" or awareness is a unitive force; it binds together the upper *yod* and the lower *yod* so that the entire universe forms one single *'aleph*. This is why God is called "the cosmic *'aleph*."[6]

The cosmos ultimately consists of two *yods* (*hokhmah* and *malkhut*), God before or above creation and God inherent in the universe. The rest of the sefirotic world is merely the *waw*, the extension or connecting link (*da'at*) by which they are joined together. Man's task is the cultivation of his own *da'at*, in the form of awareness, so that he too may become a channel for drawing together the God beyond and the God within.

The universe may be viewed from either of these two ends. When seen from the point of view of *hokhmah*, the beginning of emanation, the world is yet nothing. Here all is pure potential; no separation from the One has yet taken place. *Hokhmah*, in a well-known play on words, is *koah mah*, undefined divine energy or potential. *Hokhmah* is a pure flow of *hiyyut*, the divine life force, and nothing more. However, "potential" existence here is conceived as already defined potential. The world as it is to be, down to every final detail, already exists in *hokhmah*.

> The tree is planted from seed, and that tree bears fruit. Surely the tree, its branches, and its fruit were all there in the seed from the beginning, but in a hidden way.[7]

Though Hasidic sources refer to *hokhmah* by the Greek term *hyle*, what they really have in mind is pure form more than unformed matter.

At the other end of the sefirotic process we find *malkhut*, the presence of divinity in the things of this world. Here the physical creation has already taken place; it is God within world rather than world within God to which we now turn our attention. The sense that the world is fraught with divine presence was the essential insight of the Ba'al Shem Tov that the Maggid had found so renewing. He, however, sought for it a more sophisticated cosmological setting. Yes, the world is filled with divinity. All things are enlivened, or in fact reified, only by the presence of the *hiyyut* within them. All other properties they have about them, including substance, extension, and so forth, are merely the "veils" that cover and hide the *shekhinah*, the only real thing about them.

God has made "something" (the ephemeral phenomenal world) out of "nothing" (*'ayin*; his own Self before manifestation). Man's essential devotional task, as the Maggid and his disciples frequently repeat, is to make "nothing" out of "something"—in their contemplative lives to so strip both self and world of corporeality that it is again as it was before the process of Creation began. This "stripping," however, is really a matter of seeing through a veil of illusion—knowing that God is there in hiding. By this it becomes clear that the *process* of emanation through the sefirotic world, from hidden potential to the reality of being, is no process at all. Everything is in the end as it was in the beginning; the task of the devotee is to become aware of this sameness, to discover the hidden divinity within the world, and thus to see that Nothing, or God as he was before creation, is in fact all that exists.[8] Traditional western emanation theology has thus been swept away and replaced by a very different type of religious claim:

nothing but God is real; there is no duality of God and world, but only a false duality of God and illusion.

The issue of *zimzum*, or the contraction of the infinite God in order to allow for the world's existence, is treated by the Maggid in similar fashion. *Zimzum* was a major pillar of the new Kabbalah elaborated by Isaac Luria and his followers in the sixteenth century, a system that Gershom Scholem saw as originating partially in reaction to the cataclysm that had befallen Spanish Jewry in the preceding generations. Luria no longer accepted the old notion of graded emanations to explain the emergence of the multiform universe from the depths of the one and undivided God. He sought an explanation of a rather more dramatic and total sort. If God was alone before creation, he claimed, then God was and filled all; there was no empty space beside him. To claim that God existed alongside an eternal void would be to capitulate to an ultimate dualism, one that by implication might see evil as being co-eternal with God. Rather, he taught, the first step in creation was a contraction within the all-pervading God, one that allowed for a void within which creation could take place.

Scholem has shown how succeeding generations of Lurianists (his doctrine dominated Kabbalistic circles for some two hundred years after his death, and it is still the path followed by most Kabbalists today) could use this notion of *zimzum* in either theistic or pantheistic ways. For the Kabbalist who took *zimzum* literally, God indeed had vacated primal space, and creation was from without, the work of a transcendent God. Those who tended toward pantheism claimed rather that full *zimzum* was impossible, that even in the divine act of withdrawal his presence was confirmed, and that the void was never truly empty of God at all. For them the creation from without was more an activation of the underlying divine presence (*reshimu*), and the God who inhered in the universe was central to their religious lives.[9] It has also been demonstrated, primarily through the work of Isaiah Tishby, that the entire myth of *zimzum* is a myth of divine self-purification and of the origins of evil; the all-containing God contracts in purity before creation, leaving in the void those "roots" of evil that are to inhabit the universe there created.

The Maggid, as will be expected, follows those Kabbalists who do not take *zimzum* literally, those who believe in the continued presence of divinity in space even after the primal contraction. He goes farther than his predecessors, however, reducing them to a gracious act of a loving father-God who performs it in a semi-illusory way in order to allow psychological "room" for his child to resist.

> Since it was the primal will of God that the righteous among Israel exist in each generation, He contracted His brilliance, as it were, just as a father reduces his mental level and speaks of childish things with his small child . . . *zimzum* took place for the sake of Israel, and it was love that brought it about.[10]

> A teacher studies with his pupil. If the pupil is greatly concerned with what his teacher is saying and pays close attention to him, the teacher may open the gates and reveal his wisdom. Even though he may be able to share all of his abundant wisdom with him, a student who is almost a peer can attain to nearly all that his teacher has to offer. If, however, the student is dull and slow to understand, the teacher has to contract his great wisdom and teach him on his own level. Were he to offer him too much, trying to reveal to him the most profound depths, the student would only become confused and turn aside from learning. Then he would not even acquire that bit which is within the range of his abilities. Thus must a teacher reduce his wisdom down to his student's level . . . *zimzum* took place so that the world could properly exist. Without it we would not be able to bear the brilliance of His light, and our existence would be negated.[11]

The last phrase here will be of interest to us a bit farther along, but for now we are interested in the change in *zimzum* itself. The concept has here been psychologized: it is the human *mind* that must be left room to exist alongside the great light of God, rather than the world itself that must perforce exclude him. Here the potential Gnostic sting of *zimzum* has been removed; we are no longer speaking of the world's origins and the roots of the demonic, but rather of God's abundant love and his patience with man's small-mindedness or his willingness to allow for our humanity. Once again, as with the *sefirot*, a myth that accounted for a degree of distance between God and man has been undercut, allowing for a full immediacy of divine presence. The father's mind, we must realize, is not *really* reduced to childish dimensions; it is rather by a willful act of compassion that he offers the child the appearance of proximity to the child's mental level. This is done, of course, in a pedagogic context: the father hopes bit by bit to expand his child's mind.

We have approached early Hasidism to this point very much from the perspective of its *theology*, seeing the development of doctrine as would the intellectual historian. Here we must say that such a point of view will not do for us. These changes in formulation of ideas accompany and reflect a change in the modality of religious experience of those who bear them. We shall not be so naive as to try to define which of these changes first, the doctrine or the experience; here as elsewhere in the history of religion a good case could be made for either. But we must remember that Hasidic thought is promulgated against the background of an intense and ecstatic feeling of the all-pervading presence of God. The prayer-life of the earliest conventicles was denounced for its wild shrieks and uncontrolled jumping and shaking; there was about them an aura of spiritual frenzy that was compared (and not only by enemies) to both madness and drunkenness. We will now do well to bear this *Sitz im Leben* in mind as we examine some selections of teaching from the Maggid's school in which the horizons of western religious living seem most radically to be expanded. We begin with a passage of devotional instruction:

> The proper intention with which to recite the word "One" of the *shema'* ("Hear O Israel the Lord is God the Lord is One") is that there exists nothing in the entire world except for God, whose "glory fills all the world." The main intent is that man make himself into absolute nothing. There shall be nothing of him but his soul, which is "a part of God above." Thus is there nothing in the world but God who is One. This is where one's thoughts should be turned while saying "One": the whole world is filled with His glory and there is no place devoid of Him, be He blessed.[12]

This call for spiritual self-annihilation is of course common to many mystical literatures; by its very nature it also calls forth an immediate revision of traditional cosmology. If annihilation of self and world leads to a "higher" state, it must perforce also lead to a greater "truth" in understanding what the world really is. Devotion and cosmology (statements of "you should feel" and statements of "the world is") are often combined with one another in the sources:

> This is a high rung: when a person constantly considers in his heart that he is near to his blessed Creator and is surrounded by Him on all sides. He should be so attached to Him that he has no more need to reassure himself that this is the case: he should rather see the Creator, blessed be He, with his mind's eye, and that He is the "place of the world." This means that He was before He created the world and that the world stands within the Creator, blessed is He. He should be so attached that his sight is chiefly upon God, other than seeing the world first and the Creator only second. . . . Such a person merits to have the "shells" fall away from him. It was they that had brought darkness, separating God from man and blinding the mind's eye from the sight of the Creator.
>
> Think that the Creator, blessed be He, is endless and surrounds all the worlds that His blessed influx flows downward from above by means of channels throughout the worlds. We are ever walking about in God, blessed be He, and we could not make a single movement without His influx and life-flow.[13]

Note that the language remains very much that of western theism: God is primarily referred to by the term "Creator," even though the worldview here has rather little to do with that which is usually called Creation. The exhortation to ever concentrate our sight on God rather than on the world could easily be supported by passages of a more moralizing intent throughout medieval pietistic literature. The sense that every movement of the human body is controlled by God also has its well-known precedents in the philosophical (or antiphilosophical) literature of medieval Judaism and Islam. The full constellation, however, remains startling. Here the notion that all is God is approached with a radical enthusiasm that is previously unknown in Jewish sources.

The final statement of this, the "All is God" spoken plainly, is that which we should most be surprised to find within Judaism. The wide freedom of interpretation permitted within the tradition, combined with the various philosophical and mystical influences upon later Judaism, might eventually lead to a carefully guarded formulation that in fact meant nearly the same thing—but surely pious Jews could not say it in just so many words. Even within the loose dogmatic structure of Judaism that would seemingly have to be perceived as heresy. It is especially interesting, then, for us to quote from a precious document that was never intended for publication, an early nineteenth-century letter from one important HaBaD Hasidic disciple to another, in which he outlines the real meaning of Hasidism and the reasons for its persecution. The letter reflects an inner controversy within that particular school, the details of which are not essential for our purposes here. The writer is Rabbi Yizhak Isaac Epstein of Homel (1780–1857):

> Listen, please, my beloved friend! Do not say that this is, God forfend, heresy and philosophy. . . . And all Hasidim . . . have this faith. And it is generally sensed when reciting the Eighteen Benedictions. That is to say, after all the goodly meditations while reciting the songs of praise and reciting the *shema'*, with the higher and lower unification, then it is sensed that, in Yiddish, all is God. . . .
>
> All Hasidim share this truth. As for the opponents . . . they do not have this faith except in exceedingly great concealment, exactly as it was when Israel was in Egypt. Even though God to them also is the single object of faith, they have nonetheless no room for this faith that all is God.[14]

The letter is written in a thorough mixture of Yiddish and Hebrew, as was common for letters between scholars at the time. No particular note is taken of this fact. When he first comes to the key phrase, however, he says "in Yiddish," meaning "I am telling you this in plain Yiddish, in which there can be no misunderstanding." The letter is significant because here in private (alas!) communication he was able to shed all the Hebrew circumlocutions ("the whole world is full of His glory," etc.) and say exactly what he meant: *Als iz Got* (alles ist Gott).

The fact that this document comes from within the HaBaD/Lubavitch school is no accident. Among the many disciples of the Maggid, it was Shneur Zalman of Liadi (1745–1813), the great systematizer of Hasidic thought and the founder of HaBaD, who maintained the greatest consistency in promulgating this aspect of his master's teaching. The second portion of his *Tanya*, even now the daily read spiritual guidebook of HaBaD

Hasidim, is a brief tract on mystical cosmology. It works chiefly around the notion of *zimzum* and the contemplation of God's oneness, forming a contemplative exercise to accompany the recitation of the *Shema'*. It is structured, however, as an exposition of a biblical verse, one that has a long history in the realm of Jewish mystical speculations: "Know this day and set it upon your heart that the Lord is God in heaven above and on the earth beneath; there is none else" (Deut. 4:39). In the course of Shneur Zalman's reading it becomes quite clear that the concluding phrase is rather to be taken as "There is nothing else," for nothing but God may be truly said to exist:

> Now behold, after these truths, that anyone who carefully considers the matter [will realize] that every created and existing thing should really be considered as nought when compared with the power of the maker and the breath of His mouth in the creature, always giving being and bringing it forth from nothingness. All these things appear to us to be extant and real only because we cannot conceive or see with the eyes of the flesh the power of God in His creatures or the breath of His mouth in them. But if permission were given the eye to see and conceive the life and spirit flowing by the word of God into every creature, the physical aspect of creatures and their substance would not be seen by us at all. They are completely unreal in the light of the life-flow and spirit within them. Without this spiritual essence they would be as nothing, quite as they were before the six days of creation. And the breath/spirit flowing into them out of the mouth of God alone takes them constantly out of nothingness and non-being, causing existence. Therefore it is said: there is nothing without Him" (Is. 45:6)—literally.[15]

Shneur Zalman's disciple Aaron of Starroselje, another important systematizer of Hasidic thought, emphasized a strand in the Maggid's thought that distinguished "God's point of view" from the limited perspective of man. From God's point of view, taught R. Aaron, there has been no *zimzum*, there is nothing outside of God, and the phenomenal world may not be said to exist. It is only from man's viewpoint that this world has existence. Of course, it is from within our own perspective that we must conduct our religious lives. More on that below.

It was not only in the Maggid's school that the new experience of Hasidism was giving birth to surprising ways of religious speaking. A younger contemporary of Shneur Zalman, and one often thought to be his very antithesis as a type of Hasidic thinker, was arriving through somewhat different formulations at many of the same ideas. Rabbi Nahman of Bratslav (1772–1810) was the great-grandson of the Ba'al Shem Tov and the founder of a unique sect within the Hasidic community, one for which he still stands as first and only master.[16] Nahman was a theologian of paradox, one who filled his traditional-sounding homilies with contradictions so intense that they seemed to force conventional theology, even Kabbalah, to a breaking point. Note first how he subverts the meaning of an old adage, originally meant to show how impossible it was for man to truly know his maker:

> Eternal life belongs only to God, who lives forever, but he who is included in his root in God also has eternal life. Since he is included in the One and is One with God, he lives eternally just as God does. . . . The basis of this inclusion within God is knowing Him, as the sage says: "If I knew Him, I would be Him." The core of a person is his mind; where the mind is, there is the whole person. One who knows and attains to a divine understanding is really there. The greater his knowing, the more fully he is included in his root in God.[17]

Frequently Nahman's teaching involves a dialectical movement through stage after stage of religious discovery, doubt or challenge, and new integration within an expanded faith. In one of the homilies in which he speaks of this ascent, he describes its highest point in the following way:

> When one finally is included within 'eyn sof, his Torah is the Torah of God Himself and his prayer is the prayer of God Himself. There is a Torah of God, to which our sages have referred as follows: "I was first to fulfill it"; "The Holy One, blessed be He, clothes the naked, visits the sick" etc.; "How do we know that the Holy One, blessed be He, puts on tefillin?" There is also a prayer of God, of which the sages say: "How do we know that the Holy One, blessed be He, prays? From the verse: 'I shall grant them joy in My house of prayer'" (Is. 56:7).

We thus find that there exist a Torah of God and a prayer of God. When a person merits to be included within ʿeyn sof, his Torah and his prayers are those of God Himself.[18]

The Talmudic sages had told these tales in the course of humanizing God; the biblical God is transformed by them into a picture of the ideal rabbinic Jew, studying Torah, performing the commandments, and even saying his prayers. Little might they have thought that a mystic of a millennium and a half later would use their descriptions as an avenue of identification with God in a wholly different manner, claiming through his prayer and study to so ascend through the rungs of being that his own study and prayer be those of God. There is almost no distance that need be traversed between this position and the much more shocking version of the same formulation reported in Nahman's name by his faithful (and usually rather conservative) disciple:

> I heard from Rabbi Nathan: . . . our master said . . . that you have to reach such a state of self-negation that you come to God's Torah and prayer and are able to say: "May it be my will!"[19]

Prayer here has reached its apex and transformation: so intently has the worshiper said "May it be *Thy* will" that his own will is finally utterly negated, and he may fully identify with the will of God. Behold where all this pious talk of humility and self-abnegation has finally led! Here Hasidism, indeed Judaism, comes as close as it ever has to violating that ultimate taboo of western religion, that of the devotee proclaiming "I am God."

At the psychological-devotional root of this entire complex of ideas stands the experience of the negation or transcendence of self, and the discovery, in the wake of that experience, that it is only God who remains. One would expect that this apex of mystical transformation would be greeted with great if trembling exultation. Indeed, that is the case in certain of the Hasidic accounts. There are some that see this as the source of prophecy as well, including indications that ecstatic prayer, following such an experience, is overtaken by a state of divine possession, one in which "the *shekhinah* speaks though his mouth." At the same time, we can find in any number of Hasidic renditions of this mystical moment a great hesitation, a hesitation that seems to treat negation of self as more a danger than a blessing. We have heard the Maggid say that *zimzum*, of the sort he proposes, must take place, else "our existence would be negated." But is not the negation of our existence precisely the goal of the religious life he so avidly preaches? Why not, to use a metaphor commonly found in these sources, stare directly into the sun and be blinded by its light? Nahman too warns us that we must maintain an awareness of the void whence God has departed, lest "the space not be empty and all would be *'eyn sof* (endless God)."[20] But what could be better, from the point of view of an unequivocal mysticism? Here Hasidism totters at the brink and returns, refreshed and renewed, but on the road to that compromise that would make it synonymous with ultraorthodoxy only a few generations later. It is upon this return and compromise that we must now seek to focus our attention.

It is possible in viewing any period in the history of Kabbalah to see the imperfect grafting of a mystical branch on the nonmystical tree of biblical/rabbinic Judaism. Insist as the mystic may that his views represent the true intent of the earlier sources, and weave as he may a seemingly convincing thread of argument through an impressive array of such quotations, the necessary transformations of earlier meanings can always be found. Whether it is "nothingness" that has reappeared as "the Nothing" or creation that has taken on the new garb of emanation, the mystic in Judaism is ever a daring reinterpreter of the original sources. At the same time, most of the mystics were deeply committed to maintaining the normative in the daily life patterns of rabbinic Judaism. Hasidism has in common with the Kabbalistic writings of the thirteenth century (including the Zohar) a need to *defend* what each saw as the authentic rabbinic tradition, the one against the inroads of medieval rationalism and the other against an array of enemies, including heretical mysticism, petrified Talmudism, and, after the turn of the nineteenth century, the advent of modernity. Reinterpretation was thus to function in part to underscore the value of the normative, to strengthen it by a deepening of its meaning. Given the nature of Judaism, the norm at issue was the *halakhah* or the life of the commandments.

The old Kabbalah had devoted a great part of its energies to just that: the literature of *sodot ha-mizwot* or esoteric rationales for the commandments occupies a major part of Kabbalistic writings. Hasidism, however, turned aside from this literary genre (with a few noteworthy exceptions) and devoted rather little of its intellectual attention to the command-ments themselves, despite its full commitment to a life pattern that was entirely within the traditional rabbinic mold. It tended, as Rivka Schatz-Uffenheimer has noted, to focus its attention on the two areas of contem-plative prayer and the worship of God through the uplifting of corporeal things, while avoiding the rather major question of interpreting the com-mandments.[21] The fact is that the commandments constituted a problem-atic *datum* for the radically spiritualized value system that Hasidism was proposing. It ultimately was for this reason that Hasidism was forced to retreat from its own mystical insights.

The old Kabbalah had preached a carefully graded ascent to God through the many rungs of being. In the course of such a journey, an uplifting of the commandments through successive grades of spiritualization could prove an appropriate accompaniment to the mystical voyager. In each "world" or rung the same deed might gain a new level of symbolic mean-ing, providing at once a richness of texture and that constancy which the mystic so frequently seems to need. Hasidism, however, has little patience for the grades and rungs of ascent. If the Hasid seeks to rush up to God all at once in a burst of ecstatic fire, would not the commandments seem to hold him back? For one who sought to see through the illusion of mate-rial existence, must there not have been a certain impatience with a reli-gious life that kept him so very bound to earth? The commandments, after all, require the body; pure spirit cannot don the *tefillin*, wave the *lulav*, or eat the *matzah*. Their proper performance, moreover, requires a wealth of knowledge and awareness of bodily things, constant reminders of the limits of mortal existence in both space and time.

We see this tension in Hasidism through a rather frequent need by Hasidic authors to justify corporeal existence, indeed to justify God's creation of the material world altogether. Usually the justification is por-trayed in the garb of the age-old contest of men and angels. Now man is proven God's best-beloved creature because he, unlike the hosts of heaven, can make spirit out of mere matter; the fact that he can uplift the sparks of God's light from among the *qelipot* of darkness represents not only his vindication but the greatest triumph of creation itself. The Maggid was also apparently responsible for an apt if rather grotesque image, accord-ing to which the king turns away from the exquisite music of the angelic choirs in order to listen to the prayers of mortal man, his talking parrot.

But the preference for a life of pure spirit is not the only challenge that Hasidism had to meet in its defense of rabbinism. The other side of the coin, as it were, was equally problematic. The Ba'al Shem's followers had insisted that divinity is to be found throughout all of creation, that "the power of the doer in the deed" could be attested everywhere. Why, then, we may ask, in the cow and not the pig? How can one distinguish holy from profane, permitted from forbidden, pure from taboo—distinctions which lie at the very essence of *halakhah*—if all is holy? We see Levi Yizhak of Berdichev, a leading proponent and popularizer of the Maggid's teachings, struggling with this question:

> We should understand the nature of the snare by which the serpent seduced Eve to transgress God's commandment. The snake argued as follows: Were not heaven and earth created by the word of God? Is it not well known that all the worlds and everything in them were brought into being by the divine utterances ("Let there be . . .") and word? Is not the very root of their existence and life essence drawn from the utterance of God, the source of all life, whose words continue to live? If this is so, how is it possible that the Tree of Knowledge, also the creation of God's word, could be harmful and cause death? Was not it too created from the source in the Tree of Life?
>
> Therefore, said the serpent, even though God did say, "You shall not eat," etc., what place does this statement have? Was the Tree not created by the word of God? . . . If this is so, surely it gives life and not death. Even though God said, "You shall not eat," why not obey His first saying, that which created the tree, rather than this one?[22]

Of course, Levi Yizhak will find an answer to the "snake," invoking the raising up of sparks, the need to separate and purify, and so forth. But the questions here placed in the mouth of the serpent are not accidental. Some challenger, either in Levi Yizhak's circle or within his own self, was demanding an answer.

The dangers to the commandments from this embrace of God in all creation are also seen in the tendency of early Hasidism to want to expand the notion of commandment, allowing it to embrace the full range of human activities. The author of *Me'or 'Eynayim* frequently lets slip such a phrase as "eating, drinking, and the rest of the commandments," and it does not seem from the context that kashrut restrictions are what he has in mind. The Maggid himself shared in this tendency toward a limitless expansion of the rubric of *mizwah*:

> The sages said: "God wanted to lend merit to Israel; therefore He multiplied Torah and commandments for them." This means as follows: The commandments themselves are 613. But when a person fulfills "Know Him in all your ways" (Prov. 3:6) he may fulfill many many more times 613, endlessly, for all his deeds are for the sake of heaven. He is fulfilling the command of his Creator in every moment . . . that is why they say that He "multiplied" the commandments. This term applies properly to that which is without limit. If they were only 613, why would the sage have called them "multiplied"? Our interpretation resolves this question: For the one who knows God in all his ways there is no end to his commandments.[23]

If the commandments are without limit, however, what place is there for the very specific commandments of the tradition? Why not celebrate the presence in some other and more original way? Here one cannot but sense, as did some of Hasidism's more astute opponents, that religious enthusiasm is on the verge of spilling over into religious anarchism.

The Talmudic sages, in the course of claiming that there was no life of piety outside of the commandments, had expended much effort in the projection of rabbinic *halakhah* back onto the heroes of the Bible, much as we have seen them ascribe it to the Lord himself. In this the patriarchs were a particular problem, having lived before the Torah was given and thus seemingly having been unaware of the divine commandments. Not so, concludes the dominant rabbinic voice on the subject: Abraham observed every one of the commandments, even down to restrictions promulgated by the rabbis themselves. The echo of anti-Pauline polemic is not hard to trace in this Talmudic dictum. Now in Hasidism we find the rabbis challenged (by reinterpretation, of course!) on this uniquely touchy of subjects. The demurral is heard through several voices in the Maggid's school. The rabbis do not mean that Abraham knew all the laws and commandments, but rather that through his love of God, his single act at the *'aqedah*, or circumcision, he did all that we do as we follow God's commands. Once again Levi Yizhak expresses the challenge with particularity:

There are two ways to serve God: one is a service by means of total dedication, and the other is the service through the commandments and good deeds. The difference between them is this: one who serves through dedication alone, without commandments and deeds, is truly in the Naught, while the one who serves by means of the commandments is serving Him through some existing thing. The commandments are in existence. Therefore, the one who serves in dedication and is wholly within the Naught cannot cause divine blessing to bow down upon himself: "he" does not exist, but is fully attached to God. The one who serves through deeds, however, is still attached to being, and thus he can bring blessing forth.

Now, within the service of God through commandments and actions, there may still be both of these aspects of non-being and being. In doing that which is pleasing to the Creator alone, one may be said to be in a state of Naught, while he who does that commandment in order to bring blessing down upon himself is yet attached to being. In fulfilling the Creator's will one is intending to reach the Naught, while that self-same commandment also binds you to existence, since the commandments partake of existence, and you draw forth blessing. Thus there are people who sustain themselves through their deeds.

Our sages tell us (Yoma 28b) that our father Abraham observed the entire Torah, even the details of how to prepare Sabbath food on a festival, before the Torah was given. We have tried to understand how he came to know the Torah. By separating himself from the corporeal and looking into his own 248 limbs, each of which corresponds to one of the 248 commandments and receives its life from that source, he was able to know them all. Each of the limbs receives its life from a particular commandment, and without it that limb could not be: thus he saw that the head is sustained by *tefillin* and all the rest; he knew the entire Torah before it was given.

It was for this same reason, however, that Abraham was not able to serve God through the commandments before he entered the Land of Israel. Outside the land he was not able to fulfill those commandments which apply only to one living in the land itself; thus various limbs in the system of correspondences would have been lacking. . . . Therefore, as long as Abraham was outside the land, he served God through total dedication alone: he cast himself into the fiery furnace and underwent various other great trials, all before he entered the land. When he entered the land, however, he was able to fulfill the commandments and thus be a complete being, one possessing all his limbs. At that point he turned to the commandments as his way of service. In the Land of Israel he no longer needed to be dedicated unto death, for he had the commandments. As for the binding of Isaac: there too he was fulfilling an explicit command of God.

As long as Abraham was outside the land, he was serving God from the place of Naught and could not bring blessing upon himself. In the Land of Israel, when he turned to the commandments and was thus attached to being, he could bring blessing forth. Therefore Scripture says: "Go thee from thy land" (Gen. 12:1) and RaSHI commented: "For your own benefit and good"—go to the land for your own good, for there you will serve God through the commandments and bring forth the flow of blessing, while outside the land you served Him through dedication and cling to the Naught, thus arousing no blessing. . . .

Now he who serves God through dedication alone sees Him with his very eye, while he who serves God through commandments and actions sees Him through a glass, since his means of service is an existing thing. This is the meaning of: "After these things, the word of God came to Abram in a vision saying" (Gen 15:1)—he saw God through a glass. And God said to him: "Fear not"—do not be afraid because you are serving Me by means of commandments and not through dedication alone; "your reward is very great"—by serving in this way you will bring forth blessing.

So when the sages said that Abraham fulfilled all the commandments, they were referring to that period when he lived in the land—but outside the land he served through dedication. In our case, however, even though we are outside the land, we are able to serve by means of the commandments—for the Torah has already been given.[24]

A number of motifs come together in this most surprising teaching. The correspondence between the commandments and the limbs of the body is frequently discussed in both later Kabbalistic and Hasidic works; the notion that Abraham learned Torah from within is an interesting mystical adaptation of the rational Abraham known in medieval philosophical writings. But by far most significant here is Levi Yizhak's recognition that there is another way of service and one that, from a purely mystical point of view, might even be preferable to the life of the commandments. The reader is even further tantalized by the notion that it is the purely spiritual service that is appropriate to life outside the land, in fact the locus in which Hasidim found themselves. The rather lame postscript to the effect that the situation changes once the Torah has been given is hardly very convincing.

The projection backward may also be related to a projection forward; there is a good deal of discussion in the same circles about the rabbinic belief that the commandments will be unnecessary after the final redemption. Both Scholem and Schatz-Uffenheimer have pointed to such statements as evidence of the deep-seated ambivalence toward the commandments that is to be found throughout this literature.

In the case of Nahman, ever the most daring and paradoxical of the lot, it was not only remote past and anticipated future without the *mitzwot* that could be romanticized. While returning from his famous journey to the Holy Land in 1799, he was captured by pirates and had some rather realistic fears of being sold into bondage. The worst of such fears for a pious *Hasid*, so it would seem, would be the inability to live as a Jew. Nahman, however, managed to overcome these terrors:

> He had reached the understanding of how to serve God even if he were, God forbid, not able to observe the commandments. He had attained the service of the patriarchs who had served God before the Torah was given, fulfilling all the *mitzwot* even though they did not observe them in their ordinary sense. Just as Jacob fulfilled the commandment of *tefillin* by stripping the sticks and so forth, so did he come to understand how he would fulfill all the *mitzwot* in this way if forced to do so in the place where he might be sold, God forbid.[25]

This confidence that such a purely spiritual Judaism was attainable in this world might have been comforting to the young rebbe at the moment, but it would do little to assuage his greater fears or the fears of those around him as to Hasidism's ultimate commitment to life within the rabbinic order. Surely for Nahman, who already saw the start of western "Enlightenment" among the Jews of Russia, it was the very opposite pole that needed strengthening. No wonder that he, and especially his disciple Nathan, pulled back from such dangerous formulations. No wonder that HaBaD, the very heart of a cosmic radicalism as it emerged from the Maggid's teachings, placed the very physical fulfillment of the sacred act at the core of its religious teaching. The mystical enthusiasm of the Ba'al Shem and the Maggid had brought them to the edge of the transcendence of their own specific religion, a transcendence which, as some saw well, was also its potential destruction.

NOTES

1. *Ben Porat Yosef* 55a.
2. *Toledot Ya'aqov Yosef* 7a.
3. *Zawa'at RIVaSH* (Cracow, 1896), 3b.
4. *Zawa'at RIVaSH* 14b; *Liqqutim Yeqarim* 17d.
5. This insight is originally that of Gershom Scholem. Cf. *Major Trends in Jewish Mysticism* (New York, 1954). 341ff. Here is as good a place as any to say that this essay, like all contemporary studies in the field of Jewish mysticism, is much indebted to the work of Scholem and his students in Jerusalem. With regard to Hasidism the latter include particularly Joseph Weiss and Rivka Schatz-Uffenheimer. Several of the sources quoted in this article have been previously discussed, in one context or another, by these scholars.
6. *Me'or 'Eynayim* (Jerusalem, 1966), 16d–17a. I have translated a major portion of this work, the homilies on Genesis, in *Upright Practices and The Light of the Eyes* (New York: Paulist Press, 1982, 1998). I am currently at work on a full translation of it.
7. *Me'or 'Eynayim* 16d–17a.
8. The Hebrew reader should see the elegant illumination of this idea, along with several other key concepts of Hasidism, in Hillel Zeitlin's *Be-Pardes ha-Hasidut weha-Qabbalah* (Tel Aviv, 1960). I have now translated this in *Hasidism for a New Era: The Religious Writings of Hillel Zeitlin* (Ramsey NJ: Paulist Press, 2012).
9. A brief and highly readable summary of this discussion is to be found in Louis Jacobs's *Seeker of Unity* (New York, 1966), chap. 3.
10. *Maggid Devaraw le-Ya'aqov*, opening.
11. *Or Torah, wa-yeze'* (Jerusalem, 1968), 24d.
12. *Liqqutim Yeqarim* (Jerusalem, 1974), 161.
13. *Liqqutim Yeqarim*, 54.
14. The letter has been translated by Louis Jacobs and published as an appendix to Jacobs's *Seeker of Unity*.
15. *Tanya*, second section, chapter 3.
16. On Nahman, see my *Tormented Master: A Life of Rabbi Nahman of Bratslav* (New York: Schocken Books, 1981).

17. *Liqqutey MoHaRaN* 21:11; cf. *Tormented Master*, 336n59.
18. *Liqqutey MoHaRaN* 22:10.
19. *Avaneha Barzel*, 44; see my discussion in *Tormented Master*, 320.
20. *Liqqutey MoHaRaN* 64:1–3.
21. *Ha-Hasidut ke-Mistiqah* (Jerusalem, 1966), 54–55.
22. *Qedushat Levi, bereshit* (Jerusalem, 1958), 7b.
23. *Or Torah* 147a.
24. *Qedushat Levi, lekh lekha*, 15b–d. (Emphasis mine.)
25. *Shivhey ha-RaN* ii:2. The reference to Jacob is from Genesis 30:37.

12

Levi Yizhak of Berdichev on Miracles

The question of miracles and the supernatural, both theoretically and practically, was never far from the mind of Levi Yizhak of Berdichev (1740–1809).[1] Before turning to this question, however, it will be important to present Levi Yizhak in a rather specific historical context.

Levi Yizhak is a leading figure of the so-called third generation of Hasidism, a disciple of the great Maggid R. Dov Baer of Mezritch, himself a disciple of the Ba'al Shem Tov, the figure around whose image Hasidism was created. In fact it was this "third" generation that established Hasidism as a dynamic popular religious movement, as historians have shown. The BeSHT, whom Levi Yizhak never met, died before any such movement carried his banner came into being, and the Maggid, while fostering the *bet midrash* out of which the most important movement leaders were to emerge, was a somewhat reluctant supporter of popularization.[2]

The Ba'al Shem Tov had indeed been known as both a clairvoyant and a miracle worker. These qualities constituted a good portion, though not all, of his growing reputation. As tales of the BeSHT were being told and collected during this era of the "third generation," leading up to the publication of *Shivhey ha-BeSHT* just after that generation passed from the world (1815), surely the accounts of his wondrous deeds were growing, both in number and in miraculous content. The Maggid, however, eschewed miracle working. He was a purveyor of profound teachings, not of supernatural acts. While legend claims that he himself had originally been drawn to the Ba'al Shem Tov in a quest for healing and had been helped and convinced by a shamanic rite the BeSHT performed for him,[3] the impressive band of followers who constituted his circle in Mezritch came to hear his teachings, not to behold wonders. Surely the Maggid believed theoretically in the power of the *tsaddik* to affect the will of heaven, of which he writes with some frequency.[4] But he seems to have felt that it was immodest or unwise to do so blatantly, except in extreme circumstances. His disciple and Levi Yizhak's friend R. Shne'ur Zalman of Liadi is quoted (in a later

HaBaD source) as saying, "In Mezritch miracles lay about on the floor in heaps; no one bothered to pick them up."[5] There was no doubt in the disciples' minds, in other words, that R. Dov Baer would have been quite capable of performing miracles, but doing so was just not his way.

Within the Maggid's circle, Levi Yizhak was among the most prominent activists and propagandists for the spread of the new movement. He was deposed from two major rabbinic posts (and possibly an earlier one as well) due to opposition, both internal and external, to his Hasidic preaching. Following the second round of anti-Hasidic bans in 1781, he engaged in public debate with R. Abraham Katzenellenbogen of Brest-Litovsk, a leading anti-Hasidic rabbi. He was poignantly defended by his friend R. Elimelech of Lezajsk as a victim of anti-Hasidic persecution.[6]

Among the large and impressive group of young seekers and devotees who gathered around the Maggid between the early 1760s and his death in 1772, certain rough distinctions may be drawn. Levi Yizhak belongs to the group of young rabbis within the Mezritch circle, people well respected for their learning in the exoteric realm as well as for their Hasidic piety and homiletical creativity. Several of these went on to rabbinic careers, serving in various communities. These included R. Shmelke Horowitz (who was responsible for bringing along several of the others), R. Uziel Meisels, and R. Issachar Dov, later of Zloczow. A second group, including R. Shne'ur Zalman, R. Elimelech, and R. Israel Hofstein, surely had the learned credentials to serve as rabbis, but instead devoted themselves entirely to spreading Hasidism, earning their living through the support of their disciples. This led to the emergence of the Hasidic court with its distinctive economic features.[7] These two groups may be roughly distinguished from yet another group of future *preachers* within the circle, men of profound intellectual ability and spiritual depth who quoted both Aggadah and Zohar quite fluently, but who did not have the same level of Talmudic education. Prominent among these are R. Menahem Nahum of Chernobyl and R. Ze'ev Wolf of Zhitomir. There were also a few spiritually impressive nonintellectuals who were accepted within the group, including R. Elimelech's brother R. Zusya of Anipol and R. Leib Sarah's.

During the first three decades of Hasidism's spread (1765–95), the Mezritch circle was in competition with several individuals and groups that lay outside it. Prominent among these were the circle of R. Yehiel Mikhl of Zloczow in Eastern Galicia, the group around R. Pinhas of Korzec and

R. Barukh of Miedzybozh, the grandson of the BeSHT. R. Barukh, the first to claim Hasidic authority by dint of family lineage, was a decidedly nonintellectual figure who saw himself primarily as heir to the wonder-working abilities of his grandfather.[8] In the Zloczow circle too there was not the disdain of miracle working that was found in Mezritch. By the last decade of the eighteenth century, such independent figures as R. Aryeh Leib of Shpola were also making a name for themselves as miracle workers, healers, and intercessors in prayer.

Levi Yizhak's major work, *Kedushat Levi*, appeared in two sections. He published homilies on Hanukkah and Purim, plus some other incidental *derashot*, in Slawuta, 1798 (reprinted in Zolkiew, 1806). The larger *Kedushat Levi 'al ha- torah* appeared in Berdichev, 1811, shortly after its author's death. Before the end of the eighteenth century, the bookshelf of printed Hasidic writings was still quite small. Books generally fell into two categories: *derashot* following the order of the Torah (*Toledot Ya'akov Yosef, No'am Elimelech*, etc.) and random collected teachings (*Maggid Devaraw Le-Ya'akov, Likkutim Yekarim*, etc.), often in brief form, including those now defined as *sifrut ha-hanhagot* or "conduct literature," i.e., instructions for moral behavior. Levi Yizhak's was the first Hasidic work dealing specifically with Hanukkah and Purim, considered two of the "minor" holidays on the Jewish calendar. Indeed there are few books in the entire prior Jewish canon devoted exclusively to these. The notable exception, and Levi Yizhak's obvious inspiration, are the writings of the MaHaRaL of Prague (1525–1609), *Ner Mitsvah* on Hanukkah and *Or Hadash* on Purim. The writings of the MaHaRaL were known to Levi Yizhak's teacher, the Maggid, and in general are thought to have had significant influence on Hasidic authors both early and late.[9] This is most likely because they felt in him a kindred spirit, one shaped by the contours of Jewish mystical thought while declining to include technical and abstruse Kabbalistic symbolism in his writings.

The main theme in Levi Yizhak's discussion of both holidays is that of the hidden miracle, or the relationship between revealed and hidden ways that God acts in history. The notion of hidden miracles is one that Levi Yizhak derives from the RaMBaN, whom he quotes copiously on this subject.[10] While it is not the purpose of this essay to offer a full history of this idea, it is fair to say that one may trace a line of thinking from

RaMBaN through MaHaRaL and into Levi Yizhak. Levi Yizhak repeatedly makes it clear that the hidden miracle, that which takes place without seemingly violating the laws of nature, is the more impressive to him. The essential Hasidic message is that God is present within this world and is accessible to people living in an ordinary state of consciousness (*katnut*). The message of the "hidden miracle" is that this world as it exists is the scene of divine self-revelation, one accessible to those simple Jews so loved by Levi Yizhak.

The treatise on Purim and Hanukkah (treated in that order) begins with this notion. Levi Yizhak quotes the Talmud's discussion of whether Israel freely received the Torah at Sinai, given the legend of God's holding the mountain over their heads as a warning against rejecting the divine word.[11] The Gemara's resolution *"hadar kibluhah bi-yemey Mordechai ve-Esther"* ("they reaccepted it in the days of Mordecai and Esther") gives him the opportunity to say that it was only the discovery that God is present within the seemingly natural world that allows us mere mortals to discover the divine presence and hence to serve God freely and joyously. The "mountain held over their heads" is thus a symbolic representation of what happens in the supernatural moment when the ability to deny God's presence is absent. Accepting the Torah in such circumstance might not carry over into ordinary time. That is why the story of Esther is told in a *megillah*, because it "reveals" (a play on *megillah/megalleh*) a this-worldly divine presence that would otherwise be hidden. Similarly, the festival is called Purim, "lots," because it takes place in the natural world, one in which the person has alternatives, and therefore free choice, about whether to discover God's presence and to accept the yoke of His service. This can only take place in the realm of *katnut*, for in the state of Sinai-like *gadlut* one is so surrounded by the intense experience of divinity that there remains no alternative but to accept it.

So too does Levi Yizhak explain the Talmud's surprising statement that "all the festivals will be canceled in the future, except for Purim."[12] The major festivals of the year are structured around the story of the Exodus and Sinai. Those were supernatural events, which there will be no need to recall in the messianic future. Nature itself will be so transformed—here Levi Yizhak quotes the prophet's vision of the wolf lying down with the lamb—that the supernatural will have been rendered superfluous. In this we seem to have a new state, not the temporary suspension of nature by the effecting of God's will (or the *tsaddik's*), but a new responsiveness of nature itself to do what is needed.

The exact quality of the hidden miracle in Levi Yizhak's treatise is not entirely clear or consistent. He seems to be looking toward a God who is ever concerned with Israel's welfare and acting in their behalf, the same as he expects of the *tsaddik*. In the Hanukkah narrative, God acts behind the screen of military activity, allowing the smaller and weaker army to defeat its enemies ("*masarta . . .*"). In the Purim story, God acts within the heart of the king to turn his will toward Israel's benefit.[13] In a particularly impressive passage he suggests the order of the year reflects an increasingly open revelation of God's presence.[14] Hanukkah is the first festival to occur within profane time (i.e., after the fall sacred season). The victory of the Maccabees could be seen as an entirely natural one, the result of military prowess. The hand of God that gave them victory remains almost entirely hidden. Next comes Purim, when Israel did not act in battle to defend themselves (he conveniently ignores the embarrassing closing chapters of Megillat Esther). Israel relied only on Esther's machinations and the king's will.[15] Here humans were less powerful, so the positive result was a greater revelation of divine interference, meaning that the miracle was somewhat less hidden. Only from there does the year proceed to Pesah, an event that took place "without arousal from below," when the hand of God in history was entirely revealed.

In these passages, *nes nistar* seems to mean the active, conscious hand of God in controlling historical events, but one exercised from behind the scenes.[16] On reflection, however, Levi Yizhak tells us that all miracles, but especially these, exist for the purpose of demonstrating to us that all of life is in fact miraculous. That which appears to be natural or ordinary (*hergel*)[17]—the rising and setting of the sun, for example—is in fact an act of divine will. That ties him quite closely to the position articulated clearly by Nahmanides in his comment to Exodus 13:16:

From the great and famous miracles, a person comes to admit the hidden miracles, which are the foundation of the entire Torah. A person has no portion in the Torah of Moses until we believe that all our affairs and everything that happens to us are miracles. There is no "nature" or "way of the world" about them. This applies to both the individual and the collective.

While scholarship has shown that Nahmanides elsewhere demonstrates a significantly more nuanced view of the role of miracles (in fact one closer to that of Maimonides than is widely thought), it seems that this passage was the crucial one in Levi Yizhak's understanding of the medieval sage. "Nature" is but an illusory outer cloak that garbs the hidden activity of the divine will in every moment of existence. If that is the case, however, then "miracle" and "nature" seem to be differentiated primarily as attitudes of the beholder. The same sunrise can clearly be described as both, depending upon the religious consciousness (or lack thereof) in the one who sees it. To be a religious human being is to appreciate "Your miracles that are with us daily, evening, morning, and noon." This seems somewhat different from his descriptions of Hanukkah and Purim. While these are hidden miracles, they nevertheless seem to be described as *extraordinary* events of divine interference. But the sunrise is not that. Of course, the banishing of *hergel* means that everything is indeed to be seen as extraordinary. But then there is no ordinary, no rule to which these events become exceptions. In other words, if *everything* is to be seen as miracle, is *anything* any longer a miracle, except in the eye of the beholder?

Another complication in Levi Yizhak's understanding of hidden miracles is the role of humans, and particularly the *tsaddik,* in bringing them about. In general, Levi Yizhak is a great believer in the importance of "arousal from below" and the central role humans play in the governance of this world. His teacher, the Maggid, had already offered a most daring reading of *retson yereʾav yaʾaseh.*[18] In the infinite and unchanging Godhead there is no specific will that determines the fate of individual persons or human events. The inner *ayin,* so central to the mystical God-concept of Kabbalah, lies beyond such concerns. But the roots of *hesed* do reach that high, for the act of emanation itself could only come about as a result of the flowing forth of divine love. That love is specifically focused on Israel and the *tsaddikim,* the ultimate goal of Creation and the ones who will restore the cosmic balance by uplifting and restoring the flow of energy to its Source. Hence their desires are of utmost importance; God's love for them permits them to implant a particular desire within the divine mind in their moments of ecstatic union.[19] The verse is thus to be read (ungrammatically): *retson yereʾav yaʾaseh* "[God's] will is made by those who fear Him."

In several particularly revealing passages, Levi Yizhak uniquely goes beyond the Maggid in this line of thought, depicting God as intentionally retiring from the scene of worldly involvement in order to extend the rule of His beloved, Israel and the righteous. God places control over the lower world in their hands, causing all things to do their bidding.[20] This position, which might be designated as a "mystical humanism," is a belief that humans do indeed control the affairs of this world, but they have that power due to an intentional act of divine withdrawal. This depends, of course, on the full self-effacing righteousness of the human actors. You need to be acting for God's sake, often characterized as the sake of *shekhinah*, rather than to show your own powers.

In the Purim story, Mordechai is seen as such a figure.[21] A mystical devotee in the way of the Maggid's teachings, Mordechai contemplated the origins and purpose of existence itself. He ascended into the place of cosmic nothingness, and there he was able to direct the flow of a hidden miracle onto the historic plane.[22] A parallel passage, *Kedushat Purim* 2, 346–47, depicts him as a sage who knew all seventy human languages, thus having access to the seventy *sarey ha-umot* and their workings. Here music enters the scene alongside language. He was able to sing the proper melody of the *sar* opposing Israel and thus to overcome its power. Another passage, KLS 354–55, depicts a similar "singing contest" between King David and Nebuchadnezzar who sought but failed to defeat the power of the Psalmist to arouse and thus shape the divine will in defense of Israel.

The recent Rand edition of *Kedushat Levi*,[23] supplied with a full index of sources, makes it clear that the Talmudic passages about the power of the *tsaddik* to undo divine decrees (*Mo'ed Katan* 16b; *Ta'anit* 23a) are among Levi Yizhak's very favorite rabbinic quotations. These passages are quoted by others of the circle as well, but nowhere as frequently as in *Kedushat Levi*.[24] Levi Yizhak's unusual emphasis upon them is part of the mystical (or is it "magical?") humanism mentioned above. He sees a world in which righteous people are called upon to take action, to shape the course of history, rather than to depend upon a God who, without man's help, is off in the realms of mystical obscurity. The venerable Kabbalistic notion of "Israel add to the power above" or that human actions fulfill a divine need is now transformed to the realm of "conducting the world." Righteous Israel are God's helpers—but in effect His surrogates—in ruling the world.

Hidden miracles, an outsider might say, are not performed, but only claimed. If the sick child is healed, or the enemy kept away from the city gates, the *hasid* can say that it was the *tsaddik's* prayers that caused this to happen. No one sees a hidden miracle in the hour when it is happening. The case of Mordechai, therefore, is a relatively easy one. The Jews were saved in otherwise unexplained ways. It must have been the efforts of the *tsaddik* that caused this to happen. But what of revealed miracles? Is the *tsaddik* called upon to perform these as well? In Levi Yizhak's treatise on Hanukkah and Purim, devoted almost entirely to the question of miracles, there is no indication that this is the case. He seems in this sense to be a faithful disciple of the Maggid, not interested in turning the wonder-working potential of being a *tsaddik* into reality.

But when we turn to Levi Yizhak's better-known work, *Kedushat Levi 'al ha- torah*, published immediately after his death, this is no longer the case. In the essay mentioned in note 2, I have pointed to a reconstructed debate among the Maggid's circle with regard to Moses' action and liability at *Mey Merivah* (Num. 20:7–14). Some voices, including that of the Maggid himself,[25] explain that Moses' sin lay in striking the rock rather than speaking to it. The *tsaddik*, they are claiming, is essentially one who has to work through speech, *dibbur*, continuing the work of *dor ha-midbar*, the generation when wonders could be effected by speech alone. I take this to mean that the power of the *tsaddik* lies in his teachings—the approach of the Maggid—rather than in supernatural deeds. This is the stance of the Mezritch school in the face of such figures as R. Baruch of Miedzybozh and others, who are presenting themselves as wonder-workers. The way to spread *hasidut,* the Maggid and his followers insist, is through its teachings, not through visible miracles.

But Levi Yizhak demurs from this view. In a most daring reading, he ascribes to Korah the notion that the coming generation, those going into the land (one has to read *ha-nikhnasim la-arets* as referring to *artsiyyut*, a commonplace in Hasidic interpretation) can be approached in the same way as "the generation of speech."

"Korah took . . ." (Num. 16:1). There are the generation of the wilderness and the generation that entered the Land of Israel. *Dor ha-Midbar* refers to speech; they accomplished everything by speaking. There are *tsaddikim* who accomplish everything by speaking and do not need to perform any deed. "The generation that entered the land of Israel" refers to action; they needed to do some deed. That is why Joshua, when doing battle with the thirty-one kings, had to perform some act with the javelin and the ambush (Josh. 8:18–19). Moses, who lived in the generation of *midbar*, needed no such act; he did it all through speech . . .

The Torah of Moses is parallel to speech, since he accomplished all by speaking. But it becomes garbed through the *middot* in the world of action as well. Of this Scripture says: "I am first and I am last (Is. 44:6), [meaning that God is present on the highest and lowest levels].

When Korah saw that this generation would not enter the Land of Israel, he had no faith that Moses' Torah could become garbed in action. . . . Korah believed only in the world of speech . . . and not that it could be garbed in the world of action.[26]

Korah denied that "the teaching of Moses is garbed also in the world of action." "Action" here refers to deeds in the physical realm that demonstrate God's power (i.e., miracles). The Korah position described here, I am suggesting, is rather close to that of Levi Yizhak's own revered teacher.

What leads to Levi Yizhak's seeming impatience with this view of the Maggid and others in his school? For this we have to turn to the best-known quality of Levi Yizhak: his love of ordinary Jews and his concern for their needs. This quality, while reinforced and perhaps also exaggerated by later legends about the *tsaddik* of Berdichev, is found readily within the pages of *Kedushat Levi* itself. A strong advocate for the spread and popularization of the Hasidic message, he is exceptionally forgiving toward the people and their lesser sins. He sees the most important task of the *tsaddik* as that of defending Israel, including their defense before heavenly judgment. He believed that ordinary Jews could not be reached by "speech" or teachings alone. They needed to see deeds done by the *tsaddikim* that would convince them of their powers. This meant a willingness to engage in demonstrable miracles, acting in a visible way that will convince people of the *tsaddik*'s powers above as well as his concern for their worldly needs.

In this internal debate within the Maggid's circle, Levi Yizhak is supported by R. Elimelech, who understands the high stakes involved. He suggests that the *tsaddik* indeed does have to act in order to convince the people, even if he will suffer punishment at God's hand because of it.

It is the way of the *tsaddik* to constantly seek out what is good for Israel, even if doing so appears to contain some bit of transgression. If it is for

Israel's good, he will do it, even accepting that he might have to suffer Hell for their sake. His entire desire is to do what is good for them. The *tsaddik* could in fact bring forth the flow of blessing just by his word, without any physical act at all, but sometimes he has to do it . . . for those who do not believe.[27]

In this matter they stand squarely against R. Shne'ur Zalman, who refused to engage in such efforts. He was engaged in creating and marketing a *hasidut* that would capture the hearts of Jews in northern Belorussia, where Lithuanian attitudes and anti-Hasidic agitation were strong. He needed to show a "pure" image of the *tsaddik*, one completely free of the magical elements that were associated with Hasidism, having their roots in the Ba'al Shem Tov himself. His Hasidism was developing away from those roots, creating a Hasidism more comfortable both for him, as a refined intellectual and spiritual person, and for those of his district.

This reading of the sources works well except for one interesting fact. We have no miracle stories about Levi Yizhak. The stories about him, written and published in an era when there was no shyness about tales of *tsaddikim* and their miracles, are all accounts of personal piety and the love of Israel.[28] Levi Yizhak indeed defies the seeming will of heaven in arguing with God to see the merits of Israel, but he does not engage in miracles to bring about their salvation.

We may thus see Levi Yizhak as a figure who stands in a middle position as Hasidism begins to spread and become a dominant force in the area where he lives. He believes both in the power of the *tsaddik* to change the decree of heaven and the importance of demonstrating that power. Only this will show that the *tsaddik* can reach out to ordinary Jews and that he cares about their worldly needs. Yet he continues to hold off from doing so. The influence of the Maggid remains very strong. Perhaps so too does his disdain for wonder-workers when he sees them in action. Levi Yizhak's strong support for both Shne'ur Zalman and the young Nahman of Bratslav in their struggles with Baruch of Miedzbozh may reflect this attitude. Although attracted by his love of the people to fulfill their needs and draw them into the Hasidic fold, in the end he remains a religious intellectual and the rabbi of a major community, one for whom the self-image of *ba'al mofet*, miracle worker, is somehow beneath his dignity.

1. A critical biography of Levi Yizhak is still a desideratum of scholarship, one I hope to fulfill together with my student Or N. Rose. Meanwhile, the volume by Samuel Dresner, *Levi Yitzhak of Berditchev: Portrait of a Hasidic Master* (New York: Hartmore House, 1974), contains some important materials. The key traditional source is Shalom Gutman's *Tif'eret Bet Levi* (Jassy, 1910).

2. This characterization of the Maggid emerges from my article "Around the Maggid's Table: *Tsaddik*, Leadership, and Popularization in the Circle of Dov Baer of Miedzyrzec," *Zion* 78, no. 1 (2013): 73–106 (Hebrew). An English version appears elsewhere in this volume.

3. *Shivhey ha-BeSHT*, ed. Rubinstein (Jerusalem, 1992), 126–29; *In Praise of the Ba'al Shem Tov*, trans. Ben-Amos and Mintz (Bloomington: Indiana University Press, 1970), 81–84.

4. *Maggid Devaraw le-Ya'akov* #179, ed. R. Schatz-Uffenheimer, 278–80; #127 (p. 220).

5. Hayyim Me'ir Heilman, *Beit Rabbi* (Berdichev, 1902), 6.

6. The texts of the debate as well as R. Elimelech's defense are published in M. Wilensky's *Hasidim u-Mitnaggedim* (Jerusalem: Mossad Bialik, 1970), 1:168–76.

7. See Immanuel Etkes, "The Hasidic Court," in *Text and Context: Essays in Modern Jewish History and Historiography in Honor of Ismar Schorsch* (New York: Jewish Theological Seminary, 2005), 157–86.

8. On R. Barukh, see the sources collected by Reuven Margaliot in *Makor Barukh* (Zamoszcz, 1931). The little volume *Butsina de-Nehora* (Lemberg, 1880), written later to burnish the credentials of R. Barukh, did not add much to his intellectual reputation. It is interesting to note that we have no *haskamot* by him, not even to his own brother's *Degel Mahaneh Ephraim*, published in 1810, while he was still alive.

9. See B. Safran, "Maharal and Early Hasidism," in his *Hasidism: Continuity or Innovation* (Cambridge: Harvard University Center for Jewish Studies, 1988), 47–144.

10. The term *nes nistar* is a coinage of the RaMBaN, thought to be one of his most distinctive contributions to the history of Jewish thought. For extended discussion of the meaning of this term in the RaMBaN's writings, as well as its later misappropriation, see D. Berger, "Miracles and the Natural Order in Nahmanides," in *Nahmanides*, ed. I. Twersky (Cambridge: Harvard University Press, 1983), 107–28; M. Halbertal, *'Al Derekh ha-Emet* (Jerusalem: Shalom Hartman Institute, 2006), 149–80.

11. *B. Shabbat* 88a.

12. *Kedushat Levi ha-Shalem*, 350–51, based on (a distorted reading of) *Yerushalmi Ta'anit* 2:2

13. *Kedushat Levi ha-Shalem*, 379–80; MaHaRaL (introduction to *Or Hadash*, ed. Bnei Brak, 1972, 59) distinguishes Hanukkah from Purim. Hanukkah was in

fact a *nes nigleh*, referring to the miracle of the lights. This was possible because Bayit Sheni still stood. Purim takes place in *galut,* where there is only *nes nistar.* Hence its heroine is named Esther, etc.

14. *Kedushat Levi ha-Shalem,* 390.

15. See *Maggid Devaraw le-Ya'akov* #14 (ed. Schatz, 27–28) and #35 (54), where the Maggid says that Israel in exile are capable of receiving only hidden miracles, those deriving from *malkhut,* indicated by the name *adonay,* but not revealed miracles, which depend on the name Y-H-W-H. On the source of this view, see Halbertal, *'Al Derekh ha-Emet.*

16. This parallels the view of the RaMBaN in his comment to Genesis 17:1. See Halbertal, *'Al Derekh ha-Emet,* 159.

17. That is why the time for lighting Hanukkah candles is "*'ad she-tikhleh regel min ha-shuk,*" playing on *regel/hergel.*

18. *Maggid Devaraw le-Ya'akov* #7 (p. 21); #161 (p. 257).

19. The *No'am Elimelech's* version of this same idea is expressed in another verse of the same psalm. "*'Eyney khol elekha yesaberu*" (Ps. 145:15) means that the *tsaddikim* gives eyes to God, causing Him to see the sufferings of this world and thus to change His decrees. *No'am Elimelech,* ed. Nig'al (Jerusalem: Mossad Ha-Rav Kook, 1978), 30 and esp. 59.

20. See *Kedushat Levi ha-Shalem,* 246, 248, and elsewhere.

21. *Kedushat Levi ha-Shalem,* 154, 348.

22. See *Maggid Devaraw le-Ya'akov* # 30 (ed. Schatz, 49). One is here tempted to ask whether Levi Yizhak is a very subtle reader of the RaMBaN with regard to the question of the human role in effecting one sort of divine interference or another. RaMBaN, following Ibn Ezra, ties the ability to effect miracles to one's level of *devekut.* Cf. the discussion by Halbertal, *'Al Derekh ha-Emet,* 167–73. My sense is that what we have here is a rediscovery by Levi Yizhak, within the general thought-world of Kabbalah, rather than a careful reading of particular sources.

23. *Kedushat Levi* (Ashdod: Hadrat Hen Institute, 2005).

24. Interesting to compare Levi Yizhak's usage of the *Mo'ed Qatan* passage with that of the *Me'or 'Eynayim.* The latter quotes it frequently, but always in an apologetic context, to show that it is not really the *tsaddik* but God who is negating the decree or effecting the miracle. Levi Yizhak shows no such hesitations.

25. *Maggid Devaraw le-Ya'akov* #84 (146–47).

26. *Maggid Devaraw le-Ya'akov* #84 (223).

27. *No'am Elimelech, Balak,* 448.

28. See, for example, *Tif'eret Bet Levi* (Jassy, 1909/10), and *Nifla'ot Bet Levi* (Pietrkow, 1911).

PART 4

Contemporary Jewish Theology

13

A Neo-Hasidic Credo

A Personal Introduction

When I turned seventy years old earlier this year, I did not realize how fully the occasion would turn into a time of reflection. While I have every hope that my productive years are far from over, there is no question that reaching this big number tells one that the final phase of life has begun. There is no more saying "late middle age" or "sixty is the new forty." The Psalmist's words, however tempered by medical advances, still resound loudly in the ears of the septuagenarian. *Yemey shenotenu shiv'im shanah.* Anything more is surely *hesed hinam*, a pure divine gift.

Although my years have been marked by a number of shifts of direction in both my writing and my professional roles, in the perspective of hindsight I now realize they constitute a single project, one that has taken many forms but nevertheless bears a consistent message. Since Neil Gillman has known me almost since the beginning of this half-century journey, and since we share a commitment to the personal nature of the theological enterprise, I thought I would offer my comments here in a more personal tone than is usual in *Festschriften*.

I was twenty years old, a senior in college, when I read Hillel Zeitlin's essay *Yesodot ha-Hasidut*, "The Fundaments of Hasidism."[1] I no longer remember whether it was Zalman Schachter or Alexander Altmann who put it in my hands, but they are the most likely candidates. To say that I fell in love is something of an understatement. I realized then and there that his words were giving expression to a deep truth that my heart already knew, and that this would be my religious language throughout my life. I promised myself (and Zeitlin) that I would translate this essay into English, a promise I only fulfilled half a century later.[2]

Although I did not yet have the term in my vocabulary, I have ever since then been a committed Neo-Hasidic Jew. Zeitlin joined with Buber, Heschel, and Schachter, whose writings and teachings saved Judaism for me, much as the Hasidic Rabbi Pinhas of Korzec once said that the Zohar had "kept him a Jew." Collectively they moved me toward a rather defined faith-stance (I intentionally choose this term over "theology"), from which I have wavered rather little. Zeitlin was the most important, and thus remains my rebbe, because he showed me the abstract truth that lay behind the mask of personalist God language, which was already problematic for me. He in turn led me to a search within the primary texts of Hasidism, one that has never ceased. My purpose here is to articulate the nature of that quest and to flesh out in specifics my lifelong project of bringing to birth a Neo-Hasidic Judaism that would have broad appeal to contemporary seekers. These seekers include many present and future rabbis, with whom I have tried to share my love of the original Hasidic sources and who I hope will open this path to others. But I write also for the many spiritually serious Jews of my and more recent generations who have turned away from Judaism and toward eastern spiritual paths in despair of finding anything useable in our own spiritual patrimony. My heart goes out especially to this latter group, and I constantly have them in mind as I write. It is for them (though I daresay for myself as well, since I am spiritually so close to them!) that I have sought to use Hasidism in creating what I sometimes call a "seeker-friendly" Judaism.

Elsewhere, most recently in *Radical Judaism*,[3] I have outlined a theological position that takes as its departure point an evolutionary approach, both to human origins and to the origins and development of religion. I take for granted that as the twentieth century ran its course, the two great century-long battles fought by traditional religious forces, one against Darwin and the other against biblical criticism, have both been decided, neither coming out the way traditionalists might have hoped. In articulating a religious language that will speak to twenty-first-century people, we have to leave both of those struggles behind us, accept their conclusions on the scientific/scholarly plane, but then seek out a way of expressing our sacred truth that reaches beyond them. In the course of doing this, I make frequent recourse to the Kabbalistic and Hasidic traditions, since I believe they provide tools that make such a transition possible. Here I would like to work in the opposite direction. Rather than beginning situationally with the present, I want to lay out what I consider to be the key principles of Neo-Hasidism. I offer both original text and my own commentary, following a format occasionally found in the Kabbalistic corpus. The comments will be historical, theological, and personal, but always with the intent of drawing forth their implications for our contemporary religious situation.

Zeitlin's introduction to Hasidic thought was published just over a century ago. A bit later he published an "interview" with himself in which he described the new Hasidism he sought to create in interwar Poland, emphasizing its continuities with and differences from the old.[4] He also wrote fourteen admonitions for members of his intended community Yavneh, a sort of Neo-Hasidic *hanhagot*. Although there is no text called a "credo," one can certainly surmise one from a reading of these in tandem. (All are included in the volume of Zeitlin's writings I have just edited.) Schachter wrote something called "A Modern Hasid's Credo" back in the 1950s, which formed the basis for many of his later writings.[5] Here is mine, in the shortest form to which I am able to reduce it. It is very much a personal statement, but one that I hope will be useful to others as well. Text and commentary should be read together.

A NEO-HASIDIC CREDO

1. There is only One. All exists within what we humans call the mind of God, where Being is a simple, undifferentiated whole. Because God is beyond time, that reality has never changed. Our evolving, ever-changing cosmos and the absolute stasis of Being are two faces of the same One. Our seeming existence as individuals, like all of physical reality, is the result of *tsimtsum*, a contraction or de-intensification of divine presence so that our minds can encounter it and yet continue to see ourselves as separate beings, in order to fulfill our worldly task. In ultimate reality, however, that separate existence is mostly illusion. "God is one" means that there is only One, that we are all one.

2. God's presence (*shekhinah*) underlies, surrounds, and fills all of existence. The encounter with this presence is intoxicating and transformative, the true stuff of religious experience. "Serving God," or worship in its fullest sense, means living in response to that presence. In our daily consciousness, however, divinity is fragmented; we perceive *shekhinah* in an "exilic" or unwhole state. Sparks of divine light are scattered and hidden everywhere. Our task is to seek out and discover those sparks, even in the most unlikely places, in order to raise them up and rejoin them to

their Source. This work of redemption brings joy to *shekhinah* and to us as we reaffirm the divine and cosmic unity.

3. That joyous service of God is the purpose of human existence. God delights in each creature, in every single distinctive form taken by existence. But we human beings occupy a unique role in the hierarchy of being, having the capacity for awareness of the larger picture and an inbuilt striving for meaning-making. We are called upon to develop that awareness to our fullest ability and to live our lives in response to it, each of us thus becoming a unique image of God.

4. "God needs to be served in every way."[6] All of life is an opportunity for discovering and responding to the divine presence. Each moment and every deed is a potential gateway to God's service. The way we relate to every creature is a mirror of our devotion to our single Creator. Openheartedness, generosity, fairness, and humility are key virtues of the religious life. Moral courage, honesty, and integrity are also values never to be ignored.

5. The essence of our religious life lies in the deep inward glance, a commitment to a vision of spiritual intensity and attachment to the One. Outer deeds are important; ritual commandments are there to be fulfilled. They are the tools our tradition gives us to achieve and maintain awareness. But they are to be seen as means rather than as ends, as vessels to contain the divine light that floods the soul or as concrete embodiments of the heart's inward quest.

6. Our human task begins with the uplifting and transforming of our physical, mental, and emotional selves to become ever more perfect vehicles for God's service. This process begins with the key devotional pair of love and awe, which together lead us to our sense of the holy. The task of proclaiming God's oneness calls upon us to be one and whole, to be at peace with ourselves. Care for the body, our own and others', as God's handiwork is also a vital part of our worldly task.

7. The deeper look at reality should put us at odds with the superficial values of the consumerist and overly individualist society amid which we live. Being, unlike our Hasidic ancestors, citizens of a free society, we

can and must take a critical stance toward all that we regard as unjust or degrading in our general culture. Caring for others, our fellow limbs on the single Adamic body or Tree of Life, is the first way we express our love of God. It is in this way that we are tested, both as individuals and societies. Without seeking to impose our views on others, we envision a Jewish community that speaks out with a strong moral voice.

8. The above principles all flow directly from an expansive Hasidic reading of Torah, classical Jewish teachings. We live in an abiding and covenanted love relationship to Torah. That involves the text, "written Torah," and the whole of the oral tradition, including our own interpretive voices. We are not literalists about Torah as revelation, but we know that our people have mined endless veins of wisdom and holiness from within that text, and we continue in that path, adding new methods to the old. The whole process is sacred to us.

9. We are Jews. We love our people, past, present, and future. We care that our people, bearers of a great spiritual legacy and also a great burden of suffering and persecution, survive and carry our traditions forward. We want this to happen in a creative and openhearted way, and we devote ourselves to that effort. As Jewish seekers, we have a special connection to Abraham our Father, who followed the voice and set off on a journey that we still consider unfinished.

10. Our world suffers from a great imbalance of energy between the typically "male" and "female" energies. Neo-Hasidism needs to be shaped by the voices of women alongside men, as full participants in every aspect of its emergence. We welcome devotion to the one God through the channels of *shekhinah* and *binah*, God as life-giving, nourishing, and protecting Mother.

11. Classical Hasidism at its best and worst is built around the figure of the *tsaddik*, a charismatic holy man blessed by God and capable of transmitting divine blessing. We too recognize that there are gifted spiritual teachers in our world, and we thank God for their presence and our ability to learn from them. We who teach and lead need to live such lives as allow us to serve as exemplars to others. But we live in an age that is rightly

suspicious of such figures, having seen charisma used in sometimes horrific and dangerous ways. We therefore underscore the Hasidic teaching that each person has his/her own path to walk and truth to discover. We encourage spiritual independence and responsibility.

12. Hasidism, like Judaism itself, believes in community. The sense of *hevrayyah,* or fellowship among followers of a particular path, is one of the greatest tools it offers for spiritual growth. The heart of such a community lies in cultivating spiritual friendships that allow you to rejoice together in God's presence as well as to talk through your own struggles and the obstacles you find in your path. Developing an ear to listen well to the struggles of others is one of the great skills to be learned from the Hasidic tradition.

13. We recognize that Torah is our people's unique language for expressing an ancient and universal truth, one that reaches beyond all boundaries of religious tradition, ethnic community, or symbolic language. As heirs to a precious and much-maligned legacy, we are committed to preserving our ancient way of life in full richness of expression, within the bounds of our contemporary ethical beliefs. But we do not pose it as exclusive truth. The old Hasidism limited all of its teachings to Jews, believing that we alone had the capacity to truly serve God, and that Judaism was the only revealed path toward such service. Thankfully we live in a different era of the relationship of faiths to one another. We happily join with all others who seek, each in our own way, to realize these sacred truths, while admitting in collective humility that none of our languages embodies truth in its fullness.[7]

COMMENTARY

1. *There is only One. All exists within what we humans call the mind of God, where Being is a simple, undifferentiated whole. Because God is beyond time, that reality has never changed.* The essential faith claim is that being is one. This is the way I understand the daily proclamation of *shema' yisra'el,* the core of Jewish liturgical practice. Note that I do not say that all being "originates" within God, as though I were offering an account of creation: it was first there, then it emerged from there. I do not believe that change has ever happened. "You are He until the world was created; You are He

since the world was created,"[8] that is, unchanged. The language we speak in explaining "creation" may sound temporal, but that is only because we are telling a story. Our existence as one, within God, is a permanent condition, an underlying truth. We still exist "in the mind of God."

It is that simple wholeness of being that we call Y-H-W-H or Being. The capitalization (possible only in English, not in Hebrew, of course) indicates that we revere it, that we accept Being as an object of worship. We fall before its majesty, its mystery, including both its life-giving and its destructive power, as did Job. *In doing so, we give to it the highest gift we humans can offer: we personify it;* we give to Being of our most precious humanity, enabling ourselves to address it as *atah*, "Thou," to render it not only object of veneration but *subject* of prayer.

I recognize that a phrase like "the mind of God" is the beginning of anthropomorphism; hence the qualification. What lies behind it is the Kabbalistic *hokhmah*, the font of existence in which all being is fully present in a not yet differentiated state. *Hokhmah* is, for the Hasidic sources, the first of the ten *sefirot*, the stages of divine self-manifestation. It is also described as *ayin* or "nothingness," meaning that no specified identity is yet present in it.[9] Like all of the ten *sefirot* of the Kabbalists, *hokhmah* is transcendent to both space and time, though it may be depicted in metaphors that derive from both.

"God is one" means that we are one. This is *sod keri'at shema'*. The rest is commentary. I have elsewhere quoted the comment of the *Sefat Emet* on this, a completely unequivocal statement of *unio mystica* at the heart of Hasidism.[10] This is where I depart most clearly from Heschel, who was strongly committed to theological personalism. You might say that we choose to read different parts of the Maggid of Mezritch. I (like Zeitlin) am mostly attracted to the abstract theology of early Hasidism; Heschel preferred the affectionate God-as-Father language that fills the Maggid's parables.[11]

Our existence as individuals, like all of physical reality, is the result of tsimtsum, a contraction or de-intensification of divine presence so that our minds can encounter it and yet continue to see ourselves as separate beings, in order to fulfill our worldly task. In ultimate reality, however, that separate existence is mostly illusion. This nonliteral reading of *tsimtsum* has its origins in the seventeenth- and eighteenth-century debates about how to understand the Lurianic myth. It was adopted by the early Hasidic masters as a key part of their mystical self-understanding.[12] It may be seen as a mystical parallel to Kant's Prolegomenon: the mind by definition cannot know or make claims about that which lies beyond its scope. We live in a mental universe shaped by individual consciousness and self-awareness. That is the way the human mind is fashioned. (The old Hasidic language would say, of course, "That is in the way God in His wisdom created us." I am not averse to such language, but I want to avoid it here in order to lessen confusion.)

But how then do I dare to make the prior statement that all existence is one in the mind of God? Does not *tsimtsum* make it impossible for me to know or assert such a thing? Here again I need recourse to Kabbalistic language. *Da'at*, best translated as "mind" or "awareness," resides within the realm of *tsimtsum*, the reduced consciousness of our ordinary mental self. But human beings are capable of insight that comes from a more profound realm of existence (or a deeper, preconscious level of mental activity). It is called *binah*, as in the phrase *ha-lev mevin*, "understanding of the heart."[13] Such insight, often coming in brief flashes and resistant to expression in the prose of *da'at*'s language, is the transcendent side of religious experience, leading us to an awareness that goes beyond the constricted consciousness within which we mortals are both blessed and cursed to live our daily lives. It dwells alongside the daily experience of "the whole earth is filled with His glory." Religious teaching, often best encapsulated in the multivocality of myth, originates in that deeper level of mind. Religious experiences, including but not limited to such flashes of deep intuition, are the primary data around which theology is to be shaped.

2. *God's presence (shekhinah) underlies, surrounds, and embraces all of existence. The encounter with this presence is intoxicating and transformative, the true stuff of religious experience.* This is the other, and larger, part of religious experience. It is the sense of divine immanence, an awareness that all of being shimmers with an inner glow that marks it as fraught with sacred character. It was well known to the Psalmist and is present in the works of all great religious poets. (Rumi, Whitman, and Tagore come to mind, along with a host of others.)

Calling this aura of holiness *shekhinah* requires a bit of historical footnoting. The term is first used in early rabbinic Hebrew much as *kavod* ("glory") is used in the Hebrew Bible, a euphemistic way of referring to God as present in the world, where use of the term Y-H-W-H or even *elohim* (the generic Hebrew word for "God") would somehow diminish divine transcendence. In Kabbalistic parlance, *shekhinah* took on a specifically feminine characteristic, serving as the mate to the blessed Holy One in the *zivvuga qaddisha* or sacred coupling that constituted divine wholeness. As this took place, *shekhinah* came to be seen as a cosmic entity or hypostasis, somehow separate from God but separate from the world as well. Indeed, the Kabbalistic *shekhinah* is precisely an intermediary between the upper and lower worlds, as I have sought to show elsewhere.[14]

Not so in Hasidism. The Maggid and his disciples go back to the insistence that *shekhinah ba-tahtonim mamash*: the divine presence truly infuses the lower, corporeal world. This means that the classic western division between matter and spirit, reaching back to Plato, is misguided; the physical world itself is filled with spiritual energy, which alone animates it. Martin Buber wrote that he loved Hasidism because it was the only western mysticism untinged by the Gnostic spirit. Of course, as Scholem has insisted, one has to read the Hasidic sources quite selectively to maintain this view, but it is fair to say that there are some texts that proclaim it clearly. They love the old rabbinic formula "He is the place of the world, but the world is not His place,"[15] which they take as implying that this world is totally contained within *shekhinah*, but that God also exists beyond in unknown ways. That means that *yihud kudsha brikh hu u-shekhintey*, the unification of primal "male" and "female" within God, is in effect the union of upper and lower worlds, the utter infusion of matter with spirit. No wonder it is intoxicating and transformative! ("Intoxicating," by the way, is a translation of the Zohar's *itbassim*, from the *bosem* of the perfumes of Eden, wafting through the verses of the Song of Songs, not the coarse intoxication of Purim and the vodka bottle.)

"Serving God," or worship in its fullest sense, means living in response to that presence. The notion of service, so essential to the devotional life in any tradition, is hard for us modern westerners to swallow. We are too afraid of the loss of both ego and freedom to see ourselves as servants. This is part of the struggle to be a religious person in our era. "Responsiveness" may help in that swallowing process. We stand in love and awe before the greatness of God (I will not argue if you call it "the magnificence of exis-

tence"), and feel ourselves called upon to respond by living a life of holy service. This is how we can mean *ana 'avda de-kudsha brikh hu*, "I am the servant of the blessed holy One."

In our daily consciousness, however, divinity is fragmented; we perceive shekhinah in an "exilic" or unwhole state. Sparks of divine light are scattered and hidden everywhere. This is our human, all-too-human, situation. We live most of our lives with ordinary, unexpanded consciousness, *mohin de-katnut.* We may have glimpses into the divine fullness in rare flashes of insight: beauties of nature, great love, great loss, and other transcendent moments in our lives briefly open the *haloney raki'a*, windows of heaven, and we see how much we are usually missing. But how do we build a life around these moments? Can we fashion a sustained and sustaining vision out of such brief and occasional glimpses?

The Talmud tells us, "Both the whole and the broken tablets were placed in the ark."[16] I like to think that the broken tablets were placed there for our generation, a time when whole tablets have ceased to function. That applies to *any* set of whole tablets. Orthodox Freudianism or Marxism are just as alien to our age as is Orthodox Judaism; there is no grand system of truth that works for us, whether you are to look up the "right" answers in the *Little Red Book* or the *Kitsur Shulhan 'Arukh*. We rather rejoice in discovering the fragments and fitting them together—each of us in a unique way—to fashion "our" truth. This does not have to lead to solipsism or chaos, as some fear. As in all ages, the sacred process requires trust in God.

Awareness of exile as the human condition is one of the great contributions of Judaism to civilization. There is nothing more eerily prescient about our tradition than the fact that we bore a notion of exile from Eden as the essential human situation centuries before historical exile was to become the dominant and formative experience of Jewish life. The Hasidic masters, building on earlier developments, understood this chiefly as an exile of the mind.[17] We are too deeply alienated from God and our own souls to be regularly aware of the ever-presence of the One in and around us. Egyptian bondage was "awareness in exile." Redemption from *mitsrayim* was release from the *metsar yam*, the "narrow straits" in which we did not have the breadth perception to get beyond our inner *katnut* or exilic mind.

This notion of the mind-in-exile appears again in twentieth-century literature, most often associated with figures like Kafka, Agnon, and Borges.

We moderns also feel ourselves cut off from the deeper wellsprings of an inner reality that we somehow know to exist.[18] Perhaps that is why the longing to reclaim ancient sources of inner wisdom has attracted so many of the best minds of the past century, stretching from the generation of Zeitlin and Buber (as well as Tolstoy and Hesse) down to seekers of our own day.

Our task is to seek out and discover those sparks, even in the most unlikely places, in order to raise them up and rejoin them to their Source. Surely this is a significant part of what makes Hasidism so attractive, both in its eighteenth-century form and in this Neo-Hasidic garb. There is a sense of spiritual adventure, in which one is ever seeking out the sparks, ever involved in that work of uplifting and transformation. In this sense I find Hasidism to be a remarkably modern, romantic religious movement, and that has much to do with my original attraction to it. The human journey is depicted as a lifelong quest, filled with struggles to find, uplift, and redeem fallen bits of the single divine Self. When you add the phrase *even in the most unlikely places*, the drama is pitched to a high point and the journey becomes fraught with danger. Indeed it is. I know from my own failures.

For us, living as we do in such a "secular" culture, the task is greater than ever. We have to raise up sparks not only from amid the conversation with the peasant in the marketplace, as the Ba'al Shem Tov taught, but from off the computer and television screens, filled with everything from blatant pornography to the less openly pornographic, but equally desacralizing, worldviews created by both Hollywood and Wall Street.

3. *This work of redemption brings joy to shekhinah and to us as we reaffirm the divine and cosmic unity. . . . That joyous service of God is the purpose of human existence. God delights in each creature, in every single distinctive form taken by existence.* This is probably my most audacious claim, one that I take directly from the early Hasidic sources. How do we dare make it? I can know what gives me pleasure or what pleases those around me. But "the *shekhinah* takes pleasure?" "God delights?" What do I mean?

Of course, such language exists in the realm of *poesis* rather than that of scientific discourse. This is the point where Gillman dismissed Heschel as poet rather than philosopher, or became annoyed by Heschel's insistence that such poetic assertion indeed has truth value or *is* philosophy.

Here I take up the cudgels for my teacher, agreeing that the traditions of *philosophia* have indeed been read too narrowly in recent generations and that the "love of wisdom" needs to be restored and made whole again by the admission of categories of human experience that come from levels of mind other than that of logic and provability. Our Western encounter with the philosophies of the East is all about this, and I believe that is the most important frontier to be crossed in the development of our self-understanding and humanity, one we need most urgently to approach. The future of theology will have much to do both with this encounter and with growing awareness of the complexity of consciousness. This will be helped by progress in the realm of brain science, but should not be reduced to it.

The western intellectual tradition fought a necessary but terrible battle to free itself from ecclesiastical domination. The scientific advance of the past several centuries would not have been possible without that liberation. The way it succeeded in that fight was through establishing a new high altar of objectivity, one that (in unacknowledged paradox) could only be approached by maintaining critical distance. This has led to a bifurcation between poetic insight and philosophic truth, separating the acquisition of knowledge and the quest for wisdom. This is part of why philosophies originating in the East, where that battle did not take place in the same way, have been so attractive.

Having said that, the assertion of divine delight is a return to the Psalmist's insight. A glimpse of beatific vision is part of the religious mind-set, including a sense that the fullness and radiance of such vision is not the mind's alone. The vision may present itself as representing an Edenic past or a glorious, not yet disclosed, future. It may be what the Zohar identifies as 'olam ha-ba', a world that is always "coming," but ever remains just a step beyond our current grasp. This window into divine joy is humbling; the greatest exultation I can feel is but its palest shadow.

So the insight that comes from expanded mind (*mohin de-gadlut*) is at once intellectual and emotional, transformative in both of those realms, though its Source lies beyond them. The truth of which it speaks is that of a universal Self that radiates its light throughout the world. That light can penetrate every human mind that is able to free itself from its *kelipot*, its self-generated defensive blinders. The light that shines through those cracks in the wall (see Song of Songs 2:9) speaks of de*light* and comes to en*light*en.

But we human beings occupy a unique role in the hierarchy of being, having the capacity for awareness of the larger picture and an inbuilt striving for meaning-making. We are called upon to develop that awareness to our fullest ability and to live our lives in response to that awareness and its call. The shining light, the calling voice—they are one and the same. The sense of religious call does not stand or fall with the personified Caller. The voice sings out to us from within the folds of the earth—*mi-kenaf ha-arets zemirot sham'anu*[19]—as much as it does from the highest heavens. It may indeed manifest itself in song or in verse or in the thundering cry of the biblical prophets. The important thing is that it makes a claim on us and our lives. Awareness of the larger picture takes us back to Job's hearing (38:4) "Where were you when I laid the foundations of earth?"

We become human when we begin to see beyond the moment, beyond the fulfillment of our immediate creaturely needs. Even though an old prayer tells us that man is no better than the beasts (the Sephardic version can't stand it and rushes in to insert "except for the pure soul!"), we detect "humanity" among our primate ancestors when we see them sublimating *eros* enough to begin to create art, to decorate beads or to paint pictures on the walls of caves. The "uplifting" that is such a key part of Hasidic teaching is surely in part another way of saying "sublimation." That same sublimation also leads us on the path of transforming desire into compassion, lust into the love of God. Being human means being able to uplift and transform.

Among the great wonders of evolution is the fact that the first creature powerful enough to dominate and determine the fate of all species on earth, the first to have the power to destroy our earthly biosphere, is also the first creature to have enough of conscience and self-awareness to hold back from doing so. Is this a coincidence?

The call has been uttered. It waits to be heard. This is the essential *mitzvah: da'at elohim*, knowing God. Acting on this *mitzvah* calls upon us to transform our lives, to work to redeem the world. Will we respond in time?

4. *"God needs to be served in every way." All of life is an opportunity for discovering and responding to the divine presence. The way we relate to every creature is a mirror of our devotion to our single Creator. Openheartedness, generosity, fairness, and humility are key virtues of the religious life.* It is not only through the specific practices of our tradition that we serve God,

but through the entire way we live in God's world. Transform and uplift every act you do, including the fulfillment of your bodily needs, to make every deed an act of worship.

This is the way of living taught by Hasidism, both the old and the new. The word *hasid* in this context is seen as derived from *hesed,* the realm of unbounded and unearned giving and love. As the world began with an act of *hesed*, so does all our world-redeeming work have to begin with *hesed*, compassion. To be a Hasid is thus to be a giver, a bestower of love. Our love of God is best witnessed, of course, by our acts of love toward God's creatures. Beware of anything that may distract you from this effort of loving and uplifting, especially of excessive religious guilt or deprecation of your sacred potential for giving. These will only lead you astray from your task of serving God in joy. The Ba'al Shem Tov understood that oppressive religion can bury the spirit. Our memory of liberation from Egyptian bondage is essential to our identity as Israel. Sometimes that bondage can be brought about by religion itself; we need to be vigilant about that danger, especially among the young. "The handmaiden at the Sea saw more than Isaiah or Ezekiel."[20] Liberation from bondage is a sacred moment, one in which God is revealed, even if that liberation is from too much stifling piety.

5. *The essence of our religious life lies in the deep inward glance.* Look more deeply; that's our message. We apply it to the three realms of person, world, and text. Look more deeply into yourself and into those around you. Do not be satisfied either with the well-defended ego that first appears or the needy, craving self that you may see next. Go deep enough to seek out the soul, the vulnerable innermost self that is the seat of true love and wonder. Cultivate those close love relationships with which you are blessed as paradigms for the way you should learn to see all human beings, each a unique expression of the divine image, and then all creatures.

World. See the natural world around you in all its magnificence, contained within the small and seemingly "ordinary" as well as within the great. Develop an eye for wonder, both in yourself and especially in those you teach. Devote time and attention to cultivating that awareness; do not take it for granted. Let it inspire you to do more to save and to protect our world.

Text. As above. Our view of Torah should be enriched rather than diminished by critical, especially literary, insights. The presence of a level on which we see the texts in historical perspective should not keep us from engaging with the many other levels of reading, including both the profound and the playful. Insight comes in all sorts of packages. "Turn it over, turn it over, because the All is to be found within it."

Ritual commandments are there to be fulfilled, but they are to be seen as means rather than as ends, as vessels to contain the divine light that floods the soul or as concrete embodiments of the heart's inward quest. "Are there to be fulfilled" is intentionally ambiguous. Neo-Hasidism can embrace a wide range of relationships to *halakhah*, varying in accord mostly with the psychological and devotional needs of the individual. There is no absolute "right" or "wrong" in this realm, not even a "better" or "worse." The values of Neo-Hasidism as outlined here are lines that barely intersect with those that define American Jewish "denominations." "One mitzvah performed with a whole heart is better than many without." "One does more, another less. Just turn your heart toward your Father in Heaven."

The Hasidic sources often quote an older play on the word *mitzvah*, deriving it from the Aramaic *tzavta* or "togetherness. A *mitzvah* is an act in which God and the person are drawn together, an opportunity to find one another in the midst of our eternal game of hide-and-seek. I rather like this reading and have lived by it for many years. I hear the traditionalist immediately rise to object. "But where is *obligation* in all this?" he (probably a "he") will ask. Go back to the credo. Read it again. There is plenty of obligation: to openheartedness, to compassion, to decency, to Torah, to the Jewish people, to healing the world, and lots more. Traditional observance is not the only way for Jews to have a culture of obligation. Classical Reform's prophetic call and Zionism's *yishuv ha-arets* are also forms of deep Jewish commitment; they are *religious*, even though some may not call them that. I say these things as a Jew who happens to care, for my own personal reasons, that the Shabbat candles be lit before dark, that I hear a hundred *kolot* of the *shofar* on Rosh Hashanah, every word of the *megillah* on Purim, and lots more. I have returned to a rather full regimen of traditional observance after many years of ambivalence. But the governing principle is personal/spiritual, not legal/obligatory, with no need to pretend otherwise.

"Keep your eyes on the prize" is my essential message here, on the end of *devekut* or spiritual openness, rather than on the means. Do not get overly caught up in the game.

6. *This process begins with the key devotional pair of love and fear, which together lead us to our sense of the holy.* We need to purify these aspects of our lives, coming to realize that all true love bears within it the love of God and that the only worthy fear is our awe at standing in God's presence. True love and fear, along with other emotions that flow from them, open channels through which God's blessing can flow into us. Inner discipline and purification of heart and mind are our constant spiritual work.

Care for the body, our own and others', as God's handiwork is also a vital part of our worldly task. The physical self is deserving of respect. The Hasidic sources go a long way toward understanding this, finding God's service in ordinary physical activities as well as in study and prayer. But they are still afflicted by the deep western/Platonic bias against the body, talking about transcending the corporeal self, "stripping off" the physical, and so forth. Neo-Hasidism's completion of this move is in harmony with the most ancient Jewish insights into *tselem elohim*, the notion that each human self, body and soul as one, is a unique embodiment of the divine image and thus needs to be protected and kept whole. A healthy Judaism needs to retain our essential values while shedding their medieval shell.

7. *The deeper look at reality should put us at odds with the superficial values of the consumerist and overly individualist society amid which we live.* A Hasidism to be lived within contemporary society, without reconstructing the ghetto walls, will have to deal in complex ways with the secularization of consciousness and its views of self, world or society, and text. On the one hand, we remain a defiant religious minority who need to stand up as a critical voice to modern capitalist society's superficial and trivialized view of human existence, bringing with it a culture of coarse materialism and the many human degradations of our consumer society. But we must also recognize the blessings of that secularization, our liberation from a society of compelled religious belief and behavior, and be wary of those forces that seek to reverse them. Hasidism's first battle was fought against socially compelled and routinized religious behavior, just as deadening to

true spiritual awareness as is secular superficiality. We have no desire to re-create premodern Jewish life or the *shtetl*, and we should avoid excessive romanticizing of it.

Historical Hasidism underwent two great struggles: first against the dominant rabbinic culture, then against *haskalah*. You might say that our situation more reflects the latter; the secularization of consciousness surely began with the enlightenment, and we continue to live in its midst. Yes, but we need to go about that ongoing struggle in a manner completely different from nineteenth-century Hasidism. What they did then is parallel to the current fundamentalist (in all three western faiths) rearguard rebellion against modernity, against Darwinism, against biblical criticism, etc. We need to understand that those battles are over, decisively lost. Our religious consciousness has to awaken from the daze of that loss and seek old/new paths for expression. Yes, there has been a cost as those battles were lost. A certain naïveté about willful divine control of things in such a way that our prayers might make them go our way no longer works for us. Yet we do not stop praying! The sense of the miraculous, *'al nisekha shebe-khol yom 'imanu* ("for your miracles that are with us every day"), is not at all diminished by evolution. This wonder remains the object of our prayers. Nor is the transcendent beauty of insight into text, our special Jewish way of reading, lessened by our knowledge of the text's human authorship. We need to allow ourselves the spiritual *freedom* to feel those things, liberating ourselves from the tyranny of our own skeptical selves (yes, tyranny exists on that side as well) that holds us back. And that freedom itself, we should recall with no small sense of irony, is a gift of modernity.

Caring for others, our fellow limbs on the single Adamic body or Tree of Life, is the first way we express our love of God. It is in this that we are tested, both as individuals and as societies. Without seeking to impose our views on others, we envision a Jewish community that speaks out with a strong moral voice. The oneness of being does not mean any less care for fellow humans or celebration of the differences between us. On the contrary, it means that we are all joined together in a bond that needs only to be discovered, not forged artificially. In caring for the other, we reassert the One.

8. *We live in an abiding and covenanted love relationship to Torah.* As readers of *Radical Judaism* will know, I do not affirm a God-initiated covenant

with the people Israel. There is too much of both anthropomorphism and religious exclusivism linked to such a notion for me to accept it. Yet I still have a sense that we exist as a covenantal community, a covenant *we* have made with our memory of transformative events recorded in our people's historic saga. Remembering that we were slaves in Egypt and that we stood at the foot of Sinai is what makes us a people, one marked by a sacred legacy and called to a sacred task. Never mind that neither of these can be affirmed by historians; they are events that transcend history. We relive them constantly, and they become the language, the echo chambers, through which we speak about many other things that happen in our individual and communal lives. Our sense of covenant with them is abiding and unbreakable. We are indeed *mushba'im ve-'omdim me-har Sinai*, under oath since Sinai to remain faithful to them.

The whole process is sacred to us. The early Hasidic masters had a bold approach to the ongoing process of reading and reinterpreting Torah. Each generation, they taught, has its own soul root and needs to discover the meaning of Torah for its own time. Teachers emerge to do that, adding to and enriching the store of tradition as it is passed on to future generations. Anyone who denies this, some of them add, denies the power of Torah itself as a living embodiment of truth.[21] Amen.

9. *We want this to happen in a creative and openhearted way, and we devote ourselves to that effort.* This commitment to the survival of Judaism as a creative force sets us apart from the ongoing traditional Hasidic community, mostly dedicated to preservation of its old ways. We believe firmly that Judaism's most creative centuries may yet lie ahead of us. We encourage ongoing creativity in realms that were familiar to the old Hasidism— Torah interpretation, music, dance—but in many new media as well. This is a vital part of "serving God in all ways."

As Jewish seekers, we have a special connection to Abraham our Father, who followed the voice and set off on a journey that we still consider unfinished. The unfinished journey is at the same time a spiritual, familial, and political one. Abraham was the classical Jewish seeker, smashing idols and trying on forms of truth until his path was revealed to him. But he is also *avinu*, the progenitor of our tribe, which must continue both to live and to maintain faith with his spirit. And since his journey was one that took him to the Holy Land, the body politic that we Jews have created there in our beloved State of Israel must also be one that shares the open-tent values of the one who set us out on our way. The true *Israel* does not begin with Herzl's vision, but one much older and wiser. Remember that Abraham was ready to risk everything, even his relationship with God, for the sake of wicked "Palestinians" in Sodom.

We are also Jews who live in the shadow of the greatest catastrophe of Jewish history, one of the darkest episodes in human history as well. This leaves us sharply aware of the depths of human evil as well as the responsibility borne by indifferent bystanders. We recognize that the Jewish people may have real enemies and promise not to be naïve about that reality; the price is one we cannot afford to pay again. At the same time, our post-Holocaust "Never again!" applies to ourselves and to all of humanity and commits us to active involvement in standing against the forces of evil in our world, wherever they may be.

10. *Our world suffers from a great imbalance of energy between the typically "male" and "female" energies.* The overvaluing of the "male" (present, to be sure in biological women as well as men) is manifest in excessive aggression, war, and rampant capitalism. All these and more are in need of healing. The old Hasidism, born of a deeply misogynist Kabbalah, saw that imbalance, but was still part of it.[22] Neo-Hasidism openly seeks to right that wrong, by welcoming both women and female energies into its ongoing creative rereading of tradition. The sages of the Talmud (b. Hullin 60a) may have already been aware of the dangers caused by this imbalance when they depicted God asking us to bring an atonement sacrifice for Him each Rosh Hodesh because He diminished the moon, giving it monthly cycles that make it less than the ever-shining sun. The ignoring of women's potential contributions to our society has indeed diminished us, and not only because they represent half of humanity. It is our male-dominated society that has brought us to the brink of self-destruction.

11. *We too recognize that there are gifted spiritual teachers in our world and we thank God for their presence and our ability to learn from them. . . . But we live in an age that is rightly suspicious of such figures, having seen charisma used in sometimes horrific ways. We therefore underscore the Hasidic*

*teaching that each person has his/her own path to walk and truth to dis-
cover. We encourage spiritual independence and responsibility.* The greatest
error of Hasidism was its turn to dynastic succession. Spiritual charisma,
as attractive and dangerous as it is, does not pass through the genes. Hasidism became committed to ultra-traditionalism, and hence became frozen
as a creative force, partly because leaders whose only legitimacy was based
on dynastic succession could offer nothing more than nostalgic preservation of the past. We do not need to repeat that error. The best examples
here are those of early nineteenth-century Polish Hasidism, where disciple succeeded master, each proclaiming openly the need to strike out on
a new path. A variety of diverse paths and teachers seems appropriate to
a Neo-Hasidism for our age.

12. *Hasidism believes in community. The sense of hevrayyah or fellowship
among followers of a particular path is one of the greatest tools it offers for
spiritual growth.* Judaism is a nonmonastic tradition. Our religion is one
designed for householders, people committed to raising families, who
nevertheless seek an intense spiritual presence in their lives. In this sense
Judaism is closest to Islam, as distinct from classical Christianity and Buddhism. The Hasidic community, like the Sufi brotherhood, is meant to create the sort of bond among householders that supports this vision. It is an
essential part of the Neo-Hasidic enterprise, where communal energies
to some degree supplant the authority of the onetime *tsaddik* and serve
as a check against potential abuses.

13. *We are committed to preserving our ancient way of life in full richness of
expression, within the bounds of our contemporary ethical beliefs.* Yes, there
are ethical limits to our traditionalism. We are not ashamed to say that
we have learned much that is positive from living in an open society that
strives toward democracy and equality. These values should become part
of our Judaism. Ultimately they are rooted in the most essential Jewish
teaching that each person is a unique *tselem elohim*, divine image. Traditions that inhibit the growth and self-acceptance inherent in that teaching must be subject to careful examination and the possibility of being
set aside. New ways of thinking that enhance our ability to discover the
divine image in more ways, or in people we once rejected, need to be taken
seriously as part of Torah.

Mordecai Kaplan was certainly right in calling Judaism an "evolving religious civilization." Our ethical norms grew as civilization progressed. We went from a literal "eye for an eye" to the payment of damages. Setting aside the biblical text, we stopped stoning suspected adulteresses or rebellious children to death. But in the course of our long struggle for self-preservation, halakhic innovation lost its nerve. We need to reassert the early rabbis' claim to a right to move boldly when faced with moral and ethical norms that we know to be behind the times.[23]

We happily join with all others who seek, each in our own way, to realize these sacred truths, while admitting in collective humility that none of our languages embodies truth in its fullness. We especially welcome shared efforts in the realm of action. We seek to join with other people of faith and goodwill to reshape our society into one based less on greed and competition and more on human goodness, and to engage with them in the most urgent task of our generation, that of protecting life on our beloved and much-threatened planet.[24]

NOTES

1. Originally published in Warsaw in 1910 and included in the posthumous volume *Be-Fardes ha-Hasidut veha-Kabbalah* (Tel Aviv: Yavneh, 1960).
2. It appears in my volume of Zeitlin's writings called *Hasidic Spirituality for a New Era* in the Classics of Western Spirituality series (Mahwah NJ: Paulist Press, 2012).
3. *Radical Judaism* (New Haven: Yale University Press, 2010).
4. "*Hasidut shele-'atid la-vo*" in *Sifran shel Yehidim* (Warsaw, 1928).
5. Published in *Varieties of Jewish Belief*, edited by Ira Eisenstein (New York: Reconstructionist Press, 1966).
6. *Tsava'at RYVaSH* (Brooklyn: Otsar ha-Hasidut, 1975), #3.
7. The number thirteen was not intentional. In fact, I tried to avoid it but failed. I take it as parallel to the thirteen *middot ha-rahamim*, qualities of compassion, and thus ask the reader to judge its author mercifully.
8. From the daily morning service.
9. This identification of *hokhmah* and *ayin* is a specifically Hasidic feature, diverging from most earlier Kabbalistic sources that identified *ayin* with *keter* and saw *hokhmah* as deriving from it.
10. See *The Language of Truth* (Philadelphia: Jewish Publication Society, 1998), or *These Are the Words* (Woodstock VT: Jewish Lights, 1999; new ed. 2012).

11. I am grateful to Shai Held for helping me to formulate this distinction.

12. A very readable treatment of this debate is offered by Louis Jacobs in *Seeker of Unity* (New York: Basic Books, 1966), 49ff.

13. I have in mind the passage from *Patah Eliyahu*, the passage from *Tikkuney Zohar* printed in Sephardic prayer books as a daily credo and recited by *hasidim* prior to Kabbalat Shabbat. Zeitlin commented on this text, reprinted in *Be-Fardes*, 147ff. This too was among my earliest readings in Kabbalah.

14. "Shekhinah, the Virgin Mary, and the Song of Songs" in *Association for Jewish Studies Review* 26, no. 1 (2002): 1–52.

15. Bereshit Rabbah 68:10.

16. B. Berakhot 8b. Of course, Neil Gillman's own book *Sacred Fragments* is named after this legend.

17. Among many other sources, see the classic formulation in Menahem Nahum of Chernobyl's *Me'or 'Eynayim, shemot.*

18. Erich Heller's *The Disinherited Mind* was "on the reading list" during my undergraduate years at Brandeis, where all my key teachers were themselves exiles. Especially formative in my own thinking was Nahum Glatzer's essay "Franz Kafka and the Tree of Knowledge," in *Between East and West: Essays Dedicated to the Memory of Bela Horovitz,* edited by A. Altmann (London: East and West Library, 1958). See my comments in the introduction to this volume.

19. Isaiah 24:16. The reading belongs to R. Nahman of Bratslav, *Likkutey MoHaRaN* 2:63. See my *Tormented Master* (Tuscaloosa: University of Alabama Press, 1969), 139.

20. Mekhilta be-shalah 3.

21. I have documented and discussed this in my essay "Hasidism and Its Response to Change," which appeared in a special 2013 issue of the journal *Jewish History,* entitled "Toward a New History of Hasidism," edited by Ada Rapoport-Albert, Moshe Rosman, and Marcin Wodzinski.

22. See the very thorough presentation in Sharon Faye Koren's *Forsaken: The Menstruant in Medieval Jewish Mysticism* (Waltham: University Press of New England, 2011).

23. The Conservative rabbis' Committee on Law and Standards' rejection of Rabbi Gordon Tucker's *teshuvah* regarding homosexuality, even as one of several legitimate alternatives, is an example of this failure of moral courage in the adjudication of *halakhah*. To cite another example, our inability to insist on the stunning of animals before Jewish religious slaughter is a blight on our moral courage.

24. I am grateful to my students Ebn Leader, Ariel Mayse, and Or Rose for important contributions to this essay. I shared the credo with participants in a conference on Jewish theology at Hebrew College in the fall of 2011. I am grateful for their input as well.

14

Restoring the Aleph

Judaism for the Contemporary Seeker

The Zohar, the greatest work of Jewish mysticism, is deeply concerned with the nature of exile and the exilic situation in which God, the cosmos, and the Jew all find themselves. In one of his more profound comments on this situation (Zohar Hadash 38a), the thirteenth-century author suggests that the divine name that accompanied Israel into exile was itself a broken one.[1] The Zohar knew and accepted the ancient tradition that "wherever Israel is exiled, the divine Presence is exiled with them."

The name that accompanied them was אהיה, pronounced EHYEH, God's "I am" or "shall be." The name, however, was broken: The *aleph* of EHYEH remained above in the heavens, while the three letters היה HYH joined themselves to Israel. But in this configuration of the verb "to be," the *aleph* is the indicator of the future tense. Its departure means that Israel in exile loses hope, becoming detached from a sense of its own future. All that remains is HYH, that which "was," the memory of past glory, past intimacy with the Holy One, the cosmic Aleph. Exile becomes truly serious when it causes us to lose hope.

Why should we feel hopeless as we think about the future of Jewish life in the new millennium before us? We have come through this most unspeakably complicated century of Jewish history a strong, proud, and free people. For the first time in nearly two thousand years, we can say that Jews are no longer oppressed by any regime for the crime of being Jewish. Popular anti-Semitism still exists, but not on a scale to constitute a significant threat. Israel is living through an era of prosperity and is looking forward to a time of real peace, even as terrible costs in human life are being paid along the way.[2] Jews in North America have achieved levels of material success and acceptance by the established powers of this society that go beyond the immigrant generation's wildest dreams. Even the final taboo against mingling with Jews, that of accepting them into the family circle, is breaking down. Surveys show that few Christian families, especially those of older American Protestant stock, object any longer to their children marrying Jews.

Ah, but there's the rub. Intermarriage, it turns out, was not quite what we had in mind. We sought full acceptance in America. That meant elite schools, executive positions in old companies, moving into the "right" suburbs, even joining the country club. But somehow we naïvely thought it would stop there. Jewish boys would take Jewish girls to the country club dance or at least would come home to marry Jewish women after a few "flings" on the other side. Now we discover that there are no "sides" any more. Young Jews growing up in this country after 1970 are almost fully integrated into American white upper- and middle-class society, which, with but rare exceptions, embraces them with open arms.

For the vast majority of American Jews under forty, this is the fourth (now fifth) generation since immigration. These are Jewish kids, or half- or quarter-Jewish kids, whose grandparents were born mostly in urban East Coast American cities. Few of them live in those cities any more, and a great many are scattered to other parts of the continent altogether. To these Jews the "old country" is Brooklyn, Philadelphia, or Baltimore. Their grandparents' tales of childhood are as likely to be about baseball games as they are about pickles or herring from the barrel. Jewish knowledge is rare in that second generation; most were too busy Americanizing to care much about the bits of Jewish lore or practice their parents had dragged with them from across the sea. The fourth generation has no direct tie to the world of East European Jewish life and its spiritual and cultural riches. All that belongs to history. The natural ties to *Yiddishkeyt,* including the rhythms of the Jewish year, the inflections of Jewish speech, even the humor that we Jews over fifty (including the important group of children of Holocaust survivors, whose memories are still more vivid) remember so well, are no longer a part of this younger generation's psyche.

From the 1920s through the 1960s, Jews were among the great proponents of melting-pot ideology. Here we were, part of a new nation being forged in America. Forget the old hatreds and divisions of Europe! Those were code words for us; we hoped they would mean "Leave anti-Semitism behind."

"Who wants to visit Europe?" an immigrant uncle of mine used to proclaim, as the first relatives ventured forth as tourists in the 1950s. "We ran away from there!"

Here we would help to create something better, fairer, less hateful, more humane. Ethnic divisions would recede with the passage of time. Even racial divisions, we thought somewhat naïvely, would eventually fall away like so many relics of backwoods prejudice.

In the late 1960s the pendulum began to swing the other way. Ethnicity was rediscovered by America, thanks significantly to the "black is beautiful!" cry that came forth from African Americans toward the end of the civil rights generation. Distinctiveness and pride in origins took the place of full integration as the final goal. Latinos were just beginning to become articulate as a minority, and they too clearly wanted to hold on to some of their old ways, including language. But if black and Latino were beautiful, so were Italian, Polish, Armenian, and all the rest, including Jewish. For us, this era in American cultural history coincided with the shock therapy in Jewish awareness offered by the Six-Day War, leading to a major renewal of Jewish life over the course of the succeeding two decades.

This renewal was heralded by the growth of the Jewish counterculture, best known through the Havurah movement and the *Jewish Catalogs*. But it includes such mainstream phenomena as the growth of day school education; the development of Jewish Studies programs in colleges and universities; a great array of books, ranging from fiction to scholarship; magazines such as *Moment* and *Tikkun*, and much more. It includes the new pride (and sometimes militancy) of Orthodoxy and the inclusion of Orthodox concerns on the general Jewish agenda. It is represented in a significant shift in both style and priorities within the organized community, from the greater funding of Jewish education to the observance of kashrut and Shabbat at public communal functions.

Then came the 1990s, opening with the devastating news of the National Jewish Population Survey. Was the whole Jewish renewal movement, in all its phases, both too little and too late? Such qualitative observers as Charles Silberman and Leonard Fein, celebrators of the spirit of renewal, were now swept aside by dour figures-don't-lie predictions based on the ever-increasing rates of intermarriage, the surprisingly low rate of conversions to Judaism, and the high dropout rate of Jews themselves.

The fear begins to mount that Jewish counterculture types are our version of aging hippies, that the "new" and supposedly dynamic Judaism of the *havurot* and *minyanim* is in fact serving only a small closed group of rabbis' kids and alumni of Jewish summer camps. Even a day-school education is viewed as far from inoculation against intermarriage as we raise a generation that lives in a very nearly unbounded open society (for upwardly mobile and educated whites, which happens to include most Jews).

That is why we are afraid. We see a decline in numbers, in loyalty, in knowledge. Those of us raised in this tradition were taught to value one *mitsvah* over all others: ושננתם לבניך. "Teach them to your children." Even among Jews where there was rather little left to pass on, the transmission of heritage, especially in the years following the Holocaust, was the greatest imperative of Jewish life. We were raised to see ourselves as a link between our parents and our children, our grandparents and our grandchildren, passing a legacy from each generation to the next. In Jewish families all over this country there is a feeling that the chain is being broken. We stand dumbfounded as we see whole limbs falling off the tree, the end of Judaism or Jewish awareness in branches of our own families.

If Judaism is going to survive in this country, it will do so because it meets the needs of new generations of entirely American Jews, including Jews who have some non-Jewish relatives and ancestors on their family trees. Rail as one may against this utilitarian/psychological approach ("They should be serving God—or standing loyal to tradition—rather than having their 'needs' met"), those who work in any form of outreach to younger Jews know it to be true. These needs are partly social and communitarian, the need for small community and intimacy in the face of mass society; partly familial and recreational, the need for "safe" day care for toddlers and high-quality squash and tennis courts for upper-middle-class Jews and their friends. But above all the need Judaism can answer is the spiritual one, a dimension of life that continues to have great and perhaps even increasing significance in American life.

The term "spirituality" is one with which most Jewish thinkers, including rabbis, were quite uncomfortable only a decade ago. Imported into English from the French chiefly by Roman Catholics, it seemed to Jews to evoke monastic life, otherworldliness, and the awesome silences of vast, dark cathedrals, all so alien to the values and experiences of children of

East European Jews. Increasingly, it has come to be associated with eastern forms of meditation and the tremendous influence they have had on Americans over the course of recent decades.

If these associations with "spirituality" were strange and alien even to rabbis, the generally more secular communal activists and "doers" standing at the helm of Jewish organizational life saw them as dangerously solipsistic, a self-absorbed turn inward that would lead to fragmentation rather than to greater communal strength. In fact, the only Jewish group that was sufficiently poised to deal with the needs of many Jews in this era was HaBaD. For the Lubavitch Hasidim, "spirituality" translated precisely into *rukhniyes* (*ruhaniyyut*), a well-known term in Hasidic parlance, and precisely that which Hasidism had to offer.[3] This Jewish version of spirituality meant a life devoted to *avoides* (*avodat*) *ha-shem*, the service of God, but marked by an inward intensity (*kavone; kawwanah*) leading to attachment to God (*dveykes; devequt*) and ultimately to the negation (*bitel; bittul*) of all else. Of course, for the HaBaDnik, as for any Hasid, this *avoide* was to be carried out through the usual Jewish means of Torah and *mitsvot*, including full commitment to the halakhic way of life.

Hasidism, in other words, comprises a Jewish version of the "spirituality" that so many in America are seeking. It does so, however, in a way that insists upon uncompromised acceptance of traditional norms, a way of life attractive to a few but probably impossibly alienating to most young American Jews in the twenty-first century. It is hard to believe that we are to build the Jewish future by a return to the life patterns (including role of women? style of leadership? norms of dress?) belonging to the eighteenth or early nineteenth century. This "Amish" pattern for Jewish survival is the way of a few hardy souls who join the core of those raised within it, but it offers little attraction for the many.

But let us return to "spirituality." Now that we have found a Jewish language for it, let us examine more closely what it means and why it has become the cry of our age. Spirituality is a view of religion that sees its primary task as cultivating and nourishing the human soul or spirit. Each person, according to this view, has an inner life that he or she may choose to develop; this "inwardness" (*penimiyyut* in Hebrew) goes deeper than the usual object of psychological investigation and cannot fairly be explained in Freudian or other psychological terms. Ultimately it is "transpersonal," reaching deeply into the self but then extending through an inward reach beyond the individual and linking him/her to all other selves (to all other Jews, the Hasidim would say) and to the single Spirit or Self of the universe we call God. God is *experientially* accessible through the cultivation of this inner life, and awareness (*daʾat*) of that access is a primary value of religion. External forms, important as they are, serve as instruments for the development, disciplining, and fine-tuning of this awareness. The Hasid may see them as divinely ordained forms but still recognize that they are a means (indeed, a gift of God to help us in our struggle), not an end in themselves.

Such is, in fact, the shared theology of vast numbers of seekers in our era. Though pursuing the quest through a variety of symbols and traditions, we contemporary seekers are joined by a series of shared sensitivities that transcend the differences between our systems of expression. We understand "being religious" not primarily as commitment to particular symbols or even as faith in a specific set of principles, but as openness to a deep well of inner experience. This includes experiences in nature, in solitude, those induced by meditation and silence, or some quite spontaneous. Moments like these offer us insight into the wholeness of being, expressed by Hasidic tradition as the realization that "the whole earth is filled with His glory" or "there is no place devoid of Him," but by Hindu and Buddhist philosophy without reference to God as "that which is, is."

It is the truth of such moments, translated into teachings through one language or another, that nourishes our lives as seekers, that gives us the strength to go forward. It is the love for and unity with all creation in such moments (whether those are moments experienced, imagined, or merely striven for) that underlie our ethical and moral lives and tell us how to live.

Whether our spirituality is Jewish or Christian, Buddhist or eclectic New Age, you will probably hear us talking about living in harmony with natural forces, following the voice of our deepest inward nature, and seeking to shape a human society that appreciates more and destroys/consumes less of nature's bounty or of God's gifts. A shared spiritual language of this age is beginning to emerge, one that transcends the borders of the traditions in which we live and where we may have gained our original impetus toward the spiritual life.

Together, we share a sense that the world urgently needs this new spirituality; we are as committed to it as we are to our individual traditions.

Living in an age of ecological crisis, we understand that nothing is more important for humanity than a shared religious language, reaching across the borders of traditions, that will make us more sensitive to the natural and physical world in which we live, which is itself the domain of the sacred. In the coming century, all the religions will have to be drawn upon to create such a language in order to transform human consciousness for the very survival of our world.

This "new" universal spirituality of the late twentieth century is most commonly lightly dressed in Indian or Tibetan garb and thus accompanied by belief in reincarnation, karma, and various charts of spiritual energies or stages in the process of enlightenment. Western elements, too, are added to the mix of this ever-evolving raiment in which the spirit is to be clothed. The commonality of theological and ultimately experiential substructure across religious and cultural lines also makes it possible for some seekers (and not only those to be dismissed as "flighty" or unstable) either to turn from one tradition to another in the course of a lifelong quest or to combine elements that seem (at least to the outsider) to originate in entirely different and even contradictory social and historical contexts.

Over the course of some thirty years as a Jew committed to my own form of religious quest within Judaism, I have met many Jews who have chosen or needed to explore their spiritual lives through a variety of non-Jewish, mostly eastern, spiritual paths. Among them I have come upon some remarkably profound, honest, and open seekers. I urge us to see such seekers not as "apostates" or as rejecters of Judaism, nor as the duped victims of "cults" (though such do exist; they come in eastern, Christian, and even Jewish versions), but as Jews loyal to at least one aspect of our people's most ancient ways.

Among the spiritually wandering Jews I have met over these three decades are faithful children of Abraham, doing for themselves what we are taught our first ancestor did. They have rejected the superficial idolatries of their own time and place (those of Washington, Hollywood, and Madison Avenue; even those of complacent, semi-assimilationist suburban Judaism, rather than those of Ashur and Ur) and have gone off to the desert, seeking in it the secret places that flow with milk and honey. Though the terrain they explore may be alien and sometimes even objectionable to us, their need to do so and the growth that takes place over the course of such exploration should be familiar and not entirely surprising to us as Jews. Given the generally low level of spiritual seriousness in most liberal synagogues in our country, it is little wonder that Jewish seekers feel a need to turn elsewhere in quest of profound religious truth.

For the generations born or raised since the end of the Second World War, religious quest has been prominent among Americans in a way it had not been earlier. This is true among Jews in somewhat higher numbers, but it is true of general culture as well. Such serious students of American cultural norms as Peter Berger, Robert Bellah, and Martin Marty have tried to document and explain this phenomenon. The attraction of Americans to serious religion in recent years runs the whole gamut, from fundamentalist and evangelical Christianity to the quasi-eastern, from charismatic Catholicism and HaBaD Judaism to the New Age and experimental in all (and no) traditions. Among Jews it includes *ba'aley teshuvah*, those who have found their way into a more intense and spiritual, but also more observant, Jewish life; and the much larger group who have turned elsewhere for their spiritual satisfaction, sometimes to Christianity and a neo-Sufi version of Islam, but primarily to eastern religions. Generationally this group runs from Allen Ginsberg and Baba Ram Dass (a.k.a. Richard Alpert), who came of age in the 1950s, to students currently on campus and living near campus in such centers as Berkeley and Santa Cruz, California, Cambridge and Northampton, Massachusetts, and several points in between.

Why has this generation turned so much to seeking? Some of it has to do with being the first to grow up in the aftermath of both the Holocaust and Hiroshima. Life in the nuclear shadow has given us an insecurity paralleled in few earlier generations. As in the aftermaths of previous cataclysms of human history, life seems particularly precarious. Pictures of mass burial pits and endless bodies again inhabit our imagination. The notion that at any time some lunatic (for a while he was even named "Dr. Strangelove!") might come along and "push the button" has forced us to reach somewhere for ultimate meaning. We need something that will enable us to go forward, to bring children into the world and work to improve human life, even in this ever-so-threatened generation. The shift over the past decade from nuclear war to ecological disaster as the focus of our fears has not essentially changed this situation.

A second motivating factor in the search for meaning among American Jews is surely the high level of material success that many have attained over the course of these four generations. As members of the financially highest-achieving ethnic or religious group (on a per capita basis) in this society, we are brought face-to-face with questions of values and priorities. "Is this all there is?" we find ourselves asking. Wealth, achievement, and glamour do not in themselves bring happiness or fulfillment, as a significant portion of our newly active Jewish leadership has found. They also do not protect us from the personal crises that most require spiritual meaning. Wealthy and powerful Jews still face death, infirmity, divorce, alienation between parents and children, even the ennui and emptiness that ensue when you seem to run out of deals to make, resorts to visit, entertainments to enjoy, obstacles to conquer. Life has to have some greater meaning, some value beyond that of our own seemingly endless, and ultimately somehow trivial, achievements.

Where do we seekers turn for such an ultimate value? Prior generations might have had an easier time believing in a God who had supreme power over His creation and was thus the source or guarantor of absolute values. But that sort of religion is hard for us. Will we trust a Deity who did not prevent the Holocaust (or slaughter in Rwanda, starvation in Ethiopia, or the AIDS epidemic) to reenter history and save us from destruction at our own hands? Conventional western-type faith in an all-powerful Creator God seems difficult unless it is explained in a highly sophisticated— and compromised—fashion. No wonder it is rejected by large numbers of seekers, including many Jews.

On the other hand, the well-known western alternative to religious faith seems even more discredited. Our trust in humanity, and especially in the modern pseudo-religion of scientific progress and the conquest of evil through systematic human knowledge, is severely tested in the late twentieth century. Our memories include Nazi scientists in the land of reason and morality, emerging in the century after the Categorical Imperative and Absolute Spirit. It is hard, even fifty years later, to believe in the "progress" wrought by modernity and its achievements. Added to these are the economics and politics that complicate and often corrupt the "pure" advance of scientific thinking. We are happy to support science's advance, to be sure, especially insofar as it alleviates suffering and contributes to the world's survival. But we cannot turn to it as a source of ultimate values.

Today's seeker is one who takes the accomplishments of science for granted; the old battles between the religious and scientific worldviews on life's origins read to us like ancient history. But we also understand that we need not look to the scientific community as our provider of meaning. Often we try to broaden the scope of science by integrating into it the wisdom of the ancients, whether in accepting traditional Chinese and homeopathic medicine or in speaking about rungs of consciousness that may preserve memories of countless past lives and generations, much like the rungs of the tree or molecules of DNA preserve genetic "memory."

There has been a sense throughout this period that we needed to be rescued by another source of truth, by some deeply rooted wisdom attuned more closely to the moral and spiritual needs of a much-battered humankind. Over the course of these past several decades, that source of truth has mostly been the wisdom of the East, in various Indian, Japanese, and Tibetan forms. The insecurity of the West about its own achievement, including the basis of its moral life, makes us more open (and not for the first time) to learning from other civilizations. The heart of this eastern teaching is a profound nondualism, an acceptance of all that is, and a timelessness, fostered by meditative silence, that allows one to transcend daily worries great and small. When seen anew from the heights of this compassionate yet detached mind-set, life regains the value it had lost in the battle-scarred decades of violence and degradation through which all of us have lived.

We far fewer seekers who have made Judaism the path of our quest find some similar and some different formulations. We, too, look toward the contemplative and inward portions of our tradition. "Jewish Meditation," reconstructed from many fragments of nearly lost practices, has elicited great interest in recent years.[4] The theological language to which we are attracted is largely that of the mystical tradition, though few would find it accurate to designate ourselves as "Kabbalists" in a literal sense. It is the abstract notion of Deity, combined with the richness of metaphor and symbol, that makes the Kabbalah attractive. The highly simplified mystical language of the early Hasidic sources, one that speaks of fullness and emptiness, of the ever-elusive God beyond and the spirit of Godliness that fills all existence, seems especially well suited to the contemporary need. Most have found that regular patterns of observance, especially the rhythms of Shabbat and weekday, of life according to the sacred calendar, offer unfathomable spiritual rewards.

These seekers include those who have "gone all the way" and joined Hasidic or other ultraorthodox communities and others who have sought a less rigid structure, often gravitating toward Reconstructionist or "Jewish Renewal" circles. At their best, the latter have sought to create a "maximalist" version of liberal Judaism, as intense as Orthodoxy in its demands but more universalistic in perspective, emphasizing a renewed prophetic commitment and Judaism's demand for justice and care for the downtrodden as key portions of that maximalist agenda. Whether such a "muscular" and demanding liberal Judaism can take hold is a key question in thinking about our collective future.

The serious seeker, today as always, is open to taking on spiritual disciplines, even of the most rigorous kind. We are not talking about an easy push-a-button or drop-a-pill experience-craving pseudo-spirituality, one that seeks only "highs" and takes no responsibility for the deep valleys that lie between the peak experiences.[5] All the traditions recognize that discipline and regularity of practice are essential building blocks of the spiritual life. Their routine and the very ordinariness of doing them day after day, even when they seem empty, provide the counterpoint to the spiritual mountaintops of great insight that appear occasionally in their midst. But the disciplines we seek, whether old or new, are those that seem helpful to us, those that offer us the tools and framework within which to engage in the task of spiritual growth and self-development that each of us must ultimately face alone. When a practice is there just because it is traditional, done that way just because it always has been, today's seeker may be expected to question. Turn as we do to ancient paths of wisdom, we inevitably remain late twentieth-century Americans, for better and for worse: practical, somewhat impatient, wanting a hand in shaping things, not content simply to accept them and pass them on. We are open to hard work, but for our efforts we expect to get results.

A number of years ago my family and I were living in Berkeley, California. Around the corner from us was, of course, a spiritual or New Age bookstore. The front of the store was decorated with a huge sign, in inverted pyramid form. The top line read, in large block letters: SCIENTOLOGY DOESN'T WORK. Beneath that, in slightly smaller letters, it said:

INTEGRAL YOGA DOESN'T WORK. Then, again slightly smaller: CHRISTI-
ANITY DOESN'T WORK. After going through six or seven more would-be
spiritual paths the sign concluded, again in large letters: YOU WORK. Seeing
this sign reminded me of a definition of Hasidism that Abraham Joshua
Heschel had passed on in the name of the Kotsker rebbe. When asked
what Hasidism was all about, Rabbi Mendel of Kotsk replied: "*Arbetn oif
zikh*"—"to work on yourself."

Being a seeker means understanding that there is work to do. In the first
instance this is spiritual work, which means the transformation of the self,
opening oneself to become a channel through which divine light shines
or cosmic energy flows. This work requires a training of the mind in the
twin tasks of awareness and responsiveness. Awareness, *da'at* in the Hasidic
sources, means a knowing and constant remembering that all things and
moments contain the Presence, that everything can lead us back to the
one. It is intellectual, to be sure, but an act of mind is colored with all the
eros of the first biblical meaning of "to know," as the Hasidic sources not
infrequently remind us. Responsiveness is that state cultivated over years
of inward prayer or meditation, where the heart is always half open, ever
ready to respond to the lightest knock on its gate by the Beloved.

Inevitably the seeker in these generations must also deal with the question of the relationship between personal and societal transformation.
Each of us feels challenged by the social ills that still surround us: pov-
erty, racism, injustice, the destruction of the planet. Few would say these
matters are of no concern. Even the eastern religions, often stereotyped
in the West as totally unconcerned with alleviating the sufferings of this
world on the material plane, begin to take on a measure of worldly and
practical responsibility when imported and reshaped by westerners. All of
us who seek, no matter how specific our symbol system or spiritual language, are universalist in our concern for humanity and its earthly home.

The question for us is often one of priorities and faith in our own capa-
bilities to effect change. Should I spend my time in demonstrations or
political party work to change the opinions of others, or should I work first
to make sure my own inner garden is free of weeds? Given the shortness
of my life and the limits of my strength, where should I put my energies?
These questions are unresolved for many a contemporary seeker; most of

us tend to shuttle back and forth among priorities as our lives go on and as specific demands present themselves.

We also seek religious community. The lone work each of us has to do cannot thrive without the support and understanding of others. But the communities we need have to be made up of those who understand and share our search. The American synagogue, even at its best, seldom had that character in the previous generation. It was too concerned with propriety, respectability, and public image to be very welcoming to those few and often "different" Jews who were seeking on the spiritual plane. That is beginning to change in some places as a new generation of rabbis and synagogue leaders are discovering the seeker in one another. Many synagogues have been quietly remade in recent years into warm and supportive communities that in *havurah*-like fashion serve as extended family to their members. The next step for communities like these is to seek out the seekers and make room for them, working with them to create a shared language of personal religious expression.

Judaism is not is not an easy path for the contemporary seeker, even if it happens to be his or her ancestral tradition. The reasons for this are manifold and the mix varies from person to person, but it behooves us to examine a few of the serious stumbling blocks that lie in our way as we think about educating for a Jewish future with the potential spiritual seeker in mind.

First are the external difficulties. Judaism is a highly verbal tradition, and its language is Hebrew. Nobody says that you have to learn Pali or Tibetan or Japanese to be a good Buddhist. True, those are the languages of scripture, commentary, and the contemporary faith communities. But texts may be translated, as many have been, and a language and culture barrier to the native Buddhist cultures of Asia may help in the western Buddhist's somewhat naïve re-creation of the faith, rather than harm or challenge it.

Significantly, few of the eastern teachers who have come to the West in recent decades have insisted that their western disciples learn the languages, fully absorb the practices, or assimilate culturally to the world from which their teachings came. They are realistic in this regard; recognizing the cultural distance involved, they have chosen to "go native" in the West and create indigenous forms of Buddhist or Hindu spirituality, very much a mirror image of what Roman Catholicism learned to do in Mexico or in parts of Africa.

For Judaism, particularly because our traditional mentality was so shaped by oppression, minority status, and the struggle for group survival, such transcendence of the cultural/ethnic context is almost unthinkable. To do the Jewish spiritual life seriously, you really do have to know Hebrew. Our prayer traditions are highly verbal and tied to the intricacies of language; they just don't work in translation. So much of our teaching, including the deepest insights of the mystical and Hasidic sources, is caught up in plays and nuances of language that translation of such sources, while it is to be increased and encouraged, will never be quite adequate.

Because we are right here in the West, the seeker living cheek-by-jowl with various ongoing Jewish communities, it is all the more difficult to create a Judaism of one's own. There seems always to be someone down the street or in one's synagogue (sometimes even if you are the rabbi!) telling you that what you have created is not authentic, not Judaism as it once was and ever should be. The Havurah/Jewish Renewal movement has tried to fight this, creating small independent communities that are neo-traditional in form but often quite revolutionary in hierarchy of values. Unfortunately, these, too, have undergone a certain weakening as the 1960s have turned into the 1980s and 1990s. Such communities constantly need to examine whether they are truly agents of positive change and rebalanced Jewish intensification for their members, or whether they have not become convenient clubs for those who want less, rather than more, of one or another (including the financial!) sort of commitment. In recent years those communities have suffered from the well-known struggles of new communities in our society over issues of leadership and empowerment: Does "egalitarianism" mean that those with more experience or greater knowledge of the tradition should not serve as teachers and leaders for those who come seeking to learn?

But a new commitment to Judaism as a spiritual path involves deeper problems as well. I alluded earlier to the question of God and the use of the word "God" in a contemporary spirituality. Now we have to examine this question more closely. It is clear that a person can have a spiritual life without believing in God. That is precisely what Buddhism provides, at least on a rarefied theoretical level; I daresay that is a major reason why it is attractive to so many Jews. The emphasis of Buddhist spiritual training is on attentiveness, on attitude, on an approach to reality rather than on a personal Subject who is the goal of one's spiritual life. By contrast, even the most spiritualized form of Judaism is focused on knowing, loving, and obeying God in one way or another. Is it in any way conceivable that one can seek to have a Jewish spiritual life without believing in God?

Let us not rush in too quickly with our negative answers. The question is more complex than it appears, and a contemporary response requires a good deal of subtlety. How do we reply to the Jewish seeker who says:

Yes, I am a religious person. I believe in the oneness of all being. I feel a connection to something eternal and infinite that is present in my own soul and in yours. That's what my quest is all about. But I can't call it "God." That means that I don't consider it to be a willful, personal being. It is not someone I want to worship, someone to whom I can address prayers. Certainly the language of the synagogue, that of God as King of Kings and myself as His supplicating servant, is not one I like or see any reason to adopt.

Or to another who says:

I am grateful for the inordinate gifts that nature has bestowed on me. I have health, sustenance, meaningful work, a loving partner, friends, and family. Sometimes when I walk on a beach or am alone outdoors on a beautiful day, I feel overwhelmed by gratitude and by a sense of inadequacy to express the fullness with which I feel blessed. That is about as close as I can come to prayer. But the prayer that wells up in me at such moments is addressed to life itself and to no one in particular, surely not to "God." And all this has nothing to do with the synagogue, the cantor and choir, or uncomprehended Hebrew chants that feel like they come from another time and another place.

These are not at all the voices of the Jewish atheist of a couple of generations ago, the "old Left" Marxist sympathizer who believed that religion was the opiate of the masses and wanted no part of God, synagogue, or religious life. We are confronted now with a religious agnosticism (and sometimes atheism) on a massive scale. Does Judaism have the resources to respond to such a generation? Or will it cause these seekers to turn elsewhere, concentrating its efforts on those who do not question or who have found a way, usually because of long-standing emotional commitments and the ability to reinterpret texts almost automatically (rather than because of truly different beliefs), to stay within the fold of Jewish forms of expression?

A Judaism for the seeker in this generation will have to reexamine a number of givens of our tradition. How certain are we that we need to insist on the personalist metaphors, mostly those of male parent and ruler, that have constituted the heart of Jewish prayer language for so many generations? The theology of *Avinu Malkenu*, God as Father and King, is problematic not only because of the single-genderedness of these terms. We in this psychological age understand the divine parent as a projection, a cosmic superego figure that we impose upon ourselves and accept because of our felt need for an externalized center of societal and individual self-control. But once we let that cat out of the bag, the control no longer works as well. Once I lose my naïveté about God as Father, it is hard for me to use those words again, to fully reenter the now broken myth.

It is true that *becoming* a father helped me bridge the gap for many years. The realization that God loved me in the same way that I loved my then-helpless infant child from the moment I saw her did much to sustain in me the language of Jewish faith. But it is hard to leave faith in the hands of the volatile parental metaphor, one toward which we all have a complicated network of emotional reactions and which changes profoundly as we go through the course of our lives. And "king" is even harder than "father" in a world where kings no longer radiate ancient glory, but are either powerless figureheads, men who dress once a year in garb of state, or else petty despots who remind us mostly of the ugliness rather than the glory of earlier times.

Of course, classical Judaism had other metaphors for God. The Beloved, the God of such Kabbalistic poetry as *Lekha Dodi* or *Yedid Nefesh*, is a tempting one to seek to restore. But here, too, I hesitate. The same question of the possibility of religious language in a psychologically self-conscious age comes directly to the fore. God as Cosmic Lover will work in some very special moments. We will always find ourselves on guard, however, asking about what it means to long for the Lover of the Song of Songs when the "real" issues of love and erotic self-fulfillment are so painfully obvious to us on another level. The fact that we are a tradition without monasticism or celibacy must also mean that we cannot be naïve about love. We may have exhausted the resources of our old language for speaking both to and of God. We may need to create a new language, as the Kabbalists did in the Middle Ages. Meanwhile, perhaps we should say: "Unto You Silence Is Praise." Silence may create in us the condition out of which a new prayer language might be born.

We will also have to ask ourselves how fully wedded we are to the vertical metaphor for the divine/human relationship, one that almost completely dominates in our classical sources. By the vertical metaphor I mean the notion that God dwells "in heaven," while we humans are "down below" on earth. This notion is, of course, derived from ancient beliefs about the gods as sky dwellers. As mature and sophisticated in our faith as we may think we are, it is difficult for us to outgrow the notion of "God above," an idea that God "resides" in some vague place on the other side of the sky. Every time we read a psalm about "God in heaven" or tell the tale of Moses ascending the mountain to reach God, we reinforce the myth of verticality. We do so also by such abstractions as referring to someone who is "on a very high rung" of spiritual attainment or even negatively by referring to someone who is not serious about religion but merely trying to "get high."

I am not one who believes that we can or should get rid of all the vertical metaphors in our religious tradition. We would be terribly impoverished and for no good reason. But it is important to see through this language and thus to be freed of its total hold on us. We can do so most easily by turning to the other great metaphor of religious tradition, that of inwardness. Rather than seeing all humanity climbing up the great mountain, let us imagine ourselves as journeying down into the depths, seeking to draw water from our innermost well. Instead of ascending rung after rung, we are peeling off level after level of externals, reaching toward a deeper vision of the universe. Of course, this, too, is a metaphor, but the presence of a second way of seeing our journey helps to release us from the singular hold of the first.

But once we have let ourselves question the vertical metaphor of our ancient cosmology, a great deal more is questioned as well. The God above might come down onto the mountain once, at a particular place and time, to talk with those gathered there. Since God is outside the world, revelation is an unusual event. But can the God within, the one who speaks to every human heart, have the same relationship of "choosing" with the Jewish people? If God is none other than the innermost heart of reality, is not all of being equally an emanation of the same divine Self? Is Judaism not just our own human symbolic language into which we Jews render the universal inward God's silent, preverbal speech, just as others translate it into verbal symbols of their own heritage? And can the internal God be the source of authority in the same way as the Fellow on top of the mountain, the One who could, according to the Midrash, hold it over our heads, even as we agreed to receive Torah, saying: "If not, here you will be buried"? Most basically, it would seem that the God within is not other than ourselves in the same clear way as the God above. The vertical metaphor allowed for distance: "If you do not do good, I will turn far away, rising to the seventh heaven, far beyond your ability to reach Me." But the hidden God buried deep within the self feels more like one who ever longs to be discovered, and the process of finding God is not to be clearly distinguished from the deepest levels of self-discovery. What we are likely to find is the truth of the mystics: The individual self and the cosmic Self are one. The Judaism that will emerge from a turn inward will then be something like a version of what Aldous Huxley and others have called the *philosophia perennis*, a single truth that underlies all religions, though expressed and taught in the specific symbolic language of the Jewish tradition.

The theology that will speak to today's seekers will be a Jewish nondualism, a spiritual vision that seeks to transcend the most basic barriers between God and world, self and other. This is not the religion of God the Creator, who fashions a world outside Himself and sits over it in judgment. It is rather that of God the One who enters into the dance of multiplicity, who dons the coat of many colors, and thus is to be found and discovered throughout the world, amid the great richness and diversity of existence.

This is also not the religion of God the Revealer in its classic form: the God who makes manifest His arbitrary will, backed by threat of punishment and promise of reward. Rather, it is the God of that beautiful maiden dwelling in the castle who, according to the Zohar, reveals a bit of her face to the lover who passes by her gate day after day.[6] *We discover ever more of*

God's self and will as we seek to live in God's presence. Torah is not a finite body of laws and teachings, codified in details of praxis down to the nth degree. It is rather an endless well of wisdom, present in the texts, commentaries, and traditions of our ancestors, to be sure, but living in us only because we keep our hearts open by our own practice. It is the presence of divine energy that we find within, renewed each day, that makes our teachings living Torah and not dead letter.

The first Hasidic masters knew this well and taught it unceasingly. This voice was lost in later Hasidism's rush to preserve tradition.[7] But it is our task to recover and renew that voice. It should speak out from within a deep commitment to practice and love tradition, warning nevertheless against Judaism's greatest inner danger: the overly zealous commitment to detail and form. This zeal can sometimes result in a loss of broader perspective and deeper openness, even the openness to God.

This God is also not one who redeems as the traditional metaphor depicts it, looking down from the heights of heaven to lift Israel from Egypt or to send a messiah who will save the world from humanity's worst violent and self-destructive urges. We speak rather of a God who dwells within the unquenchable spark of freedom that lives within every human heart, the one who inspires the Moses in us to rebel against every Pharaoh. It is the divine voice in us that calls us to maintain our undying faith in the full liberation of humanity, in both flesh and spirit. It is through our deeds that God brings about redemption, being manifest within us and triumphing over our own desires to escape and avoid the true fulfillment of our divine/human selves.

What I am proposing for the Jewish seeker, deriving from my own quest which is essentially similar to his or hers, though conducted within the sphere of our own people's religious language, is a Jewish mystical humanism. It is humanistic in that I believe humans are the essential actors in the historical, political, and social spheres. For better or worse, it is we who are charged with the task of saving this world and we who are also the agents of the world's destruction. In this drama, there is no *deus ex machina* who will protect us from ourselves. But it is very much a mystical or spiritual humanism, not secular in any way. On the contrary, I seek to expand the bounds of the holy, to find the One manifest everywhere, to understand that each of us is not just a separate willful being but a spark of that divine light. It is by finding those sparks in one another and drawing their light together that we discover and articulate the deeper truth about this world in which we live. That truth understands that there is ultimately only one Being, present in each of us, longing to know its own source and draw together the uniqueness of each being and the singularity of the Source from which we all come and to which we all return.

"Why do it through Judaism?" the seeker often asks. My answer comes not in absolutist terms; it cannot, Judaism is a hard path, but it is one toward which we have a special obligation. We have just been through an age that sought to turn its back on many of the most profound and ancient of human teachings. Modernity "knew better" than the wisdom of prior generations, and traditional ways of knowing and living were cast onto the trash heap of history. The era emerging is one that seeks to rediscover truths long neglected; we are more willing now, and will be more willing in the next century, to relearn this wisdom of great antiquity and depth. This age will need the energies and teachings contained in all the great and venerable traditions of humanity.

Among these are perhaps eight or ten truly great religious traditions, developed over the course of human history. Several of them have hundreds of millions of followers. We, diminished both by genocide and assimilation, are a small people bearing a great tradition. Most of its heirs do not care about this legacy. Others love it so much and hold on so tightly that they cannot let it move forward into the new and universal age that stands before us. And so I would say: If you were born a Jew, or if you are drawn to Judaism, perhaps it is not just by chance. Perhaps what the human future needs of you is your reading of, you encounter with, this great portion of our shared spiritual legacy. You can raise up sparks that belong to your soul alone, reveal worlds that can be found by no other. The tradition waits for you to discover it.

Our sages say that Abraham the seeker was like a man wandering from place to place when he came upon a בירה דולקת, a burning tower. Can it be, asked the seeker, that the tower has no master? Then the master peered out and said: "I am the master of the tower." The term הציץ, "peered out," leaves no doubt that it was from within the tower itself that the master revealed his face to the wanderer. Abraham discovers that this world, in the very midst of its conflagration, contains the divine presence. Is it any wonder that my teacher, the late Abraham Joshua Heschel, when he told this story in one of his books,[8] sometimes intentionally mistranslated the phrase to mean "a tower full of light"? We find God in the light, in the beauty of life in this world, as we find God in the fire, in our world's suffering and conflagration.

Finding divinity within the world will lead us toward the understanding that God (YHWH in Hebrew) and being (HWYH) are One and the same, two perspectives on the same reality. We will come to see that even this most basic of all dualities, the distinction between God and world or God and self, is less than the whole of truth. Thus the *bet* of בראשית will be replaced by *aleph*, the *aleph* of אנכי, I am," the beginning of the Ten Commandments. This restored *aleph* will also turn out to be that of אהיה, "I shall be," the one that returns our hope and renews our future.

It is also, as it happens, the *aleph* of אברהם, Abraham, the father of all Jews and all seekers. May the seekers of today be faithful children of that earliest father, not only in questing after truth, but also in seeking to pass their truth on to future generations. In this way, our ancient legacy will not be lost but infinitely enriched and renewed by this generation of seekers, as we live it, reshape it, and help it continue to grow.

NOTES

1. Based on the text of Ezekiel 1:3.
2. Ah, the dreams of Oslo!
3. I render the terms here both in the Yiddish colloquial of Hasidic speech and in the more "proper" Sephardic and accepted scholarly versions.
4. It would be interesting to make a study of "Jewish meditation" as a growth industry over the course of the past twenty years. The bibliography in Mark Verman's book, *The History and Varieties of Jewish Meditation* (North Vale NJ: Jason Aronson, 1996), would be a good place to start. Such a study would be an object lesson in the interpenetrating influence of Orthodox Kabbalists (Aryeh Kaplan), critical Judaica scholars (Moshe Idel), and New Age teachers (Zalman Schachter-Shalomi), all in the shadow of the growth of eastern meditational practices in the West during this period.
5. The emphasis here is an address to several friends, thinkers and writers who are my seniors by a generation, who continue to attack the recovery of spiritual life in Judaism in the most distorting terms. Let me make it quite clear to them that neither I nor any responsible voice I know is advocating (1) the abandonment of commitment to social justice, (2) a druglike euphoria in which we lose any sense of borders and therefore the ability to distinguish right from wrong, or

(3) entering closed *havurah* cloisters where we will ignore the rest of the Jewish community and leave it to its sorry fate.

6. Zohar 2:99a–b. Included in Daniel Matt's *Zohar: The Book of Enlightenment* (Mahwah NJ: Paulist Press, 1983), 124f.

7. A particularly interesting and dynamic notion of Oral Torah, as a teaching fashioned of the deeds of the righteous in each generation, is to be found in the *Sefat Emet*, a key Hasidic work by Rabbi Judah Leib Alter of Ger (1847–1904). In several places he identifies Oral Torah with the "eternal life You have implanted within us" of the concluding Torah blessing. My edition of that work, including selected texts, translations, and contemporary personal responses, is *The Language of Truth* (Philadelphia: Jewish Publication Society, 1998). More recently, my students and I have done the same for earlier Hasidic teaching in *Speaking Torah: Spiritual Teachings from around the Maggid's Table* (Woodstock VT: Jewish Lights, 2012).

8. A. J. Heschel, *God in Search of Man* (Cleveland: Meridian Books, 1959), 112–13n6, 367.

15

A Kabbalah for the Environmental Age

An irony of history is that Kabbalah, jettisoned by generations of Jews as so much backward nonsense, is now making a comeback. In an age when modernity itself is being questioned, this renewal of interest in mystical aspects of Judaism is both spiritually exciting and potentially dangerous, even explosive. The danger lies in the deep connection found between Kabbalah and both the xenophobic and the messianic elements of Jewish tradition. When mystical faith supplants political judgment or when medieval views of the difference between Jewish and gentile souls are reflected in social policy attitudes of Israeli power-brokers, the entire Jewish people is endangered. But the promise of the mystical tradition and its potential contribution to a Judaism that could appeal to many seekers is so great that this writer, along with many others in our time, is willing to take the risk.

I am certainly not a Kabbalist in the traditional sense, nor do I aspire to be one. The old system, *qua* system, does not work for me. The mythic universe of Kabbalah, for all its beauty, belongs to another age. Whether we look at its hierarchical structure, at the Jewish exclusivism and spiritual racism implied by its doctrine of the soul, or at the passive-subject role assigned to the feminine, I for one do not believe that a return to the mentality of the ancients is the solution to our current woes. Instead, our age is very much in need of *a post-Kabbalistic Jewish mysticism*, one richly nourished, but not dominated, by the old language and structure. That new Jewish mysticism, Kabbalah in a universalist and pluralist key, has been slowly emerging over the course of the twentieth century, a process that has more recently moved into high gear. This new pace and high degree of interest is part of a much broader world-wide reexamination of the great spiritual traditions, a seeking out of ancient wells of wisdom that might sustain us in a new and unprecedented period in human history.

Humanity is in urgent need of a new sort of piety, a religious attitude fitting to an environmentally concerned future that is already upon us. This new mining of ancient religious truth is being applied to all the traditions. As a Jew who has been studying and teaching Kabbalah and Hasidism for forty years, I believe that our tradition has much to offer, if we combine deep examination of the sources with a willingness to choose carefully among them and update their teachings when necessary. Among the elements I seek is *a Judaism unafraid to proclaim the holiness of the natural world*, one that sees creation, including both world and human self, as a reflection of divinity and a source of religious inspiration. It is in this spirit that I turn to Kabbalah, seeking to learn from, but also to adapt and transform, its vision. The essential truth of mysticism, that all beings are manifestations of the same one, and that the unity of being can be discovered by a disciplined training of the mind toward insight, is one that our age both longs and needs to hear. The understanding that God is the innermost reality of all that is, and that God and universe are related not primarily as Creator and creature, but as deep structure and surface, is key to the Judaism of the future. But the ways in which we develop and act upon that insight will have to be appropriate to our own age.

The magnificent architectonics of the kabbalists' vision cannot be fully articulated here. Their grand picture of the inner universe, in which the One that encompasses all being opens up to reveal itself as ten, is the beginning of the kabbalistic system. The ten *sefirot* (literally: "numbers") are stations in the flow of energy from the One into the many. The ten-in-one cosmos is a way of responding to the eternal mystical question, "How do the many proceed from the One?" The kabbalists say: "Very slowly and subtly. Let us show you the process." As one gets further into Kabbalah, it turns out that each of the ten *sefirot* contains all the other nine and the whole process of tenfold manifestation repeats itself four times as one journeys through various upper or inner "worlds." There is thus a basic "grid" of four hundred rungs, each discussed with great finesse in the highly refined symbolic language of Kabbalah. Other versions of the kabbalistic "map" have the ten *sefirot* open themselves further to reveal more decades, becoming hundreds, thousands, and so forth. Later Kabbalists redivide the ten into five configurations of *sefirot* that each exists in six modes or stages, leading to a system of staggering and overwhelming complexity.

For the initiate, the *sefirot* also serve as rungs or marking points of the mystic's inward journey. His goal (it only also can become "hers" in very recent times) is to reverse the journey of God from unity into multiplicity, going back to make the many into one again. The kabbalist who "ascends" those rungs ideally "uplifts" the lower worlds, taking them along on the journey back to oneness. In this way they, along with the mystic's own soul, may be included again in the one. This is the kabbalistic concept of *tikkun*, the restoration of the worlds to their original harmony as carried out in this "uplifting" activity of the mystical life. Each person is a microcosm, also built in the same pattern of the *sefirot*, so that cosmology and psychology, our ways of understanding life's origins and our own innermost selves, are quite identical. God's cosmic journey into multiplicity and your inward journey into unity are mirror images of one another.

This "great chain of being" approach to spirituality can be appreciated more than ever by postmoderns, not only for its beauty but for a certain dimly perceived accuracy as well. According to the ancient myth, each human being contains the entire universe. All the rungs of descent (and potential ascent) are contained in each soul. But that is true, even in de-mythologized form: all of our ancestors, each stage and mini-step in the evolution of life that brought us to where we are today, are present within us. The DNA that constitutes the life identity of each of us exists indeed *zekher lema'aseh bereshit*, "in memory of the act of Creation," linking us back to our most remote origins.

Part of our work as self-aware, articulate beings is converting that biological "memory" into consciousness and building a holy structure (i.e., a religion or a civilization) that articulates and *sanctifies* those links between past and future. In this way, the actual fact of all our pasts' presence within us is converted into a basis for meaning, for expression of our deep rootedness in all that is and has come before us. The memory of the entire universe lies within each and every one of us. Hopefully, the values represented by that ongoing project of civilization building will lead us forward as well, helping us realize that we must be faithful transmitters to all the many future links in the evolutionary chain, just as we are the grateful recipients of the efforts of all that have fought the ongoing struggle to bring us to this moment. All of the upper and lower "worlds" of the kabbalist here become manifest in human terms, as generations that lie before and behind us but also as multiple layers of human self-awareness that we seek to peel back in search of our deepest and truest selves.

Creation and Revelation, according to esoteric Judaism, are two different but parallel manifestations of the primordial Torah or the creative wisdom of God. We might think of this as universal Mind, the wisdom that is manifest both in the ways of nature and in the deepest soul of human beings. At the heart of these twin self-revelations of the One, as understood in Jewish language, lies the barely whispered breath of the four semi-consonants *Yod He Waw He*, the verbal noun that tries to express the divine Self. In the hierarchy of language, this is the supreme word. Too holy to be spoken aloud except by the high priest on the Day of Atonement, it is the word that stands closest to the silence that surpasses all language. This name is an impossible conflation of the verb "to be"; hence the God of Exodus, where the name is introduced, says: "I shall be whatever I shall be," meaning that the elusive Self of the universe will ever escape definition. Those four letters are really a term for being—HaWaYaH—itself. But because they are mere breath (for there is no really consonantal "hard" sound in any of them), they also stand for the birth of language itself, the emergence of the word from the universal silence beyond; from what we Jews call the eternal Torah of God, the wordless truth that "was" before Creation.

God *is* Being: Y-H-W-H, when existence is seen from a fully unitive, harmonic, and all-embracing point of view—a perspective that ever eludes us mere humans, located as we are in particular identities of time and space. The small self and its limitations keep us from seeing the great Self at work both within and around us. But then the letters, like pieces in a puzzle, are mysteriously rearranged and HaWaYaH, existence itself, reveals itself to be none other than Y-H-W-H, the great name that proclaims so powerful a unity of being that it could be spoken only there, in the innermost holy chamber of the holy Temple.

Kabbalah is a tale of origins, an account of how the many come forth from the One and how we may embark on the return journey to oneness. But our beginning point of understanding has to take us beyond Kabbalah, back to the biblical tale of origins. The Kabbalists' universe depends entirely on the much older biblical creation tale, the ingenious opening chapter of Genesis that for nearly twenty-five hundred years served as chief source for the West's understanding of natural, including human, origins. The account of how God in six days spoke each order of existence into being is now of only antiquarian interest as an actual account of how the world came to be, though it remains alive for us as a liturgical text and a source of religious creativity.

But I would like to lift the veil behind Genesis 1 and ask just what it was that this magnificently penned single chapter managed to accomplish. The old Mesopotamian and Canaanite creation myths, now barely recalled, were well known to the biblical authors. They include the rising up of the primal forces of chaos, represented chiefly by Yam or Tiamat, gods of the sea, against the order being imposed by the sky gods. The defeat of that primordial rebellion and its bloody end is well documented, as scholars have shown, in a number of passages within the Bible: in the prophets, Psalms, Job, and by subtle implication even in the Genesis text itself. That tale of origins was a part of the cultural legacy of ancient Israel. The fact that it is reflected even in postbiblical midrashic sources shows that it had a long life, continuing even into the Zohar of the thirteenth century. The original readers/hearers of Genesis 1, in other words, knew of another account of creation, one of conflict, slaughter, and victory, "the survival of the fittest" among the gods. What is striking about this account is precisely the *absence* of those elements of conflict: Genesis 1 offers a purely harmonistic version of the origin of creatures, one where everything has its place as the willed creation of the single Deity and all conflict has mysteriously been forgotten.

Our civilization has been transformed over the past century and a half in no small part by our acceptance of a new tale of origins, one that began with Darwin and is refined daily by the work of life scientists and astrophysicists, the new kabbalists of our age who claim even to know the black hole out of which being itself came to be, speculating on the first few seconds of existence as our ancestors once did on the highest triad of the ten *sefirot*, or rungs, of divine Being. The history of living creatures is again depicted as a bloody and violent struggle, the implications of which for human behavior—even for the possibilities of human ethics—have hardly gone unnoticed. We too are urgently in need of a new and powerfully harmonistic vision, one that will allow even the weakest and most threatened of creatures a legitimate place in this world and protection from being wiped out at the careless whim of the creature who stands, at least for now, at the top of the evolutionary mound of corpses. A beautiful attempt at articulating such a vision was made by Brian Swimme and Thomas Berry a few years ago in *The Universe Story*. Such a vision more willing to base itself in part on the biblical/Judaic legacy would also be a welcome contribution.

But let us return for a moment to the old creation tale. While I no longer believe it in any literal sense and do not look to it, even through reinterpretation (each "day" is a geologic era, etc.) as a source of information about geohistory, I claim it still as a *religious* text for me as a Jew and for us as a people. We still read it in the synagogue and its closing section is the introductory rubric for our most precious and best-beloved sacred form: the observance of the Sabbath. "Heaven and earth were finished, and all their hosts . . ." What then does the text mean to me? What underlies the myth, or to what truth or value am I pointing by so privileging this ancient text?

The text says that before there were many, there was only the one. Before the incredible variety and richness of life as we know it could come to be, there had to exist a simple self, a source from which all the many proceeded. I refer not to some single-celled amoeba that existed in the ocean hundreds of millions of years ago. I read the text on a different level by asserting that *the primacy of the one to the many is not necessarily temporal in meaning.* Sacred myth describes a deep and ineffable reality, one so profound that it is not given to expression except through the veil of narration, through encapsulation in a story. And stories, given the need for a sequential plot, require time. So the precedence of the One over the many, placed into story form, comes out sounding like: "In the beginning God created . . ." Its meaning, however, is that the One underlies the many— then, now, and forever. A dimly perceived but awesome, deep structure links all things and ties them to the root out of which they all emerge. Multiplicity is the garbing of the One in the coat-of-many-colors of existence, the transformation of Y-H-W-H, singularity itself, Being, into the infinite varieties of H-W-Y-H, being as we know, encounter, and *are* it.

The Genesis "creation" story is really a tale of the origins of multiplicity, a biblical attempt to answer that eternal question of mystics to which the later account of the *sefirot* was also addressed: "How do the many proceed from the One?" This reality is symbolized by the beginning of the Torah with the letter *bet*, long a subject of speculation within Jewish tradition. *Bet* is numerically "two"; its positioning at the beginning of Torah indicates that here is the beginning of *duality*. From now on there is not just "God" but "God and . . ." This meaning is dramatically reinforced by the emergence of Creation in what are repeatedly described as pairs: light and darkness, day and night, heaven and earth, upper and lower waters, sun and moon, male and female, and all the rest. Behind all these twos, however, behind the *bet* of *bereshit bara'* ("In the beginning God created") lies the hidden, singular, silent *aleph*. This One, representing the absolute oneness of being, the One after which there is no "two," is to be proclaimed at Sinai in the opening letter of *anokhi*, "I am," the very heart of revelation. So there are two ways in which the One is revealed. One leads through the path of infinite multiplicity and diversity, the one as manifest within the many, God in creation. The other is the invitation to the return journey, revealing to us the *aleph* that underlies all being, the One to which we all return, both in the ecstatic silence of mystical journey and in the ultimate ego transcendence of death.

This One, I believe, is the only Being that ever was, is, or will be. It is the One that undergoes the only sacred drama that really matters: the bio-history of the universe. *I believe that it does so as a conscious and willful Self.* From those first seconds of existence, through the emergence of life in its earliest manifestations, and along every step, including the seeming stumblings, missteps, and blind alleys along the way of evolution, it is this single Being that is evolving, entering into each new life form, ever carrying within itself the memory of all its past. I thus seek to re-vision the evolutionary process, not as the struggle of creature against creature and species against species, but as the emergence of a single life energy, a single cosmic Mind that *uses* the comparative adaptabilities of all the forms it enters as a means of ongoing striving ever forward into richer and more diverse forms of life. The formless Self searches out endless forms, delighting to rediscover its own identity anew in each of them. That constant movement of the One, expansive in all directions at once, is at the same time directed movement, pointing toward the eventual emergence of a life form that can fully know and realize the One that lives in all beings. This creature, the one in whom the self-knowledge of Being can be ultimately fulfilled, is thus the *telos* of existence.

In this process, the emergence of humanity with its gifts of intellect, self-awareness, and language is indeed a major step forward. Judaism has always taught a distinction between humans and other forms of life, a sense in which the human stands beyond the vegetative and animal realms out of which we emerged. Each creature embodies the life energy and hence the presence of the One, but only humans are called "God's image" in our tradition. This means that we are the first to have the mental capacity to recapitulate the process, to be self-conscious about our roots within the One. The implications of that potential are tremendous if we understand the mystical journey back to oneness as a central value within human existence, the "opposite" that complements our drive toward progress, growth, and forward movement. But surely our being "in the divine image" is not meant to give us license for the rapacious destruction of all so-called "lower" forms. God forbid! That would be the model of the "species eat species" view of evolution. Although we are indeed by design and necessity eaters of the "lower" species, we still seek a life of harmony and balance with them. The Bible provides two models for defining humanity's role in relation to the natural world. One is that of Genesis 1: humans as stewards, the viceroy who is to "rule over the fish of the sea, the birds of the sky, and all the beasts who roam the earth." But if we look into the Psalms, the concluding chapters of Job, and other scriptural sources, we find another option. I quote from Psalm 148, using a recent contemporary adaptation by Stephen Mitchell in *A Book of Psalms, Selected and Adapted from the Hebrew* (1993):

> Praise God upon the earth,
> whales and all creatures of the sea,
> fire, hail, snow, and frost,
> hurricanes fulfilling his command,
> mountains and barren hills,
> fruit trees and cedar forests,
> wild animals and tame, reptiles, insects, birds,
> creatures invisible to the eye
> and tiniest one-celled beings, rich and poor, powerful
> and oppressed, dark-skinned and light-skinned, men and women
>   alike,
> old and young together.

Here the Psalmist envisions us as *part* of the universal chorus of praise, rather than isolating us as the final creation of Friday afternoon, with the message of "stewardship" that accompanies it. A true understanding of the unitive vision being proclaimed here would lead us beyond the demands of "stewardship," the ethic usually derived from the biblical tale. Life's meaning is to be found in discovering the One, and that means realizing the ultimate unity of all being. It is in *yihud*, discovering and proclaiming the underlying oneness of all existence, that our humanity is fulfilled.

We are of the One; each human mind is a microcosm, a miniature replica of the single Mind that conceives and becomes the universe. To know that oneness and recognize it *in all our fellow beings* is what life is all about. But that recognition leads us to another level of awareness. The One *delights* in each of the infinite forms in which it is manifest. To play on that lovely English verb, this means that the One sends its *light* into each of these forms. Vegetative forms indeed experience this gift most in sunlight, stretching toward it as they grow. We humans are privileged to experience that same radiating light energy as delight or love.

The One *loves* the many. The coat-of-many-colors in which Being comes to be garbed is a garment of delight. We, as the self-conscious expression of Being, are called upon to love as well, to partake in and give human expression to, the *delightfulness* of existence. This is expressed in Jewish liturgy in the order of daily prayers. The blessing of God as the source of nature's light is directly followed by a blessing for God's love. The One does nothing different in the interim between these blessings. God does nothing different in giving light to all creatures, plant and animal, and in giving love to human beings and holy communities, assemblies of God-seekers wherever they are. As humans who are creatures of love, we receive the divine life flow in the form of love, turning toward it and being fulfilled by it just as naturally as plants stretch toward the light. Nature experiences this shining as light; we humans receive it as love. But as recipients of love we are called upon (Dare I say "commanded"?) to love as well.

I am also fully willing to admit that we may still be at an early stage in an ongoing evolution of aware beings. Perhaps our period will be looked upon in the distant future by creatures no more willing to demean themselves by the word "human" than we are comfortable being called "ape," as a primitive life stage. Surely they will not be wrong, those wise beings of the future, in seeing our age as characterized by nothing so much as pretentiousness and self-glorification on the one hand and wanton consumption and pillage of the earth's resources on the other. Let us hope that we leave room for that wise future to emerge.

Discovering the presence of the One within the natural order and therefore the sacred quality of existence itself is exactly what our father Abraham did, according to Philo of Alexandria, the hidden grandfather of all Jewish philosophy. This One manifested itself to him in terms of law: Abraham felt that he was being taught how to live in harmony with the forces of nature. Moses' Torah, according to Philo, is the lawgiver's attempt to legislate for a whole human community the life of harmonic insight with the God of nature that Abraham had already found for himself. I have tried to show elsewhere that certain writings of the Hasidic masters, unaware of the ancient precedent, continue this trend. Levi Yizhak of Berdichev, the eighteenth-century Hasidic master, introduces his treatise on hidden miracles, or the miraculous within nature, with precisely this claim: Sinai allows the entire people to apprehend that which wise old Abraham had already discerned on his own.

The law that teaches us how to live in harmony with the natural world should be one of eternal principles and countless new applications. Its most basic teachings should demand of us that we live ever at the cutting edge of sensitivity toward the suffering we cause God's creatures. We need to be aware of the rest and reinvigoration that we should give to the soil. So too should we avoid the waste of living resources, for each is the embodiment of divine presence. We may not take the endless material gifts with which we are blessed any more casually than we would take God's *name* in vain. We may not take the One's great gift of holy *water* in vain. Or *air*, source of *nishmat kol hai*, the sacred breath of life. To rest on the laurels of forms our ancestors created long ago or boast of their progressivism in the tenth or sixth century BCE is very much not to the point. What is the point of observing *shemitah*, the sabbatical year, but using earth-destroying pesticides? Of insisting on the humanity of *shechitah*, kosher slaughter, but hoisting and shackling and refusing to stun animals to lessen their awareness before they die? Of washing the bugs out of our lettuce while investing our greenbacks in multinationals that daily destroy entire forests? The challenge before us is to be as aware and insightful for our times as the Torah was in its day. How can we *today* create a civilization and a law that will be such a *torat hayyim*, a teaching that enhances life? And what will it demand of us? Surely a return to the reverence for air, water, fire (by limiting the amount that we, including our automobiles, burn!), and soil would be a good place to start.

Another potentially useful rubric within tradition for proclaiming this insight is the parallel between the ten divine utterances (of "let there be . . .") in Creation and the ten "commandments" (the Hebrew might be better rendered as "speech acts") of Sinai. This is another way of expressing the unity between the revelation that lies within Creation and that which is manifest in Torah. The presence of the One that underlies all being is depicted as pure verbal energy: God is the One who ever unceasingly says, "*Yehi!*" ("Let there be!"), speaking the world into being. But at Sinai, those ten *yehi*s are translated into imperatives for us; the inner "law" of God's presence in nature is now manifest in the form of imperatives that can govern human existence, bringing us into harmony with the ten words within ourselves as well as within all creatures. And since the ten "commandments" are the basis of all the 613 yeas and nays that comprise Torah, all of it is tied through them to the ten cosmogenerative utterances of the One. This parallel is a great favorite of certain mystical teachers. Creation and revelation are two deeply interrelated manifestations of the same divine Self, one showing us that all existence is fraught with holiness, the other instructing us on how to live in the face of that awareness.

Here the language of Kabbalah may be useful again. These two tens, the utterances and the commandments, are both versions of the ten *sefirot*, those primal numbers that allow us deeper entree into the "secret" of existence. We manifest that secret by turning outward and inward toward the world around us, seeing it in all its awesome beauty and recognizing how deeply we are a part of all that is. We then ask (in good Jewish fashion): "What does this awareness *demand* of us?" Here we have the beginning point of a new Kabbalah and a new Halakhah ("path" of religious practice) as well. This praxis, one using and adapting the rich forms of Jewish tradition, should be one that leads us to a life of harmony with the natural world and maximum concern for its preservation.

All this talk must seem terribly mythical to readers of a more scientific bent of mind. Perhaps it also seems obscure and irrelevant to some of those most keenly aware of the several immediate threats to global existence. Let me assure you that I share that sense of urgency. Life has so evolved that the fate of the biosphere itself is now determined by human actions. We are masters not only over our own species but also over those we consume, as so many others have been. The very existence of our planet as a fit habitat for *any* living thing has now fallen into human hands.

With this increase in human power comes a manifold increase of responsibility. It is the future not only of our own offspring that we threaten each day with a million decisions weighted with political, economic, and competitive baggage. The land itself, the *adamah* from which we humans derive our name, is threatened by us, the earth, and all that is upon it. The changes needed in collective human behavior in order to save us from self-destruction are stupendous. Belief in their possibility stretches our credulity as much as it is demanded by our need for hope. Our economic system, including the value we place on constant expansion and growth, will have to change. The standards of consumption, created by our wealthiest economies and now the goal of all others, will have to be diminished. Effective world government, perhaps even at the cost of some of our precious freedoms, will have to triumph over the childish bickerings and threats that currently characterize world affairs.

Hardly believable, indeed. But consider the alternative. If any of this deep-seated change is to come about, religious leaders and thinkers need to take an early lead. A seismic shift in the mythical underpinnings of our consciousness is required; nothing less will do the trick. That shift will have to come about within the framework of the religious languages now spoken by large sections of the human race. Experience tells us that newly created myths do not readily take hold; they usually lack the power to withstand great challenge. But a rerouting of ancient symbols, along channels already half-cleared by the most open-eyed thinkers of earlier centuries, might indeed enable this conversion of the human heart of which we speak.

In the emergence of a new tale of origins, we Jews, who have for so long been bearers of the old tale, have a special interest. The new tale will need to achieve its own harmony, summarized with no less genius than was possessed by the author of Genesis 1. It will need to tell of the unity of all beings and help us to feel that fellow creaturehood with trees and rivers as well as with animals and humans. As it brings us to awareness of our common source, ever-present in each of us, so must it value the distinctiveness and sacred integrity of each creature on its own, even the animals, or fish, or plants we eat, even the trees we cut down. If we Jews are allowed to have a hand in it, it will also speak of a human dignity that still needs to be shared with most of our species and of a time of rest, periodic liberation from the treadmill of our struggle for existence, in which we can contemplate and enjoy our fellow feeling with all that is. This sacred time also serves as a model for the world that we believe "with perfect faith" is still to come, a world of which we have never ceased to dream.

16

Abraham Joshua Heschel

Recasting Hasidism for Moderns

Abraham Joshua Heschel is generally seen as an American Jewish religious thinker. When he is taught, it is primarily in the context of American Judaism. His mature works were published here, and his greatest impact was on Americans, Christians as well as Jews. In the public realm, Heschel is best remembered for his friendship with Martin Luther King Jr., his marching at Selma ("my legs were praying!"), and his leading role in opposition to the war in Vietnam. In addition to his great lifework as a theologian and Judaic scholar, he made important contributions to Jewish/Christian relations (especially in connection with Vatican II), religious education, and the shaping of the American rabbinate. His voice, alongside that of Elie Wiesel, was among the first to be raised for the plight of Soviet Jewry, years before this became a subject of international Jewish concern. Through us, his students, he has been (along with Martin Buber) one of the two most important intellectual/theological influences and models for the Jewish renewal movement, beginning with the *havurot* of the late 1960s. Heschel helped us to recover and articulate a sense of spirituality within Judaism. Translating that religion of spiritual insight and sensibility into one of imperative and action was Heschel's greatest task, and it remains ours.

But Heschel, both the man and the thinker, was formed in Europe. When he arrived in America in 1940, at the age of thirty-three, the three major shaping influences on his life were already in place: the Hasidic world of his childhood, the (mostly Jewish) intellectual community of Berlin and the disciplines studied at its university, and the experience of living for five years in, and finally being booted out of, Nazi Germany. Of course he was influenced and refined further by the land in which he lived in the second half of his life. But I believe that for Heschel, the American experience was seen largely through one or another of these three lenses that he brought with him from Europe.[1]

Hasidic Warsaw was the first part of that European experience. Heschel was the scion of several of the great Hasidic families of Eastern Europe. For at least five or six generations, virtually all of his male ancestors had been Hasidic rebbes. Raised to continue in the family tradition, it was at first assumed that young Heschel, who was a Talmudic as well as a spiritual prodigy, would be a great figure within the Hasidic world. On his mother's side, he was most closely related to his uncle, the Novominsker rebbe, whose court had moved to Warsaw where Heschel was raised, and on his father's side to the Kopyczienicer branch, who were centered in Vienna, but also to the Czortkow and Husiatyn branches of the Ruzhin family, the descendants of the Maggid of Miedzyrzec. These were all Ukrainian and Eastern Polish dynasties.[2] Members of Heschel's family were culturally immigrants to Warsaw, where Hasidic Jewry was dominated by Kotsk and Ger, to which he had no family connection. As a Hasidic youth in Warsaw, he was, however, taught in the Gerer schools and had a personal tutor who was a devoted Kotsker Hasid. Hence the very different worlds that Heschel late in his life referred to as Miedzybozh and Kotsk came to dwell together in his soul.[3] Heschel left this world behind, however, as an adolescent, something of a rebel, seeking the kind of education that his extended family obviously would have preferred that he do without. The Hasidic world of Warsaw was too narrow for him; he saw the small-mindedness that necessarily resulted from the tremendous effort expended to shut out the modern world. He also experienced the competition and frequent bickering that went on among the various dynasties, all of them led by men who were there because of their lineage, but few of whom retained the charismatic qualities that had first made the progenitors of their lines into rebbes.[4]

Hasidism thus existed for Heschel as something that belonged to his past, a world to which he no longer fully belonged. Yet it seems he still felt that Hasidism *belonged to him*. Heschel may be seen as part of a rather remarkable group of *rebbeshe eyneklekh*, descendants of Hasidic rebbes who, though no longer part of the community, took pride in their Hasidic legacy and continued to view Judaism through Hasidic eyes.[5] This group includes such diverse figures as historian Shmuel Abba Horodezky, psychologist and novelist Fishel Schneersohn, novelist Yohanan Twersky, and memoirist Malka Bina Shapira. Heschel's understanding of Judaism was in many ways a Hasidic one. The books he chose to teach in seminars and the sources he quotes in his late theological writings include works that were specifically either Hasidic in origin or key to the Hasidic library.[6] *The Sabbath* is a work possible only against the background of Hasidism. The grand entryway into *God in Search of Man,* the language of depth theology, the journey through awe, wonder, and mystery—all draw on the Hasidic consciousness. Heschel retained much affection for, and a certain loyalty to, Hasidism throughout his American years. At the same time as he was writing his widely read theological classics (*Man Is Not Alone,* 1951; *Man's Quest for God,* 1954; *God in Search of Man,* 1955), he was also publishing, in Hebrew, meticulously researched historical articles on the early generations of Hasidism.[7] Some of this renewed interest in his own closest roots, of course, was sharpened by the terrible sense of loss Heschel felt after the Holocaust.

In 1944, when the dimensions of European Jewry's loss had become clear, Heschel was invited by the leadership of YIVO, the Yiddish Scientific Institute in New York (itself a recent transplant from Vilna), to deliver a memorial lecture. This magnificent piece of Yiddish oratory, *The East European Jew* (published in Yiddish in 1946), was expanded and translated as *The Earth Is the Lord's* (New York: Henry Schuman, 1950). Along with Roman Vishniac's photos of Polish Jews, this work served as the most significant *kaddish* for the Holocaust that was available to most American Jews for nearly twenty years. In it Heschel overcame any distance, either geographical or critical, that the Berlin years had placed between him and the world of his childhood. In the early postwar years, Heschel came to see himself as one of the last who really understood that lost universe; he was the lone survivor in the tale of Job, the one who says, "I alone have escaped to tell thee." His readoption of the name "Joshua" during or immediately after the war, a change that made his name instantly recognizable to Polish Jews as that of a Hasidic rebbe, was certainly part of this, a partial willingness to reassume the mantle of family heritage. Heschel had a mixed attitude toward reemergent Hasidism as it existed in New York in the postwar years. He remained personally close to his surviving relatives (some of whom had preceded him to America), leaders in that community, but maintained a silent truce with them on questions of religious values and priorities.

Looking in retrospect at Heschel's mature thought, we may say that the key themes of his complex writings are the loftiest mysteries of existence as perceived, celebrated, and challenged by the questioning religious mind. He seeks to create an inspired phenomenology of religious living around such themes as the mutual relationship of God and person, our human need for God, and the question of whether God has any need for us. Ever fascinated by the claim that each person is God's image, he reflects profoundly on the nature of humanity and the role of community and leadership. Seeking out the point of interconnection between human society and the divine, he reexamines and clarifies the place of prophecy, revelation, and commandment, as well as the human response to these in prayer and the power of deeds. Although all of these mighty questions are addressed from a specifically Jewish (and often biblical) point of view, they are framed in a universal human context, addressing the non-Jewish reader as well as the Jew.

It is Heschel's universalism, including the fact that he was loved and appreciated by so many non-Jewish readers, which makes him a uniquely American phenomenon. It was widely felt that Heschel was no mere apologist or defender of tradition, but a person of authentic spiritual experience, rooted deeply in his own Hasidic background. But what did Heschel learn from the Hasidic traditions he knew so well with regard to these central themes of his future thought? What does it mean to claim Heschel as a neo-Hasidic figure? Heschel positioned himself as an eloquent representative of the classical Jewish tradition as a whole. He studied and taught Maimonides and Abarbanel as well as the Ba'al Shem Tov. His original academic work was on the prophets, who presumably precede the distinction between *hasid* and *mitnagged*. He refused to be publicly critical of any aspect of the tradition. In dealing both with Christians and Jews, Heschel saw himself as a spokesman for Torah in the broadest sense, for the religion of the Hebrew Bible, for the Word and People of God. He never referred to himself as a "mystic," seemingly accepting the cultural bias against that word that reigned in 1940s and 1950s America. Although he wrote scholarly articles on the early history of Hasidism, he did not place himself in the role of the movement's defender and refused to be sidelined as a representative of "the mystical tradition." He disliked sectarianism and saw beyond denominational distinctions. Although close to the leadership of the Conservative movement, he was as critical of it as he was of Orthodoxy, Reform, and secularism. He was not called upon to champion Hasidism at the expense of any other Jewish movement, nor would he have wanted to do so. Yet still there is, I would claim, a distinctly Hasidic cast to Heschel's Judaism. How is it present in his thought, and in what ways, if any, was he at pains to transform or universalize it?

In answering these questions one must make use of all of Heschel's varied writings, published in four languages and over the course of his lifetime and later. But Heschel's first published work, a collection of poems called *Der Shem Hamefoiresh: Mentsh* (Warsaw: Indzl, 1933)[8] is of special significance. The title itself, translated as *The Ineffable Name of God: Man*, sets the tone of religious humanism that so characterizes all of Heschel's writings. Many specific themes developed later make their appearance in the poems collected in this clearly highly personal and revealing volume.

It is in five areas that Heschel's roots within Hasidism may be seen as significant. First, his work is Hasidic in that it maintains a sense of wonder about God who fills the universe. The biblical exclamation, "The whole earth is filled with His glory!" and the Zohar's, "There is no place devoid of Him!" become twin watchwords of the Hasidic consciousness. This is the core religious experience of the Ba'al Shem Tov, around which all of Hasidism crystallized: there exists neither time nor place where God cannot be found by one who has the inner training and courage to open the eyes to see. From the *Upright Practices* of Rabbi Menahem Nahum of Chernobyl:

Believe with a whole and strong faith that "the whole earth is filled with His glory!" and that "there is no place devoid of Him." His blessed glory inhabits all that is. This glory serves as a garment, as the sages taught: "Rabbi Yohanan called his garment 'glory.'" His divine self wears all things as one wears a cloak, as Scripture says: "You give life to them all."[9]

To see this, and to show it to others, is the task of the *zaddik*. Listen to young Heschel's bold self-description in the poem "Intimate Hymn":

I have come to sow the seed of sight in the world,
To unmask the God who disguises Himself as world.

Like many of the lines in Heschel's poems, this one has to be read quite carefully. The Yiddish *"kh'bin gekumen zayen zeyen in der velt"* is a line of great power and daring. The "I have come" formula is attributed to the Ba'al Shem Tov in numerous sources, explaining the meaning of his mission. It is a kind of formulation familiar in the speeches of other great religious teachers as well. Young Heschel does not appropriate it lightly. The line reveals that he thinks of himself as having a mission of bringing religious awareness to others. The notion of "unmasking" the God "who disguises Himself as world" is a precisely Hasidic way of seeing the God/world relationship, expressed much more boldly here than in Heschel's later writings.

But the statement of young Heschel's mission is also connected to Psalm 97:11, "Light is sown for the righteous," one of the biblical verses most often quoted and interpreted in Hasidic writings. The divine light (*or ha-ganuz*) is hidden, sown into the ground, buried behind the mask of nature, waiting for the *zaddik* to reveal it. I am here, Heschel says, "to sow sight," to help others discover that hidden light. A true rebbe is one who can discover that light and make it visible to others. It is a line the Ba'al Shem Tov could well have used about himself.

For the biblical authors, prophets and Psalmists alike, it was clear that the wonders of Creation were a primary testament to the workings of God. To know God, one needed to appreciate and revere His handiwork. This view of nature as a testament to God diminished significantly in the Talmudic age, and it may be said that both the Kabbalists and the Hasidim sought to restore it to its place of primacy. The Kabbalists (I refer to the sefirotic Kabbalah of the thirteenth century) did so by means of symbolism: nature is glorified through the fact that images of the natural world (often taken from the landscape imagery of the Psalter or the Song of Songs) are included in the symbol clusters used to describe aspects of the divine self: *sefirot* are streams and rivers, nut trees and gardens; aspects of the Godhead are described as sun and moon, sky and earth, etc.

In Hasidism the restoration of nature is done directly, without need for the symbolic bridge. All the world is a cloak or mask, which hides behind it the great light of God. Hasidism sings the glories of all Creation, but especially the forest, so much a reality in the Eastern European landscape of the eighteenth century. This is the forest to which the Ba'al Shem Tov, as a child, would run away from *kheyder* (school) to be alone with God. This is the forest of Rabbi Nahman's tales, where one can truly lose and find oneself. This is also the forest of Heschel the student, who covers his head in reverence when going for a walk in the local woods, and who writes in a poem called "I Befriend Forests":

You are a soul incognito,
My beloved tree . . .

As I step lightly into the forest
How tree-like I become!
"Grandfather! Grandfather!" I call to the spruce
Your offspring has come to you.

In the Yiddish, "My beloved tree" is *Sertse mayns, O boim*. The choice of the Slavic word *sertse* for "beloved" is unusual; it contains an echo of Levi Yizhak, who was known to use that term in a parable about a lovable drunk who calls everyone *sertse*. Here that love is extended into the natural world.

The sense of wonder, which Heschel so well understands to be basic to all religious consciousness, may be traced right back to Abraham, in a famous passage from the ancient Midrash of Genesis that Heschel quotes several times:

> Abraham may be compared to a man travelling from place to place who came upon a *birah doleqet* [usually translated as "a burning palace," but Heschel insisted that it could also be rendered "a palace full of light"]. Could it be, he said, that there is no one to care for the palace? The owner looked out at him and said: I am the master of the palace. Similarly, since Abraham our Father wondered: Could it be that there is no one to care for the world? The blessed Holy one looked out at him and said: I am master of the world. (Bereshit Rabbah 39:1)

Here is R. Mordecai Joseph of Izbica (d. 1853/54), originally a disciple of the Kotsker rebbe, on that same passage:

> [The prayerbook] says: "He does wonders . . . renewing each day the work of Creation." But what renewal is there if Creation is renewed each day? Doesn't the renewal itself become habitual? What then is left of it?

> The fact is, however, that God makes the habitual into something new, bringing wonder into the hearts of those who hope in Him, so that of each thing they say: "Who created these?"

> Thus it was with Abraham our Father, of blessed memory. The world had gone on for some time before he came along, with no one asking or wondering about its conduct. *In Abraham's heart there was very great*

wonder. "Might you say the palace has no owner? Who is the palace's owner? When God saw that his questions were not those of the natural scientist, but that he truly wanted to know "Who created these?" *in order to serve Him,* and had rejected all worldly pleasures for this sake, the blessed Lord had to reveal Himself and show him that He was indeed Master of the palace.[10]

Both in evoking wonder as a key to the growth of religious consciousness and in distinguishing scientific approaches to nature from that of the devotee, Heschel is faithful to these roots in Polish Hasidism. Though Izbica Hasidism broke off from that of Kotsk, this passage is a faithful reflection of the Kotsk/Ger tradition in which Heschel was first schooled.

Heschel the mature thinker, viewing the American cultural landscape, was profoundly disturbed by the secularization of consciousness among modern Jews (and moderns in general). Heschel wanted to re-create for moderns a Jewish life centered on God. For Heschel, the real and ultimate religious question was the only one that mattered. How do we become aware of God's presence in our lives, of God's passionate and compassionate concern for us? How do we awaken ourselves to respond to the divine call? What will we *do* about it? The cultivation of *da'at,* of a true religious mindfulness that goes deeper than intellectual understanding, is the central subject of many an early Hasidic work and may be seen to be the goal of Heschel's writings as well. He wanted Jews to experience God more fully and to be less shy in talking both *to* God and *about* God. To lead them to this, he had to write about theology in an evocative and passionate way, demonstrating his faith as he expounded on it. For all of this, one may say at least metaphorically that Heschel had the writings of the Hasidic masters open before him. The "God intoxication" that makes Heschel so distinctive among twentieth-century religious thinkers came directly from Hasidism, both its teachings and its nostalgically re-created example.

A second aspect of Heschel's Hasidism is his understanding that God, God's existence, and divine providence are not to be proven. Although he sees himself as a philosopher (a point long debated among his students and critics), logical argumentation was hardly his forte. Heschel saw himself as engaged in redeeming the word "philosophy" itself from the hands of those who had rendered it dispassionate and "objective," those so caught up in the analysis of argument and critical "distance" that they were forced into indifference to the horrors of our age. The person of faith does not argue but *witnesses*. The God of Hasidism, despite all the pantheistic formulations, is also the God of Abraham, not that of Aristotle. For this God, postulates mean nothing. The God of Abraham is the God of living faith, not a God whose existence has to be assumed for philosophic reason.

Here Heschel stands counter to the neo-Kantians of his age. He does not seek a God whose existence will be presumed or postulated in order to provide a basis for moral absolutes. Heschel believes that the real existence of God does in fact demand moral absolutes, to be sure. But the reality of faith comes first, and it is one to which the person of faith can and must always testify, but which he or she cannot prove. Heschel's work and life collectively constitute that testimony, of which he said in an early poem:

> How miniscule my offering,
> My gift, my way of honoring
> Your presence. What can I do
> But go about the world and swear
> Not just believe—but testify and swear.

The Jew as witness who testifies to God's greatness is key to the Hasidic legacy of Ger. The festivals are frequently described by the *Sefat Emet*, the key writing of that tradition, as times of special witnessing, connecting the term *mo'ed* (festival) with *'ed*, meaning "witness."[11] Its author's son, Rabbi Abraham Mordecai of Ger (who was rebbe while Heschel studied in the movement's schools), noted that the concluding two paragraphs of the daily liturgy, the *'alenu*, each of which begins with the letter *'ayin* and ends with the letter *dalet*, form the work *'ed*, serving as the two required witnesses testifying to the sincerity of our prayers. Both Sinai itself and the daily recitation of the *shema'* are taken in the Ger tradition as moments of universal witness.

> God has chosen the Children of Israel as His own portion. One might think that this would make for a greater distance between God and the other nations. But actually just the opposite is true. This was God's deeper plan: to bring all nations near to Him by means of Israel . . . for they are God's emissaries, to bring all creatures near to Him.

Abraham Joshua Heschel | 333

This is the meaning of: "The Lord spoke all these words, saying: 'I am the Lord your God'" (Ex.20:1-2). . . . The intent is that Israel speak these words, drawing them into rung after rung, until all creatures are brought close to God. The life-force of all is in the Torah, and all are to be redeemed by the power of Torah. This is the meaning of "saying" in that verse: every one of Israel has to bear witness to the Creator each day. Twice a day we say "Hear, O Israel." These words shine forth to all the world, to all who are created. . . . This becomes the oral Torah, of which we say: "Eternal life has He emplanted within us." The words of Torah were absorbed into their soul . . . their very selves became Torah.[12]

Here is Hasidism, a highly particularist and exclusivist reading of Judaism, veering as close as it ever does to the universalist edge. The Oral Torah is the Torah that we speak, proclaiming God's truth before the world each day. Heschel, an avid reader of the *Sefat Emet*, would have rejoiced at finding such a passage. That is the level of testimony of which each Jew is capable, daily bearing witness to the world, not just believing but testifying and swearing. Or, in the words of Rabbi Nahman of Bratslav: "I *am* a 'know what to answer the heretic!'"[13] R. Nahman means to say that his life itself, not only his teachings, serves to refute the heretics' claims. Heschel would agree that life itself is testimony. So would Kierkegaard, whom Heschel regarded highly enough to compare to the Kotzker.

The third point is that Heschel knows the world is in need of great charismatic religious figures. Such people can have tremendous power and effect upon those around them. Heschel grew up nourished by tales of such people, "with my mother's milk," as he used to say. In the classic Hasidic tradition, of course, the transformative power of the holy man's words affected not only people but also God. "The blessed Holy One issues a decree but the *zaddik* can cancel it" (B. *Mo'ed Qatan* 16b) is a widely quoted Talmudic dictum that underlies the popular Hasidic belief in the efficacy of wonder-working rabbis' prayers. It seems rather clear that Heschel was not one to take this belief too literally. Without some rebellion, at least on this level, he never could have left Warsaw. Well trained to the Kotsker's critical view of Hasidism, he saw such claims as being of very varied merit. Later, of course, he was also enough of an insider to the years of post-Holocaust trauma, when such claims seemed so utterly hollow, that he could not trumpet them. But this does not mean that he abandoned the Hasidic faith in charismatic leadership and its role in human religious community. Much of his intellectual life, after all, was devoted to the prophets, their experience of God, and their message. It is hard to imagine that images of the Hasidic masters, especially of the Kotsker, did not cross his mind as he read and considered the prophets.

I would like to suggest that the prophets served a similar role for Heschel to that served by the Hasidic masters for Martin Buber. Each of these men had to look elsewhere—Buber to Hasidic Eastern Europe, Heschel to ancient Israel—for examples of the holy and charismatic figures that they strove to become and knew were so much needed in our day. The Hasidic masters were too close for Heschel to use as his primary example; he knew too much of their failings to put them on the sort of pedestal that the more distant Buber could. Heschel could have been a Hasidic rebbe, after all, but had chosen not to become one. But the figure of the prophet, the topic of Heschel's doctoral dissertation in Berlin in 1936 and a major book (*The Prophets*) in 1962, emphasizing the experience of pathos and identification with God as the core of the prophetic phenomenon, surely bears echoes of such religious figures as Heschel knew them in the Hasidic setting. The Hasidic yearning for *true* charisma is alive and well in Heschel.

As for the claim that the true Hasidic master could negate the divine decree, Heschel was able to reread it in the spirit of R. Levi Yizhak, who insisted that the decree that the *zaddik* can nullify (or better here: "transform") is nothing other than Torah itself! Nullification of destructive heavenly decrees is not the object of the *zaddik*'s powers; rather, it is the transformative renewal of God's eternal message:

A basic principle in God's service: we . . . believe in two Torahs: written and oral, both given by a single Shepherd. . . . The written Torah was given us by Moses, God's faithful servant, in writing etched on the tablets, black fire on white fire. The oral Torah given to Moses is its interpretation, including "everything a faithful student is ever to discover." This means that the oral Torah given to us essentially follows the interpretation of the *zaddikim* of the generation. *As they interpret the Torah, so it is.* This great power has been given us by the Creator out of love for Israel, His chosen people. All the worlds follow their will in Torah. Thus did the sages say: "The Holy One issues a decree, but the *zaddik* may nullify it."[14]

It does not seem far-fetched to say that this is what Heschel sought to do for his own era: to be the charismatic voice that had survived and come to the new world, rearticulating the truth of Torah in a new language for a new generation. By the time of *Man Is Not Alone*, Heschel had accepted the obligation not to flee from this attractive, yet terribly frightening and overpowering, role. The legacy he had left behind in Warsaw had indeed caught up with him. Thoughtful readers of Heschel's essay "Did Maimonides Believe That He Had Attained Prophecy?"[15] have been tempted to pose the question rather of the essay's author. Did Heschel consider himself a prophetic figure? There were certainly ways in which he cultivated that image, especially during the 1960s, the heyday of his activism on the historical stage. The insight of Elie Schweid that the *study* of prophecy becomes a central preoccupation in modern Jewish thinkers—Ahad Ha'Am, Buber, Kaufmann—who would wish to reclaim the prophetic mantle but dare not do so, certainly applies to Heschel, perhaps even more than to others.[16]

A fourth area of obvious Hasidic influence is Heschel's great belief in the Hasidic virtues of *hesed* and *simhah* as key to the spiritual life. When we heard Heschel read the famous passages in the *Toldot Ya'akov Yosef* or the *Kedushat Levi* about the proper *mokhiah* (preacher or chastiser), who brings people back to God *be-derekh ha-hesed* ("by means of kindness") rather than by harsh threats, we understood that Heschel saw his own role in this way. He never berated Jews for not being observant, but tried to show them the light and beauty that he found in the religious life. He saw his job as helping people to open their eyes in a deeper way, and he knew that this could only be done by positive example, not by anger or judgment. In this sense I think it fair to say that he did indeed take on the role of rebbe, however reluctantly, for liberal Jews. There is something very much Hasidic, in the original sense of Hasidism (before it became a weapon against modernity and sometimes revealed an angry face), present in this approach. Hasidism understands anger, even righteous anger, as a negative characteristic, emerging from too strong a pull to the left side or the presence of too much black bile in the system. It has to be countered by the activation of *hesed*, divine love or compassion, for which Hasidism is named, after all. To be a *hasid* is to be an *ish ha-hesed*, something Heschel tried to exemplify all his life. This is found in his writings on education and of course formed the basis for his commitment to reasserting the voice of religion in powerful nonviolent movements for social change. In Martin Luther King he saw *gevurah shebe-ḥesed*, if I may say it in Hasidic language—the tremendous power that lay hidden in acts of love.

On the side of negative evidence, it is noteworthy how remarkably little interest we find in sin in Heschel's writings.[17] While Heschel speaks very often of *mitzvot*, and religious action and obligation are key to his system, he very seldom mentions sin. When he does, it is clear that he is not speaking of an ontological category. "To the prophets, sin is not an ultimate, irreducible, or independent condition, but rather a disturbance in the relationship between God and man; it is an adverb, not a noun."[18] Despite a certain attraction to the thought of Christian neo-orthodoxy (for the seriousness with which it treated both God and Scripture), Heschel never accepted the key notion of Karl Barth and his followers that man is filled with or "conceived in" sin and therefore in need of salvation. Here he saw a great gulf between Judaism and Christianity. In fact, because there is little sense of sin, there is little need for eschatology in Heschel's system. The redemption of which we are in need comes about through our response to God's call and our actions. "Creation/Revelation/Religious Action" may be seen as the triad around which *God in Search of Man* is written. If there is a salvific teaching here, it is more we who are "saviors of God" than the other way around.[19] The great sense of sacred partnership is key to Heschel's reading of Judaism, and it is the potential glory of the human being and the high source of the human soul that he seeks to help us discover. Concentration on sin would have been a distraction from this. But that choice comes from his Hasidic background, where mitzvah (sometimes playfully derived from the word *tsavta* in Aramaic, meaning "that which brings God and the person together") is central, but excessive worry about one's sins (*de'agat 'avonot*) is to be avoided. Serving God in joy and wholeness is the goal, and over concern with sin keeps one from it. In this sense, Heschel is very much a *ḥasid* and not a *mussarnik* in his understanding of the human being. Compare the place of sin in Heschel and Rabbi Joseph B. Soloveitchik, for example, and you will see the difference between a *ḥasid* and a *mitnagged*'s readings of Judaism.

Now I come to the fifth and final point, which really forms the heart of my reading of Heschel's *oeuvre* altogether. The most powerful and distinctive motif in Heschel's theology is that encapsulated by the phrase *God in Search of Man*. Heschel knew a God who is concerned with and affected by human actions. God creates each human in the divine image so that we may fulfill the role of partnership with God and so that we may discover God's presence within the world and within our own souls and respond to it, with heart but primarily by deed. God awaits this response.

I came to understand the literary source of this conviction through an assignment that Heschel gave me in the years I was privileged to study with him. Since I was interested in Kabbalah, he had me read a book called 'Avodat ha-Qodesh ("The Divine Service"), a kind of *Summa Kabbalistica* by Rabbi Meir Ibn Gabbai, an author born in Spain in 1481, who survived the expulsion and lived his adult life somewhere in the Ottoman Empire. The key theme in that book, repeated and defended in chapter after chapter, is *ha-'avodah tzorekh gavoha*, "worship fulfills a divine need." The notion is not new in Ibn Gabbai, who is seldom an original thinker. It can be clearly traced back to Nahmanides, the great thirteenth-century rabbi who lent credibility to Kabbalah by including its secrets within his widely read Torah commentary.[20] Both Nahmanides and Gabbai use this notion in fierce anti-Maimonidean polemics, opposing the philosophical coolness of the philosopher's God who remains unaffected by human actions on the lowly material plane.

Heschel was fascinated by this debate between philosopher and Kabbalist, and he sought to trace it back a step farther, rooting it in the struggle between the two great schools of early rabbinic thought that he outlined in his *Torah min ha-Shamayim*, now so ably translated and presented to the English reader by Gordon Tucker.[21] RaMBaM versus RaMBaN becomes Rabbi Ishmael versus Rabbi Akiva, with the latter as proto-mystic, religious romantic, lover of the supernatural, and one who insisted that God is indeed strengthened or (God forbid!) weakened by the loyalty and deeds of Israel. While Heschel clearly identified with aspects of both Akiva and Ishamel as he portrayed them, on this matter of the *mitzvot* as religious actions and their ability to affect God, he was clearly an Akivan.

Whence did this notion of God's need for the *mitzvot*, rarified into *God in Search of Man*, come to Heschel? Heschel learned about the secret and mysterious power of the *mitzvot* in the Hasidic world. The special love and devotion that Hasidic rebbes lavished upon the *mitzvot* is legendary; Heschel was surrounded by this in his childhood. Although Hasidism by its second generation had abandoned the complex infrastructure of Lurianic *kavvanot* or mystical intentions for prayer and most of daily life, certain particular *mitzvot* were still treated as mysterious sacraments, with only partially understood *kavvanot* retained for them, but with the promise that the *zaddik*'s performance of them could take the heavens by storm and affect the divine will, even to the point of changing ill decrees in heaven, a concern very central to the original intent of the Ba'al Shem Tov.[22]

Heschel was not, as we have said, a naïve or literal believer in the power of the *zaddik* to repeal the decree of heaven. But he was also unwilling to abandon this dramatic sense of the cosmic importance of human deeds, which added so much to the value of humanity and the sense of divine/human partnership. He thus chose to undertake a very interesting shift in the way he read this part of the Hasidic/Kabbalistic legacy. When Hasidic rebbes spoke of *sodot ha-mitzvot*, the commandments as sublime secrets, *razin 'ila'in*, they usually were referring to such mystery-laden religious acts as *teqi'at shofar*, the blowing of the ram's horn on the New Year, *na'anu'ey lulav*, the waving of the palm and other branches on Sukkot, or *tevillah ba-mikveh*, immersion in the ritual bath. Rebbes would prepare intensely for these sacred moments, often turning back to the old *kavvanot*. Surely these all needed to be done *le-shem shamayim*, "for the sake of heaven." On the simplest level, that was defined in Kabbalistic language as *le-shem yihud qudsha brikh hu u-shekhinteyh*, "in order to unify the blessed Holy One and His *shekhinah*."[23] Heschel was surely impressed by the power of such religious performance and the serious devotion it entailed. But now he made a brilliant and transformative move: Heschel agreed with his Hasidic tradition that God longs for us to do the *mitzvot* and that heaven itself is moved by our deeds. But he applied this first and foremost to the *mitzvot beyn adam le-havero*, to the commandments that regard the way we treat our fellow humans. God *needs* you to do the *mitzvot* indeed—to feed the hungry, to care for the poor, to sustain widows and orphans. These were the essence of *mitzvot* for Heschel. It is primarily through these that you become God's partner in the world. As a traditionalist, of course, Heschel never denied the importance of ritual observance. His works were often used as a buttress to defend it. But if you look at the key thrust of the latter part of *God in Search of Man*, combined with *The Prophets* and several of his essays, it is clear that what God seeks of us in the first place are those *mitzvot* that demonstrate human decency, compassion for the oppressed and needy, and a response to the prophetic call for justice restored to God's world.[24]

Heschel takes the Kabbalistic/Hasidic view of Judaism and its commandments most seriously. He understands that it gives an infinite depth of meaning to the religious act that no claim of the spontaneous celebration of God's presence (Buber) and no debate about autonomy or heteronomy (Hermann Cohen) could ever provide. Here one is doing something for God, offering a gift of mysterious and unfathomable significance. But Heschel's creativity lies in the great subtlety with which he treats this theme of "the deed," which serves as the climax of his philosophy. Heschel is no Kabbalist; he does not want to say in any coarse or simplistic way that the *mitzvot* fulfill a divine need. But he does want to say that human actions done in holiness, deeds that seek to fulfill God's will in this world, are an infinite source of blessing to God and to the world. Here are his words on the subject, from the concluding page of *Man Is Not Alone*:

> Piety, finally, is allegiance to the will of God. Whether that will is understood or not, it is accepted as good and holy, and is obeyed in faith. . . . All the pious man's thoughts and plans revolve around this concern, and nothing can distract him or turn him from the way. . . . His preoccupation with the will of God is not limited to a section of his activities, but his great desire is to place his whole life at the disposal of God. In this he finds the real meaning of life. . . . In this way, he feels that whatever he does, he is ascending step by step a ladder leading to the ultimate. In aiding a creature, he is helping the Creator. In succoring the poor, he fulfills a concern of God. In admiring the good, he reveres the spirit of God. In loving the pure, he is drawn to Him. In promoting the right, he is directing things toward His will, in which all aims must terminate. . . . The glory of a man's devotion to the good becomes a treasure of God on earth.[25]

Torah and commandments, as Judaism classically knows them, are part of this, to be sure. But the boundaries of good deeds are expanded beyond all limitation. Heschel has subtly turned around the order of priorities. Yes, the *mitzvot* are indeed divine need, he says, but it is in the first case these commandments—the life of goodness and justice—that God needs of us. In doing this, of course, Heschel is restoring the link between the Hasidic masters he knew and the prophets of ancient Israel. The God who needs us to live holy lives, to be His witness in the world, by loving goodness and doing justice, is a God who is rooted in Isaiah and Jeremiah as well as in the Ba'al Shem Tov and Levi Yizhak. The message is a biblical one, one that the world can again learn from us, one that needs to be shared and made real by marching in Selma, by speaking out against unjust war.

Heschel sought to rescue the notion of *mitzvot tzorekh gavoha* from the obscurantism of the mystics and to bring it back to what he believed was its first source—the teachings of the prophets of Israel. The "missing link" in Heschel's *oeuvre*—perhaps left unwritten due to his sudden death—is the step that traces *tzorekh gavoha*—already extending from Hasidism to RamBaN to Rabbi Akiva—back to Isaiah, Amos, and Micah. In other words, I am claiming Heschel's version of prophetic Judaism, including the pathos with which the prophet identifies with the will of God, as an expression of his neo-Hasidism. He comes from that place in the Hasidic tradition that loves the commandments, seeing them as God's great gift to us as a means to be close to Him, even as a meeting place between the divine and human spirit. Not mere requirements of the law code or ways to fence about our evil urge, the *mitzvot* are the means by which we reach toward transcendence. Ever the man of expansive vision, Heschel understands this to mean that God in His love for all of us humans calls upon us to do transforming deeds, to act in ways that will at once make our lives holy and the world more whole. The hope of humanity is that we can, and will, still respond to that voice, one that has never ceased calling out to us.

NOTES

1. A great deal of detailed information on Heschel's European period can be found in Edward K. Kaplan and Samuel H. Dresner, *Abraham Joshua Heschel: Prophetic Witness* (New Haven: Yale University Press, 1998). See genealogies on x–xi.

2. Novominsk is a later offshoot of the Koidenov/Lechowicz dynasties, a Lithuanian-Bellorussian form of Hasidism. The history of the dynasty is treated in Wolf Rabinowitsch's *Lithuanian Hasidism* (New York: Schocken, 1971) and in a small (uncritical) volume, *Mi-Gedoley ha- torah veha-Ḥasidut,* vol. 20, by A. Y. Bromberg (Jerusalem: Ha-Makhon le- Ḥasidut, 1962/63). The rebbes of Kopyczienic were a branch of the direct descendants of R. Abraham Joshua Heschel of Opatow (Apt, 1754/55–1825), Heschel's namesake and founder of the line.

3. Heschel's ancestor, the Rabbi of Apt, settled in Miedzybozh, the home of the Ba'al Shem Tov, in his later years. This gave Heschel a direct familial association with what may be called the birthplace of Hasidism.

4. It was the Kotzker influence on Heschel that caused him to question the validity of inherited Hasidic authority, possibly as early as his own adolescence, when he turned aside from the opportunity to succeed his father as rebbe. See discussion of the rebbe's role, including frank discussions of pretense ("imitation") and its dangers in Heschel's *Kotzk: In Gerangel far Emesdikeyt* (Tel Aviv, 1973), 423ff., 438ff.

5. I am grateful to a conversation with Nicham Ross for this insight. Schneersohn was a direct influence on Heschel, as documented by Kaplan and Dresner (see their index). So too was Hillel Zeitlin (1871–1942), the first important neo-Hasidic writer in Hebrew. Zeitlin was shunned by most of Hasidic Warsaw, including Ger, but was close to the Novominsker, at whose table young Heschel surely met him. See my discussion in "Three Warsaw Mystics," *Kolot Rabbim: The Rivka Schatz-Uffenheimer Memorial Volume* (Jerusalem: Magnes, 1998), English section, 1–58.

6. These seminars included the writings of Kabbalist Meir Ibn Gabbai (b. 1481), the *Shney Luḥot ha-Brit* of Isaiah Horowitz (1565–1630), the section *'amud ha-tefillah in Sefer Ba'al Shem Tov,* and *Qedushat Levi* by Levi Yizhak of Berdichev. On Heschel's use of sources, see the important dissertation by Michael Marmur, *Heschel's Rhetoric of Citation: The Use of Sources in God in Search of Man* (Jerusalem: Hebrew University, 2005).

7. These studies have been collected and translated under the title *The Circle of the Ba'al Shem Tov*, ed. Samuel Dresner (Chicago: University of Chicago Press, 1985).

8. Heschel, *The Ineffable Name of God—Man*, trans. Morton M. Leifman (New York: Continuum, 2004). See also the earlier unauthorized and "freely rendered" version by Zalman M. Schachter (privately printed, 1973). The translations below are my own.

9. The full text is found in my translation of Menahem Nahum of Chernobyl, *Upright Practices and The Light of the Eyes* (Ramsey NJ: Paulist, 1982).

10. *Mey ha-Shiloah, tazri'a* (Jerusalem, 1995), 1:109.

11. For further information on Ger, see Arthur Green, *The Language of Truth: Teachings from the Sefat Emet* (Philadelphia: Jewish Publication Society, 1998).

12. *Sefat Emet, Yitro*, 1880. Translation and comment in *The Language of Truth*, 106ff.

13. *Ḥayyey MoHaRaN* 2:7:13. Discussed in Arthur Green, *Tormented Master: A Life of Rabbi Nahman of Bratslav* (Tuscaloosa: University of Alabama, 1979), 317.

14. *Qedushat Levi, Yitro*. Emphasis mine. Translated and discussed in my essay "Teachings of the Hasidic Masters," in *Back to the Sources,* ed. Barry W. Holtz (New York: Schocken, 1984), 376ff.

15. Louis Ginzberg Jubilee Volume, 1945. English translation in A. J. Heschel, *Prophetic Inspiration after the Prophets*, ed. Morris Faierstein (Hoboken: Ktav, 1996).

16. Eliezer Schweid, "Prophetic Mysticism in Twentieth-Century Jewish Thought," *Modern Judaism* 14, no. 2 (1994): 139–74.

17. Some of this analysis emerged in a conversation with Shai Held, whose recent book on Heschel treats it more fully.

18. Abraham Joshua Heschel, *The Prophets* (New York: Harper Perennial, 2001), 229.

19. *The Saviors of God* is a remarkable religious work by Nikos Kazantzakis. Heschel referred in teaching as well as in *Torah min ha-Shamayim* to the remarkable references to God being exiled and redeemed in the early Sukkot poem *Ke-Hosh'ata Elim*.

20. See RaMBaN to Exodus 29:46. The Chavel edition (Jerusalem, 1959–60) ad loc. quotes an array of Kabbalistic supercommentators on Nahmanides, including Ibn Gabbai, but without much understanding. In general, the Kabbalistic passages in Nahmanides are frequently misinterpreted in this edition, with the force of their symbolic language totally ignored. The same distortions carry over in the available English translation as well, which can simply not be trusted on any issues of Kabbalistic content. On Nahmanides as a Kabbalist, see H. Pedaya, *Ha-RaMBaN: Hit'alut; Zeman Mahazor ve-Text Qadosh* (Tel Aviv: 'Am 'Oved, 2003).

21. Abraham Joshua Heschel, *Heavenly Torah as Refracted through the Generations*, ed. and trans. Gordon Tucker and Leonard Levin (New York: Bloomsbury Academic, 2006).

22. This has been best demonstrated by Immanuel Etkes in his important study, *The BeSHT: Magician, Mystic, and Healer* (Hanover: New England University Press, 2005).

23. In classic Kabbalistic terms, this refers to the restoring of unity between divine male and female, which effected the *hieros gamos* that unites the upper worlds. But Hasidism emphasizes the indwelling quality of *shekhinah* to such an extent that it is surely fair to say, at least for some Hasidic authors, that the *le-shem yihud* formula meant restoration of an unbounded union between this earthly world and the divine. There is also a very significant debate within the Hasidic sources as to whether one is to seek any earthly blessing as a result of such devotion. The more extreme pietistic strain opposes any seeking of material reward for 'avodat ha-shem. Surely the highest form of worship is for God's sake; do it "like the servant who seeks not to receive reward," as an early Hasidic source intentionally misreads the well-known passage in *Pirkey Avot* [*Degel Mahaneh Ephraim, Haftarat Ki Tetze* (Jerusalem, 1963, 253)]. Quoted in A. Green and B. W. Holtz, *Your Word Is Fire* (Ramsey NJ: Paulist, 1977). True worship requires utter selflessness, as though you did not exist in this world at all. But all those lofty pronouncements coexist with the *zaddik* as we know him in social context, a side of Hasidism that also has its intellectual defense. The *zaddik* cares so much for the world, loves his people so dearly, that he wants to bring them

blessings. This is, after all, why Hasidism forced the ancient Jewish *zaddik* figure out of hiding. The *lamed vav*/thirty-six hidden righteous could have sustained the cosmos by their prayers without being known to anyone; perhaps they could have done so better if left undisturbed. By proclaiming the virtues of the public holy man over the hidden one, Hasidism precisely wanted him to serve as a link between the upper and lower realms, to be the conduit of divine bounty in human beings living in the world. This point is made most forcefully by R. Levi Yizhak in a homily in which he contrasts the piety of Melchizedek, who serves God for the pure sake of "Nothing," with Abraham, who serves in order to bring blessing into this world (*Qedushat Levi lekh lekha*). I believe the true subject of this homily is an inner Hasidic debate on this subject, and it is likely that Melchizedek is serving as a stand-in for Dov Baer of Miezedyrzec, Levi Yizhak's *rebbe*, or his friend and in-law R. Shneur Zalman of Liadi, who was famous for refusing to pray for this-worldly matters.

24. Heschel avoided giving expression to the rather obvious reverse side of this claim, the notion that God needs you to do these *mitzvot* because He has no other way of accomplishing them. That would have been too thoroughgoing a religious humanism for Heschel and would have deeply offended his traditionalist ethos. God's calling upon us to do, to give, to open our hands to the needy is itself a call of love. In a recent essay I treat the relationship between this love and divine need.

25. Abraham Joshua Heschel, *Man Is Not Alone* (New York: Farrar, Straus and Giroux, 1978), 294.

17

Personal Theology

An Address to Rabbis

I would like to address you, both hearers and readers, from an inner place that is not the locus of most rabbinical convention speeches or journal articles. My opening פסוק for this address is Psalm 42:8: תהום אל תהום קורא לקול צנוריך כל משבריך וגליך עלי עברו, which I will translate for our purpose as "Depth calls out to depth, a voice seeking your channels, as all the mighty waves and breakers pass over us." By this I mean to say that I want to speak דברים היוצאים מן הלב, trusting that they will find a channel, a way into your hearts as well. Let all the crashing waves of our seas' surface pass right over us, and enter with me into תהום, our shared deep "undersea" places.

The topic I was asked to discuss here is "Personal Theology."[1] Because I was originally not given a full description of what was meant by this pregnant phrase, I have been allowing it to roll around in my mind for these past several months, and now I will want to talk about it in several ways, which I hope will all come together.

First is the need for a rabbi to have his/her own theological stance. In the course of your rabbinic education—an ongoing process throughout your lives—you encounter many compelling teachers and visions of reality. What do you take from them? What do you reject? What does your own experience as person, as Jew, or as rabbi cause you to question or perhaps refine in a personal way? What is the window into Judaism that you and you alone can offer to a congregant, a seeker, a potential convert? This sorting out of readings, teachings, and positions eventually will coalesce into what may be called a rabbi's personal theology.

I would say that this need for a personal theology, one that I fully endorse, is secondary to a more basic need for a personal religious life. The point may seem obvious, but it is truly not so. Let me spend a bit of time explaining what I mean by the rabbi's need to have a religious life.

As you all know, we liberal rabbis minister to a highly secularized Jewish community. With the notable exception of some Jews-by-choice, personal piety is not a common phenomenon among those who join our congregations. As you also know, it is especially around the life cycle and the quest for legacy—something to pass on to the next generation—that Jews find themselves turning to rabbis and synagogue communities. The birth of a child, education in the tradition, celebration of life's milestones, tragic losses of life or misfortune, the aging and illness of parents, death and mourning—all of these bring Jews back from their secular pursuits to seek out wisdom and consolation from their tradition and the personal support and affection of rabbis and other clergy.

Rabbis are expected to meet Jews in such moments with empathy, drawing on a deep well of caring, having an ability to give and to be present to people with whom they otherwise may have little relationship. At such times the traditional phrases of piety do not suffice, nor does the attempt at purely intellectual teaching. The rabbi has to be seen, above all, as genuine, truly caring, and not merely professional. Indeed "professionalism" at such times can be seen as "slick" or superficial.

The ability to be present as a full human being in such moments can only come out of the rabbi's own inner religious or spiritual life. To live a life of giving to others, you need to be nourished by God's presence in your own life. Otherwise, your well will quickly run dry. To *hold* people, in their pain as well as in their joy, to pastor in an almost literal sense, you as a rabbi have to be able to draw on a great, indeed endless, reservoir of strength that is really not your own at all but God's, in which you are rooted by your own faith. For a rabbi, cultivating and probing the depths of spiritual life is nothing less than a survival skill.

So teaching students to become rabbis, helping each one grow into his or her own rabbinate, as we like to say it, includes instructing them on how to develop their own inner lives. This includes prayer, both communal and personal. Spiritual direction and counseling also have a place. Continuing all of these throughout your rabbinate should help keep you open to that reservoir of strength and inspiration. But in our tradition the inner life is also very much nurtured by study of the sources, learned and discussed in openhearted ways, so that each rabbi's spiritual life is rooted directly in the text and language of the ages. The rabbinate is the western world's original tradition of lifelong learning. Staying close to Torah as a great font of living waters should be an ongoing source of nurture to our own inner gardens, hence to the rich plantings we can pass on to others. A personal theology is not a series of positions on key issues, and hence it cannot be taught in theology courses alone. Rather it is our reflection on our own inner lives, an attempt to understand where we are, each of us, in our own Jewish growth and what we experience within ourselves, including both the presence and absence of God. A theology divorced from the inner life becomes a barren exercise of mind.

This brings us to a second sense of personal theology. Each of our theologies, whether we realize it or not, is in part an articulation of our own journeys through life, amplified through the medium of tradition's voice. Jewish theology in its most native form is narrative theology. Neither the Torah nor the Talmud articulates a *concept* of God. They tell us stories about the One who called to Abraham, about the One who brought us forth from Egypt, about the One we encountered standing before the mountain. "Do you want to know the One who spoke the world into being?" asks the Talmud. "Then study Aggadah: narrative, stories."

We share a common story. We are all Jews. All of us, in each generation, as we recite at the *seder*, came out of Egypt. To someone who unexpectedly seems close to us, feels like a soul sister, we will say, "We must have been standing next to each other at Mount Sinai." (There was, you see, mixed seating, or at least mixed standing, at Sinai.) Not that this is *history*, of course, but that is entirely beside the point. It is *ourstory*. The point is best expressed in Buberian language. It may not be "his-story," in the impersonal third person objective sense, but when turned into first person plural it is "ourstory," and that's what matters. Our shared mythology. "That's our story, and we're stickin' with it!"

But each of us then takes that collective story and makes it our own, individually and uniquely. Yes, you too have come out of Egypt, or need still to come out of Egypt, or most likely both. What is the particular מיצר, narrow strait, that comprises your מצרים? With whom can you talk about that? Might you dream of a religious community where you could be challenged to ask—and free to answer—such a personal question? Part of the classic rabbinic definition of a חבר in Avot de-Rabbi Nathan's comment on ועשה לך חבר is one שיגלה לפניו כל מצפוני לבו, one "before whom you can reveal all the secrets of your heart." That sort of "spiritual friendship" is what my ideal of חבורה is really all about.

What is my Egypt? How will I come out of it? I am particularly moved by a comment of Rabbi Nahman of Bratslav on the phrase וגם צדה לא עשו להם —" They made no provisions for the way." When you're about to leave Egypt, he says, don't stop to ask, "But how will I make a living out there?" If you do, you'll never get out.

Another passage: God calls you and says לך לך —go forth, for your own sake, following RaSHI, or go unto your true self, in the Hasidic reading. But how does that work in my own life? What is my journey? Where will I find my promised land? What if I don't? How many times will I have to go back and forth to the *negev*, that place of dryness, before and even after I get there?

Or another: I am there with Mother Rivka, the first person of whom we are told ותלך לדרוש את האלהים. What do I mean by seeking out the One? What is it that I am seeking? What do I want of God?

A personal Jewish theology, a personal engagement with these stories, makes a great demand of us. Such a reading of Torah forces us to confront the most powerful questions of our lives. But that confrontation is not only demanding. It is entirely *intimate* as well. These are questions addressed to our most private self, to the place within us that is deeply hidden from most others, protected by defensive walls, often hidden from our own busy selves most of the time. These personal questions, amplified by the echo chamber of religious language, are all about דברים המסורים ללב, דברים בין אדם לעצמו.

This, then, is the second meaning of personal theology. Not just a theology that belongs to you alone but one that is all about your most intimate and secret inner places. Yes, theology is in that sense a personal enterprise. If I share my theology with you, I am sharing something of my deepest self.

If I have spent a *shabbat* at your congregation, you have heard me share my interpretation of לכה דודי. I call it a flirtation song with the נשמה יתרה. I do not believe, you see, that the "extra soul" we have on *shabbat* comes floating down from heaven at 3:42 in the winter season or 7:29 in the middle of summer—at least in our Boston climate! I believe that soul, the most intimate and therefore vulnerable part of ourselves, is there within us all week long. But it is afraid to come out. It fears being trampled by the pace at which we live, shouted down by the loudness of our encounters in the hustle-bustle of ordinary life, of חול. But on ערב שבת we promise it:

"It's all right. You can come out now. I promise, for the next twenty-four hours, to live at a slower pace. No rushing, no fighting, no screaming. No despair over the stock market or the business cycle. I promise not to get depressed by watching politicians on television. It's safe in my *shabbat* world; you can come out now." So we say to *her*, נשמה, *anima* (in a text originally written by and for men):

. . . התנערי, מעפר קומי . . . רב לך שבת בעמק הבכא . . .

התעוררי התעוררי . . . מה תשתוחחי . . . לא תבושי ולא תכלמי

We say to this vulnerable (hence feminine) place within the soul: Come out of hiding. Let me, the conscious self, join with you, the hidden soul-self, in this mystical marriage, as God unites with Israel, as heaven unites with newly created earth. Let us all become whole together. Personal theology: a theology of intimacy.

But there is a third meaning of the phrase "personal theology" that we cannot avoid discussing here, and this may be the true heart of our investigation. I refer to the theology of God as divine person. *The Personhood of God* is the title of my teacher Yochanan Muffs's beautiful little book on the subject.[2] In my case, I need to ask what we still mean by such designations, indeed how we can use them at all, once we accept that all our personified images of God may be seen as projections from the human onto the divine. Does such awareness mean a rejection of all such language and its emotional content? If so, where do we go as religious Jews? Is there still an attachment possible to the God language of our Torah that will make for a sense of continuity? What do we say to the critic who says, as one did upon reading my *Radical Judaism*, that "his God is not the God of Israel."[3] The fact that the same was said of the RaMBaM as well as Mordecai Kaplan is of some comfort, but insufficient as a response.

I want to tie this back to our prior elucidations of "personal theology" and talk about the connection between them. Can one be personal about one's religious life without personifying? Can there be intimacy with a God who remains abstract, even elusive, the God of אהיה אשר אהיה? Or can we give ourselves permission to personify again in a post-critical mode? If religion is all about that which makes us human, how can we invoke the notion of צלם אלהים without falling back into a religious language that does not reflect what we really believe?

If this talk sounds more like a שיעור in selected texts than a lecture, you will understand the way I seek to do Jewish theology. I read the sources from within, weaving them together and seeking to stretch them, to make them open enough to embrace the meaning I find within them, rather than applying them to a structure that comes from without. In this (as in some other matters) I am a devotee of the Zohar rather than the RaMBaM, R. Nahman of Bratslav rather than Moses Mendelssohn or Hermann Cohen, Heschel rather than Kaplan. I fully acknowledge that I am "working" the sources, seeking to pull them in the direction I want them to go. But I have come to understand that in the course of that intense engagement I am giving them the power to "work" me as well. Pulling the tradition in my own direction is an act of engagement, one in which I of necessity make myself vulnerable to being pulled as well. As a *darshan*, you do not work the cold magic of interpretation on inanimate sources to make them say what you want. You rather engage with tradition as a living body, either as Jacob wrestling with the angel or as the troubadour suitor of that maiden high in the tower who, according to the Zohar, reveals her face only to the one who truly loves her. We wrest meaning from the text in a struggle that is also an act of love. I sometimes wonder about Jacob, supposedly the most beautiful human since Adam, and that all-nighter with the angel, twin, or alter ego. Wrestling or making love? Are we sure we know where the border lies? Straddling that border between wrestling and lovemaking defines our relationship with the tradition, maybe even with God.

One of my current favorite *pesukim* of the Torah comes up in a surprising place, the end of פרשת תצוה. Exodus 29:46:

וידעו כי אני ה' אלהיהם אשר הוצאתי אותם
מארץ מצרים לשכני בתוכם אני ה' אלהיהם.

Read in the Hasidic mode: Whatever Egypt you have come out of, you have been brought forth by God. Realize that! You have been liberated from that מיצר, that constraint, narrowing, or squeeze—even if it was the squeeze of unhealthy religion—because God seeks you out as a dwelling place. Know that your freedom has come about to give you the opportunity to fashion your life as a משכן, a home for the שכינה. (Of course ושכנתי בתוכם is read as בתוכם ממש, not just "in their midst" but within each of them.)

Yet the Psalmist says אדני מעון אתה היית לנו בדור ודור. You have been a dwelling place for *us* in each generation. This is one of the verses quoted when the rabbis say הוא מקומו של עולם ואין העולם מקומו. We dwell within God, are surrounded by God, rather than the other way around.

Can both of these be true? Can we fashion and be God's dwelling while we also dwell within God? As rational propositions, it would seem not. The law of contradictions would seem to apply. Either we dwell in God or God dwells in us. But in experiential terms, these two only represent different modes of religious experience: the One who seems to embrace us and surround us from without, becoming our dwelling, and the One that wells up from within, seeking a home within our heart, are the same One.

פתחו לי שערי צדק אבוא בם אודה י-ה

Open the gates for me, that I may come in to praise the Lord. פתח לנו שער בעת נעילת שער Open the gate for us as it is about to close! Like Kafka's Josef K. in *The Trial*, we stand before the gates, needing to call upon God, or upon someone, to let us in.

קול דודי דופק פתחי לי

The sound of my Beloved knocking, "Open up for me!" *We* are the ones with our doors shut; it is we who have to open them to let God in. קמתי אני לפתוח לדודי. I need to rise up myself, of my own accord, אני קמתי, to open for my Beloved.

Can both be true? Can I stand before a closed gate while at the same time having my own door locked to the One who is knocking, seeking to come in? Logical contradiction has no place here; we are seeing the same experience from two angles, both of which are psychologically and spiritually quite real.

Those of you who grew up in traditional synagogues will remember one of my very favorite liturgical texts, אנעים זמירות or שיר הכבוד, something I much miss in modern prayer books. I love it because, after due apologies, it is the most blatantly pagan Jewish text I know. A part of that apologetic introduction, referring to the prophets, reads:

דימו אותך ולא

כפי ישך וישווך לפי מעשיך

המשילוך ברוב חזיונות הנך אחד בכל הדמיונות

(In Israel Zangwill's classic translation:)

> They told of Thee, but not as Thou must be.
> Since from Thy work they tried to body Thee. To countless visions
>   did their pictures run,
> Behold through all the visions Thou art one.

ויחזו בך זקנה ובחרות ושער ראשך בשיבה ושחרות

זקנה ביום דין ובחרות ביום קרב כאיש מלחמות ידיו לו רב

> In Thee old age and youth at once were drawn, The grey of eld, the
>   flowing locks of dawn.
> The ancient judge, the youthful warrior,
> The man of battles, terrible in war.

The poem is based on a series of midrashim claiming Israel saw God twice: at the Reed Sea, God appeared to them as a youth, while at Sinai they saw God as an elder. The context determines the way God is seen. Who wants to be led into battle by a tottering old God? But who wants to receive law and wisdom from a young whippersnapper of a deity? Some versions of this trope fashion it around the Torah's ראו כי אני אני הוא ואין אלהים עמדי (Deut. 32:39). Why is אני repeated? Just because you see multiple visions, do not think that I am more than one. אני הוא בים, אני היא בסיני.[4]

Can the same God be both זקן and בחור? But of course! These are different spiritual moments, each with its own needs, like building a משכן while we dwell within God, like standing before the gate while we ourselves are the closed door.

The midrash is cautious in its language: נראה "appeared." Is the change in God or in them? This would seem to make all the difference. Are we talking about grand-scale supernaturalism, the greatest miracle of revelation, that God can know what each heart and each moment needs, then change appearance accordingly? Or are we simply saying that all our images of God are human projections, reflections of our own need?

תיקו. There is no answer to that question. As in our previous examples, both are true at once. Yes, God creates us in the divine image. Yes, all our images of God are our projected creation. There is a kaleidoscopic hall of mirrors here, but you can look into this kaleidoscope from either end.

Referring to the visions of Isaiah and Ezekiel, our sages said גדול כוחן של נביאים שמדמין צורה ליוצרה. "Great is the power of the prophets, who liken the human form to its Creator."[5] But that's not really what the prophets were doing! In their most intense visionary moments—Isaiah 6 and Ezekiel 1—they were in fact likening the *divine* form to that of man. But that was perhaps too much for the sages to acknowledge. So they said it backward. But the point is that in depicting God in human form, we are uplifting the human rather than diminishing the divine. Yes, the hall of mirrors can be opened from either end.

Can we try it this way? *We are created in the image of God and we are obliged to return the favor.*

Let me turn to yet another favorite midrash, *Bereshit Rabbah* 17:4: Y-H-W-H asks Adam to name the animals. You recall that the creation of humans did not win much favor with the angels, apparently God's unchallenged favorites until then. But God said to them, "Look how smart this new human is! At that, God paraded a series of four-footed creatures across the stage. "What are these?" the divine voice asked. Having no part of the world of flesh and blood, the angels were dumbfounded. Then God asked Adam: "What's this one? What's this?" Adam blithely replied "This is called a dog. This is called a cat." "And what should you be called?" God asks. Adam replies, "I should be called Adam, earthling, because I was taken from Adamah." "And what should I be called?" God asks.

Now this is the great moment. The human is being asked to name the divine, to give Y-H-W-H, breathy abstraction itself, an identity, a way of being known, becoming manifest in the human realm. Adam could have said *anything*. But without missing a beat, he says לך ראוי ליקרא אדוני כי אדון אתה על כל מעשיך. "You should be called Lord, for You are lord over all your works." It is we, in other words, who have set up the master/servant relationship with the divine, clearly a projection from human society. Why? Because that was what we needed: someone before whom to bow, to whose authority to submit. It was not that God needed—or needs—to be מלך; it was rather we who needed to be עבדים.

Do you see what I'm doing here? I'm suggesting a theology that sees through the personal, understands that it is all metaphor, and yet remains affectionately bound to it. Demythologize and remythologize. Both the RaMBaM and the Zohar understood that the reality of Y-H-W-H lies beyond all description in human terms. Maimonides chose the apophatic path: saying less about God is saying more. Purify your theological language, attempt to come as close as you can to the abstract truth. Get rid of myth. The Zohar, recognizing the same truth and inadequacy of language, takes the opposite strategy. Drown them in metaphor! Make *everything* a metaphor. Of course God is an elder on the throne—Daniel saw Him that way! But so too is God mother, warrior, sun and moon, fountain and river, myrtle branch and *etrog*, bridegroom and bride. With so much metaphor, and with the metaphors switching and flowing together at every moment, you couldn't possibly freeze a single one of them and mistake it for *the* truth. Dress the mystery of Y-H-W-H up in an endless variety of mythic garments of glory.

I recognize that this series of human metaphors is the rabbis' way—*our* way—of giving texture to the intimacy of religious experience. Personal theology requires that. Religious experience, taking us to our most intimate and vulnerable places, demands a language that can speak to our human, all-too-human self. Nothing less than the language of person will do. *We give to God the greatest gift we know how to give: that of our humanity.*

I proceed with lessons from two Abraham Joshua Heschels, both having very much to do with this sense of personal theology. The first is from the Apter Rav, Professor Heschel's ancestor, the founder of the line. On Deuteronomy's (10:12) מה ה' אלהיך שואל מעמך—What does Y-H-W-H your God ask of you? He noted that the word מה is numerically 45. So too is the word אדם. The simpler *hasidim*, when they heard this, must have understood him to be saying: God wants you to be a *mensch*. But to his closer disciples—one of them quotes this in his name, he said that he was referring to the Adam of Ezekiel's vision. ודמות כמראה אדם עליו מלמעלה An image like that of man was upon the chariot. What does God want of you? Adam! That is the Adam God wants of you—that you place the image of man atop the chariot.[6] Yes, projection is a *mitsvah*.

His great-great-grandson, surely not by coincidence, published a book of poems entitled מענש–דער שם המפורש, *Man: The Divine Name*. The greatest lesson I learned from Heschel, with whom I had the privilege of studying quite closely, came as תורה שבעל פה. "Why," I heard him ask, "is the Torah seemingly so obsessed with the problem of graven images?" If (with the Maimonidians) you believe it is because God has no image, then all these images are merely errors. But why, then, is idolatry such a great sin? The point, he said, is that God indeed *does* have an image. You, a human being, are God's image. You cannot *make* God's image; you can only *be* God's image. The medium in which you need to do that encompasses the canvas of your entire life. To take anything less than a full living, breathing person and declare it God's image is למעט את הדמות, to diminish God's image in the world. That is the true sin of idolatry.

You will have noticed, since I have been quoting old rabbinic and Hasidic sources, that all the varied images until now are those of males. But of course there need to be female images as well—and not just because it is politically correct to say so. I am a disciple of Ben Azzai, who told his friend Rabbi Akiva that he had a greater principle on which to base the Torah than "Love your neighbor as yourself." Ben Azzai's כלל גדול was Genesis 5:1–2 זה ספר תולדות אדם . . . בדמות אלהים עשה אותו זכר ונקבה בראם, "This Torah is the book of human generations . . . as they—or we—were made in God's image, created male and female." (We don't know, of course, where Ben Azzai meant to end that proof text, but I insist on reading him this way.)

Yes, this means that men and women are both equally created in God's image. But I take it to mean more than that: all of us, created in God's image, are both male and female. זכר ונקבה בראם (Not ברא אותם). Read not: "He created them all, male and female," but: "He created them all male and female!" Feminine images of the deity are not needed only by women. In the deeper spirit of third wave feminism, all of us are both male and female, and we respond to images of both genders in complex and subtle ways.

The Kabbalists were masters of the subtle use of this gender-based complexity. That is one of the things I learn from them, though adapting it to our very different egalitarian values. Among the clusters of symbols (= *sefirot*) that constitute the heart of Kabbalistic language, none is as fully developed as that of the tenth, called שכינה, מלכות or ישראל כנסת. The mystics have built upon a well-known rabbinic designation for the indwelling God, שכינה, that happens to be grammatically feminine but is nowhere in the old rabbinic sources described in female terms. In identifying her with כנסת ישראל, an idealized representation of the Jewish people, long described in מדרשים on שיר השירים as the bride of God, they create a female hypostasis, a divine entity that is part of the one indivisible God (they insist on their monotheism, after all!) and yet longs for Him, goes into exile with Israel, weeps for Her children in the persona of Rachel or Jerusalem, and all the rest.

She stands in a liminal place between the upper and lower worlds. When seen from above, from the viewpoint of the mysterious One, She is purely receptive, receiving the flow of divine blessing like an empty receptacle, the sea into whom all the rivers flow, the moon receiving the light of the sun. But when seen from below, from our earthly perspective, She is אם כל חי, compassionate mother of all life, God as sustainer and nurturer, the One through whom all blessings flow. It is not accidental that this transformative development in Jewish theology took place in thirteenth-century Christian Spain. My article on the subject is entitled "Shekhinah, the Virgin Mary, and the Song of Songs."[7] That tells you a great deal, but for our purposes it is just a long historical footnote. I celebrate the fact that Judaism has been enriched through contact with other traditions.

The real meaning of "male" and "female" in Kabbalistic language is what they call משפיע and מקבל, giver and receiver, so-called active and passive partners, to use the metaphor of human sexuality, but those terms are hardly adequate. As lovers, we know that we are all both givers and receivers, indeed that our own greatest pleasure may lie in giving to the other in ways that entirely blur the clarity of who is giving and who is receiving. Let us not be too embarrassed or prudish to learn from that lesson. It is true in other forms of love as well, including our love relationship with God, as the Kabbalists insist.

We human creatures are receivers, and we need to recognize that. God blows the breath of life into Adam's nostrils, an act that is repeated in each birth, indeed in each moment, with every breath we take. Life is a gift; Y-H-W-H, נשמת כל חי, the breath of all life, is משפיע and we are all מקבלים. This is the usual midrash on שיר השירים. Gratitude is the beginning of religious consciousness.

But that is only the first step. The purpose of Kabbalah is to turn us all into משפיעים, givers. The true goal of religious awareness, of our inward journey, is to awaken and activate the source of divinity within the self, the God who is immanent within our souls. Gratitude leads us toward this inner awakening, the discovery of our נקודה פנימית, longing to be joined to her source in the mysterious beyond of Y-H-W-H. Bringing out and cultivating this inner point, making it the object of the way we live, fashioning our lives after it, is all part of what it means to be a religious person. It is *personal theology!* In the interpersonal domain, רשות הרבים, especially, this means discovering that generosity of spirit is our true natural state. There are psychological studies to back this up, but we know it as religious people; it is a truth revealed to us. We are here to become givers. We are obliged to give back, to the human community as a whole as well as to all the more specific communities—including the Jewish community—that have made us who we are, that have blessed us with all the material and cultural gifts we have received. This sense of becoming a giver recaptures and provides a much-needed spiritual foundation for the entire agenda of תיקון עולם, in which the Reform movement has shown such great leadership. Those of you who know and read me are aware that I am a strong supporter of that agenda. I accept no either/or between the revival of Jewish spirituality and our understanding that we are judged by our worldly deeds. But also in the spiritual domain, רשות היחיד, there is a way of giving back to the One who gives us life. That has to do with the mystery of כוונה, the direction of our spiritual energies. Life, like breathing, is a great circle. We receive; we give back. כל הנשמה תהלל י-ה—every breath goes back to Yod Heh, the highest divine name, the deepest inner divine place, which is also נשמת כל חי, ever breathing that breath back out into us, renewing the first breath of life. In a startling reading of the well-known Hallel verse (Ps. 118:23), the Maggid of Mezritch declares מאת ה' היתה זאת היא נפלאת בעינינו to mean "Y-H-W-H, the Giver, has turned into a *zot*, a female, a receiver. How wondrous in our eyes!"[8] Yes, we are capable of giving; God is capable of receiving our blessing.

Here we have arrived at the fourth and final way in which theology is personal, the one that unites them all. God looks into us and finds a mirror, divinity reflected back, offered by each of us in our own way. For those of you who know my favorite Rabbi Nahman story,[9] each of us brings back our own portrait of the king. We embody the divine persona. I do not fear incarnational language as long as it is about all of us, not just one of us. We are the image of God because we contain a font of divinity, flowing forth from within, to be a reflection of God's presence in the world. In us the divine מקור חיים is inexorably attached to בשר ודם, a fact that makes us subject to terrible temptations, but also leads to the greatest exaltation of the divine/human spirit, the ultimate moment of *personal theology*.

NOTES

1. In the gap between the oral and written versions of this essay, I see that the Festschrift for Neil Gillman is also (and most appropriately!) entitled *Personal Theology* (Boston: Academic Press, 2013). My article there, "A Neo-Hasidic Credo," may be seen as a companion to this piece.
2. Yochanan Muffs, *The Personhood of God: Biblical Theology, Human Faith, and the Divine Image* (Woodstock VT: Jewish Lights, 2005).
3. Daniel Landes, "Hidden Master," *Jewish Review of Books* 3 (2010). See my response to him and our ensuing correspondence in *Jewish Review of Books* 4 (2011) and the online forum *Jewschool* (http://jewschool.com/2011/03/04/25656 /the-greenlandes-debate-continues/).
4. See my article on this series of midrashim, "The Children in Egypt and the Theophany at the Sea," *Judaism* 24 (1975): 446–56.
5. *Tanhuma Hukkat* 6; *Be-Midbar Rabbah* 19:3.
6. Quoted by Zvi Hirsch of Zydaczow in *'Ateret Zevi, parashat aharey mot*.
7. "Shekhinah, the Virgin Mary, and the Song of Songs: Reflections on a Kabbalistic Symbol in Its Historical Context," *AJS Review* 26, no. 1 (2002): 1–52.
8. *Maggid Devarav le-Ya'akov*, ed. Rivka Schatz-Uffenheimer (Jerusalem: Magnes Press, 1976), 76.
9. I discuss it in *Tormented Master* (Tuscaloosa: University of Alabama Press, 1979), 355–60. It also serves as the introduction to *Seek My Face* (Woodstock VT: Jewish Lights, 2003). I have recently had a third opportunity to reflect on it in *Ha-Hayyim ke-Ga'agu'a*, ed. Roee Horen (Tel Aviv: Yedi'ot, 2010), 91–99 [Hebrew].

Source Acknowledgments

I am grateful to these publishers for granting permission to reprint the following articles, which originally appeared in their publications.

1. "Introduction to *Jewish Spirituality*." *Jewish Spirituality*, vol. 2, edited by Arthur Green (New York: Crossroad, 1987). Reprinted with permission by The Crossroad Publishing Company. www.crossroadpublishing.com.

2. "Sabbath as Temple: Some Thoughts on Space and Time in Judaism." Reprinted with permission from *Go and Study: Essays and Studies in Honor of Alfred Jospe*. Washington DC: B'nai B'rith Hillel Foundations, 1980.

3. "Some Aspects of Qabbalat Shabbat." Reprinted with permission from *Sabbath: Idea, History, Reality*. Beer-Sheva: Ben Gurion University, 2004.

4. "Judaism and 'The Good.'" Reprinted with permission from *"Theoria: Praxis,"* ed. L. Swidler. *Journal of Ecumenical Studies*. Leuven: Peeters, 1998.

5. "Bride, Spouse, Daughter: Images of the Feminine in Classical Jewish Sources." Reprinted from *On Being a Jewish Feminist*, edited by Susannah Heschel, copyright © 1983 by Schocken Books, a division of Random House LLC. Used by permission of Schocken Books, an imprint of the Knopf Doubleday Publishing Group, a division of Random House LLC. All rights reserved.

6. "The Children in Egypt and the Theophany at the Sea." Reprinted with permission from *Judaism: A Quarterly Journal of Jewish Life and Thought* 24, no. 4 (Fall 1975), American Jewish Congress.

7. "The Song of Songs in Early Jewish Mysticism." Reprinted with permission from *Orim* 2, no. 2 (Spring 1987). New Haven: Yale University Hillel.

8. "Around the Maggid's Table: *Tsaddik*, Leadership, and Popularization in the Circle of Dov Baer of Miedzyrzec." Reprinted with permission from *Around the Maggid's Table: Tsaddik, Leadership and Popularization in the Circle of Dov Baer of Miedzyrzec*. Zion, 2013 (Hebrew). English version original to this volume.

9. "Typologies of Leadership and the Hasidic *Zaddiq*." *Jewish Spirituality*, vol. 2, edited by Arthur Green (New York: Crossroad, 1987). Reprinted with permission by The Crossroad Publishing Company. www.crossroadpublishing.com.

10. "The *Zaddiq* as *Axis Mundi* in Later Judaism." Reprinted with permission from *Journal of the American Academy of Religion* 45, no. 3 (September 1977).

11. "Hasidism: Discovery and Retreat." Reprinted with permission from *The Other Side of God*, edited by Peter L. Berger. Garden City NY: Anchor Press/Doubleday, 1981.

12. "Levi Yizhak of Berdichev on Miracles." Original to this volume.

13. "A Neo-Hasidic Credo." Originally published as "A Neo-Hasidic Life: Credo and Reflections," reprinted with permission from *Personal Theology: Essays in Honor of Neil Gillman*, edited by William Plevan. Boston: Academic Studies Press, 2013.

14. "Restoring the Aleph: Judaism for the Contemporary Seeker." Originally published in the CIJE Lecture Series. New York: Council for Initiatives in Jewish Education, 1996.

15. "A Kabbalah for the Environmental Age." From *Tikkun* 14, no. 5. Copyright 1999, *Tikkun Magazine*. Reprinted with permission of the copyright holder, and present publisher, Duke University Press.

16. "Abraham Joshua Heschel: Recasting Hasidism for Moderns." Reprinted with permission from "Abraham Joshua Heschel: Recasting Hasidism for Moderns," by Arthur Green. *Modern Judaism* 29, no. 1 (2009): 62–79.

17. "Personal Theology: An Address to Rabbis." Reprinted with permission from "Personal Theology: An Address to Rabbis," by Arthur Green, CCAR *Journal*, 2012.

Bibliography of the Published Writings of Arthur Green

BOOKS

Your Word Is Fire: The Hasidic Masters on Contemplative Prayer. Coedited with Barry W. Holtz. New York: Paulist Press, 1977.
———. 2nd ed. New York: Schocken Books, 1987.
———. 3rd ed. Woodstock VT: Jewish Lights, 1993.
———. Dutch trans. The Hague: East-West Publications, 2003.
Tormented Master: A Life of Rabbi Nahman of Bratslav. Tuscaloosa: University of Alabama Press, 1980.
———. 2nd ed. New York: Schocken Books, 1991.
———. Woodstock VT: Jewish Lights, 1992.
———. *Ba'al ha-Yissurim.* Hebrew trans. Tel Aviv: Am Oved, 1981.
———. *La Sagesse Dansant de Rabbi Nahman.* French trans. Paris: Albin Michel, 2000.
———. Russian trans. 2007.
Upright Practices and The Light of the Eyes: Homilies on Genesis, by R. Menahem Nahum of Chernobyl. Edited and translated. New York: Paulist Press, 1982, 1998.
Jewish Spirituality. 2 vols. New York: Crossroad Books, 1986–87.
Devotion and Commandment: The Faith of Abraham in the Hasidic Imagination. Hebrew Union College, Efroymson Lectures of 1986. Cincinnati: Hebrew Union College Press, 1989.
Seek My Face, Speak My Name: A Contemporary Jewish Theology. Northvale NJ: Jason Aronson, 1992.
———. *Baqqeshu Fanai, Qire'u Vi-Shemi: Emunato shel Mehapes.* Hebrew trans. Tel Aviv: Am Oved Press, 1997.
———. 2nd ed. Published as *Seek My Face: A Jewish Mystical Theology.* Woodstock VT: Jewish Lights, 2003.
———. Dutch trans. 2006.
Keter: The Crown of God in Early Jewish Mysticism. Princeton: Princeton University Press, 1997.
The Language of Truth: Teachings from the Sefat Emet by Rabbi Judah Leib Alter of Ger. Philadelphia: Jewish Publication Society, 1998.
These Are the Words: A Vocabulary of Jewish Spiritual Life. Woodstock VT: Jewish Lights, 1999, 2012.

————. Dutch trans. Amsterdam, 2001.

————. Italian trans. Firenze, 2002.

————. Nine entries reprinted in *The Jewish Lights Spirituality Handbook*, ed. S. M. Matlins. Woodstock VT: Jewish Lights, 2001.

————. Hebrew version (rewritten), *Eleh ha-Devarim, Leksikon le-Ruhaniyyut Yehudit.* Tel Aviv: Yedi'ot, 2008.

————. Portuguese trans. Rio de Janeiro, 2014.

EHYEH: A Kabbalah for Tomorrow. Woodstock VT: Jewish Lights, 2002.

————. Spanish trans. Buenos Aires, 2015.

Ha-Shekhinah, ha-Betulah ha-Kedoshah, ve-Shir ha-Shirim (Shekhinah, the Virgin Mary, and the Song of Songs). Jerusalem: Yeri'ot, 2004.

A Guide to the Zohar. Stanford: Stanford University Press, 2004.

Radical Judaism: Rethinking God and Tradition. New Haven: Yale University Press, 2010. Hebrew translation Tel Aviv: Yedi'ot, 2015.

Hasidic Spirituality for a New Era: The Religious Writings of Hillel Zeitlin. Mahwah NJ: Paulist Press, 2012.

Speaking Torah: Hasidic Teachings from around the Maggid's Table. 2 vols. Woodstock VT: Jewish Lights, 2013.

Judaism's Ten Best Ideas: A Brief Guide for Seekers. Woodstock VT: Jewish Lights, 2014.

Arthur Green (Library of Living Jewish Philosophers). Ed. Hava Tirosh-Samuelson. Leiden: Brill, 2015.

ARTICLES: HISTORICAL/PHENOMENOLOGICAL

"The Continuing Redemption of Rabbi Nahman." Review-Essay of J. Weiss, *Mehqarim be-Hasidut Bratslav. Conservative Judaism* 29 (1975).

"Rabbi Nahman Bratslaver's Conflict Regarding Leadership." In *Texts and Responses: Studies Presented to Nahum N. Glatzer.* Leiden: E. J. Brill, 1975.

"The Children in Egypt and the Theophany at the Sea." *Judaism* 24, no. 4 (1975): 446–56.

"The *Zaddiq* as *Axis Mundi* in Later Judaism." *Journal of the American Academy of Religion* 45, no. 3 (1977): 327–47.

"Sabbath as Temple: Some Thoughts on Space and Time in Judaism." In *Go and Study: Essays and Studies in Honor of Alfred Jospe*, ed. Raphael Jospe and Samuel Z. Fishman, 287–305. Washington DC: B'nai B'rith Hillel Foundations, 1980.

"Rabbi Nahman's Journey to the Land of Israel." In *Essays in Honor of Alexander Altmann.* Durham NC: Duke University Press, 1981.

"Hasidism: Discovery and Retreat." In *The Other Side of God*, ed. Peter Berger. Garden City NY: Anchor Press/Doubleday, 1981.

"Bride, Spouse, Daughter: Images of the Feminine in Classical Jewish Sources." In *On Being a Jewish Feminist*, ed. Susannah Heschel. New York: Schocken Books, 1982.

"Judaism and Mysticism." In *Take Judaism, for Example*, ed. Jacob Neusner. Chicago: University of Chicago Press, 1983.

"On Translating Hasidic Homilies." *Prooftexts* 3, no. 1 (1983).

"The Zohar: Jewish Mysticism in Medieval Spain." In *An Introduction to the Medieval Mystics of Europe*, ed. Paul Szarmach. Albany: SUNY Press, 1984. Reprinted in *Essential Papers on Kabbalah*, ed. Lawrence Fine. New York: New York University Press, 1995.

"Teachings of the Hasidic Masters." In *Back to the Sources: Reading the Classical Jewish Texts*, ed. Barry W. Holtz. New York: Summit Books, 1984.

Contributions to *Encyclopedia of Religion*, ed. Mircea Eliade. Five entries on Hasidism. New York: Macmillan, 1987.

"Typologies of Leadership and the Hasidic *Zaddiq*." In *Jewish Spirituality*, vol. 2, ed. Arthur Green. New York: Crossroad Books, 1987.

———. "Eine Tradition auf der Suche nach Autoritaet: Die Rollen des Weisen (Zaddiq) im chassidischen Judentum." Abridged German trans. In *Weisheit: Archaeologie der literarischen Kommunikation III*. Munich: Wilhelm Fink, 1991.

———. Hebrew trans. In *Zaddik ve-'Edah*, ed. David Assaf. Jerusalem: Zalman Shazar Centre, 2001.

"Hasidism" and "Spirituality." Contributions to *Contemporary Jewish Religious Thought*, ed. Arthur Cohen and Paul Mendes-Flohr. New York: Scribner's, 1987.

———. Hebrew trans. In *Leqsiqon ha-Tarbut ha-Yehudit Bi-Zemanenu*. Tel Aviv: Am Oved Press, 1986.

"The Song of Songs in Early Jewish Mysticism." *Orim: A Jewish Journal at Yale* 2, no. 2 (1987): 49–63.

Perush Shir ha-Shirim le-Rabbi Yishaq Ibn Sahula. Critical edition with introduction and notes. *Jerusalem Studies in Jewish Thought* 6, no. 3–4 (1987).

"The Current Hour in Hasidic Research." In *Hasidism Re-appraised*, ed. Ada Rapaport-Albert. London: Littman Library, 1996.

"Three Warsaw Mystics." *Kolot Rabbim: Essays in Memory of Rivka Schatz-Uffenheimer,* ed. Rachel Elior. Jerusalem: Magnes Press, 1997.

Contributions to *Oxford Dictionary of the Jewish Religion*, ed. Geoffrey Wigoder. Sixteen articles on Hasidism. New York: Oxford University Press, 1997.

Review of *Gates of Light* by R. Joseph Gikatilla, English trans. by Avi Weinstein. *Journal of Hebrew Studies* 36 (1995).

Review-Essay of Elliot Wolfson's *Through a Speculum That Shines: Vision and Imagination in Medieval Jewish Mysticism. History of Religions* 36, no. 3 (1997).

Review of Moshe Idel's *Hasidism: Between Ecstacy and Magic. Journal of Religion* 77, no. 1 (1997).

"Judaism and 'The Good.'" In *Theoria: Praxis*, ed. L. Swidler. Leuven: Peeters, 1998.

"Abraham Joshua Heschel: Recasting Hasidism for Moderns." *Tikkun* 14, no. 1 (1998).

Review of M. Rosman, *R. Israel Ba'al Shem Tov*. *History of Religions* 40, no. 2 (1999).

Reply to Alon Goshen-Gottstein (Reviewing *Keter: The Crown of God in Early Jewish Mysticism*). *Kabbalah* 5 (2000).

"Shekhinah, the Virgin Mary, and the Song of Songs: Reflections on a Kabbalistic Symbol in Its Historical Context." *Association for Jewish Studies Review* 26, no. 1 (2002): 1–52.

"Some Aspects of Qabbalat Shabbat." *Sabbath: Idea, History, Reality*, ed. Gerald J. Blidstein. Beersheva: Ben Gurion University, 2004.

"Hasidism" and "Eco-Kabbalah." In *The Encyclopedia of Religion and Nature*. 2 vols., ed. Bron Taylor. New York: Continuum, 2005.

"Introduction to the Zohar." In *The Pritzker Edition of the Zohar*, vol. 1, trans. Daniel C. Matt. Stanford: Stanford University Press, 2003.

"Intradivine Romance: The Song of Songs in the Zohar." In *Scrolls of Love: Ruth and the Song of Songs*. ed. P. Hawkins and L. Stahlberg. New York: Fordham University Press, 2006.

"Shekhinah." In *Encyclopedia of Love in World Religions*, ed. Yudit Greenberg. Santa Barbara: ABC-CLIO, 2007.

Contributions to *The YIVO Encyclopedia of Jews in Eastern Europe*. "Piety"; "Dov Baer of Mezritsh"; "Elimelekh of Lizhensk"; "Levi Yitzhak of Berdichev"; "Ger Hasidic Dynasty"; "Radomsk Hasidic Dynasty"; "Nahman of Bratslav"; "Satmar Hasidism"; "Shne'ur Zalman of Lyady." New Haven: Yale University Press, 2008.

"Abraham Joshua Heschel: Recasting Hasidism for Moderns." *Modern Judaism* 29, no. 1 (2009): 62-79.

"Hillel Zeitlin and Neo-Hasidic Readings of the Zohar." *Kabbalah* 22 (2010).

"Hasidism and Its Response to Change." *Jewish History* 27 (2013), special issue: "Towards a New History of Hasidism."

"Elie Wiesel in the Context of Neo-Hasidism." *Essays in Honor of Elie Wiesel*. Boston: Boston University, 2013.

"*Ga'agu'ey ha-Elohim el ha-Adam*" (On Rabbi Nahman's Tale of the King and the Sage). *Ha-Hayyim ke-Ga'agu'a*. Ed. Roee Horen. Tel Aviv: Yediot Ahronoth, 2010.

"Around the Maggid's Table: *Tsaddik*, Leadership, and Popularization in the Circle of Dov Baer of Miedzyrzec." *Zion* 78, no. 1 (2013): 73–106 (Hebrew).

ARTICLES: CONTEMPORARY THEOLOGY

"The Experience of Sinai." *Variant* 4, no. 3 (1964).

"Notes from the Jewish Underground: Psychedelics and Kabbalah." *Response* 2 (1968). Reprinted in *The New Jews*, ed. James Sleeper and Alan Mintz. New York: Vintage Books, 1971.

"After Itzik: Toward a Theology of Jewish Spirituality." *Worship* (1971). Reprinted in *The New Jews*, ed. James Sleeper and Alan Mintz. New York: Vintage Books, 1971.

"Response to Richard Rubenstein." *Conservative Judaism* 28 (1974).

"The Role of Mysticism in a Contemporary Jewish Theology." *Conservative Judaism* 30 (1976).

"Neo-Hasidism and Our Theological Struggles." *Ra'ayonot* 4, no. 3 (1984).

"Jewish Studies and Jewish Faith." *Tikkun* 1, no. 1 (1986). Reprinted in *Tikkun: To Heal, Repair, and Transform the World: An Anthology*, ed. Michael Lerner. Oakland CA: Tikkun Books, 1992.

"The Real Challenge of Orthodoxy." *Reconstructionist* 52, no. 2 (1986).

"Keeping Feminist Creativity Jewish." *Sh'ma* 16/305 (1986).

"Judaism and Spirituality: A Jewish Mysticism for Our Age." Proceedings, Brandeis University Institute for Distinguished Community Leaders, 1987.

"Scholarship Is Not Enough." *Tikkun* 2, no. 3 (1987).

"Finding God in an Israel That Isn't Zion: A Response to Arthur Cohen." *Sh'ma* 17/327 (1987).

"Judaism as a Spiritual Language: A Jewish Mysticism for Our Age." *Manna* 19 (1988).

"Rethinking Theology: Language, Experience, and Reality." *Reconstructionist* 54, no. 1 (1988).

"Toward a New Theology of Revelation." Materials from the Critical Issues Conference II. New York: CLAL, 1988.

"Twin Centers: Sacred Space and Sacred Time in Judaism." *Reconstructionist* 55, no. 5 (1990).

"God, World, Person: A Jewish Theology of Creation." *Melton Journal*. Part One: Winter 1990; Part Two: Spring 1991. An alternate version appeared in *Journal of Theology* 96 (1992).

"Speaking in Thunder." *Tikkun* 6, no. 3 (1991). Revised reprint in *Celebrating the Jewish Year*, ed. P. Steinberg. Philadelphia: Jewish Publication Society, 2009.

"The Problem of Evil." *Reconstructionist* 57, no. 3 (1992).

"The Aleph-Bet of Creation: Jewish Mysticism for Beginners." *Tikkun* 7, no. 4 (1992).

"What Is Jewish Theology?" *Torah and Revelation*, ed. D. Cohn-Sherbok. Lewiston NY: Edwin Mellen Press, 1992.

"God, Prayer, and Religious Language." *Imagining the Jewish Future*, ed. D. Teutsch. Albany: SUNY, 1992.

"God, World, Person: A Jewish Theology of Creation." *Journal of Theology* (Dayton) 96 (1992).

"Is There Really a God?" *When Your Jewish Child Asks Why*, ed. K. Olitzky et al. New York: Ktav, 1993.

"Some Words on the Words of Prayer." *Worlds of Jewish Prayer: A Festschrift in Honor of Rabbi Zalman Shalomi-Schachter*, ed. S. Harris-Wiener and J. Omer-Man. Northvale NJ: Jason Aronson, 1993.

"New Directions in Jewish Theology in America." The Third David W. Belin Lecture in American Jewish Affairs. Ann Arbor: The Jean and Samuel Frankel Center for Judaic Studies, 1994. Reprinted in *American Jewish Identity Politics*, ed. D. Moore. Ann Arbor: University of Michigan Press, 2008.

"Judaism for the Post-Modern Era." Samuel Goldenson Lecture, 1994. Cincinnati: Hebrew Union College Press, 1995.

"Our Days of Awe." Preface to a new edition of S. Y. Agnon's *Days of Awe*. New York: Schocken Books, 1995.

"Restoring the Aleph: Judaism for the Contemporary Seeker." CIJE Lecture Series. New York: Council for Initiatives in Jewish Education, 1996.

"What Do American Jews Believe?" Contribution to *Commentary* symposium. *Commentary* 102, no. 2 (1996).

"A Kabbalah for the Environmental Age." *Tikkun* 14, no. 5 (1999). Revised reprint in *Best Contemporary Jewish Writing*, ed. Michael Lerner. New York: Jossey-Bass, 2001. Revised reprint in *Religion in a Secular City: Essays in Honor of Harvey Cox*, ed. A. Sharma. Harrisburg: Trinity, 2001.

"Theology on the Far Side of Myth." With Or Rose. *Sh'ma* 32/587 (January 2002).

"To Learn and to Teach: Some Thoughts on Jewish-Buddhist Dialogue." In *Beside Still Waters*, ed. H. Kasimow, J. P. Keenan, and L. K. Keenan. Boston: Wisdom, 2003.

Afterword to *A Benedictine Legacy of Peace: The Life of Abbot Leo A. Rudloff*. Weston: Weston Priory, 2005.

"Judaism and Creation Theology." *Sh'ma* (December 2005).

"God!" *European Judaism* 39, no. 2 (2006).

"Mystical Sources of the Healing Movement." *Healing and the Jewish Imagination*, ed. William Cutter. Woodstock VT: Jewish Lights, 2007.

Contributions to *My People's Passover Haggadah*, ed. D. Arnow and L. Hoffman. Woodstock VT: Jewish Lights, 2008.

"These Are the Journeys: Tales of Our Wandering. Reflections on Parashat Massa'ey." *A Modern Men's Torah Commentary*, ed. Jeffrey Salkin. Woodstock VT: Jewish Lights, 2009.

"A Neo-Hasidic Credo." *Personal Theology: Essays in Honor of Neil Gillman*, ed. William Plevan. Boston: Academic Press, 2013.